Cover Illustration by **Simon Brett**
http://www.simonbrett.co.uk/

A DOCTOR WHO FAN ANTHOLOGY

YOU AND WHO

CONTACT HAS BEEN MADE!

VOLUME ONE

EDITED BY J. R. SOUTHALL

You and Who Contact Has Been Made
A **Doctor Who** Fan Anthology

First published 2013 by Miwk Publishing

This edition first published 2015

Copyright © the respective authors 2013.

You Will Be Reading...

- 7 Introduction
- 11 The First Doctor Who
- 103 The Second Doctor Who
- 178 The Third Doctor Who
- 251 The Fourth Doctor Who
- 387 The Fifth Doctor Who
- 451 The Sixth Doctor Who
- 495 The Seventh Doctor Who
- 540 Afterword by Tom MacRae
- 543 Index

Meet the authors of **You and Who**, read more stories and get involved in the next **You and Who** book, at:

youandwho.weebly.com

Find out more about **Watching Books** at:

watchingbooks.weebly.com

Introduction

The Five Faces of Doctor Who repeat series in 1981. The first Target Books issues in 1973 and 1974. Twenty Years of a Time Lord, Longleat, 1983. The launch of **Doctor Who Weekly** (latterly **Monthly**, and now **Magazine**) in 1979. All significant moments in the lives of the viewers of **Doctor Who**, the kinds of moment when a viewer becomes a fan.

But these aren't the end of the story, nor barely even its beginning. Because the above-mentioned events are all triggers, the kinds of thing that make us realise that we're more invested in this silly old show than perhaps is normal or desirable or even sane. And as triggers, they wouldn't exist if we didn't already possess a latent desire to see and know more about the programme they are celebrating. **Doctor Who** is the kind of series that attracts that type of adulation.

So what is it about **Doctor Who** that encourages us to want to connect with it and celebrate it in the way we do?

That's a very good question, and one that goes back almost as far as fandom itself. It's the question that the first volume of **You and Who** stories attempted to get to answer, and it is of course the reason we're here again. But this time, there's a difference. This time, we are also here to celebrate the fiftieth anniversary of **Doctor Who**, fifty years of the show we all adore. And so **Contact Has Been Made** (Volume One of which concentrates on the original run of **Doctor Who**, while Volume Two looks forward to the revived series and more) will be attempting to answer that question by asking the fans themselves to look back over those entire fifty years, and identify the moments in every single broadcast story that have sparked and nurtured and developed that burgeoning fandom into something solid and real.

I well remember my own tipping point, my first Target book adaptation (it was *Planet of the Daleks*, not necessarily the novelisation held in the highest esteem among fans at large, but the one I nevertheless have the fondest memories of). That was when **Doctor Who** became something that didn't just occupy 25 minutes in the week any more, but became something that I could spend time with whenever I wanted to, at my own leisure (the school day permitting, of course). My fandom became proactive, rather than reactive – and that's a huge step. A kind of 'Bingo!' moment, if you will.

Nowadays, it's easier to access the show itself, what with the internet, multi-channel television and Digital Versatile Discs and so on, but that doesn't make the thrill of connecting with the show any less vital (as I hope these two volumes will demonstrate). Indeed, whether it be through **Doctor Who Confidential** (rest in peace!), **Doctor Who Magazine** or perhaps even a book very like the one you're holding in your hands right now, whatever it was that triggered your fandom into activity, I hope you'll recognise the symptoms in the stories people have contributed to the selection contained herein.

Speaking of which, I'd like to take a moment to thank all those who've put aside their valuable time to put their thoughts and memories into prose for **You and Who** – including Tony Green, whose essay on the subject of *Spearhead from Space* I held over from the first book in order to use as a starting point when assembling this one. But of course, he's not the only one; every single person who has contributed to this book has directed their efforts towards creating a kind of collective memory of growing up with **Doctor Who**. And all for charity too. Bravo to each and every one of them. There will be names you recognise, but many you won't – and there will be those you might want to read more from too; if so, you should pop along to the **You and Who** website and check out what else they have to offer.

Compiling these books has been a humbling but extremely rewarding experience, and I hope the joy I felt in doing so is reflected in the reading of them. But I guess you'll just have to carry on if you want to find out...

For Mother and Omes

ORIGINAL PUBLISHER'S NOTE:
This book would not have been possible without the generosity and goodwill of the many contributors. The authors of each of these essays have given up their time to help a good cause.

BBC Children in Need began in 1980 and is one of just three regular UK charity telethons. Over the years they have raised more than £600 million. This is an awesome achievement and the money goes to help children not just in the UK but around the world. Children with mental, physical or sensory disorders, victims of abuse, famine, neglect and circumstance all benefit from the goodwill of the people who support the charity; people like you. In purchasing this book you've helped to change a life and we thank you for your support.

To all the authors and especially to J.R. and Chris for their incredible hard work, we offer our sincere thanks and appreciation. None of this would be possible without fandom.

R.P.M. (The Miwk Men)

The First Doctor Who

The first Doctor Who was played by William Hartnell.

No, strike that. Doctor Who was played by William Hartnell.

When Hartnell took the role, and **Doctor Who** began broadcasting on the 23rd of November 1963, the role had not been played by any other actors previously. There had been no regenerations, no mentions of a second heart, no appearances from the Daleks, and no long line of leggy companions from which the creators of **Doctor Who** could take their inspiration.

When **Doctor Who** began broadcasting in November 1963, it was brand new. There were no rules, no boundaries, no limits and no history from which to draw. This might seem obvious now, but it's worth repeating.

And why is it worth repeating? Because other shows, your **Coronation Street**s and your **Blue Peter**s and your **Casualty**s, have a well-defined history and format to draw upon. Their lives began with a very firm idea from the programme-makers of what they wanted and where they wanted to go, and even today, years later, the new programme-makers, the ones who have taken over from the ones who took over from those original programme-makers, know exactly what kind of a show they're making.

Nobody has ever known quite what kind of a show they were making when they were making **Doctor Who**, and back in 1963, back before *The Tomb of the Cybermen* and *Genesis of the Daleks* and *Blink*, they would have had even less of an idea. No idea at all, in fact. Can you even begin to imagine how scary, and yet how exciting, that must have been?

For most of us reading, or having written in, this book, our experience of the first Doctor Who will not have been of watching his tenure live on transmission. That's how long the show's been going, how great its legacy is. It began before many of our lifetimes did. Most of them, in all probability.

Due to the short-sightedness of the BBC's employees back in the mists of time, many of the first Doctor Who's stories have been lost, never to be returned. *Marco Polo*, *Galaxy 4* and *The Daleks' Master Plan* will likely never be complete in the BBC's archives. So our experience of these stories will have come to us in a variety of different ways, through the Target books, the BBC Audio soundtracks, or even the fan reconstructions of Loose Cannon and others. And on DVD too, of course – those stories that we are lucky enough to still have, that is. We're fortunate to be able to experience most of it at all.

What do we find when we do? That it was a period of courage and experimentation, learning and consolidation, of the kind we'll never see again. That it was a wonderful, ground-breaking, myth-making era, that's what.

Where It All Began
An Unearthly Child by **Si Hunt**, 35, Sawbridgeworth
First story: **Full Circle**

You might at one time or another have tried to recall who the very first person in **Doctor Who** was. It actually wasn't the policeman, shining his torch around a darkened junkyard on what our imaginations insist is not a cramped studio interior but a chilly November night. It wasn't that cheeky student who peers over the shoulders of his two more glamorous Coal Hill classmates and pulls a face like Kenneth Williams, although he may well be the first camp person in **Doctor Who**. It wasn't even Jacqueline Hill or William Russell, riffing off each other in a scene which, call me ungrateful, somehow seems over-rehearsed, knowing this was their second crack at it. No, the very first person in **Doctor Who** was me. Every time I watch.

There are in fact a number of seldom-acknowledged firsts in *An Unearthly Child*. It's the first time the Doctor talks to camera for a start (and you thought Tom Baker was bad), as the Doctor peers straight at the viewer and challenges the intruders behind him to, 'Go and fetch a policeman.' It makes you realise not just how perfect Hartnell is as the Doctor, but how perfect he *looks*. Face craggy, eyes darting around, squinting then focussing, suspicious, devious. Somehow there is nothing positive whatever in his manner or actions, yet we are drawn to him, like a beguiling wizard. It's the first (and last) time Susan wears her marvellous Bob Dylan hat, for shame. And it's the first and last time that the viewer, through the eyes of the camera in that opening sequence, discovers the TARDIS. Today, the effect would be lost as the journey through the gates of 76 Totters Lane (which are actually pushed open by us as we pass through! Brilliant!) would be swift and motion-controlled. Back in 1963, one really feels as if one is cautiously approaching the thing through the darkness. The police box is highlighted as significant firstly by virtue of the fact that it is inexplicably and mysteriously the focus of our attention – another oddity lost to a twenty-first century viewer, to whom the police box itself is actually alien. And secondly by the ringing hum which fills our ears. What is it? Why is it humming? Is it dangerous? Just as our heads are filled with questions, we blur-fade to somewhere else entirely. It's a special sequence to us not just because the **Doctor Who** theme music has oddly been left running, as if they forgot to turn off the tape, but because we, not some unrelatable authority figure or unwitting heroine, *we the viewer* have discovered something unearthly and unexplained and possibly wonderful. **Doctor Who** challenged us to question what we know and venture into the unknown from the very beginning.

The greatest strength of this episode for me is the story, fairytale-like in its timelessness. Two school teachers follow home an erratically behaving student and find that she lives in a police box in a junkyard which whisks them off into time and space. That's it, right there. A premise that immediately sounds more exciting than any new show that has been invented since. As with the TARDIS, a plot device to beat them all, it feels like **Doctor Who** was first to the blocks with the best series premise, and every other series which followed feels contrived. It's a warm idea, but paradoxically this episode itself is cold and edgy. It simply wouldn't be half as effective if it opened on a bright summer's day. There's something dangerous and at the same time magical about the darkness, particularly when it's cold and foggy. Like Bonfire Night, similar nights in our lives make us remember, and perhaps that's why revisiting this particular episode has become something of a pre-occupation of mine down the years. When I was a naive young student, my dad once bought me a book at a convention stall. I wouldn't swear the author hadn't personally talked him into the purchase (I took little convincing; Dad wants to buy me a **Doctor Who** book - let's make him happy!). The book was called **Timeframe** and it contains the claim that **Doctor Who** began at exactly 5:16:20 on the 23rd November, 1963. I was amazed – they even knew the time to the second! It never occurred to me back then that, unless the author had the foresight to jot down the exact time **Doctor Who** was on back in the day, this was probably made up, so I endeavoured to watch the first episode at exactly that time every year from that moment on. This brought its fair share of problems, as people would inevitably choose that exact time to ring me up or call round for a chat. I'm ashamed to say that I shunned a few people down the years just so I could watch a video at a precise time! These days I'm a little more balanced (!) and relaxed about when I re-watch *An Unearthly Child*, but the point is that I wanted, and still want, to remember those humble beginnings and immerse myself back into the world of November, 1963 at this time every year. **Doctor Who** is part of all of us and it's important to remember where you came from. Where it all began. And luckily, *An Unearthly Child* is an episode that never seems to wear out.

And that's why it's so powerful. It's so definitely a *start* (imagine if **Doctor Who** had just begun with the Doctor in the TARDIS, to enable them to show them in any order, like **Friends** or **He-Man**) and so definitely the first steps of a journey, that it thoroughly enables us to go back and acknowledge the birth of something so amazing and so immense that it's still going, fifty whole years later. Blimey, that's quite something, isn't it? Just to make you feel old, the *halfway point* of **Doctor Who**'s history is now *Remembrance of the Daleks*! I digress, though. This was once the only episode of the production-coded story that anybody talked about, before it came into vogue to remark how wonderful the neglected three episodes were. But that really isn't the point – from *The Cave of Skulls* onwards **Doctor Who** suddenly starts to do what would become normal **Doctor Who** things – running from monsters, introducing villains, escaping from places. In a way that's part of what makes *An Unearthly Child* so joyful – it's the one episode of the series that prefaces it, and all rules are off. There truly would never be an episode like it again. **Doctor Who** as the series we know starts from the moment Ian and Barbara touch the alien sand, hear the cry of strange birds and see them wheel in another sky, albeit one on their own planet but centuries in the past.

But the single thing I love most about *An Unearthly Child* is the way it *takes off* – literally and figuratively. It's essentially the story of the Doctor, Susan and their new friends setting off for adventures. The story of leaving. Yes, they will bend history later to make out that there were pre-Ian and Barbara landings (Quinnis and all that jazz) and no-one is pretending here that this is the TARDIS' maiden voyage, but the key thing is that at this point, the TARDIS is essentially a stationary abode. Susan is enjoying Coal Hill School, and there's no sign the Doctor wants to leave London; he's even given the ship's location to the school as a permanent address! Such emphasis is given to that monumental first take-off, violent enough to cause what looks like a milkshake to be whipped up into Susan's face and to make Ian do a bizarre dance around the console room, that it's clear that this is the very beginning of the voyage. *Our voyage*. My favourite moment is at the end, when we see the police box sitting slightly askew on an alien-looking landscape, its light steadily flashing. There is no music, just the whistling wind. We then cut back to the inside, Ian and Barbara unconscious. The Doctor is looking grave, his best, 'Well, I've done it now,' face. And outside, a shadow falls. There is very much the sense of a ship having tethered its moorings with no way back; a journey into the impossible that is still going. And then, as the titles roll, I always think of what's to come – Marco Polo, and Skaro, and Skonnos and Segonax and Sycorax and Slithergees and sleeping seas and screaming companions and what a wonderful life it's been with **Doctor Who** in it. I always think of that, and I always think that it all began here. With a junkyard, a police box, two school teachers and me.

The Anatomy of a Classic
The Daleks by **Wayne W. Whited**, 40, Dayton, Ohio
First Story: **The Invasion of Time**

From the moment that Barbara turns around to see a sucker arm menacingly coming towards her, and her piercing scream of terror echoes as the screen fades to black, a classic was born. But now, fifty years and nearly a thousand episodes later, the definition of the word 'classic' has become diluted within the personal interpretation of our 'favourites'. The very mention of the term brings about thoughts of *Pyramids of Mars*, *Fury From the Deep*, *The Caves of Androzani*, and so on. But has the real meaning of 'classic' been lost to fandom, or is it still there hidden in the flood of great stories that have been produced throughout the last five decades?

First we must explore exactly what is necessary for a story to be considered by a fan to be a 'classic'. When asked, most would say that the requirements are: a well-written script with witty dialogue and well-rounded characters; great acting from the main cast, with perfect chemistry, and a terrific guest cast; outstanding production values and imaginative direction.

Of course, the aforementioned stores fall into this category. Each are cherished and remembered by the fan collective for exactly these three reasons. However, we mustn't forget a fourth and final category: to be enjoyed and beloved by the viewer.

It is with this fourth category where the definition of 'classic' becomes blurred. For every fan that cries *City of Death*, another shouts *The Horns of Nimon*. For every *Genesis of the Daleks* that is adored, another finds *Timelash* exciting and fun. Because of this discord among fans, a new question must be asked. Exactly whom sets the standards that define which stories have earned the distinction of 'classic'?

Let's examine one specific story that the vast majority of fans consider a true classic - *Genesis of the*

Daleks. First we must investigate whether or not such a story fits into our four categories of definition. The opinions of most fans will agree that it is one of Terry Nation's finest scripts: the origin of the Daleks, with an age-old struggle between two factions near the brink of destroying one another. It features memorable characters, such as Davros and Nyder, who would become embedded within the folklore of the series. There is a perfect chemistry between the leads Tom Baker, Elisabeth Sladen and Ian Marter, and powerful performances from guest stars Michael Wisher and Peter Miles, along with a talented crew behind the scenes, including David Spode, Barbara Kidd, John Friedlander and Peter Day. Special mention must go to David Maloney for his outstanding direction, bringing out the excitement and suspense from Nation's story. And finally, of course, it holds a special place in the hearts of a great majority of viewers and fans, their attention never waning even through repeat viewing.

With the facts of this story now before us, are we able to determine exactly why this highly praised story has been awarded the status of 'classic'? Perhaps it's because of David Maloney, whose direction is revered by so many? Or maybe it's the combination of the three leads, whose sparkling performances are beloved by both old and young? Could it be Michael Wisher's portrayal of the maniacal creator Davros, a character that would survive into even the current series? Perhaps it is a combination of everyone involved in the creation of the story, each putting their heart and soul into six weeks of television that would continue to live on with repeat showings, video and DVD releases, audio CDs, and the enduring presence of its themes and characters throughout the last 38 years, since its original broadcast?

I think perhaps we are looking in the wrong direction. The television series is a constantly evolving, ever-changing entity, regenerating literally to keep up with the times. What makes an accepted classic such as *The Evil of the Daleks* any more qualified than the more recent story *Daleks in Manhattan*? Both are very similar in storyline and production value. Is it even fair to compare the two? Both are products of their times, but they are *different* times – forty years apart. Both stories have their following. There are those who adore the stories for everything we have already mentioned above and more, and there are those loyal fans who loathe the stories, unwilling to even attempt a second viewing. Neither are wrong.

It is with this assessment that I believe that each and every one of us is qualified to determine which stories deserve to be named as a true example of 'classic' **Doctor Who**. It is up to us to make our own opinions, to decide which stories are the best examples of perfection and which ones get placed back onto the shelves never to be inserted into the DVD player again. Most importantly, it is up to each of us to accept and respect one another's choices – even if we strongly disagree. Just as the Doctor, Susan, Ian and Barbara had to come to terms with their differences in order to survive on the planet Skaro and learn to work together as a whole, we admiring viewers must come to accept one another in all our diversity.

Whether it's *The Daleks* or *Time-Flight*, *Spearhead From Space* or *Nightmare of Eden*, *The Curse of Fenric* or *Love & Monsters*, it's all part of that fantastic show they call **Doctor Who**. And that we can all agree we love.

All In The Family
The Edge of Destruction by **Anthony Zehetner**, 39, Sydney, Australia / First story: **Day of the Daleks**

Doctor Who thrives on adversity. Often serendipity arises out of adversity. In the fiftieth anniversary year, we will have our only BluRay from the classic series because *Spearhead from Space* was shot entirely on film. Strikes necessitating studios under tent tops fortuitously worked for the solely affected serial, the appropriately circus-themed *The Greatest Show in The Galaxy*. When Patrick Troughton's last season ran short, an extra episode was constructed, with our regulars at the mercy of the TARDIS. As in *The Edge of Destruction, The Mind Robber* explored the innovative terrain of the TARDIS interior (the Power Room) and what life on board would be like.

The Edge of Destruction is a curiosity. It is the only serial featuring just the principle cast. Had it been lost, it would have been elevated to mythical status, like *Mission to the Unknown*, which featured none of the regular cast. It is bookended by two of the series' most revered stories: the first appearance of *The Daleks* and the epic grandeur of *Marco Polo*. Yet it is by no means poor.

A mystery abounds and its placement near the genesis of the series means that the viewer does not yet trust this unpredictable Doctor and his shadowy Ship. The TARDIS is the fifth character in the story and its interior is not as decidedly reassuring as its constabulary facade. Nigel Robinson's novelisation goes further in a scene where the TARDIS appears to breathe, reconfiguring its passageways and almost smothering Ian; a claustrophobic scene which chillingly comes to life in William Russell's brilliant narration. It would be 38 years until the TARDIS was personified completely on screen in *The Doctor's Wife*. *The Edge of Destruction*'s legacy is felt in the portrayal of the TARDIS's horrendous maze of corridors in *The Invasion of Time, Logopolis*, *Castrovalva* (and to a lesser extent in *Terminus* and *Frontios*), *The Doctor's Wife* and the enticing *Journey to the Centre of the TARDIS*. The power which resides beneath the Time Rotor's central column was first mentioned in the third serial and became a vital plot point in the denouements of *Boom Town* and *The Parting of The Ways*.

Episode two, *The Brink of Disaster*, naturally completes the thirteen-part trilogy of stories which make up the first 'Act' of Season One, mirroring **Doctor Who**'s initial commissioning of thirteen episodes. However it is inconceivable now to think of the series ending at this point. There is more character exposition in this story than in the series opener, *An Unearthly Child*, and *The Edge of Destruction* offers a breather after the frenetic and fraught second story, *The Daleks*. It is *The Edge of Destruction* which crystallises the dynamic of the TARDIS crew and makes us care about each one of them.

Serendipity arises again with the simple, yet functional, use of striped bandages of differing designs to convey healing following the Doctor's head trauma. Less effective is the hand-drawn 'Fast Return' text on the TARDIS console (apparently never intended to be seen on screen) which regrettably further spoils the *deux ex machina* ending. That the lives of its occupants may be placed in jeopardy from a faulty circuit is either metaphorical, reductionist or lazy writing. The fact that the concept of the Fast Return switch has been revisited several times since, notably in *Seasons of Fear* and *Neverland*, may mean writer David Whittaker ultimately has the last laugh.

Susan's dressmaking scissors appear impossibly large and Carole Ann Ford's captivating scene shows how brilliant an actor she can be, given the material. Alas, both character and actress's potential were never fully realised.

Just as *An Unearthly Child* is referred to by some fans as *100,000 BC* and *Mission to the Unknown* as *Dalek Cutaway*, *The Edge of Destruction* is often referred to apocryphally by its working title, *Inside the Spaceship*, or even *Beyond the Sun*, used (incorrectly?) on the first edition of the 1974 BBC Enterprises sales catalogue **A**

Quick Guide to Dr Who. *Beyond the Sun* is now believed to have been the working title of *The Daleks*, rather than *The Mutants* – or indeed even *The Survivors,* before Terry Nation's formal commissioning of *The Daleks*! Ian's remark that the Doctor's heart (singular) 'seems fine,' reverberates with Roberts Holmes's decree on a duodenary regeneration cycle in *The Deadly Assassin*; no one knew that a throwaway line would have far-reaching consequences for the show's mythos. Susan mentions the planet Quinnis (and would do so again 37 years later with Big Finish), tantalising us with the promise of earlier adventures between their flight from Gallifrey and arrival on Earth. These controversies often incite great arguments in fan circles and this published volume will surely not be exempt either.

The Edge of Destruction has it all, and was the first story to do so. I am glad that it survived being wiped, unlike *Marco Polo* (of which it contains the only few frames of introduction), and remains an icon of early **Doctor Who**, appropriately filmed at Lime Grove Studio D. It contains some of the best thrills, ideas, acting, mystery and warmth of the entire series; key elements which define the series and concepts it would return to repeatedly. This serial is also the earliest existing with soundtracks dubbed into Arabic and Spanish, for overseas sales. Like the good Doctor, this 'filler' serial not only saved the day, it added layers to the mythology of the show, never outstayed its welcome and remains a fitting example of good triumphing over adversity. Serendipity indeed!

A Journey Without Cathode Ray

Marco Polo by **Steve Herbert**, 44, Bristol, UK
First story: **Planet of the Daleks**

In a **Doctor Who** that was first broadcast in February 1964, more than four years before I was born, the first Doctor went back to Cathay in the Himalayas in 1289 and encountered Marco Polo, the war lord Tegana and the lady Ping-Cho. *Marco Polo* was the first purely historical **Doctor Who** adventure, a mainstay of the 1960s show, and in 1966 *The Highlanders* would be the last. (*Black Orchid* in 1982 would be the only modern attempt at a purely historical **Doctor Who**, and quite a good one too. It's a shame that none have graced our television screens since. And equally a shame that the new series has never had one.) So why my fascination with this story, long ago lost from the BBC's television archive, and one I've thus never been able to see properly?

All that remains of *Marco Polo* these days are the scripts, a number of photographs, and the audio soundtrack – preserved at the time by fans of the show, who captured the audio on reel to reel tape. It was back in 1973 when I would have been aged five, and my earliest encounters with the Doctor and Jo Grant were during the final episode of *Planet of The Daleks*, when my interest in the show was born; throughout my whole life it has continued to grow, to such an extent that from my late teens I experienced fandom for the first time.

In 2003 I went to Panopticon, the biggest convention I've ever been to, just after the BBC released the *Marco Polo* soundtrack on Audio CD. I had the CD and a personal CD player with me, so it was at this convention that I was listening to the story for the very first time. There was an interview panel featuring one of the show's original companions, Carole Anne Ford, and within the course of this interview the subject of **Doctor Who** reconstructions was bought up. This was totally new to me; I had no knowledge that such things existed. But here at this convention I learned something new, about how fans would reconstruct the long lost missing episodes using a mixture of existing photographs, surviving video clips, computer generated sequences created especially for the reconstructions, and the manipulation of photographs to look like they were stills from the missing episodes when in fact they were from something else entirely. An incredible amount of work for a few people to put together to reconstruct a missing **Doctor Who** serial. Later on at the convention I was queuing up for autographs, hoping to get the cover of the *Marco Polo* CD signed by Carole Anne Ford, when just as I'm a few people away from reaching her, it's time for her to go. Just my luck. Still, there would be another time, surely?

When I got home I looked up Loose Canon on the internet, sent an email, and they emailed me back. I then sent off a video cassette (yes, a video cassette; the likes of Blu-ray discs were many years off, and although DVDs were available, these reconstructions were unofficial and fan made, and you were only allowed to have them on videotape), requesting *Marco Polo*, *Mission to the Unknown* and *The Daleks' Master Plan*, the three stories I most wanted to see out of what was available. Soon after, the tapes arrived on my doorstep, and I was able to enjoy these missing gems in this exciting new format. Although *Marco Polo* was recorded in monochrome in the early days of **Doctor Who**, it was here in this reconstruction in full colour. During the serial's production, a number of colour photographs were taken on set, and that's how Loose Cannon had decided to make their reconstruction. Here was another reason to fall in love with the serial, seeing the costumes in full colour.

Loose Cannon's reconstruction included a making-of documentary, the kind of feature that would regularly appear on the BBC DVDs, providing a fascinating look back into how this lost classic came to be, and showing how much work went into creating it. The documentary would so easily not look out of place on a DVD release of *Marco Polo*, if only it wasn't a lost story. And although lost it might be, thanks to the efforts of Loose Cannon and the original reel to reel audio recordings, the story lives on.

A few years later I discovered there was going to be a convention focussing solely on *Marco Polo* itself, this time in Cardiff where they were now filming the new series, and I would finally get the chance to met Carole Anne Ford. This brilliant little convention, attended by so few, really was a gem of an event, and it was here I met William Russell (Ian), Carole Anne Ford (Susan), Mark Eden (Marco Polo), Zienia Merton (Ping-Cho) and Waris Hussein, who directed six of the seven episodes, as well as the thoroughly larger-than-life Derren Nesbitt (the Warlord Tegana). This was one of those events you just don't forget, filled as it was with memories of this classic 1964 adventure that began at The Roof of the World.

If there's one thing I would like to see in the future, it would be Steven Moffat (or a future producer of **Doctor Who**) having the insight to go back and make a purely historical adventure.

The second thing is maybe more unlikely, but the BBC have wiped so many episodes of **Doctor Who**, and there are always so many rumours of episodes returning. But all I want is is the return to the BBC's archives of just one classic **Doctor Who** serial, seven episodes from 1964; I that too much to ask for?

Finding the Keys
The Keys of Marinus by **Grant Foxon**, 26, Telford, UK
First story: **Ghost Light**

Growing up in a pre-internet, post-Soviet Union world where **Doctor Who** had disappeared overnight, along with so many Eastern European dictatorships, in 1989, I was left in a curious position; in fact if I were a big Squeeze fan it could be said that I'd been left 'up the junction.' Disowning the imported mainstream American rubbish that was being marketed for children, like all great revolutionaries I stood tall in adversity with 'my exiled TV show.'

Until 1994, my **Doctor Who** viewing was limited to the VHS releases, and a taped copy of *The Five Doctors* with the Peter Cushing **Dr Who and the Daleks** film on the end (good old long-play). Then we got cable, and UK Gold opened up new doors; I was able to watch all the stories from between 1970 and 1989, but doing so only made the 1960s stuff all the more revered and sought after in my insatiable hunger for **Doctor Who**. Very soon, Patrick Troughton became my favourite Doctor, and with each 1960s story I discovered I became happier and happier.

When *The Keys of Marinus* was finally put out on VHS it was one of those six-part releases that came as a double-pack, but the nice video covers had gone. In their place were the horribly dull swirly covers with a photograph of the Doctor – but *nil desperandum*, this was not going to stop my enjoyment. For *The Keys of Marinus* was a story I had seen no clips of and very few stills, and so I bought the video from Woolworths and took it home.

Wow ... an alien world that for once was not monotonous, that had different cultures and a cool new villainous race in the Voord. A real gem of a classic that contained all of the essential elements and several truly wondrous set pieces such as 'the sea of acid.' I was hooked like a William Burroughs character on heroin, and the two of us have had a love affair that has lasted many years and will no doubt continue on, as I have the story now on DVD and the picture is even tastier than before.

I know that I am probably in a minority when I say that, when I think of the Hartnell era, this is one of the first stories my mind goes to as a stalwart of that period, but it is nevertheless true.

Aztec Cameca
The Aztecs by **Paul Stuart Hayes**, 41, Tullamore,
Ireland / First story: **The Ribos Operation**

Doctor Who seems to have been with me from a very early age. Having an older brother who was hooked on the show, it was probably inevitable that I too would be drawn into the mysterious world of the Time Lord sooner rather than later. One of my earliest TV memories actually comes from *The Sun Makers*. I can clearly remember 'the little bald man going down the plug hole,' as I crudely put it at the time. It is surprising to find that, although my brother is some six years older than me (and still is, I might add), he only started watching the show a little over a year prior to my doing so.

I have watched the show solidly from Season 16 onwards, but for a good few years I thought little of **Doctor Who**'s past history. That was until I was in my early teens, and my brother suggested that we should watch the show in its entirety, from the very beginning, viewing one episode a night.

For the most part, we had to make do with ropey fourth generation video copies (quality that would have had the Restoration Team running for the hills in terror), but William Hartnell's impressive performance in those early stories still shone through regardless of the incessant dropouts and picture breakups. I instantly warmed to the cast and could see the dynamic of the 'crowded TARDIS' working perfectly, when it clearly did not during the Peter Davison era. Even though I was a child of the 1970s who could not remember life without a colour TV, the fact that **Doctor Who**'s early years were in black and white did not seem to faze me at all. If anything, the monochrome nature of it merely added to the show's mystique.

The first few stories were enjoyable and passed quickly, but around the corner there was a stumbling block in *Marco Polo*, lying in wait and ready to trip us up.

We had agreed beforehand that we would listen to the audio recordings of any missing episodes, but the sound quality of the tapes available for *Marco Polo* at the time were incredibly poor. Regardless of this, the two of us duly sat in front of my brother's tape deck for nearly three hours over seven nights, listening to the inaudible muffled tones. I don't think either of us caught a single word nor had we the slightest idea what was going on at any stage in the proceedings. All we could do was just sit there with looks of concentration painted on our faces, each pretending to the other that we understood it all.

That was obviously the low point of watching the first season. The high point, for me, was undoubtedly *The Aztecs*. This was a story that I eagerly anticipated, mainly due to the fact that until a few weeks before we saw it, I was under the misapprehension that the entire story was missing from the archives. For this reason, *The Aztecs* took on a kind of mythical quality to me and I could not wait for *The Keys of Marinus* to finish so that I could watch it for the first time.

The first thing that struck me on viewing the story was Barry Newbery's marvellous set design. For the money he had on offer, he clearly did a remarkable job recreating the 15th century Mexican setting. It was also nice to see Barbara getting a weightier role in this story, as she seemed to me to have been somewhat short changed in the previous stories. She took on the reins as the ipso-facto lead actor and to my mind, gave a sterling performance.

That being said, it was not Jacqueline Hill's splendid contribution that currently has me hunched over my laptop in the middle of the night, madly typing away. The person responsible for my nocturnal ramblings is of course John Ringham, for his role as the High Priest of Sacrifice, Tlotoxl. Looking back on the character now, I can clearly see the parallels between it and Olivier's *Richard III*, but at the time I was entirely ignorant of this angle and was completely enthralled by his dark and malevolent manner. To my mind, his character was far more menacing than the majority of the more archetypal monsters from the Hartnell era.

As the first episode ended, with Tlotoxl's ominous words, 'This is not Yetaxa! This is a false Goddess, and I shall destroy her!' still ringing in my ears, I asked my brother if we could watch the second episode straight away. However, my pleas fell on stony ground due to the lateness of the hour, forcing me to wait until the next evening. After an infuriatingly long day at school and with homework quickly out of the way, I found myself once again in front of the television and on this occasion with enough time to watch the remaining three episodes in one sitting.

It was interesting to see the romantic interlude between the Doctor and Cameca unfold as the story progressed, with it serving as a light relief from the main action. It was also nice to see the Doctor out of his comfort zone, if only for a short while. We knew it was doomed to fail, but the scenario was played out quite beautifully. From my own personal point of view, it was particularly amusing to see that although the Doctor was an old man from another world, he still appeared to be more successful with women than the spotty teenager sitting at home watching him.

One hundred enjoyable minutes spent in front of the television aside, *The Aztecs* has given me many things. The first is my love of history and especially the lost civilizations of South America, but the most important lesson *The Aztecs* has taught me is to not share cocoa with a Mexican lady.

A Desperate Venture
(or, How Those Sensorites Made Me High)

The Sensorites by **Anthony Townsend**, 40(ish), London
First story: **Day of the Daleks**. Probably

It would be of no surprise to those who know me that I have an inclination toward bald, bearded men. What may be a surprise is that the bald, bearded men I hold most affection for aren't the types that now congregate in several of Tom Baker's old haunts in London's Soho, but the bald, bearded men of another planet and another time altogether. The 28th century, in fact.

This is not an easy admission to make. The inhabitants of the Sense-Sphere seldom engender love from my Whomosexual chums; more commonly derision is flung in their direction. I guess this is understandable, as few can defend the shortfalls of the story from whence they came, but it does hold a very special place in my heart. Not from viewing the serial, or from devouring the novelisation. It began with one picture.

Let's wind back a decade or three. When I was young my family moved. A lot. We never stayed anywhere long; constantly changing towns, schools and friends due to my father's itchy feet. When I was nine the biggest change of all happened: we came to the UK. Here I fell in love with **Doctor Who**, completely and utterly. I had seen it from time to time before then, watching occasionally back in New Zealand, cushion poised ready to thrust in front of my face at the echoing roar of Aggedor or the gnashing teeth of Drashigs. However, when my parents decided we would emigrate to England we fortuitously arrived just in time for that spectacular repeat series transmitted to whet the appetite for Davison's debut: **The Five Faces of Doctor Who**.

I became obsessed. There he was, a link from my past, who was the perfect role model for this strange, foreign child who didn't like sport or climbing trees, who was quiet and reserved and had spent so much time travelling (but not, unfortunately, time-travelling) that he had never built the long-term friendships or sense of self that are so important. Here was something that would give me comfort and a sense of continuity wherever we went, especially as besides the regular series on the telly there were books! And a monthly magazine! As I moved schools, my passion helped forge fleeting friendships with fellow subdued, bespectacled non-sporty types who had the same penchant.

Now, you are probably saying to yourself, apart from all the moving about this is not an unusual story. Many of us spent our time obsessing on a Time Lord's travels whilst our peers showed off on the sports pitch or objectified the opposite sex. Think you are special, you say? Where is the twist? Why have I read this far and not skipped to the far more enlightening and eloquent musings around *The Reign of Terror*?

The answer is this: I discovered **The Doctor Who Monster Book**. And in that incredible tome I found something that inspired me. A picture of ... well, guess what? Something about that image ignited my imagination. Perhaps it was their simplicity, possibly their mystery, or maybe, just maybe, I actually fancied the Sensorites in some strange way? Puberty is strange.

Whatever it was, something made me reach for the nearest malleable substance. Luckily this was a packet of Plasticine modelling clay, so I set about creating a model Sensorite. It wasn't too difficult – three inches high, orange skin, blue jump suit. Considering the photo was black and white, not a bad guess. After that I made a model of Peter Davison: yellow coat, yellow hair, eyeless, but not completely appalling. With each figure I tried to improve on the last, mixing colours to get the correct hues, diligently sculpting the shape of the nose and brow, ensuring each of my figures was as accurate as possible. Well, I had a lot of time on my hands. Once finished, I used clear nail lacquer to protect them, the only varnish I could easily get my hands on. I probably spent my early teens getting inadvertently high from the fumes.

I made masses of them - Doctors, companions, monsters, Bessie - everything **Doctor Who**-related it was possible to create. Sitting at home most evenings over the next few years whilst my family watched **Howards' Way** or **Bergerac**, poring over pictures from **Doctor Who Monthly**, working on Omega's mask or the sixth Doctor's coat. I lived on the edge of Dartmoor with few friends and even fewer social skills. Don't judge me.

It was several years before I got to do something I never thought possible. I got to meet someone who had actually worked on **Doctor Who**, David Banks, touring in the epitome of modern theatre, *The Ultimate Adventure*. To mark this auspicious occasion I gave him one of my model Cybermen. He adored it so much he promptly auctioned it off for charity at the next stop on the tour. But more importantly he did something that changed my life. He passed on my name and address to the winner. David Banks pimped me out.

Soon after I got a letter from Glasgow, beginning a correspondence. My pen pal came to visit. He invited me to a convention. I met other fans from around the country. There were *so many other fans*! One invited me to That London. I went. Regularly. These people who shared my passion also showed me it's okay to be me, to love the things I love, and be attracted to people who look like Sensorites. Or something like that, anyway. Eventually, incredibly, I was invited to leave the wilds of Dartmoor for the lights of Brighton, and begin a new life.

This magnificent chain of events is why my love for those bald beardies is unconditional, and spreads to **Doctor Who** as a whole. It is not just about the programme, but the opportunities it brings us, as fans, to come together and indulge our shared passion, meeting people who enhance and perhaps even change our lives, and appreciate how from the most seemingly inconsequential activity great things can occur.

The Sensorites changed my life. I bloody love those Sensorites.

Gimme Some Truth
The Reign of Terror by **Kate Du-Rose**, 40, Manchester
First story: **The Leisure Hive**

What's in a name? A Du-Rose by any other name? In a book about fictional stories I present a true story, just as the Reign of Terror is true. A story handed down to me by my family about my surname. Way back in the 1790s my family were French aristocracy, or in another version were Huguenots. Whichever is true, they fled persecution in France to England and presumably lived happier ever after. This story may not be factual. Most family stories are a mixture of maybes and perhaps; a multi-generational game of Chinese Whispers, but what is there not to like about being descended from French aristocracy and their desperate, possibly romantic struggle to escape Madame Guillotine?

This is one of the reasons I love the Reign of Terror. I have always been a fan of history and a sucker for historical stories. When we were taught history at school I always pictured myself there, whether it was the court of King Henry VIII or a spinner in a mill during the industrial revolution. When we did Shakespeare in English I always volunteered to read. I have books of history on my e-book reader, both 'proper' history and historical fiction.

When I watch *The Reign of Terror* I imagine my family there, sharing in Barbara, Susan, and Ian's plight. Maybe they are just off-camera. Perhaps in the next rotting cell. Perhaps they escaped just before the Doctor and his party arrive. It's just a tiny family story but it is a tie-in to the events on screen that are the same mixture of fiction and fact that my family's story is.

Sadly **Doctor Who** historicals are generally viewed as very unpopular, and despite being part of the original remit of the show, they were phased out after only a few years of the series' run. Nowadays, history in **Doctor Who** is just used as a colourful backdrop, or a necessary evil in order to meet some famous person of the past. The important rule is that **Doctor Who** is about *monsters* and not history. To quote the man himself, 'Is no-one interested in history?'

I heard once that history is just the facts tidied up, the messy bits forgotten. The winners ensuring that they fought the good fight, and showing that the other side were evil and deserved to die. **Doctor Who** does exactly this, providing a safe snap-shot of history, grafting in the Doctor and company as people to root for. We know they will get out safely no matter what happens. And the same occurs with me. I know my family make it out of France safely or I wouldn't have my name.

The other interesting thing for me about *The Reign of Terror* is the fight against the odds for me to see it. I knew it existed long before I watched it, but I was not alive when it was shown in 1964. Due to two episodes not existing it was never shown on the looped repeats by UK Gold in the 1990s when I got back into **Doctor Who**. It was the very last **Doctor Who** video to be released in 2003 for the 40th anniversary year, and this was the first time I was able to watch it. Even with two episodes missing (which I didn't get to hear until three years later when the soundtrack came out on CD) I still loved it. Whenever there are rumours of lost episodes being found I always hope for an historical such as this or even *The Massacre of St Bartholomew's Eve*. I know it's a minority view.

I could if I so desired research my family tree, and with a lot of detective work I could probably find out the facts about my family history. I could have my family set out before me and know exactly who they were, where they lived and how they died. I prefer, however, the 'true' story of their escape to England over any boring old facts, and so the Du-Rose family name and its stories will be passed on to the next generation to accept or dismiss as they choose.

The best bit of this story is that on the very day I write this the postman has delivered a shiny DVD of *The*

Reign of Terror, and not only does it feature all four episodes looking their very best (right at the end of the range again, but this time in the 50th anniversary year) but the two missing episodes have been animated to complete a visual version of the story. I am very happy that my unloved historical 'biography' is being treated in this way. Perhaps there is still some future hope for those poor Huguenots after all.

So now my true story is ended, and I am off to Paris to see my family (and the Doctor) escape Robespierre again. *Au Revoir*.

Land of the Giants
Planet of Giants by **Jo West**, 41, Surrey, UK
First story: something with the fifth Doctor in it

My Doctor is Peter Davison. I grew up seeing the odd episode but as a family we were never particularly into **Doctor Who**. I did quite like the ones I saw though.

Years went by and I married a man who loved **Doctor Who** but I still didn't see what he and others saw in it. We'd sit down with our daughter and watch the new series when it came back and she loved it. At a very young age she could name all the actors who played the Doctors.

By the time I'd seen some older stories (with most of the Doctors) I quite liked them. Matt Smith is my favourite and I really like Colin Baker even though he was horrible to Peri early on, but the ones I had seen with William Hartnell I just didn't like. I just thought he was a bad actor who always fluffed his lines.

One day my husband put on *Land of the Giants* for our daughter. I wasn't going to watch it but suddenly got really engrossed in it. I'm not sure why I liked the story so much, but the special effects and the attention to detail were amazing. Just to think what they managed with such a small budget; effects with everything in proportion, the grass, sink, telephone. And it got me looking at William Hartnell in a very different way. Now I see that what I thought was unprofessionalism with the fluffed lines and pauses; it was all part of his charm.

So now I love **Doctor Who** and class myself as a fan. I'm watching all the episodes (the ones that exist) in order. We're already on to Jon Pertwee and I'm loving it. The Master's getting annoying now, and UNIT. I wish he was travelling more.

And I know it's not called *Land of the Giants* but it really annoys my husband so I'm not going to stop doing it.

The First Video on the Bookcase

The Dalek Invasion of Earth by **Tom Henry**, 28, London / First story: **The Five Doctors**

The long sun-drenched summer of 1995 was my most intense year of **Doctor Who** watching. I watched the show on a loop. Whilst other children were outside playing in rivers or doing things with hula-hoops, I was watching Colin Baker shout at his companion, 'The tree won't hurt you!'

This continued even the week that my dad (of sorts) brought home a snooker table. He used to work as a Marie Curie carer and occasionally he would get a freebie. We never questioned the morality of this arrangement. Well, not to his face. Perhaps a full-sized snooker table was a little ostentatious for a three bedroom house on a Birmingham council estate, but it didn't have any legs. The only room in the house that could fit a legless snooker table was the living room, and that was a close call. We could barely move around it. So it was sitting on a snooker table that I ordered my **Doctor Who** VHS collection from my favourite story to my most disliked.

I would often take all the videos off the revolving bookcase and put them back on again in a different order, alphabetically or chronologically or in the order of the colour of the spine. Now, I had a problem. Only two-thirds of the bookcase was easy-to-reach, the other videos were against the back wall, amongst the mess of wires and plugs that connected the TV to the video machine. So getting the stories of the mid-to-late 1980s or those in the latter stages of the alphabet or the videos with the story titles written in blue would involve a perilous reach-around in which the home entertainment system could fall on your head. I thought that if I had easy access to the stories I liked then the amount of time I spent scrambling would be minimised.

The first video on the bookcase was the William Hartnell story *The Dalek Invasion of Earth*. Looking back, I am surprised at my choice. It's not the greatest ever story and there were many others that I enjoyed a great deal more. Indeed, for long sequences it's barely even competent. This is unsurprising considering it is written by Terry Nation, **Doctor Who**'s greatest writer of schlock, of B-movie adventures of escapes to danger and derring-do. The plot of this story only has the barest connection with sanity. The Daleks are hollowing out the Earth so they can drive it around the universe and they are defeated by the Doctor nuking Bedfordshire. Nation often got lucky in that his scripts were passed to a brilliant design team, a cast playing it for real and a production team pulling out all the stops.

This is largely what has happened here, only *The Dalek Invasion of Earth* was directed by Richard Martin, the word slapdash in human form. **Doctor Who**'s reputation for creaking floors and wobbling walls, of ludicrous giant insectoid creatures created in an afternoon, of reflections of cameras and boom mike shadows and shots of floor manager's feet was largely cemented in Richard Martin's inglorious list of fluck-ups of 1965.

So, what is the appeal of *The Dalek Invasion of Earth*? The answer lies in the flipsides of these two men. Martin's strength was in not seeing **Doctor Who** as a show with limitations. His stories are filled with things to which any responsible director would have said, 'That's a bit outside the budget,' or, 'We haven't got the time to do that effectively.' The Slyther, for example, the giant stationary upholstery monster, was not in Nation's original script. Only 1980s producer John Nathan-Turner competes with Martin for displaying **Doctor Who**'s 'We can do anything, anywhere, anytime,' worldview from the other side of the camera. I've never much cared for competence, anyway.

But perhaps the key lies with Nation's script. His broad brushstrokes mean that the dystopian Earth of the

22nd century is uncompromisingly bleak; broken families, plague, hardened and humourless people living in fear and misery. This world may be ruled by motorised dustbins, but this isn't a joke. However, when the oppressors have been vanquished, then it's time for love and hope and beauty all over again. One glorious moment comes when the Doctor, William Hartnell acting his Edwardian socks off, hears the chimes of Old Big Ben, which has miraculously survived alien occupation, places his hand on the shoulder of one of the survivors and says, 'Just a beginning, just a beginning...' Nowhere else in **Doctor Who** shows such terrible lows alongside such glorious highs. Perhaps any story with these swings of tone is going to feel illogical. This is **Doctor Who**'s **Miracle on 34th Street**, only with Daleks.

A problem arose with my filing system. I was never satisfied. I would often swap stories around as they were re-evaluated on their twentieth or thirtieth viewing. But *The Dalek Invasion of Earth* would remain the first video on the bookshelf for the entire duration. It certainly lasted longer than the snooker table, which, after a brief spell down the side of my bed, was finally placed behind the shed, and left to rot away. As far as I know it lies there still; it didn't come with us when we moved in October 1996. *The Dalek Invasion of Earth* did, but it never captured the same place in my heart. By then I was leaving **Doctor Who** behind. Well, comparatively. I was beginning to be teenage and I needed **Doctor Who**'s daft and optimistic worldview far less than ever before. In my adult life, I needed that worldview all over again. It's about time I reorganised the DVDs on my bookshelf...

Dr Who & the Black (and White) Market

The Rescue by **Antony Wainer,** 42, Bath, UK
First story: **Robot**

In a time before the internet (what did we do without it?), when a first class stamp was 17p, and Dido was a planet not a singer, the fourteen-year-old me was watching on television an episode of **Doctor Who** first transmitted on the 2nd January 1965. This episode, called *The Powerful Enemy* saw the Doctor and his friends meet a new friend and defeat the not-so-powerful Koquillion. Today, this would be a normal occurrence where the DVD release of this episode is freely available, but not so in 1985. In 1985, this fourteen-year-old was watching *The Powerful Enemy* on VHS, in a domestic video player, in his bedroom.

Now I never, ever saw myself as a video pirate, because I did not wear an eye patch and the sea reminded me of **Jaws** (and that still was not a good thought to a fourteen-year-old). But I was the original video pirate, the original space cowboy, because I swapped **Doctor Who** VHS videotapes (never sold) and I was good at it!

By 1985 *The Powerful Enemy* and *Desperate Measures* were the fifth and sixth episodes of **Doctor Who** starring William Hartnell I had seen. Yes the picture wobbled, yes the dialogue was running at a different speed to the action and yes William Hartnell was largely unfamiliar, but the beauty of this recording was that it was not out to buy in the shops. This copy had fallen through my letterbox, courtesy of a VHS tape (£1.99) and an SAE (17p), and lots and lots of love for the programme.

VHS tapes whizzed around the country like emails to an inbox. You have to remember that all this was happening when YouTube did not exist, when the last **Doctor Who** story people had seen televised was a Colin Baker story and at a time when most people called *The*

Crusade, *The Crusaders*. The need to see old **Doctor Who** was rife and *Desperate Measures* were needed to enable you to do so.

You see I was a smart fourteen years old and I made pen pals as friends, but not any old pen pals, pen pals who lived in Australia. These friends (they are like Twitter friends, you do not actually know them) also had old **Doctor Who** on VHS tape too, because **Doctor Who** was being shown there nightly, and to this fourteen-year-old that was an opportunity not to be missed. Each week I would send off a batch of VHS tapes and a couple of weeks later they would land (they were heavy) through the letterbox with a thump!

By 1987 I think I had every episode of **Doctor Who** that the BBC had themselves. It was my own archive of the past glories of the show, all on VHS, all in transmission order. When the then-producer of **Doctor Who** John Nathan Turner went on *Open Air* in 1987 and said, 'The memory cheats,' this sixteen-year-old was smart enough to know a little bit better.

I was very particular about the quality of my tapes. *The Rescue* was a really good example of a tape I wanted to 'get again.' You could not really hear the dialogue for a start! *The Green Death* was another example. 'I have in my hand a piece of paper,' went the dialogue at the beginning. I know this because I would check the quality of every single copy of *The Green Death* I ever received to see whether it was better than the one before. 'Come on lads, keep it moving. We must not keep our lords and masters waiting,' was another.

In a recent DVD release of *Revenge of the Cybermen* fans talk about buying old **Doctor Who** on the black (and white) market. This was something I knew nothing about and I was never offered a copy of a **Doctor Who** story with a price tag on it – quite the opposite in fact. All the fans I knew were keen to swap VHS video tapes because of their love for the show. This was not a world in which an episode would be repeated. If you missed it, chances are you missed it forever. So for me, like many others, fans were trying to remember adventures passed and times gone by.

Beyond *The Rescue* and *The Gunfighters* and *Genesis of the Daleks*, the most exciting video pirate was the person (who cannot be identified – let us just call her Mr Bennett) who had *Shada* on VHS. Oh what a joyous day that was, when *Shada* fell through the letterbox. This wasn't just a **Doctor Who** story, like *The Rescue*, that I had never seen before, this was a Tom Baker story I had never seen before. Picture the scene, the sixteen-year-old me, watching Koquillion's (sorry Mr Bennett's) copy of *Shada* on a ropey TV and from an even more ropey VHS copy. The excitement was immense! The memory did not cheat; Tom was still the best Doctor and *Time and the Rani* was still rubbish (sorry John, you stick to your **Open Air** story and I will stick to mine). Naturally *Shada* was wonderful and the collection was complete.

But what of the underrated *The Rescue*? Well, it is not so bad, beautifully restored onto DVD for the 42-year-old me to enjoy. But I still have those tapes of *The Rescue*, I just cannot get rid of them! *Desperate Measures* in 1985 needed desperate actions, and that's just what I did. The legacy of 27 years remains intact. Nearly three decades on and my VHS tapes are different to the DVD releases. My VHS of *The Five Doctors* is complete with an introduction by Terry Wogan, Peter Davison at the end, and the on-screen 0171 numbers to call and pledge money to **Children in Need**. As Terry says at the beginning of my VHS, 'You won't believe it, I promise you...'

What Has The Romans Ever Done For Us?

The Romans by **James Gent**, 36, Cardiff, UK
First story: **Destiny of the Daleks**

I have confessions to make. Firstly, I was a fickle fan. Not for me the vigil of keeping the spirit of the show alive during the wilderness years by consuming the novels and audios, contributing to fanzines, building a library of VHS releases. I didn't even make it to *Survival*. My faith wavered during the troubled Colin Baker era and dissipated when I went to secondary school in 1987, for the very moment my hormones kicked in coincided almost exactly with **Doctor Who** returning to the box looking more like a Children's BBC production than ever; it was embarrassing. My **DWM** subscription lapsed and my small collection of stories on VHS began to gather dust. It was 'kid's stuff.'

It was roughly halfway through this abstention that I was nonplussed to receive, as a Christmas present from a brother, the double tape of *The Rescue* and *The Romans*. Hang on, hadn't I grown out of this? - and look, boring black and white stories, too! Another confession - I freely bought into the fallacy that 1960s **Doctor Who** was slow paced and the historicals were flops. This is the story of how one humble videotape made me a fan reborn.

It all began when I left the security of University for the uncertainties of adult life, unconsciously drawing myself back to all those toys in the attic I'd previously discarded. With the nostalgia fad for all things 1970s, there was no better time to be in a state of arrested development, and I went from lapsed fan to born-again evangelical, as those old tapes got dusted off and - deep joy for me, Herculean labour for my housemates - I worked my way through all the stories I had never seen, thanks to second-hand shops and UK Gold.

I'd worked through rejection and denial and moved on to acceptance, but *The Romans* was to be my true epiphany. That unloved gift must have been glaring accusingly from the shelf just once too often, and I plucked it down with a weary, resigned, 'Okay, let's do this. How bad can it be?'

How had this story earned such indifference that it had sat unseen all these years? As an impressionable young fanboy, I gorged myself on Peter Haining's thumping hardback bibles and Jean Marc Lofficier's briskly efficient **Programme Guide**. The tone of Jeremy Bentham's take on the older stories in **A Celebration**, and the occasional **DWM** feature on the 1960s serials, was so academic and respectful, it fostered the impression that the series' early past was something to be revered rather than enjoyed, like Shakespeare at school.

A story like *The Romans* ticks all of the boxes that once had it and its stable-mates marked down in these Gospels of Received Wisdom as 'purely of historic interest'; it features a Doctor who supposedly fluffed more lines than he got right, two companions who looked like the people you'd least want to travel in time and space with - cardigan-wearing teachers! - and it's an historical, aka 'the boring ones with no monsters.' It wasn't just *The Romans* that was due a re-assessment, it was my whole perspective on the show.

About five minutes into the story, with the TARDIS team enjoying a impromptu holiday, I realised I'd conned myself, and it just got better and better. *The Romans* was such a riot of laughter and high drama, it provoked an instant, fulsome recant of all my misgivings for 'vintage' **Doctor Who**.

Dennis Spooner's witty, engaging script, performed by a cast at the top of their game, proved that all human life was here! *The Romans* leaves us with no illusions as to the reality of life in imperial Rome, which was pretty cheap for the great unwashed; Ian gets put through his paces as a galley slave, and we share Barbara's revulsion at being offered as a concubine for

Nero's court. Meanwhile, Derek Francis' Nero immoderately embodies greed and gluttony, his appetite extending to the carnal as he joins the ranks of Barbara's unwanted admirers – Barbara was the Peri Brown of her day!

The stakes for Barbara and Ian are very real, Vicki is a resourceful, bright companion and the Doctor is on wily, mischievous form, revealing a hitherto unknown talent for fisticuffs and revelling in the comedy Spooner's script presents for Hartnell the Ealing veteran – for this last reason alone, it justifies the release of existing stories on CD as the quality of the script proves it holds its own on audio.

Since the series returned in 2005, *The Romans* has proved its value once again, as a lesson not to be blinded by distinctions such as 'classic **Who**' and 'Nu**Who**'. A key element in the new series' success in appealing to a broad audience was putting humour and sentiment front and centre of the format. *The Romans* covers it all, it hits all the bases. Stick an open minded, intelligent 'classic **Who**' virgin in front of *The Romans* and I'd wager they'd be surprised at how many recognisable ingredients from the new series are present and correct – place it beside *The Fires of Pompeii* and, dramatically, they're cut from the same cloth, give or take added pathos in the latter.

The ultimate clincher that we're really watching the same programme can be found in the scenes between Ian and Barbara that bookend the serial. The teachers' frisky horseplay casually debunks the myth that the old series was a chaste and epicene affair, with 'No hanky panky in the TARDIS.' If that's not a loved-up couple in honeymoon mode, my name's Maximus Petullian.

What has *The Romans* ever done for us? Proved that the past, whether of Imperial Rome or 1960s Lime Grove, isn't such a different country after all. We can pigeonhole and classify all day, but at heart it is still the same show it always has been.

Life with the Zarbi
The Web Planet by **David O'Brien**, 46, Saffron Walden
First story: **The Claws of Axos**

Ricky had everything. He was the only person I knew that had **Pong**, one of the first video games. He also had 30-minute versions of the two Dalek movies on his Dad's film projector. Our joint enthusiasm for science fiction stemmed back to when my family and I had moved into a block of flats where Ricky lived. It was 1974 and we would sit on the cold, hard floor of the downstairs lobby, read comics and discuss anything that attracted our interest from TV and cinema to the latest toys, magazine and books. It was here that he first showed me a copy of the **Radio Times** 10th Anniversary **Doctor Who** Special and my passing interest in this show grew into something more. Aside from the magazine's cover, there was one image that burned into my memory that day: a two-legged ant-creature standing on a lunar surface. There was something about it which was familiar, but I had no idea why. The feeling soon passed as we went onto the next of Ricky's seemingly endless collection of things.

The following year, my interest in the programme became deeper, after a chance purchase of *The Three Doctors* novel got me hooked. Not long afterwards, I came across the book **Doctor Who and the Zarbi**. The collage of bee-men and giant ants from the 10th Anniversary Special, amidst planets and fiery stars, adorning the cover offered a genuine outer-space adventure! Disappointingly, the content featured no journey through space, but the book nonetheless drew me in with its alien environment, the like of which I hadn't seen the TV series equal. There were also illustrations throughout the book, the first of which showed 'Doctor Who' (as he was referred to) piloting 'Tardis' from a **Flash Gordon**-style rocket-ship control panel. To a nine-year-old it felt as though I had missed a truly exciting era of **Doctor Who**, where he steered the TARDIS like a rocket to mysterious moonscapes, where aliens really did look *alien* rather than men in rubber costumes.

I still had the sense of *déjà vu*, that I had felt the previous year. Only this time, the long buried memory surfaced. I was unable to shake off the haunting image of an old man in front of a blue, pointy roofed house, surrounded by *bumble bee men* and *giant ants*. It *must* have been a real memory because of the similarities with **Doctor Who and the Zarbi**. I reasoned that perhaps it was simply an earlier cover for the novel.

'Ice Warriors versus Cybermen' proclaimed the cover of issue 16 of **Doctor Who Weekly**. That was enough to get anyone excited. Except me. I was more interested in: 'The Doctor is trapped on THE WEB PLANET,' accompanied by an insert photo of a Menoptera! Standing in the newsagents, I flicked to the article and eagerly pored over every beautiful photograph - it was everything I had ever imagined, those five years ago. When part two was published the following week, I read both articles alongside the novel and imagined watching the show as it unfolded on TV. Although by now, I knew more about the early series, it still felt as though I had missed a golden age of **Doctor Who**, with sets that could no longer be matched.

1982 was a very good year. I went abroad for the first time, started taking a serious interest in girls and getting into music in a big way. 1982 got off to a flying start with a new series of **Doctor Who**, featuring a new Doctor. The added bonus came during the airing of *Earthshock* when the review show **Did You See?** broadcast clips from several early episodes, including from *The Web Planet*. I waited patiently for the story that had weaved itself through my life like no other. Watching in stunned silence I heard the Menoptera speaking in their bizarre tones for the first time and once again, I wasn't disappointed.

It was another eight years and the start of a new decade before I finally got to see it on home video. Of course there were problems; creaking stage floor, missed-cues, and yes, banging into cameras. But I lost myself in the story, as I always had done. For the first time, I experienced the otherworldly sound effects and the planet-scape was still incredible, considering it was filmed in such cramped conditions and on a relatively small budget. Even the actors realised their characterisations away from the norm – from the creepy voice of the Animus to the balletic movements of the Menoptera.

The final part of my life with the Zarbi occurred in the 1990s. My friend Alan was moving into a new house and several of us helped him to sort through items to be thrown away. He knew I had an interest in **Doctor Who** and handed me something that made me catch my breath. Looking up at me was the white haired old man and his 'blue house' surrounded by amongst others, Zarbi and Menoptera – the first **Doctor Who Annual** which dated from 1965. The final part of my lost memory. Sometime in my past, I had obviously seen this book and it had sat in my subconscious, until Ricky's magazine awoke the memory. This annual, printed before I was born, turned out to be my earliest memory of **Doctor Who** – perhaps even predating my vague recollection of watching *The Claws of Axos* as a five-year-old.

I'm aware of how fandom views this story, but I continue to enjoy *The Web Planet*. Its image had the power to stay in my young mind long after more beloved stories had faded. I admire the ambition and foresight of people who had created something so very different. Even today, such audacious experimentation is rare, and television is the poorer for it.

A Thousand Words of Compliment and Love
The Crusade by **Andrew Orton**, 30, Durham, UK
First story: **The Brain of Morbius**

Episode three of *The Crusade*, *The Wheel of Fortune*, features the best scene in **Doctor Who**. I'd like to talk to you about it.

In a blatant attempt at orgiastic self-promotion, I'd like to mention that I've recently been writing a book about **Robin of Sherwood** (**Hooded Man,** Miwk Publications, coming 2014; *buy it*), and as a result I've been doing a fair bit of research into Richard I of England in the process. One knock-on side-effect of this is an unexpected and unasked for knowledge of the politics of the medieval Levant, hence me now writing about *The Crusade*, because I find suddenly that it fascinates me.

The complexity of what's going on in *The Crusade* is incredible. Years of war and conflict over the governance of Jerusalem had culminated in Richard, King of the English, sodding off to the Holy Land to have a fight with Saladin, and unexpectedly finding him to be a bit of an honourable chap. The crucial scene here is one that nobody ever mentions, and which I want to talk to you about, because its intricacy and importance make me stare open-mouthed with something approaching veneration. It unfolds toward the end of *The Wheel of Fortune* (not the game show). It is simultaneously a discussion of the gender politics of medieval Europe, casual racism, the religious implications of The Divine Right of Kings, the world-weariness and attrition of war, and the political and religious situation of the Levant in the twelfth century, with overtones of court intrigue, farcical theatrical misunderstanding and conscious treachery and danger for the leads. It covers anger, resentment, pride, amusement, danger, authoritarianism and disappointment. Oh, and love. The play of emotion and historical detail is enormous, and it does it in about three minutes. It also contains the two best guest performances in the Hartnell series, in Julian Glover and Jean Marsh.

At the start of the scene, the Doctor and Vicki are considered friends of both the King and his sister; at the end they are welcomed by neither. Vicki has been pretending to be a young man at court, Victor, and her guise has now been uncovered. The King's sister, Joanna, comments favourably on Vicki's appearance, and the pleasure she feels at the boyish page being revealed as another woman at court. Leicester is less concerned, humouring dryly Joanna's care with an ironic, 'a fair rose of England.' He has more political matters (concerning both the King's ambition and his own) on his mind. Joanna's personal side is cast light on in an exchange which draws attention to the importance of the difference between being a male or a female at court.

Joanna then consults privately with the Doctor and Vicki, asking them whether they have learned anything of the King's intentions towards her during their time with him. The Doctor is placed into an awkward position: he will ensure Joanna's ire if he does not tell her the King's plans, but will incur the King's anger if he does tell her. The Doctor maintains his silence, claiming he does not want to steal the King's thunder. Joanna storms off angrily to talk with Leicester.

As the Doctor and Vicki debate their circumstances, the King enters. It's clear to the viewer, but not the King, that Leicester has told Joanna of the King's plans.

Richard is attempting to sell his sister to Saladin's brother Saphadin. The King wants her to be married to a man that she has never met, and whom due to her prejudices she despises; all for the sake of a land dispute guised in a religious conflict. Just to put this in context, the entire future of Western and Middle Eastern civilisation is being decided in one man's attempt to marry off his sister against her wishes. Joanna's response to Richard is the clash between a man who acts purely for political endeavour and a woman reacting entirely according to her personal emotional responses.

> Joanna: I will speak with my brother!
> Richard: Oh?
> Joanna: What's this I hear? I can't believe it's true. Marriage to that heathenish man, that infidel?
> Richard: We will give you reasons for it.
> Joanna: This unconsulted partner has no wish to marry! I am no sack of flour to be given in exchange!
> Richard: It is expedient, the decision has been made.
> Joanna: Not by me and never would be!

Richard's attempts to placate her are futile, for Joanna is appalled at the thought of her brother selling her like an object. Richard attempts to pass off his actions by acting the King, and discusses the difficulties of maintaining a protracted war in unfamiliar surroundings.

> Richard: Joanna, please consider. This war is full of weary, wounded men. This marriage wants a little thought by you, then you'll see the right of it.
> Joanna: And how would you have me go to Saphadin? Bathed in oriental perfume, I suppose? Supient, tender and affectionate, soft-eyed and trembling, eager with a thousand words of compliment and love? Well, I like a different way to meet the man I am to wed!
> Richard: Well if it's a meeting you want...

> Joanna: I do not want! I will not have it!

Note the elegance of David Whittaker's script as Joanna sarcastically outlines her role. Joanna storms from the room, and the King follows, angrily ordering his courtiers away as he does so. And then comes the breathtaking moment with a righteously outraged King Richard:

> Richard: Joanna, I beg you to accept.
> Joanna: No!
> Richard: I entreat you, Joanna!
> Joanna: No!
> Richard: Very well. I am the King. *We command you!*
> Joanna: You cannot command this of me.
> Richard: *Cannot*?!

While the mock-Victorian third-person exclamation, 'We command you!' is marginally absurd, Julian Glover squeals out his last word '*Cannot*?!' with amazing force, overtaken by the scene and his incredulity at what he, the King of The English, is hearing. He's never before had his authority questioned as publicly and openly as this. Brilliantly, Jean Marsh is more than a match for him, and refuses, calling upon the higher authority left open to her: the Pope, whose influence is more than that of any man, due to his precedence at the top of the Divine Right of Kings. Joanna is certain that the Pope will not allow her marriage to what she calls an 'infidel.'

> Richard: You defy me with the Pope!
> Joanna: No, you defy the world with your politics! The reason you and all your armies are here is the reason on my side. You are here to fight these dogs, defeat them. Marry me to them and you make a pact with

> the Devil. Force me to it and I'll turn
> the world we know into your enemy!

Here we get the more political reasons for Joanna's disapproval. Aside from the casual racism in calling the Muslims 'dogs,' the reference to the Devil speaks perfectly to the medieval interpretation of Saladin's religion as being the antithesis of Christianity. Having called upon religion and reason, Joanna again attempts to flee, assertively, from the argument. Richard moves to strike his sister but stops himself, and Joanna, maintaining her dignity at court, walks away, intent on avoiding the casual misogyny exhibited by her brother. The problem is, the King believes it to be the Doctor, not Leicester, that broke his plans to Joanna.

> Richard: Who gave away my plan?
> The Doctor: Your majesty, if you believe that I...
> Richard: You are not welcome in our sight.

And we end on a big fat close-up of William Hartnell's fantastic 'affronted' face.

In one scene, we've taken in such a huge range of emotions and arguments, and expounded greatly on the political landscape of the medieval age. I love that **Doctor Who** can do all that in one scene, and in a story that everyone forgets about, even if they're somehow conscious that it's a story other people like. What's perhaps most impressive is that this was written by the same man who had previously written the tense psychological thriller *The Edge of Destruction*, and would go on to write the James Bond pastiche *The Enemy of the World*, futuristic Cyberman 'drama' *The Wheel in Space*, and gung-ho army action-adventure *The Ambassadors of Death*. If one thing is true of Whittaker's scripts, it is that the motivations of his characters are defined and significant to his plots.

I wish he'd written more historicals. Fifty years after it was first broadcast, I'm writing a book about the same period in history, which discusses the same characters; and the depth of detail that I now see that *The Crusade* delves into makes me love it all the more. And so I say: *The Crusade* has the best scene in all of **Doctor Who** in it. Go and watch it. Marvel.

P.S. Unasked-for *The Crusade* trivia: one of the British agents who is unmasked in the James Bond film **Skyfall** is called Ben Daheer.

Goo Goo Ga Joob

The Space Museum by **Andrew Hickey**, 34,
Manchester, UK / First story: **The Five Doctors**

The Space Museum was broadcast on April 24th, 1965. It doesn't sound all that long ago, but it's still twenty-five million, one hundred and twenty-five thousand, one hundred and twenty Earth minutes.

We watch **Doctor Who** these days with all sorts of ideas about what it 'should' be, and stories like *The Space Museum*, which simply don't fit those preconceptions, get short shrift, and as a result the whole Hartnell era tends to be ignored by the majority of fans as some sort of failed attempt at doing the series that is only interesting as an example of people working towards the 'proper' way of doing things.

So the normal view of *The Space Museum* is that the first episode is 'dark' and 'disturbing' and therefore very good, while episodes two through four are rubbish. Now, if you actually *watch* the thing, without a preconceived idea as to what the show should be doing, this is not a conclusion you'd come to. In fact, what you'd realise is that it's four different styles of programme, in different genres, even though the plot is largely continuous between the four episodes. The lack of consistency is a feature, not a bug.

So episode one, the one that's universally praised, is clearly a wonderful piece of television, and it does have all the creepiness and strangeness that everyone attributes to it, but it's also *funny* – 'Doctor, we've got our clothes on!' 'Well I should hope so my dear boy,' is still one of the great dialogue exchanges of the series.

And this is where people go wrong with the story, because the next episode is one of the great comedy episodes of the series, and the fact that people have taken the tone of the first episode as the tone of the story blinds them to what's actually happening here. Yes, there's some terrible dialogue and wooden performances, but just look at how the Doctor works in the story. He comes in and refuses to take all of the genre trappings seriously. When he's having his mind read he reveals that he's a walrus (two years before John Lennon), he hides in the Dalek and parodies its voice (and says he's the master, six years before Roger Delgado) - he treats the whole thing as a joke.

Fans like to talk about how the Doctor, in Tom Baker's years especially, but throughout the show, bursts into a standard genre story and disrupts it. Here we have the Doctor *bursting into a dull **Doctor Who** story and disrupting it*, and it gets ignored because it's a Hartnell story and so they can't be doing anything that clever. All the dull 'space' talk is precisely the kind of thing people who didn't watch **Doctor Who** then would have thought **Doctor Who** was like all the time, and the Doctor won't take even that at all seriously, and his mere presence in the story disrupts it and makes it strange.

Then we have the episode with no Doctor, and we're into a 'help the young rebels overthrow the corrupt government' story of a type we've seen a million times, and we're likely to dismiss it as clichéd ... but this was the first time **Doctor Who** had actually done that, and we've suddenly got a show which is taking the side of youth revolution against the old order, even though its lead is a crotchety old man. A different genre again, and the closest **Doctor Who** comes for many years to an actual political statement.

And then there's episode four, which, fair enough, is a bit poor.

The people who dismiss this story, then, seem to be doing it from an ahistorical perspective - the story changes from one kind of thing to another (when it was never intended to be watched all in one go, but over four weeks between *The Crusade* and *The Chase*), and some of the things it's doing for the first time are things we've seen 'before' - a decade or two after this story.

And this is why Hartnell gets dismissed by so many people, completely unfairly. Look at the man's performance here, the way he moves between giggling maniac and utter seriousness, the way he uses the camera and always knows exactly how to position himself within the frame. This is a world-class actor, and he's playing the Doctor as a more multi-faceted character than he ever gets to be again.

Yet he's dismissed because he sometimes stumbles over his words. Now, even ignoring the extent to which this was a deliberate choice (and obviously he *did* fluff his lines, quite a lot), in what world is that *bad* acting? In the real world, people stumble over their words, pause, stutter and utter malapropisms. If you actually listen to most people talk, they can barely get through one coherent sentence at a time.

Yet Hartnell is regularly criticised for these same things - he is, in effect, criticised for giving a more realistic, naturalistic portrayal than any of his successors in the role. Because **Doctor Who** fans as a group want something that is as close to how they remember Pertwee or Tom Baker being (or, in the case of new series fans, to David Tennant) as possible.

But no other Doctor could have pulled off *The Space Museum* anything like as wonderfully as Hartnell does. Where Tom Baker would have walked in and hammed the whole thing up, or Sylvester McCoy would have shouted and rrrrrolled his rrrrrs, Hartnell is utterly unlike anything on TV before or since.

The Space Museum is not a story that should need defending. It's utterly of its time, but it was meant to be. It's funny, it's clever, and it has the best Doctor in it.

Chasing the Dream
The Chase by **Michael Seely**, 41, Norwich, Norfolk, UK
First story: **Planet of the Spiders**

Can you remember your first time? I can, vividly. It was down on the carpet at a friend's house, one dark Sunday afternoon, November 1985. His grandparents were away so we had the house all to ourselves - three of us - me, Darren and Mark. Young teenagers, ready for a spot of experimentation. Sontaran experimentation, actually, but Darren couldn't find the tape. He had lent it to Kevin. I wasn't sorry, for Darren had something else up his sleeve - well, on the shelf actually.

Darren had just started going to a local **Doctor Who** group. The one in Norwich was remarkably sane, and lacked the sort of personality disorders prevalent in forums these days. I couldn't yet go. The club met every other Friday night in the middle of the red light district. You could select a VHS tape to take home and watch. 'But don't copy,' they said. 'It's sort of illegal.' Typed labels hinted at monochrome magic and fuzzy CSO beauties. Most of them were quite watchable - in that you could watch them without seeing the world as a fuzzy bit of CSO for a few hours afterwards. I didn't have a video player, and getting 'video time' at a friend's house was rare. My mate Martin had a video, but it was a freakin' Betamax.

Having heard tales of the treasures Darren had seen at the Club, and at home, my chance had finally come. I had seen what was typed on the label of this cassette. *The Chase*. Daleks! Black and white! Hartnell! 'It's too long,' Darren said. I wasn't going to be denied. 'Let's watch bits of it,' I said. Mark groaned. He wasn't into **Doctor Who** as much as we others were. Tough. He would have to sit very patiently, as my dream came true.

This was my first pirated video, my first glimpse of a story not yet twenty years old, which I had heard a few things about from my dad, and seen pictures from in the magazine. Repeat seasons of classic **Doctor Who** stories were now non-existent. The show was off-air, and rumour had it that when it did come back, that would be the end of it. Videos were being released, but they might as well have been on another planet as far as I was concerned. As for black and white stories, they were *never* going to be repeated, or released on video. This was the month *The Seeds of Death* came out on tape.

After a few agonising moments, listening to the screeching of the tape fast forwarding, accompanied by Mark's sighs, Darren hit the play button. And there was Ian and Vicki, sitting on a sand dune, talking about castles. The sun set rather quickly on Aridius. That sand storm looked brilliant! I never knew the first Doctor had a hat - oh, I'd forgotten what he sounded like. Why is the picture going berserk? That *An Unearthly Child* repeat was such a long time ago. Daleks coming out of the sand! End credits are a bit dull. The Aridians tell the Doctor and Barbara (she's nice...) their sad tale. 'The Doctor looks bored,' quipped Darren. So did Mark.

More fast forwarding. Daleks kill! That Aridian took his time dying. The Mire Beast is a bit on the floppy side. What sort of jaunty music is this supposed to be? We skipped the Empire State Building as I wanted to see the Marie Celeste - one of Dad's tales. Dad remembers the Doctor rowing away from the boat, commenting on the name of the ship. That doesn't happen. We wondered why that bloke emerged from a cabin oblivious to the racket a little earlier. 'Taking a dump?' Mark muttered. Hollow Daleks!

The TARDIS was just beautiful. That console, never bettered. Those roundels, so big, and different-looking walls! Shame about the scanner. Manky old TV set. It doesn't have a proper landing sound.

We saw a few bits of Dracula and Frankenstein going mad, the android Doctor telling the Daleks, 'Don't fuss so,' and heartless Darren skipped on to *Planet of Decision*. And there they were - the Mechonoids. Just beautiful. Shame about their wobbly antennas. For some reason I told Mark an anecdote I once read about them -

as if he cared. Don't worry, Mark, we were only one year from watching pornos around your house, and two years from - well, best not said. There was Peter Purves! That little puff of smoke kills a Dalek? Lame. And so was Vicki. Bloody hell, she's wet. Push her off that 'high' roof. Barbara's pants... The battle between the Daleks and Mechonoids was the highlight. The way the city dissolved into smoke was amazing - how did they do that? That's a Fungoid?! That's a jungle?! Ian and Barbara's farewell. 'Oh, it's just photographs,' Darren told me a few days earlier. I see what he means.

And that was it. I had seen something special. Had I been a smoker, I think I would have needed a packet of twenty when the tape finished. Mark was already a smoker, and needed one out of sheer boredom. He was a colour TV lad, after all. He would have liked *The Sontaran Experiment.*

All I had to do now was to get my own copies, on audio tape, alas. Darren wasn't keen to spend two and a half hours in silence taping *The Chase* for me, as keeping his family quiet was a tall order. But he did manage to do one for me - *The Sontaran Experiment.* Okay. My first 'olde timey' **Doctor Who** audio, with a few bits from another story thrown in on the other side. Sorry *Tubular Bells*, needs must. That was a bootleg too.

The next time I did it on Darren's carpet, it was on a Sunday morning, and in front of his grandparents too. They didn't seem to mind, and neither did I. It was *The Ambassadors of Death*. Mark stayed at home.

Out of Time
The Time Meddler by **Sam Hemming**, 29, Exeter, UK
First Story: **The Time Meddler**

I have an overly romanticised view of my first memories of **Doctor Who**. In January 1992, an eight-year-old boy who was too young to have remembered the tail end of the McCoy era, switched on a black and white TV in his parents' spare room and began watching the first episode of *The Time Meddler*.

Looking back through the rose-tinted glasses of retrospect, I love the fact it was on a black and white TV. It somehow feels more 'authentic' to me to have seen an episode originally transmitted in black and white on a black and white set. Silly, but there you go. Since that day, I've been hooked. And while I do love *The Time Meddler* as a story, it was later stories in that repeat run in the early 1990s that really cemented my love for the series - most especially *The Mind Robber*, the highly imaginative and odd story that was repeated next. But all the elements of the series were there in *The Time Meddler* - the eccentricities, the anachronisms, the sense of justice, the time travel, the light-hearted moments, and contrastingly the ever-present spectre of death.

To my eight-year-old mind, the anachronistic nature of this story in particular really fired my imagination - what was a digital wristwatch doing in the time of the Battle of Hastings? On this note, my first ever cliffhanger was the final part of the puzzle that made me fall in love with the series - this old man, my new friend, the Doctor, walks into an eleventh century monastery, which judging by the chanting we've heard for the last ten minutes, should be teeming with monks. What he finds is a gramophone, now skipping, which really shouldn't be there. An amusing cliffhanger, but also one which made me want to carry on with this series, to see what happens next, a feeling which has lasted 22 years and counting. And I believe that this is one of the biggest strengths of

Doctor Who – by the nature of the concept of the series, almost anything is possible, and it is not tied down by the format that many other sci-fi space-exploration series have – necessitating ideas like the holodecks and time travel in **Star Trek** for example, which widened the scope of that series.

Part of me is also quite pleased that I became a fan in the 'wilderness years' in between series. I was almost ashamed to be a fan then, and would rarely admit to it at school, because of the extremely unfashionable image it had at the time. I look back today, with almost an over-saturation of **Doctor Who**, feeling utterly spoilt by all the **Doctor Who** that I have at my fingertips, with being a fan almost approaching 'fashionable', and I thank the fates that something made me go upstairs that Friday in 1991 to start this journey.

Galaxy Four, Aged Four

Galaxy 4 by **Kevin Jon Davies**, 51, London, UK
First story: **The Web Planet**, maybe?

It was the fizzog at the window that did it. That ugly mush sent me scurrying behind the armchair in terror as the scary music kicked in and the credits rolled. 'Look out, it's back again!' teased my uncle Cookie, and I believed him. I dared not peek. For years afterwards, I relived that seminal moment in 1965, and wondered: did they really fade up a picture of that monstrous face again, just as the second episode ended?

I'd been looking forward to this new **Doctor Who** story, *Galaxy 4*, since seeing an alarming photo at a neighbour's flat. Auntie Jean, my Mum's workmate from her days at the library, had a nice coffee table, unfamiliar biscuits and a newspaper (or was it a magazine?) with this horrifying picture of a squat little robot injecting **Doctor Who** right in his bloomin' leg!

By the time of my fourth birthday that June, I'd already been aware of the show for several months. Mum reckoned she watched it from the very start, sometimes with me on her lap. My Nan used to buy me strips of water transfers with colourful pictures I recognised; the TARDIS, Daleks, Mechonoids and those giant ant things; the Zarbi. I'd definitely seen an episode at my friend Gillian's jelly and ice cream party, where her parents had turned off all the lights and we'd watched **Doctor Who** in the dark! What an atmosphere! This was an inspired idea on their part; feeding our imaginations and seeding my lifelong devotion.

That August, at Selfridges in London, I'd been further traumatised by meeting a big red Dalek in person. It towered over me, gliding through the Saturday shoppers, as I took refuge behind my Dad. He'd carried me aloft through the crowded exhibition plugging the new Dalek movie and I'd been hypnotized by black and white clips playing on little screens in a mock up of their control room. We had to move along eventually to let others have a look. Several Daleks stood sentry nearby, safely behind some railings whilst another, more alarmingly, was strung up from the ceiling, as if it might fly!

But the notion that really had me in its grip was the image of that horrible little dome-shaped robot, jabbing the Doctor in the leg (with what, a needle, wasn't it?) and as kids, weren't we *all* terrified of inoculations?

Luckily, come Saturday, my fears proved unfounded and no such scene occurred in the show. The photo had lied! The ray gun-toting, glamorous blonde Drahvin women eventually turned out to be the real villains. The monstrous face at the window was revealed to be from one of a race of a friendly aliens and their little robot Chumblies swiftly became my favourites. Cookie even taught me how to draw one in chalk on my blackboard. He and my great aunt Rose were the creative ones in the family, encouraging my various artistic endeavours. It was Cookie's 8mm film camera on which I made my first home movie, over a decade later.

It wasn't until about that time, 1976, laughing about these traumatising childhood memories with the first **Doctor Who** Appreciation Society president, Jan Vincent-Rudzki, that I learned the identity of the terrifying face at the window. Apparently it was a Rill. Jan was a bit older than me, so He Knew These Things. I'd never seen a picture of a Rill, because it wasn't even in that bible of proto-fandom, the **Radio Times** 10th Anniversary Special. To our dismay, it soon became common knowledge that many of these early, half-forgotten episodes were sadly missing from the archives.

Jan had been given a rare film clip of a Chumbley whilst helping the producers of 1977's **The Lively Arts**: *Whose Doctor Who* documentary. He'd eventually shown me the prized snippet in 1993, whilst I was directing the 30th anniversary BBC1 tribute documentary **Thirty Years In The Tardis**. Shame we never got around to arranging its inclusion in the programme.

It was whilst fulfilling this lifelong dream of 'playing at **Doctor Who**' within the confines of BBCTV Centre, that I first met Jessica Carney, William Hartnell's granddaughter, who'd been researching his life for a posthumous biography. On a visit to her flat in Tooting, I was privileged to pour through Hartnell's personal scrapbooks and albums, including one presented to him after he'd made an appearance at RAF Culdrose, in July 1966. And there was a photo of an actual Chumbley at the same airshow! It was fascinating to finally see one in such sharp detail. I could clearly see the ridges in the dome-shaped shell, formed by the moulding process in the semi-translucent fibreglass.

But even more exciting was the relatively recent news that a complete episode of *Galaxy 4* had just been discovered and returned to the archives. I couldn't wait to relive the continuation of that awesome cliff-hanger and see the Rill face that had haunted my childhood nightmares. By the time you read this, the third episode, *Air Lock,* should be out on an official BBC DVD, ready to be enjoyed all over again by the fans. Okay, I'll admit it's more than a little hokey, but for those of us who were watching that first broadcast, it's an important bit of nostalgia. I loved the wobbly radiophonic sounds and how the lights flashed in the Chumblies' domes when they communicated.

Oh yes, and finally, at a party in 2004, I actually got to meet a genuine Drahvin, the wife of William ('Schhh, you know who') Franklyn; Susanna Carroll. She was still a lovely lady, but disappointingly, no longer toting her ray gun.

Into the Unknown
Mission to the Unknown by **Christian Tarpey**, UK
First story: **Terror of the Zygons**

I've never seen *Mission to the Unknown*, but then again if you're under fifty you won't have either. Nor will an awful lot of other people, and that's because it's one of those all too common things, a missing episode. In fact I'd go as far as to say it's one of the most missing episodes ever. One of only three (the others being *Marco Polo* and *The Massacre of St Bartholomew's Eve*) stories where not a single frame of video footage is known to survive, not even telesnaps. It's also only one of two stories offered for overseas sale but never bought, meaning it's unlikely it'll ever be found. But luckily the most important thing is that it still does exist in the form of an audio recording, and there are a few photos taken for the press covering the leaving of Verity Lambert, making reconstructions or just the audio track the only way many people, including myself, will ever experience it. But what I sometimes wonder though is, is that a bad thing?

Take a look at the release of *Tomb of the Cybermen* for instance. Before 1992 it was hailed as one of the greatest, most atmospheric stories ever made, a sort of Holy Grail of missing episodes that fans were desperate to see. But when it was discovered and hastily released to video tape a lot of people were disappointed. The video revealed some slightly dodgy acting, inconsistent Cybermats, and that the Cybermen needed a little more help than they'd like to admit when throwing a man to the floor.

The story was so mythologised – and just generally made better in the imagination of fans – that the real thing, no matter how good it was, just couldn't live up to it. The same I think may be said about *Mission to the Unknown*. It is in itself a very interesting and unusual story in that it doesn't feature the Doctor whatsoever, and is often described as a space-age James Bond, and it's easy to tell from the soundtrack that that's what the production team were going for. It even contains the line, 'Space Security Service, licensed to kill.' Would it really live up to that on screen though? I really doubt it.

I may sound really negative about the story right now, but it honestly is one of my favourites and I wouldn't care if it turned out the jungle was made of cardboard, the spaceship walls wobbled and that Lowery's transformation into a Varga plant, which sounds quite scary on audio, turned out to be Jeremy Young writhing about trying to hide his hand in a fluffy cactus glove – if it meant I could see just a minute of the story whatsoever. But I know I'm not alone in this, with the amount of reconstructions that have been available over the years, and the many animated reconstructions and even a live action one on YouTube. I really don't think it would live up to the expectations of someone who doesn't love it already.

Mission to the Unknown is particularly important to me as it was the first ever audio-only story that I'd ever heard. I only started watching **Doctor Who** in the 1990s during the UKTV repeats, and before that had only vague knowledge that it was an old science fiction show; watching it on weekend mornings I was hooked, and found a wealth of Target novelisations and old reference books in my local library that I poured over to find out as much about the series as I could. It was here that I first saw a photograph of the delegates around a table from this story, it just looked amazing. One of the delegates had a costume made of tubes and a blotched face and another looked like a giant chess piece! But I couldn't find any other mention of the story anywhere and I slowly gave up looking.

Then of course came the internet, and a new series of **Doctor Who** in 2005 that restored my interest in the show. I remembered the strange-looking creatures from the book, and after a bit of searching and a bit of disappointment when I found that it only survived as an audio story, I heard *Mission to the Unknown* and *The Daleks' Master Plan* together. I loved them. They're from a time when science fiction was more innocent and less convoluted, where the rocket ship is referred to simply as 'the rocket ship,' and can be fixed using a tool box full of spanners and a wrench, where everyone talks in received pronunciation and villains are so confident they feel safe enough to announce their evil plans over a loud speaker system that can be heard by passing Space Security agents. To someone like me, who doesn't really like big budget Americanised modern sci-fi, this is really refreshing. Don't get me wrong, I like the new series, but it's just nice to take a break from cinematic twisty-turny shows once in a while, and swap some CGI for dubious model work and MP3-players for tape recorders the size of a suitcase. Even though you can't watch *Mission to the Unknown*, it's just so obvious from the soundtrack that the whole thing is easy to imagine.

It's such a novelty and I really admire the bravery of the production team, to not only have a story with no mention of the Doctor whatsoever, but to introduce a new cast of characters, make me care about them, mercilessly kill them all off and then not reference any of this the week after. And all in a glorious 25 minutes, that no one will probably ever see again.

The Trojan Submission
The Myth Makers by **Andrew T. Smith**, 26, Gateshead
First story: **Dimensions in Time**

Subject:	You and Who Entry
From:	JR@mercifuleditor.co.uk
Date:	Wednesday, January 30, 2013 2.27 pm
To:	drew42@procrastimail.com

Hi Andrew,
Are you still alive? The deadline is tomorrow and I haven't heard from you since November.
Hope all is well,
JR

Subject:	RE: You and Who Entry
From:	drew42@procrastimail.com
Date:	Wednesday, January 30, 2013 11.46 pm
To:	JR@mercifuleditor.co.uk

Hi JR,
I'm really sorry, but I still haven't finished my entry on The Myth Makers for **You and Who**. To be honest, I'm struggling with it and thought it only polite to email you to explain why. I think my main problem is to do with the personal spin you asked us to put on these articles. You see, I've never actually seen or heard The Myth Makers. I'll get round to it, though. I promise.

I have read the story's Target novelisation. Twice, in fact; which is rare for me when it comes to that range. I'm one of that annoying generation of **Doctor Who** fans who joined the show during that period in the mid- to late-1990s when just about *everything* was available to watch, read or hear. I can absolutely understand the appreciation for the Target books during an era when re-watching the programmes upon which they were based was not an option, but to me they always felt kind of pointless. I know; I was spoiled.

For one reason or another, I'd never gotten around to reading *The Myth Makers*. I can't remember what did eventually prompt me to pick it up, but when I did, Donald Cotton's prose won me over by the first page. At the outset of the book, an old man directly addresses the reader and proceeds to tell the entire story from his first person perspective. Eventually this old man turns out to be Homer, a character who doesn't feature in the televised version of *The Myth Makers*, but who in real life was the author who extensively chronicled the Trojan War (very meta). This first person approach still feels fresh and exciting now, let alone in 1985.

One by-product of telling the entire story from Homer's perspective is that the character has to run backwards and forwards between the Greeks and the Trojans. This could easily have felt contrived, but the result instead adds to Cotton's already witty script, lending what could have been a tragic and blood-stained plot a farcical tone. It's silly, but it works. *The Myth Makers* didn't just remind me how good imaginative novelisations could be; it also reminded me just how flexible the format of **Doctor Who** could be when placed in the hands of a talented writer.

The first person narrative really does make this novelisation stand out from the crowd for all the right reasons. Yes, I know this device wasn't new to the range, but David Whitaker's take on *The Daleks* just turns most of the characters into arseholes. Homer is an engaging, well-rounded narrator. He has opinions and desires and the result of Cotton imbuing him with so much personality is that his descriptions of events don't just resort to that tired, 'he said, she said,' business or the same old stock metaphors. In what other context could one hope to find the materialisation of the TARDIS described as, 'a noise reminiscent of a camel in the last stages of *dementia praecox*,' or the Doctor as being, 'like the harassed captain of a coaster who can't remember his port from his starboard'? I'd take either of those over a dozen wheezing, groaning sounds or pleasant open faces.

If you haven't already, you should track down Cotton's other books. *The Gunfighters* followed *The Myth Makers* and uses the same first person style. Exploiting every Western cliché in the book, the author's sense of humour ends up on full display. Then, moving on to an adaptation of Dennis Spooner's script for *The Romans*, he pushed the novelisation format even further by structuring the book as an epistolary novel. In other words, the story is told as a series of documents; letters from one character to another, entries in journals or diaries and the like. Again this offers us the chance to engage with a side of the characters that the Target books rarely seemed to tackle in any depth; their inner, private selves. Combining Spooner's script with Cotton's wit resulted in a very funny book, but the plot took a bit of a beating in the process. Still, I'd rather a noble experiment than a phoned-in hack job and I've had a soft spot for the epistolary format ever since I first read Bram Stoker's **Dracula**. I'd love to try writing something like that one day.

That being the case, I guess this **You and Who** entry should be less about *The Myth Makers* and more a tribute to Donald Cotton himself. He was the kind of writer **Doctor Who** could have used more of. The kind who, on both script and screen, could transcend the limits of his medium and find a way to really stand out from the crowd. I wish he'd written more **Doctor Who**, or just more in general. I know Target published his epistolary children's novel, **The Bodkin Papers**, in 1986, so maybe I should track that down as well. Not until I've finished this article for you, though!

Well, I've banged on for far too long! Once again, I'm sorry about the delay and promise to have something with you just as soon as I come up with that personal angle.

All the best,
Drew

Subject: RE: RE: You and Who Entry
From: JR@mercifuleditor.co.uk
Date: Wednesday, January 30, 2013 11.53pm
To: drew42@procrastimail.com

Drew,
Sod it, that'll do.
JR

A Merry Christmas to All of You at Home

The Daleks' Master Plan by **Jim Sangster**, 42, Salford
First story: **Planet of the Spiders**

In 2013, I entered my eleventh year as a BBC staff member. Ever since I was a child I'd dreamed of working for Auntie Beeb (specifically, thanks to an interview with Sue Malden in **Doctor Who Monthly** in 1981, I wanted to work in the archives), even when the corporation I loved appeared not to extend the same respect to my favourite programme ever. In 2007, I was asked to join a team who were investigating ways to open up the BBC's factual archive, to dig deep into that rich seam of broadcasts such as interviews with survivors of the Titanic, former prime ministers or Hollywood legends. Of course we knew that what the public really wanted was access to top-notch comedies and dramas, but the problem was that there were too many commercial considerations to make that practical. But the factual stuff – well, if the BBC didn't make it available, who else would?

And this was how I came to come to terms with what some might consider the single biggest 'crime' the BBC ever committed – the wiping of all those tapes.

When technology is new, it costs more money than when it's commonplace. This is basic economics. In those early days of video, when one tape would cost about the same as a family car, it had to be reused. When the limited rights had expired and it was no longer possible to repeat a story without having to pay almost half the cost again on residuals, it was hard to justify keeping all the film copies too. Most importantly of all, the viewers were vocal in the pages of **Radio Times** that the last thing they wanted while paying for a colour TV license was to see old black-and-white programmes. Some would have us believe that it was just blinkered administrators committing cultural vandalism on a grand scale, but the vast majority of people still thought of TV like the theatre – you see the thing once, then it's gone. Only with the arrival of the home video machine did public opinion swing 180 degrees and all too late, the value of all that material that had been junked was painfully obvious. Some consolation, for what it's worth, is that the wiping of every original video recording helped to fund future programmes. You might have lost *The Space Pirates*, but its destruction probably enabled productions like *The Talons of Weng Chiang* or *City of Death*. Probably.

That doesn't mean to say I don't lament the passing of the 'missing' stories – far from it. But I don't froth at the mouth and curse the name of Pamela Nash either. Not anymore. Instead of mourning those episodes we'll never see, I just think myself lucky that we have so many that survived. You think the hit-rate for Troughton stories is bad, you try being a fan of **Z Cars**!

A curious gift from these lost classics is that there's so much we can never know for sure. It's so easy to discover these kinds of thing with 21st century **Doctor Who**, but imagine a story where what we don't know outweighs what we do, where our own imagination now plays as much a part in the creation of the story as Ray Cusick's did back in 1965. For an episode like *The Feast of Steven*, we might struggle to fully appreciate the joys of **Doctor Who** doing a **Z Cars** spoof where only Peter Purves is doing the right accent, or a farce set in Hollywood's silent era where we get to hear the Doctor moan that the place is 'full of Arabs.' But then, this was before Innes Lloyd limited the series to a formula, when the TARDIS didn't just travel through time and space, but through genre too.

The gaps have made some of us work hard to see what we can uncover. Like archaeologists, we've travelled to such glamorous locations as, er, Caversham, to explore the BBC's Written Archives. It's where the telesnaps were first found and it's where scrawled accident reports explain why William Hartnell had to be written out of episode three of *The Dalek Invasion of Earth*. We've read every bit of paperwork, studied the backs of photos for details and some of us have even tracked down elderly actors in coastal retirement homes just to ask them such important questions as, 'Which of the delegates were you?', 'When exactly did Steven change his outfit in *The Nightmare Begins*?' and 'What colour was the time destructor?' (New fact – it was red!)

There are so many things to love about *The Daleks' Master Plan* that we can still experience. The jungle sets suggest that, even though this is familiar territory for the series, Ray Cusick and his team were determined to make it the most jungly jungle they could. The surviving footage of the model Spar ship is the best model up to that point. Even William Hartnell himself – entering that difficult transition phase where even his original producer had abandoned him – appears to be delivering a Royal Command Performance. The fact that the serial was commissioned just because the mother-in-law of BBC1 Controller Huw Wheldon was a fan of the Daleks makes this a rare thing in 20th century **Doctor Who**, where it was popular with BBC management and audiences alike. That wouldn't happen again until 2005!

The mission for this and other essays in the book is to say why **Doctor Who** means so much to us. In this instance, I have to take so much of *The Daleks' Master Plan*'s brilliance on trust, because I haven't seen it. Not really. The reason why it's my favourite story though is simply that, based on the surviving evidence, it succeeded in achieving so much with so little, by relying on the talents of a small group of individuals. It's the BBC way.

The Massacre on St Bartholomew's Eve
The Massacre by **Donald Tosh**, UK

As always, when one production team hands over to another, there is a certain amount of unfinished business which is passed from the outgoers to the incomers. When Verity and Dennis handed over to John and me, one of these was a contracted but as yet uncommissioned third script from John Lucarotti. His previous two - *Marco Polo* and *The Aztecs* - had both been very successful. This time he wanted to write a story about the Vikings. Unfortunately the series had just done *The Meddling Monk* and we did not feel it sensible to go down that path so soon again. Lucarotti was not happy as he felt in light of his previous successes he should be able to write the story he wanted. But after a certain amount of disgruntled discussion he agreed to submit a story set at the time of the St Bartholomew's Massacre in sixteenth century France.

It was unfortunate that I happened to know a bit about the politics and history of that time, for when John submitted his story/script I could see that unusually for him, he had only done the very minimal amount of historical research and linked it to a story which I suspect he had had in his 'bottom drawer,' just fitting it into the **Doctor Who** world. We had a terrible argument and I told him the BBC wouldn't accept his script.

John Wiles then told me that we couldn't afford to do that, we had to have a script from him. There was a terrible impasse until Lucarotti challenged me to write a better story around the Massacre and which he would approve and would go out under his name. So I spent a week in the British Museum researching and then writing each night in my flat virtually next door, and produced the scripts which became *The Massacre*.

I sent them to Lucarotti, who dismissed them as, 'Rubbish - but - okay, you've done what I didn't think you could,' and let John Wiles read them thinking they were Lucarotti's rewrite; he approved them, and when Paddy Russell asked for some changes I did those too.

Bill loved having the Abbot to play and Peter at last had something to get his teeth into; with a splendid guest cast featuring Andre Morell, Leonard Sachs and Joan Young amongst others, it was a very happy production.

As we moved into the Studio I confessed to John Wiles that I had in fact written it.

'Oh, we all knew that,' he said. 'But as Lucarotti was content to let it go out under his name, Bill was happy, Paddy and the rest of the cast were happy and you didn't stretch the budget, so I was happy; it seemed curmudgeonly to point out that you were doing something that was strictly against BBC rules.'

Tantric Who
The Ark by **John Rivers**, 34, London UK
First story: **The Trial of a Time Lord**

Despite being a **Doctor Who** fan for the past twenty-six years, I only saw *The Ark* for the first time last year. This was entirely on purpose; even having bought the adventure on VHS, I opted to wait for the DVD release. This wasn't just because I'm snobby about picture quality, it was down to personal pleasure. *The Ark* has formed a part of a self-inflicted programme of delayed gratification. Kinky, I'm sure you'd agree.

Towards the end of the VHS release run I realised that pretty soon I was going to run out of classic **Doctor Who** to watch. The new series still only existed as a press conference, an awkwardly-staged photo in a corridor and a gnawing fear in Russell T Davies's gut. The old series was going from strength-to-strength on DVD but, missing episode discoveries aside, there was a limited supply. I therefore made the decision to slow-down on my **Doctor Who** intake. I wanted to savour every moment, because as brilliant as it is rewatching **Doctor Who** for every boom-in-shot and hand-of-Sutekh, nothing quite replaces the feeling of encountering something for the very first time.

Volumes could be written on **Doctor Who**'s stand-out surprise moments; even something naff like the Master's sudden appearance on the Matrix screen in *The Trial of a Time Lord* is memorable. As a child the memory of seeing Taren Capel disturbingly done-up like Gary Glitter in *The Robots of Death* (even more disturbing now I think about it) or the schoolgirl being the Dalek battle computer in *Remembrance of the Daleks* are burned in the brain. That element of the unknown has been vital to my enjoyment of **Doctor Who** and imagine my surprise when I realised it still existed, that a bitter, cynical 33-year-old fan could still be amazed by a story that was 47 years old.

No, it's not just Dodo's accent switch that is shocking, rather that *The Ark* feels much more recent in production terms than it is. When Tat Wood and Lawrence Miles made the point in **About Time** that it looks like an early 1970s production they're spot-on. The sets are huge and technologically advanced and you get a real sense of scale, especially when the story calls for an Abu Simbel-like statue to play a part. Plus the story actually deals with the Doctor revisiting the scene of his earlier intervention. History has of course been changed, albeit in a very straightforward way and arguably for the worse. Unlike say *The Waters of Mars*, the Doctor manages not to get all upset about it. The Monoids are a neat creation too; they're as sure-footed as a drunk Myrka, but their journey from dumb servants to ruling class works well. They're also as creepy as their cousins the Ood. However, none of these aspects of *The Ark* - not even the instant chicken wings from the Security Kitchen - come close to matching a surprising moment early in episode one.

The thing that made the hairs on the back of my neck stand up was the elephant. I sat there, mouth open, amazed. This wasn't stock footage, this wasn't something shot on safari that the Doctor, Steven and Dodo point at, this was a genuine elephant, filmed in Ealing. That the show had dared to employ a real elephant and had our heroes interact with it was astounding. It might seem silly, but I never believed that the Hartnell era - hell, the whole of classic **Doctor Who** - contained a real elephant. Of course we were still three years away from the Lulu the elephant incident of **Blue Peter**, which probably saw elephants banned from BBC studios (note - both incidences involve Peter Purves - coincidence?). I lay back on my sofa, delighted and somewhat content; **Doctor Who** had just surprised me once more.

The elephant revelation suddenly made me glad that I had proceeded with my delayed-gratification plan. Other fans had criticised me in the past ('How can you be a moderator on Outpost Gallifrey when you haven't seen all the stories?!' one dimwit asked); some admitted that they couldn't hold back and had to see everything at once. I can understand that, that need to know it all, the feeling that you're not part of the fan experience if you don't, but if you are in a similar position to me, then resist that urge!*

You simply can't do this with new **Doctor Who**, the internet renders it impossible. With iPlayer available on most microwaves and toothbrushes, you're going to have new episodes revealed to you in some way. The only alternative is waiting to see if any missing old episodes are recovered. As the years pass it gets increasingly unlikely, but then again no one thought that Episode 2 of *The Underwater Menace* or episode three of *Galaxy 4* would resurface in 2011 (and everyone wondered why it couldn't have been *Power of the Daleks*). Therefore I will jealously guard my right to take my time with existing stories. DVDs can stay on the shelf unopened, mysterious. They are full of promise and wonder, and probably elephants.

Right now that's how it is with *The Reign of Terror, The Gunfighters, The Krotons, The Ambassadors of Death, The Mind of Evil, The Masque of Mandragora, The Horns of Nimon* and *Frontios*. Eventually, the time will come when they are all known to me and like Alexander, I will weep, for there are no more worlds to conquer. Until that day though there is much to look forward to, shocks, surprises and new adventures. Like the Doctor, I'll always have somewhere new to visit and anticipate.

*Not that urge, the urge to watch unseen classic stories.

The Mandarin's New Clothes

The Celestial Toymaker by **John S. Hall**, 43, Pawtucket, Rhode Island, USA / First Story: **Robot**

Funny how perceptions and opinions change over time, isn't it?

Back in the early 1980s, everyone in **Doctor Who** fandom *knew* that *The Gunfighters* was the worst story *ever*, while its immediate predecessor, *The Celestial Toymaker*, was a *bona fide* classic that had been unjustly consigned to the skip by the short-sighted BBC. Further compounding this indignity, all four episodes of *The Gunfighters* existed within the BBC's archives, having somehow miraculously survived the purge.

Fans who had been fortunate enough to see *The Celestial Toymaker* on its original transmission sang its praises, and a lengthy archive feature in **Doctor Who Monthly** paraded before us sumptuous colour photos of the Celestial Toyroom, the Hall of Dolls, Mrs. Wiggs' Kitchen and the Dancing Floor, accompanying page after page of dialogue extracts and plot synopses. And we lapped it all up, secure in the knowledge that we'd never again see something so bizarre and spectacular in **Doctor Who**.

Then the story's fourth episode, *The Final Test*, was recovered from an Australian TV archive, and *The Celestial Toymaker* began its eventual transformation into The Mandarin's New Clothes.

Always eager to resurrect old foes to battle the Doctor once again, producer John Nathan-Turner commissioned his predecessor Graham Williams to bring back the Toymaker in grand fashion for Season 23's opening story, *The Nightmare Fair*. But when Williams requested a viewing copy of *The Final Test*, he watched it in bemusement, wondering what all the fuss was about, 'Watching people play hopscotch for twenty-five minutes.'

Perhaps wisely, Williams removed the Toymaker from Victorian nursery games to the video game arcades of Blackpool. But as fate would have it, *The Nightmare Fair* - along with the rest of the proposed Season 23 - was infamously cancelled by BBC controller Michael Grade, who felt the series 'needed a rest.'

Although *The Celestial Toymaker* was novelised disappointingly in 1986, fans would have to wait until 1991 to see *The Final Test* for themselves, when it was released as part of *The Hartnell Years*. Many were shocked to discover that the surviving episode of this so-called classic was, in fact, rather a clunker! The cleaned-up soundtrack only compounded this view. The Mandarin's New Clothes would indeed have been a more fitting title for a story that became clothed in a grand reputation, but in the cold light of decades of hindsight, turned out to be rather threadbare and shabby.

The Celestial Toymaker's basic premise is solid - being forced to play deadly versions of familiar games for your life - but poorly executed. Perhaps the many rewrites and changeover in production team accounts for this, but the absence of William Hartnell for two weeks doesn't help. Having rendered the Doctor both invisible and mute, the Toymaker talks to empty air for most of the story, and that forces the focus of these episodes onto Steven and Dodo.

Ah, yes, Steven and Dodo, possibly the most generic companions ever to enter the TARDIS. Peter Purves, as always, gives the part his utmost, but the script does him little favours. As for Jackie Lane, her Dodo truly lives up to her nickname, behaving like a naïve simpleton throughout, falling prey to Cyril's transparent ruses and frequently behaving as if these games weren't fatal! Only when the Doctor is restored does the story get back on track.

Another thing that lets *The Celestial Toymaker* down is its lapses in internal logic. For example, the Toymaker exults in finally having an opponent he can truly pit his mind against, yet spends most of the story capriciously advancing the Trilogic Game's moves and trying to disrupt the Doctor's concentration. Granted, the Toymaker is a self-professed sore loser and almost always plays with the odds stacked in his favour, but still! Similarly, if the Toymaker is such a stickler for his opponents' following the rules, why does he never reprimand his minions, who cheat flagrantly? Such arbitrary enforcement, along with Cyril's desultory explanations of TARDIS Hopscotch rules, makes watching the game-playing exasperating rather than enthralling.

The irritating thing is, beneath the fluff and parping 'comedy' music, there are some disquieting ideas and story elements at work here. In addition to the inherent creepiness of clowns and dolls, we're told that Steven and Dodo's opponents were once real people as well – and that the reason they all lose is down to their human flaws – but we're never actually shown any of this, so they remain little more than cardboard cut-outs brought to life. At least when Russell T Davies used the 'play for your life' plot device in *Bad Wolf*, he gave the opponents broadly-sketched characters and personalities so that when they died – particularly in the case of Lynda with a Y – we felt something for them. As viewers, why should we care what happens to a pair of clowns, a family of playing cards, and a blatant Billy Bunter rip-off?

Rather than the stuff of nightmares, this realm of creepy dolls, jovial jokers and deadly games is the embodiment of tedium.

Despite all this, the Toymaker has remained an intriguing enough concept that people have been bringing him back in a variety of media, where his reality-bending powers aren't hindered by technology or media watchdogs, and where he can run wild through our imaginations like an even-darker Willy Wonka, ever since.

'Pure Talbot Rothwell!'
The Gunfighters by **Michael S. Collins**, 26, Glasgow, Scotland / First story: **The Moonbase**

I don't recollect when I first realised there was something like **Doctor Who** in the world. I'd joke that my first word was 'Dalek.' I recall vividly seeing the inside of a video sleeve, promoting **Doctor Who** videos, and being terrified by Jon Pertwee's face. I must have been about three. Strange how you remember things like that, yet don't remember what you had for tea last week!

I know I was a fan by April 1990 however, as I was writing **Doctor Who** fan-fic. It pitted me, the third Doctor, Sooty and the **Why Don't You** gang against an evil witch. I'm sure it is a lost classic. I'm not sure how I *became* a fan though. I had already written about the show in 1990, but it wasn't until we moved house in 1991 that Dad bought me a videotape, in what was to be known as *The Moonbase* Incident.

It was me, the Doctor and some Cybermen. Swiftly followed by me, my bed, and nightmares. They terrified me for weeks on end, these creatures on the moon, yet something about the show had already hooked me. Maybe it was that indefinable magic folk go on about. Maybe it was genetic, being a third generation **Doctor Who** fan. Or maybe BBC Enterprises slipped subliminal messaging into old VHSs to improve sales...

My viewing continued with such delights as *The Green Death* (terrifying), *Pyramids of Mars* (more so) and *Genesis of the Daleks* (you wouldn't believe quite how terrifying!). And I was hooked. I even remember finding out that my hero, Jon Pertwee, had died just before a primary school parents' night, and lots of concerned adults thinking I was upset about the teacher's comments, only for me to cry: 'No, Doctor Who died!' I was nine.

Sadly, something far worse threatened to drive a wedge between me and my beloved series. I think it's called 'being a teenager' in scientific circles.

Ever since I had fallen in love with this quaint cult show, I was aware of how unpopular it was with my peers, and the general press. I was also becoming aware of how unpopular my type - damned young 'uns - were with older, more serious fans. The marketing of the New Adventures gave the first hints, then some of the fans I knew who read them shared their opinions quite loudly about what constituted 'proper fandom'. Even my uncle, a diehard, was fighting a losing battle in keeping my interest. I stopped watching the show.

You're probably guessing I started up again, if you're reading this!

About two years later, I'd started to become badly ill, and needed some anchor to keep my mind occupied. It might as well be that old show I used to love. An appointment with insomnia one evening in 2002 saw me in front of the TV when I happened to flick to UK Gold. *The Pirate Planet* was on. I remembered it being rubbish. Five minutes in, I thought, this isn't so bad.

Two hours later, **Doctor Who** and I had been reunited for good.

I sheepishly mentioned replacing my Target novels to my mum, only for her to show up with all of them, which she'd kept, knowing I'd change my mind before long. I even started getting the videos (and the DVDs, forgoing my cynicism of the newish format to listen to Sylvester McCoy commentaries).

In 2003, I got hold of *The First Doctor Collection*, three stories in one VHS box set. *The Time Meddler* was swiftly devoured, as I knew it was (justifiably) held in high repute. Next came *The Sensorites*, a fairly decent SF romp. I avoided the final video for several weeks, knowing of its reputation. 'Forever a true embarrassment to **Doctor Who**.' (Ian Levine) 'The script was pure Talbot Rothwell, the acting was not even bad vaudeville and the direction was more West Ham than West Coast.' (Peter Haining)

Finally I gave in. Might as well say I'd seen it! And truth be told, I hadn't laughed that much since I took ill a year earlier. I realised that, far from embarrassing, this was comedy gold. My brain could hardly take it in. If perceived fandom had gotten this so wrong, who knew what else they could have gotten wrong? I had a look through **The Television Guide** and **The Discontinuity Guide**, and mentally threw out everything I thought I knew about all the episodes they slated. From that moment on, I would judge every **Doctor Who** story by what it meant to me, and me alone.

Which is really the only way to take a show as varied as **Doctor Who**. It is the TV series for all seasons; if you don't like comedy, a tragedy will be just around the corner. I know that the story I consider the absolute nadir of the show, *Underworld,* has fans who adore it, and I am all the more happy for it. Good old *Underworld*, just don't make me watch it!

What *The Gunfighters* made me realise is that fandom is entirely subjective. I wasn't wrong for loving it as much as Ian Levine wasn't wrong for hating it. What makes this little TV show so grand is that it can fit such opposing viewpoints together, and still continue to invite new ones even fifty years on. That night I lost the stress of feeling embarrassed about personal, subjective likes. Life is too damned short.

As for Peter Haining's remarks, well, Rothwell wrote one of the finest British comedies of all time (**Carry On Up the Khyber**) and West Ham in May 1966 were about to send Bobby Moore, Martin Peters and Geoff Hurst off to help win the World Cup. So ... in a roundabout way, I think we fans of *The Gunfighters* should take them as a compliment well earned!

Putting Away Childish Things

The Savages by **Alun Harris**, 37, Hebden Bridge, UK
First story: **Nightmare of Eden**

People will tell you that growing up isn't good, that childhood is the best thing that ever happens to you. This is not true. Yes, childhood has lots going for it, but there's one thing that children simply don't have: a critical faculty. Show a small child a cartoon (preferably one with loud noises and lots of primary colours) and that child will be entranced. Show an adult the same cartoon and they'll be reaching for the ibuprofen.

Children can't differentiate. Sure, there are some things children don't like (dramas, usually, with talking but without any loud noises or primary colours) but they don't know and don't even care why they don't like them. They just don't. Simple as. This is A Very Good Thing.

Take me. Born in 1975, I was the right age to enjoy the JNT era of **Doctor Who**. *Warriors of the Deep*? I was eight. Didn't have a problem with it. Okay, even I knew that the Myrka wasn't the best thing I'd ever seen, but it didn't bother me. *The Twin Dilemma*? I watched it with exactly the same level of interest that I'd watched *The Caves of Androzani* only a fortnight before. It was **Doctor Who**, I liked **Doctor Who**, therefore I liked all of it.

I grew up. Growing up is good. I developed taste and a sense of personal preferences. I developed critical faculties.

The nice thing about growing up and becoming a jaded and cynical adult is that I still feel a tremendous nostalgia for the things I liked as a child. (Well, most of them. Even I can't cope with a programme that consists of nothing but primary colours and loud noises.) I watch *Warriors of the Deep* now and while I see its flaws (nothing to do with the lighting - whoever is going to run a weapons installation in permanent darkness?), I'm fond of it.

Doctor Who is not the best series ever made. (It's a ridiculous thing to try and compare TV programmes anyway; saying **Gangsters** is better than **Quatermass and the Pit** is like trying to say which is better - cheese or steak. Anyway, everyone knows the best series ever made is **Secret Army**.) But whilst I know it's not the best thing ever made, that doesn't stop it being my favourite. I love **Doctor Who**. I always will. The nostalgia factor plays a huge part in that, but so does developing critical faculties.

When I was eight, there were only two reference books on **Doctor Who** and the Target novelisations. Lofficier's **Programme Guide** didn't tell you anything about the stories, other than a handy synopsis which made them all sound equally exciting. The Target books were variable and didn't give you much sense of what the stories were really like (even now I'm disappointed by the reality of some of the TV versions of those books. The Doctor always takes the safety off Trenchard's revolver, no matter what happens on TV) and so all that was left was Haining, who told us what to think of every story. (And even then it wasn't Haining - it was Jeremy Bentham, who could only rely on his memories of being a child and watching the stories once, twenty years ago.)

A whole generation of fans grew up disliking historicals. No one even knew why. We just knew that they were boring.

Thank God for VHS, DVD and adult critical faculties. If you came to a historical for the first time in the 1990s you were in for a treat. Stories that you'd been told were boring were suddenly revealed to be magnificent dramas, dramas better than most of the stories either side of them.

It wasn't just the historicals that benefitted from this newfound discovery: there were others waiting to be discovered, and still are. A lot of the Hartnells weren't novelised until towards the end of the Target range, and if you were a similar age to me you'd find them the same way: when you'd been eight you were happy to read and re-read the books; the later ones were read only once or twice. Stories like *The Massacre* (which diverts some way from the original script) or *The Smugglers* remained quite mysterious. Listening to the audios was almost literally discovering a missing story (and remains the only way to experience them). And that's how I found *The Savages*.

    I used to ration the audios to one episode a night. That's partly because the episodes aren't made to be listened to (they should be seen) and partly because they weren't supposed to be engulfed in one go; they should be seen episodically. I broke that rule completely with *The Savages*. I didn't mean to, I just couldn't help it. I had to carry on listening. The novelisation doesn't make it sound like anything special, and fan wisdom has always maintained that Season Three is weak, so coming to this story almost fresh was a revelation. *The Savages* is not weak. It's not representative of a leading man on the way out, or a series which has no new ideas. *The Savages* is brimming with a strong cast, an engaging plot and a lead actor capable of delivering as much as he ever had done before (almost twice over in this one, given Frederick Jaeger's astonishing performance in the later episodes). *The Savages* was brilliant, and remains one of my favourites. But that's because I discovered it for myself. I didn't listen to received wisdom, I ignored fandom, and I came to my own conclusions. That's what we should all do. We shouldn't have to apologise for liking stories other people dislike, or for loving eras other people hate, we should rejoice in our own choices, and in the sheer diversity of a series which has been capable of so much difference over so many years. We should discover that series for ourselves.

WOTAN It be Loverly
The War Machines by **Allen Dace**, 49, Guildford, UK
First Story: **Spearhead From Space**

They say that if you can remember the 1960s then you weren't there. I was there (for most of the decade) but I can't remember very much of it. Despite that I'm not alone in considering it my favourite decade entirely for the music, cinema and television, which still delights fifty years on.

In theory I could have seen every single episode of **Doctor Who** on the original transmission. However it is more than doubtful that a four-day-old baby would have the ability to take in anything of *An Unearthly Child*. I was probably sleeping, crying or dribbling through it. My earliest memories of the programme are of Patrick Troughton's title sequence. He now looks benevolent but to this toddler that flaky smiling face seemed a horrific vision leering out of the darkness, causing a rapid change of channel.

In fact I began watching **Doctor Who** properly very neatly with Jon Pertwee's debut in 1970 and have always appreciated the (roughly) modern day earthbound adventures typical of his early years. Their template can be found in one of William Hartnell's last, *The War Machines*. This was the very first screening I saw at the National Film Theatre after joining the BFI when I moved south in 1986. Saturday lunchtime if I recall correctly with all four episodes shown back-to-back. That was another first for me in those pre-sell-through VHS days. I'd never seen **Doctor Who** on a big screen in the company of 'fans' before either. They were pretty well behaved apart from the wag who answered one of William Mervyn's exclamations back for a cheap laugh. There's always one. Much funnier was the ruthless attack on several empty cardboard boxes by a War Machine in the **Blue Peter** clip we were treated to.

I love London. I never went there until I was sixteen so during my childhood it was a glamorous, almost fictional place that existed only on film and television. A cultural hub, an historical goldmine but for me one great big location for screen adventures. Watching a **Doctor Who** story taking place in streets I have walked gave me a particular pleasure then and still does today.

The War Machines is a daft story about a mad computer that doesn't even know that **Doctor Who** is the title of a TV show and not an elderly Time Lord (not that anyone knew what a Time Lord was in 1966). It controls the title characters which are some of most lumbering clunky adversaries to threaten planet Earth at teatime. Preposterous. Yet ... this is the 1960s with marvellous iconography of the age like the futuristic Post Office Tower and new groovy young attractive nightclubbing companions. What's not to like?

Smuggled Up

The Smugglers by **Tim Hirst**, 43, Hampshire, UK
First story: **The Green Death**

A molten-bronze nugget of fan-legend, which could almost come from the sticky, subversive pages of **Auton**, has it that in 1966, Ice Warriors creator Brian Hayles was commissioned to write a story called *Doctor Who and the Nazis*. I can only assume that Terry Nation and Mel Brooks were otherwise engaged. Quite why this story was abandoned in favour of *The Smugglers* appears to be lost in the mists of time; it's probably a good thing, though *The Nazis* may have got better viewing figures - *The Smugglers* held the dubious honour of being the least-watched **Doctor Who** story until *The Trial of a Time Lord*, twenty years later.

Thanks to the painstaking work of a fan known for the purposes of this article as Harold, I've been able to watch quite a convincing version of this long-lost story, compiled from telesnaps, stills and snippets of soundtrack, glued together with narration by Anneke Wills and lovingly finished with a BBC-style DVD cover ... more of that later.

Even though we are only at 'serial CC', you've probably already read several accounts of hiding behind sofas, finding dusty Target books in junk shops, practising Venusian Aikido on your friends (such as they were), writing to Anthony Ainley and, 'Oh yes, Longleat ... it was our Woodstock you know ... yeah, yeah... I was chatting with Heather Hartnell for like, minutes.' Most fans of my vintage could write a book, never mind an essay, on those 1970s/80s memories of soggy crumpets, the football scores and Part Three of *Four to Doomsday*, never seen until the VHS release, because you were sent to your room that night for shouting at your dad for not lending you the £75 for a Denys Fisher Cyberman (it had a nose!) from the John Fitton catalogue ... or was it £45 for a 1973 **Radio Times** special? Either way, John Fitton - of Goole, which in those days was still in Humberside – was a man who probably made a healthy living from the TARDIS-sized pockets of **Doctor Who** fans. One Sunday in the autumn of 1983, I found a rare Patrick Troughton annual at a car boot sale at Newbury Racecourse. I bought it for 10p and sold it to John Fitton in exchange for £35 worth of goodies from his catalogue – including the newly released *Revenge of the Cybermen* video, complete with incorrect logo on the vac-formed cover, a mistake which annoyed my thirteen-year-old self almost as much as the Denys Fisher Cyberman's ludicrous nose.

That was my first foray into **Doctor Who** commerce. My second was only a month or two later, when I started my own 20p fanzine (I can't possibly tell you the title, it's far too embarrassing) on the back of the 20th anniversary. Hand-written, sneakily photocopied by my dad in his office, the first issue promised, 'Next Month, we reveal Katy Manning's address!' I did as well. Actually it was her agent's address, in Australia, and I don't know about anyone else but I never got a reply. In those days, you could write to the BBC and they sent you a pack, containing lots of sheets no doubt typed by BBC secretaries wearing horn-rimmed spectacles. Tantalising lists of merchandise (without telling you where you could buy it), a list of every story up to and including *Logopolis* (with Hartnell titles that I now know to be complete nonsense), and yes, actors' addresses (this is how I first heard about Turlough. Mark Strickson's address was on this list, even though he hadn't officially been announced – needless to say that gave me a good exclusive in my schoolyard fanzine – I beat **DWB** to that news by a good two weeks.) You'd also get a pile of beautiful signed postcards – the current TARDIS crew, plus the Brigadier, the Master, K9, Tom Baker … oh, how I anticipated the Nicola Bryant one.

If younger fans (the ones with 'Tennant' as their middle or surname on Facebook) don't get some of the references here, then I make no apology – it may be tedious hearing us old-timers pine for the halcyon days of

DWB and John Fitton and JNT, but come the 100th anniversary – by which time computers really will be controlled by moving around little coloured cubes like in 1980s Gallifrey stories – they'll all be at conventions on space stations reminiscing for the days of forums and Tardisodes and Timey-bloody-Wimey. The point is that people like John Fitton, JNT and the pioneers of early fanzines like **DWB** all made a contribution to the sea of loveliness and weirdness that is **Doctor Who** fandom, and that's all I ever wanted to do, leave a tiny little legacy, make my mark, give something back to the ongoing saga of the programme that had given me so much joy and inspiration.

The reason I have a DVD of *Doctor Who and The Smugglers* – and all of Anneke's missing stories – is that Harold kindly gave Anneke and me a full set when I was working with her a few years ago. Since then, I've had quite a 'journey,' as Anneke might put it. Years of being quietly envious and admiring of those lucky fans who made their living from **Doctor Who**, combined with nostalgia for a time when the programme really was my world, meant that the opportunity to publish Anneke's autobiography was too good to resist. And so began my latest, final and almost fatal foray into **Doctor Who** commerce. Should I get my dad to photocopy Anneke's book at work, like he used to with my fanzine? He'd retired by then, so I decided to set up a publishing company. It's rare that a decision is simultaneously so impulsive, brilliant and idiotic.

Months of work followed, and a year later, I published Anneke's **Self Portrait**. She had the hardest job of course – reliving her extraordinary life; anyone who has read her books will know that she writes in the present tense – she is *there*. She is, as she puts it, *in the moment*. It's not something I could do, and my life has not been nearly as eventful; but project management, raising funds, amateurish typesetting, spreading the word ... that, I could do. Over the years that followed, Anneke wrote the second book, and we toured the country promoting both titles – I'm not sure she ever quite understood why I was so taken with the unofficial tour title, 'Anneke in the UK.'

Obviously I'm not the first fan who has, in his or her professional capacity, got to know actors beyond the usual 'Remember? I met you at Manopticon in 1997! You signed my book! The one with pages in it, yes! Remember?' I always tried to remain cool and collected but occasionally, that thirteen-year-old fan possessed me and I struggled to contain the chubby little blighter... *I'm having breakfast with Mary Tamm! I'm giving Colin Baker a lift home! Matthew Waterhouse is at my barbecue! I'm on the actual TARDIS set with Jane Tranter! I'm reading Patrick Troughton's personal diary!* I believe the term among the aforementioned younger fans is 'Squee.' Even falling out with Nicola Bryant over what shall now regretfully be referred to as 'Knickergate' was a happily surreal moment for that same fan who, 27 years earlier, had ripped open that envelope from the BBC, suspected of containing the brand new Peri postcard. I'm not recounting these events to name-drop, but to make the point that, despite everything, I remain a fan, and that's all I ever was.

I messed up, there's no doubt about that. Most small businesses fail, and mine merrily joined the statistics. I never had any bad intentions – in my head I was creating a nice little business that would have seen me comfortably into old age, while keeping me close to my favourite TV show. With the benefit of hindsight I should have kept the publishing as a part-time interest – something to enjoy, rather than slave and sweat and stress over. When you set up a publishing company, people throw books at you – not literally, although I'm sure it will happen before long. In two years I published over thirty books. I should have published six ... okay, ten or twelve at the most – and kept a full-time job too.

I say this sincerely: I learned a lot from Anneke, and one particular piece of wisdom has stuck with me – and that's about reflecting other people's negative energy back at them. I believe that this way of thinking has helped Anneke to deal with some of the challenges life and fate have thrown at her. It's certainly helped me, and I've occasionally passed it on to others. Anyone who knows my views on spiritual matters will realise that I don't mean 'energy' in the same sense that Anneke probably does, but the sentiment and the mind-set is sound: other people's negative energy is their problem, not yours; just hold up an imaginary shield and deflect it back to them – do not absorb it. It's just a shame I've had to hold that shield up to a few individuals in **Doctor Who** fandom. Some of them, I thought were my friends.

I've had reason to feel bitter about fandom, and no doubt fandom has had reason to feel bitter about me. I am sorry, genuinely, to those authors, customers and suppliers who have been affected by my over-ambition, lack of organisation and pathetic self-discipline. This essay, this book, is not really a valid arena for this, so if you want to know more, please go to my website.

For me, 2013 is the year I claim back my fandom. **Doctor Who** has been my constant friend since the mid-1970s and I don't give up my friends that easily. I am still, despite being a tired, battle-weary failed publisher, a **Doctor Who** fan. I'm still that thirteen-year-old who almost wet himself with excitement when *The Five Doctors* was announced. I'm still the same fan who on May 27th 1996, spent £150 on a taxi from Swindon to Bradford, just so I could get home to watch the McGann TV movie after my car died.

My little publishing business has given me a catalogue of experiences that the thirteen-year-old me could only have fantasised about, and I consider myself extremely lucky. It would be easy to regret setting up Hirst Books, but without it I would not have spent many happy hours and days in Anneke's company, enjoying her hospitality and the tranquillity of her delightful cottage. I would not have shared in the wisdom she acquired from her extraordinary life, which you can read about in her two glorious volumes. Without the business I would not have had the opportunity to browse the fascinating library that is Colin Baker's downstairs loo, and I would not have had the pleasure of making a friend of one of **Doctor Who**'s most gentlemanly participants. Read Colin's books - all three are superb.

Without Hirst Books, I would not have met the wonderful Michael Troughton - without a doubt one of the nicest people I have ever met, and like many others I have met along the journey, a genuine friend. Michael's biography of Patrick is quite simply a gift to fandom, and I am proud that I was instrumental in bringing it about, and I'm proud of all the other titles too.

Without the business, I would not have got to know Frazer, Sylvester, Sophie and - even though I never got a reply from her in 1983 - Katy. Without the books I would not have been invited onto the set to meet David Tennant and stand in the TARDIS. In short, and without recounting a plethora of anecdotes, having this little publishing business has enabled me to *really be a fan*. It's allowed me to indulge my inner child, and despite everything, I don't regret any of it, because ultimately, I'm a **Doctor Who** fan, and I'm proud to be a **Doctor Who** fan.

And what of *The Smugglers*? Well, Anneke says it's her favourite story, and that's a good enough recommendation for me.

It's Far From Being All Over

The Tenth Planet by **Greg Bakun**, 39, Saint Michael, USA / First story: **The Visitation**

When I found out about this book, I scoured the list of available stories left to review. I figured the particular one of my favourite stories that I wanted would have been taken, and I would have to try to figure out something different. You can imagine my shock that with less than a month before the articles were due *The Tenth Planet* had not been picked. This is madness! It is one of the most influential and possibly realistic stories of the series. I can tell you are sceptical. I will do my best to try and explain my point of view.

As we know, *The Tenth Planet* is the first story to feature the Cybermen and also the last regular story to feature the original Doctor William Hartnell. I think a lot of people remember *The Tenth Planet* more for the primitive Cybermen (it is often said they look like they were put together with contents found in a kitchen sink), the slow-moving story and the fact that Mondas was a ticking time bomb. The planet would have dispersed regardless of the Doctor's involvement. To those who don't really care for this story, I would like to offer an opposing view.

When I was young, my PBS station would show all of the existing complete **Doctor Who** stories. I knew of *The Tenth Planet* but didn't see it because Episode 4 did not exist and therefore the story was incomplete. I knew the story only from the novelisation and whatever pictures I could find in **DWM** or wherever, and I loved the look of these Cybermen. This is what **Doctor Who** succeeds at; it succeeds at confidence. Sometimes it doesn't work but sometimes it works brilliantly. This is the case for these Cybermen. I have never seen anything like them before. Their faces are blank with empty black holes for eyes.

They are not evil-looking because in all honesty the Cybermen, at least in this story, are not evil. Immoral perhaps but not evil. They are survivors. It's an emotionless decision to pilot their planet back to their sister planet Earth. They do this out of necessity and not with an intent to conquer.

When I finally had a chance to watch the existing episodes in the late 1980s, I was not disappointed. *The Tenth Planet* story has one of my favourite moments in **Doctor Who**. No, not the regeneration, but rather the ending to Episode 1. Yes, the 'Cyber-plan' of masquerading as soldiers in parkas may be just a shade silly but the end of the episode, as a Cyberman leans down and the camera tilts up for our first head-on look at it, is one of my favourite moments ever in the series. The story is directed by Derek Martinus, who I think is one of the best directors to ever work on **Doctor Who**. He sees shots in stories that create a different perspective than something that is just recorded in a studio. I think he pushes the limits of shooting in a studio too, but where other directors who try this make mistakes, he succeeds.

Another thing I really like about *The Tenth Planet* is how the future is represented. Made in 1966 but set twenty years hence, the depiction of the future is tastefully handled. We don't see a bunch of people wearing reflective silver robes living in a Utopian society, what we see is a polar base that is not too far off the technology that was available at the time. There are a lot of monitors and communication devices but nothing too unbelievable. The things that aren't real, the polar base and Z-Bomb, are handled as if they were a natural progression to the technology of the 1960s. The set design is great and it works so well because it is darkly lit and cramped.

In the future there is a healthy space programme. This is also in line with what was going on in the 1980s - or more accurately what should have been. The space programme in *The Tenth Planet* feels not unlike the mission between the Earth and the moon. We see that there are no colonies on the moon, and humanity is certainly not seen to be capable of unrealistic travel to any other planets in our solar system. This mirrors quite well with what was happening in real life, with humans able to get to the moon - the exploration of space was all science-based. The NASA space programmes were very similar to this, but hit a massive setback in 1986 with the Challenger disaster after which the NASA space programme never fully recovered.

Regardless of when this story took place or who the monsters were, something amazing and magical was about to happen. When **Doctor Who** began in 1963 it was about a character called the Doctor, and there was never any intention for more than one person to play the role. But at the end of *The Tenth Planet*, all that was about to change. As little more almost than a small coda to the events of the last four episodes, the lead character completely changes his appearance. The only real indication that the Doctor was in any kind of trouble was when he let Polly know that, 'This old body of mine is wearing a bit thin.'

Just like many of the events of 1960s' **Doctor Who** the changeover from William Hartnell to Patrick Troughton had little fanfare. Hartnell makes no sacrifices, endures no flashbacks and utters no farewell words to his companions. Yet the change from one actor into another is one of the most important moments in **Doctor Who** history and begins a new era. The Doctor was right, it truly was far from being all over.

The Second Doctor Who

When it became apparent that William Hartnell would no longer be able to continue in the role of Doctor Who, the programme-makers decided to replace him with another actor. There's nothing unusual in this: any long-running programme is likely to have a sizeable turnover of lead actors. But your **Coronation Street**s and your **Casualty**s aren't named after their lead actor's character, and at the time of his departure, none of them will have had to deal with the problem in quite the same way as the makers of **Doctor Who**.

So how to overcome such a seemingly insurmountable problem?

Although it wasn't given a name and was never fully explained at the time, the concept of regeneration was born, the show's capacity for longevity was assured, and Patrick Troughton became the second Doctor Who. It was a decision that would become the stuff of which legends are made.

If the first Doctor's tenure was a time of experimentation and change, the second Doctor's tenure very soon became a period of repetition and reinforcement. Viewing figures were down, the series' original mission statement (its semi-educational remit, that had seen historical forays alternating with science fictional morality plays) had been torn up, and **Doctor Who** had become very much a children's programme with the sole aim of entertaining. Entertaining by frightening the bejesus out of the little ones, maybe, but the programme's function in the BBC's Saturday night line-up had nevertheless changed.

However, and in spite of its presence in the BBC archives being extremely depleted, the second Doctor's tenure has now become one of the most popular of all amongst classic series **Doctor Who** fans. Why is that? There are several possible reasons.

For one thing, the consolidatory fifth season of **Doctor Who** was the point at which the series' format as 'The Monster Show' really began to take root. The Cybermen, Yeti and Ice Warriors all made repeat appearances during the run of episodes that saw 1967 become 1968. Another reason might be that fans don't necessarily take too well to change, and the repetitious nature of the stories in this period may well have been the welcome familiarity that allowed for the scares onscreen.

But the most likely reason is Patrick Troughton. Together with Frazer Hines, Deborah Watling and Wendy Padbury, Troughton was the Doctor in charge of some of the best-remembered and most well-loved TARDIS crews the show has ever produced. It was a brave actor who would take over the role of Doctor Who from William Hartnell, but it was a brilliant one as well.

Daleks Have the Power...
Power of the Daleks by **Paul Butler**, 51, Fareham, UK
First story: **The Power of the Daleks**

It's Friday 29th July 2011, around 9am. I'm driving my Zaphira towards Gosport, Hampshire and the guy in the car next to me has just done a double take. A *proper* double take! It's a bit of a shock for him you see; there's a Dalek sitting next to me. Not a whole Dalek, you understand ... that would be stupid. Just the head, its eye stalk positioned so that it appears to be looking out of the window. The rest is in the back...

All in all it's a strange journey. I feel elated and, I have to admit, just a tad self-conscious at the same time. The trip is probably four miles in space; ten to fifteen minutes in time. But the number of people along that journey who notice my passenger, who point and smile (and wave!) is astounding ... and that's just the adults. Children are even more enthusiastic. As 'the scourge of the seven galaxies™,' it seems incredible that kids are not so much terrified as entranced and enthralled by the look of them – make them speak, however, and they run a mile. It's the power of a fifty-year-old television series called **Doctor Who** and, more importantly, it's *The Power of the Daleks*.

In many ways *The Power of the Daleks* has bookended my life in a manner I could never have predicted.

Back in 1966, I was four years old when *The Power of the Daleks* was transmitted. If truth be told, 46 years later, there's very little I recollect about being four. The jumble of memories of my childhood year in Sheffield are very few and even then exist in a dream-like state where I'm not sure whether they are real, constructed memories based on the stories of other people or the fantasies of a childish mind. It's hard to believe that, in the days before DVDs and multi-channel repeats, I could have such clear memories of a grainy black and white television programme that was broadcast once and never seen again. But I remember **Doctor Who** and, in particular, *The Power of the Daleks* with a bright, white-hot clarity even to this day.

For a start it was Patrick Troughton's first outing as the eponymous Time Lord and those early scenes of the Doctor, all frail and white-haired, stumbling into the TARDIS, falling to the floor and fading away to be replaced by a younger, dark-haired pretender was astounding to a four-year-old and, at the time, probably the biggest gamble any television programme had ever made with its lead character.

Looking back, the transition was not entirely successful for the four-year-old me. Though I have no memories of 'The Hartnell Years,' I had obviously been a part of them. I remember the shock realisation that the first Doctor was gone and been replaced by a bit of an idiot with a stupid hat. Those early 'comedic' scenes on the surface of Vulcan were as horrific to me as that moment when Sylvester McCoy attempted falling over and playing the spoons on Lakertya 21 years later (and I went on to like McCoy too, by the way).

So having established that it wasn't the new Doctor that kept me watching, it had to be something else. It had to be the Daleks. And, let's be honest here, David Whitaker's *The Power of the Daleks* has them at their absolute best. Maybe it's controversial to say this but I'm going to anyway. Terry Nation *isn't* the best Dalek writer. That kudos *must* go to David Whitaker who, as **Doctor Who**'s first script editor, guided Nation's original script to completion and then went on to create the classics *The Power of the Daleks* and *The Evil of the Daleks*, not to mention the wealth of back-story in the Dalek comic strips. Whitaker's Daleks are not just mechanical killing machines screaming 'Exterminate!' at the world. They have a hierarchy, they're sly and devious and much more likely to inveigle their way into a situation rather than appear all guns blazing.

I've always wondered why everyone is so quick to trust a creature with such an obvious weapon stuck on the front. It's like welcoming a small tank into your home (maybe the presence of a sink plunger next to it lulls them into believing it's only interested in DIY like an armour-plated Nick Knowles). But the four-year-old me loved them, young people today love them and here's the most amazing universal truth: no matter how old you get, that love *never goes away*!

So we turn full circle and return to that July day in 2011 and the reason I have a Dalek passenger in my car. *The Power of the Daleks* has taken hold once again. Sadly the short-sightedness of BBC management in the 1970s means that this story has been lost from the archives except for a few short clips, but July 29th 2011 is the first location day for Nick Scovell and Rob Thrush's *Power of the Daleks*, a fan-made reimagining of David Whitaker's story and I'm in it!

I have much to thank Nick for. We'd met working at Ferneham Hall (many areas of which doubled as the Vulcan Corporation base in *Power of the Daleks Reimagined)*. It dawned on me that this was the chap who'd played the Doctor in a stage version of *The Evil of the Daleks*, I'd seen with my children a couple of years earlier. United by our mutual love of all things **Doctor Who** as well as myriad of other series, it was he that had persuaded me to return to acting after a thirty year break and it was he that asked me to be a part of this fan production. I jumped at the chance.

For me, that first day's shooting will always be known as our Pertwee day. Thanks to the inestimable blagging of our producer Rob Thrush, no doubt enhanced by the powerful pull of **Doctor Who** and the Daleks, our morning would be spent at a land-locked Napoleonic fort built at the same time and to a similar design as the Solent-based one used in *The Sea Devils*, whilst the afternoon would see us filming in a Merlin helicopter supplied by HMS Sultan, home of the Royal Naval Air Engineering and Survival School. The Dalek was used at

Fort Brockhurst but wasn't required for the afternoon. Nevertheless, we removed it from the car and built it so hardened sailors could have their photos taken with it.

In the coming weeks we would work with seven Daleks, all fan-built, all beautifully made and indistinguishable from the BBC's 2005 revamps. The team led by Dalek wrangler, Stuart Currie, had undertaken to re-spray their pride and joys to match the silver and blue 1960s originals. Stuart had even designed a new identification plate underneath the eye stalk, the symbol forming a stylised R and S in tribute to Dalek voice Roy Skelton who had died in June.

I also have to say that the Daleks are the most infuriatingly temperamental creatures that ever existed. It's no wonder they are so unhinged, they can't get through doors unaided and, never mind staircases, slightly uneven floors cause them no end of problems. On Dalek days, the actors were definitely secondary in the performance pecking order as James George and I found out after an eleven hour wait to film a ten second scene involving us walking down a corridor. But, for all that, there is nothing more thrilling than appearing, as I did, in a scene with one, or turning a corner on location and finding one standing there menacing and charismatic all at the same time.

And that's the way it should be; the Daleks are the stars whether it's on screen or off ... *that* is the *true* power of the Daleks.

Memory and Loss in Three Acts

The Highlanders by **Nick 'Diskgrinder' Livingstone**, 50, Bristol, UK / First story: **The Invasion**

> Introduction. Recap *The Highlanders*.
> Act one: memories I must have had. The 1960s
> Act two: losing the Doctor. The 1980s
> Act three: paradise regained. 2000 AD

The Highlanders is completely gone. The last historical, the second Doctor's second outing, and Jamie McCrimmon's debut story, is gone, completely wiped. Left only in memory, photo stories, a full cast audiobook and a target novelisation. So not completely gone then.

I don't need to, so I won't, recap the story. I don't need to, so I won't, talk about the production, its place in the canon, or anything really much to with its actuality. Instead I want to talk about its context in my life: how this lost, bleak little serial represents key moments in my appreciation of all things Doctor.

Act one: bleakosity of the 1960s.

In the grainy black and white December of 1966, four days before the first episode of *The Highlanders* was broadcast, I turned two years old (I was born during the Dalek invasion of Earth in 2164). It's therefore unlikely I retain any conscious memories of the serial. However, it isn't beyond the realms of the Earth Alliance, that on some substrate of my being, it's imprinted. After all, both dad and mum were fans - the tiny plastic box in the corner of the living room would have been shining out the opening vortex that following Saturday, as it had all the preceding Saturdays when the Doctor was bigger in its inside.

Troughton is very much my mum's doctor, and there's no way that she wouldn't have been watching Polly being a bit of a shit to Tess, way back then. So by televisual osmosis (that's a thing, scientist in the pub told me) I was irradiated with subconscious wonder. Probably. That's my theory.

What I do remember about **Doctor Who** of that time, because my conscious awakening definitely happened between 1966 and 1970, is the deeply scary opening titles. And also Cybermen. All of it black and white, all of it bleak, all of it flickering on the same TV I watched the moon landing on (dad put all three of us in front of the telly late at night, and said "You will remember this"). The surprise being, to me at the time, the moon landing had worse production values than **Doctor Who**. Science fiction was in sharper focus than science fact.

Act two: paradise lost

The next time *The Highlanders* is in my life is the mid 1980s. Another bleak passage in the history of Britain, but this time in colour. This time bleakosity is evinced by the grim nastiness of recession and The Fall. I'm in my twenties now (as the arithmeticians among you will aver) and working on the railway, and listening to horrible northern noise music, and trying to be an existentialist, because I'd read the word in the NME. This is not a time to like **Doctor Who**, or at least not to admit to your intellectual friends that you do.

And, to be honest, I didn't. This was Colin Baker, this was Sylvester McCoy, this was Bidmead, Saward, and Cartmel. My least favourite period of **Doctor Who**: nasty violence, pantomime production values and stunt casting. (I have since recanted, by the way, and now enjoy even Saward's crass excesses.)

So what's a **Doctor Who** fan to do? In this parched desert of crap Doctor on TV? Well of course: Target novelisations. Finding out there was such a thing was the first epiphany, reading one, and finding it to be *excellent* (Cyberman voice), was the second. Ian Marter, Malcolm Hulke for the win.

So I am sure that I read *The Highlanders* novelisation. I read every Target book I could get my hands on (wrapped in the covers of some Wittgenstein *Tractatus*, secretly). So I must have? Right? Memory fails again.

Act three: paradise regained

So how was I to know that would be it for twenty years? I didn't watch any of McCoy, thinking that the Doctor would always be there, even if it wasn't on Saturdays. How wrong I was. I'm not including the TV movie. The TV movie was a massive disappointment, so I've effectively elided it from my memory. Lost it on purpose.

But then we have the Internet, and YouTube and telesnaps. And full cast audiobooks with linking narration by Fraser Hines.

Listening to the audiobook brings back memories; maybe not actual, realised memories I can get a grip on and examine, maybe. Maybe memories of memories. Memories of remembering watching, remembering reading. Remembering what **Doctor Who** meant to me.

And to end on a note of optimism (G, the most optimistic note), I have three sons who love **Doctor Who**, and are just getting into the classic series, with my memories of memories as a guide.

Professor Zaroff
(or, How I Learned to Stop Worrying and Love The Underwater Menace)

The Underwater Menace by **Ash Stewart**, 39, Reading
First story: **Destiny of the Daleks**

The panoply of **Doctor Who** stories have brought out a wide range of reactions in me; they've made me cry, they've made me laugh, they've made me shudder, they've made me think... But there are very few **Doctor Who** stories that I can honestly say have taught me a lesson. One of them is most definitely *The Underwater* Menace, and this is why...

Many moons ago, in the dark days of VHS, *The Underwater Menace* was not so much released on video; rather it was allowed to escape. It seemed it was almost an afterthought on *The Ice Warriors* release, as if they had to put it *somewhere*, so they might as well put it here. This release had several things on it. The main feature, on tape one, was the four extant *Ice Warriors* episodes, with a mini recon of the two that are missing (this dragged so much, it seemed to last almost as long as a full episode. And they dragged even more...) On tape two was a missing episodes documentary which, being somewhat of a missing episodes obsessive, I absolutely lapped up. After this, and somewhat handcuffed on to the end of the documentary, was what was then the only surviving episode of *The Underwater Menace*; Episode 3.

I watched most of the set quickly, but left *The Underwater Menace* for quite some time. I had read quite a lot about it, and most of what I'd read was seemingly unanimous: this was a turkey, with pretty much no redeeming features. The absolute lowest of the low. I should have known not to pay any heed to this, as the snorefest that was *The Ice Warriors* seemed to have been largely, and to my mind unduly, praised. I guess my reasoning was that if the more highly regarded story of the pair wasn't that good, the lesser regarded one would be even worse. So, I left *The Underwater Menace* unwatched.

But then one day, possibly as many as six months later, I found myself at a loose end, and felt like watching some **Doctor Who**. I didn't have much time, so it would have to be just the one episode. I found myself thinking, 'Ah, what the heck; I'll get it over with. I've got to watch it some time, just to see how bad it is...' and put on *The Underwater Menace* Episode 3.

It didn't start well; there was a very brief 'story so far' segment from Frazer Hines that skimmed over the preceding two episodes at breakneck speed, which didn't sound at all encouraging. And then, it started...

...twenty-five minutes later I was gobsmacked. Had I really just seen the same episode all these articles and reviews had said was so bad? Surely not... The episode I'd seen was so wonderful, and enjoyable, and full of great performances. I'd had a grin on my face pretty much from start to finish. It's always good to see Troughton on form, and here he was on tip top form.

But he had competition from Josef Furst's Professor Zaroff. Yes, he's over the top, but in the context of the story it worked perfectly. If you have a mad scientist as your protagonist, then he should be well and truly mad, and oh was Furst's performance M.A.D.! A more nuanced and subtle performance would have had much less of an impact on the story, and especially on that last scene, where Zaroff finally loses all his marbles and goes in to full-on rant mode; to this day it remains in my top ten **Doctor Who** scenes.

After I watched it, I immediately wished I'd watched it sooner. I'd let the received wisdom of fandom form an opinion for me about something I'd not yet seen; I started watching the episode expecting it to be a turkey, and finished watching it with a new beloved episode. I think I can confidently say, and I say this without any exaggeration or a lie, that *The Underwater Menace* Episode 3 is probably the single episode of **Doctor Who** I've watched more than any other. When November 23rd comes around each year, and there's time to watch an episode to commemorate the good Doctor's birthday, it's inevitably that episode of *The Underwater Menace*.

But, sadly, I can't help but notice the disdain for the story continues; when they made the announcement of Episode 2's return at the tail end of 2011, there were all sorts of people on internet forums saying that it was a little disappointing that it was an episode from *that* story recovered, rather than something more regarded, as if it were almost a 'waste' of an episode return. I've even seen a few posts suggesting that *The Underwater Menace* episodes would never be on anyone's 'most wanted missing episodes' list. Wrong! It was absolutely most definitely on my 'most wanted' list, and will remain there until the other two episodes come back.

It's sad that such an opinion persists, but I really think that once Episode 2 is seen more widely and is released on DVD, it will help to increase the story's standing within fandom, and more people will come to love it as much as I do.

Certainly, since then, every time I've seen a **Doctor Who** story for the first time (and there's even now some I've still not seen) I've paid no heed at all to what conventional wisdom states about it, and not worried if the world and his octopus thinks the story I'm about to watch is a duffer...

(...though having said that, I do wish I'd listened to the warnings about *The Mark of the Rani*; that's 45 minutes I'll never get back!)

To the Moon and Back
The Moonbase by **Nick Mellish**, 27, Norwich, UK
First story: **The Time Meddler**

The Moonbase: it's that **Doctor Who** story with the crap science, silly cliffhanger at the end of Episode 2, plot recycled from the first Cyberman story, and little else going for it, right?

Well, to address the points in order: it's a children's show about a magical machine that travels through Time and Space and you're complaining about silly science? And, again, it's a children's show about a magical ya-di-ya-di-ya-da and you're saying the cliffhanger is a bit childish? Show me a show that doesn't borrow from its past plot-wise at some point (if it ain't broke...).

Oh, and to me, *The Moonbase* is a lot more than just another story. To me, it's a story deeply rooted in **Doctor Who** mythos, or rather my fandom and love of the show. To me, it's the story that taught me all that had been lost. This was the story that led me to discover the world of missing episodes.

To recap though: it's 1992, I am about six-years-old and I'm already head-over-heels in love with this silly little show called **Doctor Who**. I have Daleks drawn in crude pencil hung up on my wall; I have nightmares about Vervoids that would make Freud raise an eyebrow; I have editions of **Classic Comics** with the staples long gone that have introduced me to the world of Shayde and comics and *The Tides of Time*; and most of all, more exciting than anything else, I have Mum and Mum likes **Doctor Who**, too. She enjoyed re-watching that one with the unicorn that doesn't exist. She liked the Monk and tells me stories about giant rubber snakes and watching 'the one with the pinkies' (turns out she meant *The Happiness Patrol*) with me when I was a baby: indeed, after a bit of poking around my memory, I can distinctly recall watching Haemovores rise from the sea and eating Weetabix whilst watching *Ghost Light*: no wonder the show had felt so familiar when I'd re-discovered it years later as a fully-grown six-year-old child!

Most exciting of all though were Mum's tales of watching her favourite Doctor, Patrick Troughton, as a child, and the one where the Cybermen were on the Moon. The Moon! How amazing was that?!

I bloody loved the Moon: I mean, of course I did, I was a six-year-old child who loved **Doctor Who** and unlike fictional planets that writers with names like Terrance or Rona had created, this one was real and man had actually visited it: we could actually, in theory, go there! That, to me, was the most exciting thing in the world. Dad used to take us in his car along the seafront to wave to it when it was full and near and big in the sky: and, once upon a time, the Cybermen were there.

A bit of research with my well-thumbed copy of the 1991 **Doctor Who Yearbook** later and we found out that this story was called *The Moonbase* (Mum had actually remembered the bit about the base, so putting two and two together was fairly easy to do!) and so we rushed off to the local video rental store, which we knew had a few **Doctor Who** serials to rent as we had already done so time and again. (My adoration of *The Five Doctors*, *Death to the Daleks* and *City of Death* can be traced back this far.)

We scanned the rows of videos to see what we could find: the second tape of *The Daleks* here (but never the first oddly enough), *Spearhead from Space* there, *The Curse of Fenric* incorrectly filed next to something called *Debbie Does Dallas* which I presumed was some sort of travel documentary, but no copy of *The Moonbase* to be found. The man behind the counter searched for it, but nothing came up, and so, defeated and with *Robot* safely stowed away beneath my arm, we trundled back home in the rain and ate cheese on toast as Tom Baker skipped and smiled away. We didn't give up of course: other trips to other shops did us no better and whenever new videos popped up in the shops, we scanned the titles quickly and soon realised that, once again, *The Moonbase* had evaded us.

And then came that day when I was re-reading the **Doctor Who Yearbook** yet again, and my eyes were drawn to a large section about missing episodes. I didn't really understand, so I read it along with Mum and soon we realised just why we could never find *The Moonbase*: it did not exist anymore.

In fact, a hell of a lot of stories didn't exist anymore, stories with fantastic names like *The Space Pirates* and *The Celestial Toymaker*. They were denied to us, and I was so upset in that way children are, when something so grossly unfair has happened and it feels like it was done just to spite them.

Years have passed since then, just over twenty of them, and it still stings to think so much is lost to us, though with time and age I understand why; that people were just doing their job and, in truth, the fact so many survive at all is thanks in no small part to people like Pamela Nash, who are so often vilified in fandom.

I've discovered better stories, like *The War Games*, *Verdigris* and *Circular Time*, and other, wonderful Doctors like Peter Davison and Paul McGann. I've somehow memorised and amassed information about that truly brilliant children's show, from co-ordinates to Gallifrey to which William Hartnell story it was where the end credits shifted from scrolling at the far left of the screen to the centre (*Marco Polo*, fact fans). But deep down, beneath Izzy Sinclair and Tooting Bec and 'Beat you, cock!' and Bernard Cribbins knocking four times, there's that little bit of childhood love for *The Moonbase* that will never die. It's there when I listen to the soundtrack CD or watch the Loose Cannon reconstruction or pick up *Lost In Time* or flick through the novelisation. It's there when clips or mute film trims are found and excitement bubbles across the Internet.

It's dear to my heart, and when people ask what story I'd like returned... Well, I scroll through lists of story titles in my head, but in the end, I picture a six-year-old boy and his mum, jumping in puddles and running on home to look out of the window at the Moon and eat dinner and play games and think about one day curling up on the sofa together and watching Patrick Troughton beat the Cybermen once and for all.

It's an image that not even furnaces could erase from my mind.

Macra & Me

The Macra Terror by **Matthew Fitch**, 37, Kenmore, USA / First story: **Inferno**

When I began watching **Doctor Who** in December of 1983, I never knew what to expect. Truth be told, I was mainly interested in the title sequence which at the time resembled Darth Vader's helmet, but was drawn in and hooked by the storyline and of course, the cliff-hangers. Never knowing what to expect, I had no idea how long a serial would run, and when *Inferno* was followed by *The Claws of Axos*, *Colony in Space*, and *Day of the Daleks*, nothing seemed wrong!

That changed one day in 1984 (I think I had just watched *The Ark in Space* Part Two*)* when my father decided to take us all to the most suburban 1980s location of all, the mall. Generally a welcome trip for me, as there were always some **Star Wars** toys, books, or magazines to look at, but I *never* expected to find what to this day is one of my prized **Doctor Who** publications, the **Radio Times** (or in my case **Starlog**) Twentieth Anniversary Special. Inside were a treasure trove of photographs, biographical information, and episodes I had never even *conceived* of before. 'Terror *of the Autons*? *The Dæmons*? What are these?' I wondered. But what really caught my attention was on page 53. That picture. The one with the large claw heading for the terrified man. The picture from *The Macra Terror*.

At that point I knew I *had* to see this serial. Imagine my disappointment upon discovering all four episodes were amongst the missing episodes also listed in the magazine. This still didn't stop me though, my first reaction being to ask my grandparents if there might be some old film cans in the attic!

After a few years, my interest in **Doctor Who** began to taper off as comic books took over as my main interest. Enter **Doctor Who Classic Comics** and some lucky clearance VHS finds at my local video store in 1993 and the flame reignited. I began snatching up all the books, magazines, and videos I could find, and was very excited to find two audio cassette titles were available, *The Evil of the Daleks* and (wait for it...) *The Macra Terror*. At last, I could at least listen to the story, and of all the original audio releases, it was the most listenable. Honestly in retrospect, some of this is probably down to its length but I didn't care. *I loved it*!

When the Australian censor clips were recovered in the mid-1990s, aside from the *Fury from the Deep* clips (my favourite classic story, by the way), the most exciting find for me was some *actual* footage of the Macra! Despite my misgivings about the R1 DVD release of *The Space Museum/The Chase*, I purchased a copy alongside the complete R2 version mainly for the documentary *Shawcraft – The Original Monster Makers*, which amongst other classic 1960s creatures includes full colour footage of the Macra prop.

And then there was *Gridlock*. I must confess, upon first viewing I was becoming slightly bored, until the Doctor made his discovery, the creatures thriving beneath the traffic were Macra. Many will say (and quite rightly, too) that *School Reunion* was where they connected to the current incarnation of **Doctor Who**, but to me it was this moment in *Gridlock* that cemented it. When the revelation was made, I actually frightened my parents who just happened to be visiting, by jumping out of my seat shouting about the Macra!

In 1999, BBC Audio began releasing off-air soundtracks of the missing and incomplete stories, and one of the most anticipated was *The Macra Terror*, even though it was essentially a straight port of the cassette release (gloriously remastered by Mark Ayers). It was here, presented in crystal clarity that I discovered one of my all time favourite quotes, and not just from **Doctor Who,** which for a time I actually used as the outgoing message on my answering machine.

> MEDOK: All right, have fun while you can *before they crawl all over you*! [my emphasis]

In 2012, BBC audio began releasing box sets of the missing and incomplete serials, Collection Four boasting a brand new edition of *The Macra Terror* and PDF files of the scripts, which prompted me to purchase the collection (and sad fan that I am, the other four!) again. I am now looking to sell off my other single releases to offset the cost of the box sets. If interested, please contact me, but be aware that *The Macra Terror* is off the table.

'In Case of Emergency...'
The Faceless Ones by **Gareth Kavanagh**, 40, Manchester, UK / First story: **The Deadly Assassin**

It seems incredible to think of it now, but there was a time when **Doctor Who** was distinctly finite in nature. It had a beginning, a middle and an end. Of course looking back now, it was little more than a chink. A moment spanning that strange, wild and wonderful time between the TV Movie, our great false dawn not being picked up, and the announcement of the second coming of the series in 2003.

But it definitely had a limit. And once you'd seen them all, that was it.

During this strange, sad-happy time which I like to think of as 'the resignation years,' both myself and seemingly much of fandom appeared resigned to the fact **Doctor Who** was never coming back to our screens. And I think we were strangely okay about this salutary fact. After all, the factoids amongst us were still sucking the marrow from the bones of the old series, thanks to stellar fan scholars like Andrew Pixley and Richard Bignell, and every now and again a telesnap or rare photo would surface. We'd even get, once in a blue moon, a missing episode turning up although to be honest, after *The Tomb of the Cybermen* even those were rather drying up.

The brutal reality as I saw it was this; that **Doctor Who** in 2003 (and probably for the foreseeable future) was always going to consist of the currently existing episodes and 109 missing ones (oh how we laugh from the comfy future where we're now only missing a paltry 106...). Nothing new was coming. Ever.

This was a bit of a problem, as by the late 1990s, I'd pretty much run out of existing **Doctor Who** to watch. Fuelled by cash tips and a willing vendor of pirate tapes in Cambridge, the official releases and the wonderful UK Gold, I'd pretty much seen every extant episode by the time the decade was out.

Well, all but one. To be precise; *The Faceless Ones* Episode 1.

Rather like a diminishing stock of Easter Eggs, you come to realise at a certain point you need to slow down and take stock before you run out. To be blunt, I needed an episode of **Doctor Who** I'd never seen, something to always wonder and marvel about in my twilight years. And *The Faceless Ones* Episode 1, through sheer luck had slipped the net, and so was destined to be that episode. The 'break glass in case of emergency' episode I promised myself I'd watch in in the event either of **Doctor Who** returning to our screens, or something more serious happening. It was an episode I was never expecting to see, a little like the BBC transmission in the event of the end of civilisation.

Of course, I'd plain forgotten that being a **Doctor Who** fan does tend to prepare you for the unexpected. Often the unexpected was not so good, rather like Bonnie Langford being cast as the new companion or Colin Baker's bold new costume. But every now and again, the surprises were wonderful. One marvellous day in September 2003 came the news I never expected to hear. **Doctor Who** was returning as a full series. No catches, no caveats. It was coming back. I remember hearing the news on the radio in my boss' car on the way back from a tedious meeting in Doncaster. The significance was lost on my Jazz FM-loving boss, but my mind was going cartwheels. The clock was ticking again. The **Doctor Who** tap was about to be turned back on.

This momentous news fairly rapidly led to two things happening. First, I coughed up for a TV Licence as my caveat was I wasn't buying one until **Doctor Who** came back (a minor irritant, although at the time I made the flippant excuse, it seemed as likely as Wales making it to the World Cup). Second, I gingerly reached for the shelf and pulled out *The Faceless Ones* and popped it in the video recorder. After all, it was no longer the final piece left to watch in our newly revitalised series.

I'll bet you're wondering what I made of this mythical final slice of classic **Doctor Who**. Let's just say, if I'd left it until the end of days, I suspect I'd have been mighty disappointed. However, watching *The Faceless Ones* Episode 1 in a celebratory mood was little short of perfect. Gatwick looks great and it feels like a proper, real place. Inspector Crosland is suitably 'inspectory,' and all the characters feel real. It's firmly rooted in the as-then, contemporary society of 1960s Britain and looking back, really chimes nicely with Russell T Davies' vision for the series. In fact; the whole idea of teenagers being kidnapped en-route to Ibiza or Kos and replaced by doppelgangers is such a Russell idea, I'm stunned we never saw the Chameleons again. That cliffhanger of the faceless beast wheezing and gasping for breath is without doubt one of *the* greatest ever. Pure nightmare stuff, the suffering and horror is starkly painted for us. In fact, I suspect Julie Gardner would have vetoed it on the spot had Russell tried to sneak in something as visceral as that into his brave new vision for **Doctor Who**.

And with that, for a while my journey through the classic series was over. Well, at least until that episode of *The Daleks' Master Plan* returned and the two in 2011, but nitpicking aside, you get my gist I'm sure. But I do like a tradition and, having completely missed *The Doctor, the Widow and the Wardrobe* in 2011 as I was working, I've made the decision to bank it for a rainy day, be it the end of days or something else.

I wonder what I'll learn from it when that day finally comes? Perhaps it won't. Perhaps **Doctor Who** will outlast me. Time, as ever will tell...

Repeat of the Daleks
Evil of the Daleks by **Tony Jordan**, 53, London, England
First story: **An Unearthly Child**

To the very best of my knowledge, I've watched **Doctor Who** from day one. So by the time William Hartnell regenerated into Patrick Troughton I'd got a very good idea of what I did, and didn't, like. Daleks - good, exciting and very scary. Historicals - boring, slow-moving and in need of being dropped. Clearly Innes Lloyd was listening to seven-year-old me.

The Power of the Daleks had a big impact. It was terrifying, especially Episode 6 and the ruthless manner in which the Daleks went about wiping out the colonists of Vulcan. The extermination effect was so overwhelmingly 'awful'; it always had me scuttling behind the sofa - more of that shortly.

When *The Evil of the Daleks* was trailed I was delighted, and nervous, in equal measure. Now, this is not the best Dalek story ever. It's not even the best of the 1960s Dalek stories; *The Power of the Daleks* and *The Daleks' Master Plan* both being superior in my view. But it's still very good, a climactic season finale. And a great way to bring about 'The final end,' or at least, as it was then thought to be.

Episode 1 of *The Evil of the Daleks* was shown on my 8th birthday. Very nice of the BBC to arrange that - time for a party, the FA Cup Final and then my favourite television programme. Now, to get back to the sofa: it's long been held by some that this was a myth, but it really wasn't, honest guv! When I was a lad, although TVs were big, the screens were small and programmes were monochrome and presented in 405 lines. All this meant that on a bright early evening, to get the best view you were quite likely to have to draw the curtains and pull the sofa forward.

Anyway, and no surprise here, the death of Kennedy at the climax of the episode scared me rigid, and the back of the sofa and I quickly rekindled our friendship once more...

As the weeks went by, at times the story plodded, but that was made up for by the epic nature of the final episode. Well, epic apart from the Louis Marx model Daleks that were used for some of the civil war sequences! But the set with the amazing Emperor and his many black-domed minions was really superb. The death of Waterfield was another 'sofa moment,' sacrificing himself as a Dalek is about to exterminate the Doctor. Real pathos there.

And then, minutes later, that was it. As already mentioned 'The final end' and a whole two-month break until Season Five. What would we give for a two-month break between seasons nowadays?!

'The Monster Season' proved to be a real cracker. Two Cyber stories, two Yeti, the introduction of the Ice Warriors – what more could a lad want? Well, the Daleks actually, please Mr BBC if that's at all physically possible. But, of course, you killed them off didn't you? (Or rather Terry Nation wanted to try and flog them to the USA.)

But on June 1st 1968, at the very end of *The Wheel in Space*, there was a genuine surprise. The Doctor lifts up one of the TARDIS roundels, places a conveniently located device that must have cost all of 1s 6½d to make on his head and the unsubtle stowaway Zoe is asked; 'Have you ever heard of the Daleks?' quickly followed by a reprise of Kennedy's extermination. Wow, talk about being caught on the hop and unable to get behind the sofa in time. But how wonderful that the Doctor could weave his thought patterns into a complete story. Would that someone could only recreate that unique feat nowadays!

And so it came to pass that on the following Saturday, June 8th, the start of the first ever repeat of an entire **Doctor Who** story began. 'Now as I remember Zoe, it all started when Jamie and I discovered somebody making off with the TARDIS...' Taking out the two Saturdays of Wimbledon, this seamlessly led us into *The Dominators* and the start of Season Six on August 19th.

Now I must be totally honest here. I'm not sure that I watched every single episode of the repeat. It was summer and overall the weather was nice. Yes, I know - bad fan. But I do very, very clearly recall one specific incident.

My parents belonged to a community sports and social centre called Hanger Hill Country Club. My mum played tennis as much as possible in the summer, indeed she was a good player, so on the afternoon of June 8th I was down there with her. There was a Television Room off the main hall, and as no-one else seemed bothered about it, I distinctly remember going in, switching the telly on and plonking myself down to watch the repeat of Episode 1 of *The Evil of the Daleks*. Even more vivid, though, is the memory that just before the end of the episode I got up and walked smartly out of the room, definitely not looking behind me. I knew what was going to happen - Kennedy was going to get exterminated, and I simply didn't want to go through that again!

That's how big an impact the Daleks and their extermination effect had on me as a kid. So much so that, 45 years on, I can still vividly remember it, and the 'Repeat of the Daleks.'

I Have To Really Want To Remember

The Tomb of the Cybermen by **Cliff Chapman**, 31, London, UK / First story: **Remembrance of the Daleks**

It's over twenty years, four rediscovered episodes and four new Doctors since the return of *The Tomb of the Cybermen*. If fandom can be defined as reading **DWM** and having a collection of tat, I just missed out on *The Ice Warriors*, so *The Tomb of the Cybermen* was the first find in my fan timeline, and it remains the most significant. It's still the only complete story from Season Five, and that features Victoria; it's the earliest complete Cybermen story and the last until 1975, the last complete story found, and the last complete story from a foreign archive (I'll be too busy crying with joy to care if this fact is hopelessly out date by publication). There have been four others recovered since, though all fragments. Only one of these feature Troughton, and none Watling. It's one of only two complete Troughton four-parters, hence **The Five Faces of Doctor Who** repeat of *The Krotons* in 1981 (scant months after I was born – can't remember it). These are facts. Since then, I've been obsessed with lost **Doctor Who**, and while *The Tomb of the Cybermen* didn't make me aware of the situation – there were books, **DWM**, even the *The Hartnell Years* and *The Troughton Years* with their curious yet uninvolvingly presented oddments – it was this that gave me that first taste of what it was like to get something back.

    The symbolism of archaeologists unearthing something terrifying and mysterious and wonderful was irresistible to fandom in the 1980s, and *The Tomb of the Cybermen* was the 'hero' find, spoken of with reverence in **DWM**, the script book, breakdowns for *Attack of the Cybermen*. The 1992 **Doctor Who Yearbook** had a complete episode guide, which, when I need to remember story order, I still visualise the layout of to this day. There were key shapes, filled for extant, novelised, released-on-VHS stories, empty for not, and yes, reader, I inked-in the empty shapes for a good couple of years, devotedly. And early on, *The Tomb of the Cybermen* got to have *two* shapes coloured in. **DWM** said so. The joy of a country of fans rubbed off with the print.

Doctor Who had been off air for over two years - an aeon when you're ten - and apart from one friend, no one else particularly liked it at school, despite the small random collection of Target Novelisations in the library. I consoled myself that I was obviously surrounded by children forced to watch **Coronation Street**. I'd come to the show via the Cushing films, remembered the first half of *The Trial of a Time Lord* very well, missed McCoy's debut year completely and became obsessed via a handful of videos in our local rental shop, a batch of novelisations, and *Remembrance of the Daleks*. But even the 1992 repeats season hadn't picked up any new fans in school. (Or perhaps it had. They just didn't want me bothering them.)

I spent my first ten years living with my mum and her parents. A few weeks before *Tomb of the Cybermen* was released, my granddad died. And so...

I think my uncle and auntie bought me the video, at some point after the funeral. It wouldn't have been on release day - it might have been a week or two later. Without a local group or the internet, there wasn't that need to make a statement of getting in there first. There was lots of **Doctor Who** still to see and any I hadn't would have hit the spot. Even then ... it was special. I'm fairly sure I watched it alone. That music, as the Cybermen awake; that perfect chemistry of Troughton, Hines and Watling. Troughton's Doctor in *The Mind Robber* and *The War Games* had utterly won me over, maybe because we had the same haircut; I'd like to believe it was deeper than that. Easily the most fascinating, so great that Matt Smith would be similarly beguiled another couple of decades later, making an army of wary fanboys slightly less grumpy that he was younger than them, especially when they'd *finally* decided to run away to London and become an actor. (Just me?)

The Tomb of the Cybermen was the best story to have, that early summer of 1992. When you've lost someone who's always been around, how nice to have something that had seemed forever trapped in the past, back in the present. I have to really *want* to remember.

An eternity passed... Then *The Lion*! And ... that was it. **Doctor Who** *would actually be announced as definitely coming back to TV* before we saw another missing episode. News of Russell T Davies' **Doctor Who** was one of the last things my Gran told me, and damn it, I only knew it wasn't just another tabloid rumour after she was gone. Then, *Day of Armageddon*! A rumour of my own to investigate (just one: a B-C hating art-collector friend-of-a-friend-of-a-friend, which came to nothing, alas), animations, and then...

Excited by the programme tease, but unspoiled by rumour, I managed to inveigle my way into the **Doctor Who** Polloi (what are all these knobs?) for Missing Believed Wiped, December 2011. I was baffled yet quietly impressed by the first few minutes of *Air Lock*, but utterly thrilled by *The Underwater Menace.* It was another Troughton at last, because he was wonderful ... because I'd come full circle. I *certainly* appreciated single episodes – of stories we already had a bit of, that few fondly remembered to boot – much more than I would have done when I was ten. It was ... logical.

At the time of writing, there are officially 106 missing episodes. By the time you read this, I hope that number's reduced. And if it isn't, well, come back here once a year. We will survive. They will survive. I hope you've had a *Tomb* moment. If you haven't ... I'll keep hoping that you will.

The Secret Lovecraft of Dr. Who

The Abominable Snowmen by **Peter Nolan**, 38,
Wexford, Ireland / First story: **The Robots of Death**

The Abominable Snowmen isn't the first **Doctor Who** story I ever saw, nor is it my favourite. In fact, I only saw it for the first time in 2009 and, even then, it's arguable that I've ever seen it at all – more *experienced* it via the remaining episode, reclaimed soundtrack, and cunningly made reconstructions. Despite its being a blistering ten-out-of-ten instalment, in a field of two hundred and thirty competitors and counting, it 'only' hovers into my personal Top 20.

It is, however, the most *me* **Doctor Who** story I've ever known.

Most fans probably have a story that feels like it was crafted especially to push all their personal buttons. Some may look to *The Lodger* and its tale of a dementedly eccentric flatmate simultaneously ruining and enriching lives (though smiling ruefully at the idea of said flatmate presenting a paper bag stuffed with cash, or any rent at all). I know some palaeontologists for whom *Invasion of the Dinosaurs* is both the best of times and the worst of times. And all the gladiatorial death rained down on disruptive supporters, secures *The Curse of Peladon* a place in the heart of Eric Cantona. Probably.

Me, I love a bit of HP Lovecraft. And, in a show that's always thrived on homage and reference and outright theft, they do Lovecraft oh so very well. My adolescence carries the eldritch stench of Lovecraft like an eau du backed-up toilet so, for my adult self, *The Abominable Snowmen* is nostalgia squared.

I actually approached Lovecraft side-on at first, before consuming every bit of his writing I could get my hands on, via the frankly marvellous role-playing game Call of Cthulhu. Amid those happy afternoons around various kitchen tables my favourite Player Character remains Richard Carson. Carson was an investigative journalist who, after some messy business early on, developed a bad case of dendrophobia and was terrified of trees. In fact, all the characters among my circle of friends quickly developed quirky paranoid tendencies. It was a brilliant excuse to go everywhere with carpet bags packed with guns and explosives and to take a Bush Doctrine approach to any conceivable threat. A mysterious invitation to attend a masked ball at a remote Louisiana plantation, for instance, would be instantly met with a plan to sneak onto the grounds with drums of petrol and burn the whole place to the ground without ever going inside. Before long our Game Master's first order of business in any session became separating us immediately from our carpet bags by ever more convoluted and nefarious means. If only they'd had Ryanair in the 1920s it would have been all too easy for him.

This is probably why Travers is one of my favourite supporting characters yet – he's the only one sensible enough, in the midst of all these baleful horrors, to keep a rifle on him at all times and to take a healthily paranoid view of everything and everyone around him. It's no wonder he survives the story, though it's slightly surprising nobody gets shot.

The Great Intelligence is one of the all time great Lovecraftian villains. I vividly remember, as a teen, meandering through a guide to the monsters of the Cthulhu Mythos. Azathoth was depicted as a formless monstrosity engulfing a mountaintop, while the accompanying text explained that it was one of the most unknowable, most alien intelligences of all, and that, if manifested on Earth by its insane cult of monkish followers – say, for example, in the Himalayas as in the illustration – within hours its writhing, ever-changing mass would suffocate the entire planet. I must have re-read that page a hundred times, so you can imagine the electric thrill I felt when the end game of the Great Intelligence's 'great purpose' was revealed.

It takes more than a monster to make a true pastiche, as any number of terrible movies will tell you. *The Abominable Snowmen* hits the mark in every department. The monastery is more than just another base under siege; its dark stone corridors, creaking doors and chambers bathed in flickering torchlight make it a character in its own right in a way no Moonbase or space station could ever hope. Their footsteps echoing in the dark, there's never a moment our heroes are left to feel cosy or safe. The desiccated, possessed, Padmasambhava, claw-like hands hovering over his chessboard in the gloomy half-light, invading the minds of his prey at will, is a tremendously compelling foe. That raises the stature of the Doctor, too, who perhaps for the first time seems *more* than just a hapless alien wanderer as he unleashes his own psychic powers in a titanic duel against a vast and ancient god.

Of course, it's all change now. The Great Intelligence, these days, is revealed to be not an unspeakable, unknowable, sanity-threatening amorphous Thing from beyond the dawn of time but, as far as I can make out, the vestiges of the mind of a dead Victorian scientist embittered by not having been popular at school. Which is a bit like the production team of 2051 doing a story that reveals the Beast in *The Satan Pit* was actually a door-to-door salesman called Kevin, fed up about a string of publishers' rejection letters.

But never mind that now. Close your eyes and stick your fingers in your ears. Let creeping dread feel its way up your spine and a horror without a name choke in your throat. Picture the indescribable nightmares of mankind's worst imaginings. Tingle with the certain knowledge that the spirit of Lovecraft is with you. For that is not dead that can forever lie on the bookshelves of your local independent bookshop or library.

Nobody Ever Talks About Zondal

The Ice Warriors by **Shauno Eels**, 45, Manchester, UK
First story: **The Web of Fear**

Nobody ever talks about Zondal.

Discussions and reviews of *The Ice Warriors* are more likely to mention the stock footage of the polar bear than the Martians' second-in-command, played forty-six years ago by an actor named Roger Jones.

I'm not going to talk about Zondal either, really. Or *The Ice Warriors*. What do you think this is – some kind of **Doctor Who** book? I'm going to talk about Roger Jones though, and in a personal way that's full of bittersweet reminiscence, frustration and strange coincidence. For me, that is. For you ... well there's a lovely essay about *The Enemy of the World* just over there, unless you want to read about how my mum introduced me to an Ice Warrior and how I tried to find him again years later for a DVD release.

I just missed *The Ice Warriors* on TV. My first real memory of watching **Doctor Who** is fixed on the repeat of *The Web of Fear* in the early 1970s. I was nearly six when I first saw an Ice Warrior and that was in *The Curse of Peladon*. As ever, the whole family were watching and I'll never forget Mum leaning over and saying, 'My friend Roger played an Ice Warrior when he was an actor. His name was Zondal.'

It was the first direct collision between the real world of **Doctor Who** production and my own life and it hit me at an impressionable age ... or else why would you and I be doing this right now?

It was some years before an introduction could be arranged, and the delay was undoubtedly beneficial to Roger's sanity and patience, had he but known it. Kids from all over the world are given their first introduction to Stratford-upon-Avon for Shakespearean reasons but mine was all about a much more recent era of history. Ionisers, not iambs. More Mirrorlon than Miranda. Yes, tights were playing a poor second fiddle to latex-covered waders as Mum parked the car and led me through that much-mocked Tudor tangle towards a kitchen shop on Sheep Street. Roger owned this shop, as my young self knew actors did when they stopped pretending to be hissing lizards.

And there he was, this tall, deep-voiced and handsome man who'd clearly been briefed in advance as to what a young **Doctor Who** fan might be like. We all went for tea and cheese on toast in the legendary Cobweb across the street, where he was charm itself as he plied me with tales of sweating away half of his body weight with a stinking coracle strapped on either side of him. Fond reminiscences were shared about Patrick Troughton, Bernard Bresslaw and Deborah Watling. He told me with remarkable candour that he'd, 'Never really made it as an actor,' and that playing Zondal was the point at which he realised that he never would. His height was against him, for one thing. He loved being in Stratford because it was an actors' town but he was happy now to be one of the townsmen rather than one of the actors. After little more than an hour we all said our goodbyes and Stratford was left behind and that was that for more than two decades.

Time passed, more strange connections with the world of **Doctor Who** crept in and out of my life and meeting Roger Jones had become just one of many happy memories that were somewhere in my head not doing a great deal. Like Ice Warriors frozen inside a glacier, if you've a taste for a laboured simile. I'd grown into a ludicrously keen theatregoer and admirer of the actor's craft and since I'd remained a **Doctor Who** fan it was inevitable that I'd eventually count Toby Hadoke among my friends. We can, did, and do pass countless hours in all kinds of places by exchanging theatrical gossip and reminiscences. Toby's knowledge of both **Doctor Who** and anyone who is or ever was in Spotlight is encyclopaedic in the truest sense (with none of the fallacious flumdummery for which Wiki and the IMDb have become notorious) which is why he soon became indispensible to the brave talents who work so hard on the **Doctor Who** range of DVDs. Always thinking ahead to future releases, he asked me how likely it was that I could find Roger Jones and either interview him or persuade him to take part in a commentary or documentary feature.

Which is why, in June 2010, I didn't make my usual day trip to Stratford to see the RSC's latest but spent a couple of days there looking for Roger. Mum was now terminally ill and it was as much to find her old friend as it was to enliven a future DVD. I was staying (next door to the Troughtons, one of whom was that evening's magnificent Romeo!) with my lovely friend Joy who was intrigued by the fact that I was in town to try and track down a former actor. When I told her which one, her face fell.

'Oh I knew Roger very well but I'm afraid he died a few years ago. Ooh no, I can't remember quite when... It was all over the Stratford Herald...'

It was? Roger, it transpired, had been very well known and well liked around Stratford. Exactly how well known I was about to begin to discover. Joy's cleaner arrived that morning, and she'd known Roger too:

'I went to his funeral in Clifford Chambers. Ooh no, I can't remember quite which year it was...'

At Clifford Chambers I scoured the churchyard for Roger's grave. It wasn't there. The man cutting the grass asked what I was looking for.

'Roger Jones? Oh I remember his funeral. Not sure what year it was, no... See that bloke walking down the lane over there? He'll know...'

'That bloke,' turned out to have been Roger's business partner for seventeen years, and he was able to tell me so much. But not the year of Roger's death, or where he was buried. It seemed that everybody I met in Stratford had memories of Roger to share. Everybody from tailors to waitresses agreed that he was a lovely man. Nobody could remember when he'd died, although they all knew how: he'd been driving home very late one night and suffered a heart attack at the wheel of his car. Far too young. But exactly how young...?

The Stratford Herald would be sure to enlighten me. After all, as many people had told me, Roger's sudden death had been widely reported...

Over the next few months I scanned every page of every edition of the Herald published in a ten-year period. Nothing. Not a single mention of Roger Jones's life or death. I'd have to look elsewhere. Fortunately Roger's father the formidable and distinguished Brigadier O. L. Jones had passed on to his son the traditional family middle name of Luxmoore, which would at least distinguish *my* Roger Jones from the hundreds of other Rogers Jones that the world has seen. That was the theory, anyway.

Registrars in Warwickshire were unable to help. Roger's death was sufficiently recent to be subject to certain restrictions under the Data Protection Act. Nevertheless, thanks to the current popularity of genealogy and with the help of bright, dedicated souls like Norma Hampson I began to piece together enough of his life history to be of potential interest to whoever was selected to write the production notes for the DVD release of *The Ice Warriors*. I learned that his mother had rejoiced in the strange and rather appropriate maiden name of Petronella Snowball. I found out which ships had taken Petronella and the infant Roger away from war-torn Britain and brought them safely back. All very interesting stuff to me but hardly what the DVD-buying hordes were hungry for.

I had a lovely and unexpected chat about *Upstairs Downstairs* and *Smith* with the actor George Innes and his wife, who revealed that they were off to Stratford the following day. A lovely town, I agreed, but I was bit fed up with it, having spent far too long in the library there trying to find a particular actor's date of death. Of course, they were curious to know which actor.

'Oh you won't have heard of him,' I assured them. 'He had a very short career in the 1960s. Name of Roger Jones...'

Which is how I came to learn where and when Roger trained as an actor: he'd been George Innes's friend and flatmate at the Old Vic Theatre School in Bristol! The young Jones had been a great friend of the young Tom Stoppard. He'd been the student everyone tipped as Most Likely To Succeed on account of his talent and good looks but for various reasons things hadn't quite worked out that way. Poor Roger had been at least as handsome as he was tall, which is a far too distracting combination for the stage, even now. It was equally unhelpful to a promising career in front of the fairly static TV cameras of the time. He really had been unlucky. I learned a great deal that afternoon but as was now traditional, Mr Innes couldn't quite pin down the date of Roger's death to a precise year.

Deadlines for the DVD of *The Ice Warriors* were beginning to loom and I was no closer to having those all-important dates that would go in brackets after Roger's name on the subtitles. I had his date of birth, and a couple of possibilities for a date of death but no way of checking for sure (this was just one of many reasons why a career in journalism never beckoned) until I remembered that a lovely and funny friend, Will Ingram, was an avid mapper of his own family tree. Surely he'd know a shortcut or two? Will duly shook his spear and found the final date within 48 hours of being asked ... which left me about the same amount of time before the deadline passed. Thanks to Will, Roger wasn't going to be the forgotten and largely unknown member of the cast of Serial OO.

If you aren't already reading about *The Web of Fear* you may have noticed that, having found Roger's 'dates,' I haven't actually told you what they are. That can be the privilege of the forthcoming DVD. The commentary's already in the can and pays its own tribute to him. The production subtitles are being written, very fittingly, by that splendid authority on Shakespeare Martin Wiggins who is, of course, a denizen of Stratford-upon-

Avon. And back in Stratford is where Roger's story, as the buzzword buzzards would say, finds some 'closure.'

Not long after Mum's funeral I found myself back at the Royal Shakespeare Theatre, whose physical appearance was altered by the Design Lords when they banished it to planet Stratford in the form of a fire station. Roger had appeared in quite a few plays there during his career and been in the audience for a great many more. And in a way he still is - on seat 49C in the new main auditorium there is a smart black plaque dedicated to him. It reads:

IN MEMORY OF ROGER JONES 60S RSC ACTOR
A CREATIVE LIFE

Remembered for the career he longed for in the town he loved? The rest of us should be so lucky.

Future Imperfect

The Enemy of the World by **David O'Brien**, 46, Saffron Walden, UK / First story: **The Claws of Axos**

1981 was a sombre time for me. As the year began, *Woman* and *Imagine* were in the top 10 – both having become requiems for one of the great poets of the modern era. There were race riots, rising unemployment and a view amongst my peers at school that however hard you studied, there would only ever be a dole queue at the end of it. Small wonder then that the anthem of the year would be the elegiac *Ghost Town*, sung for a lost past, to a society no longer sure of itself.

At the time I lived in Thamesmead, made famous as the dystopian setting of **A Clockwork Orange**. The vast concrete structures which, in the summer of 1976, had seemed like a futuristic paradise were by now losing their attraction. It became a hard place – a concrete scar across traditional working class North West Kent. The people who moved to Thamesmead from the overcrowded inner-London back-to-back dwellings were sold an illusion of an escape to a better life. This self-styled 'Town of the Future' would be viewed in the *actual* future as an example of the failures of the past.

The school I attended had more of the look and feel of a factory than a place of learning, with bored children and disillusioned teachers getting through the day as best they could. For me, the boredom lay in the fact that none of the other children seemed to share any of my interests. It seemed that if you weren't a football fan, fighting with other schools or hanging around on street corners, there was precious little else to do.

So I buried myself in the things that comforted me the most – music, drawing and **Doctor Who**. Because as much as I disliked the world in 1981, it was quite a year for the programme – although it may not have seemed like it at the time. There was, after all, the longest break between seasons that there had ever been and a very popular Doctor bowed out in the downbeat *Logopolis*. I was sorry to see Tom go, but relieved that someone else would breathe new life into the programme again. I recall as clear as if it were now, how I would walk along the concrete bridge that separated the two main parts of Thamesmead on my way to school and imagine what the new season would be like. Every episode was laid out in my imagination and I would run through them in meticulous detail.

It was the year that the **Programme Guide**s by Jean-Marc Lofficier were released. These two paperbacks opened up the rich history of the show as never before. Now, I could be an expert too! There was the novelisation of *An Unearthly Child*, followed by the repeat season **The Five Faces of Doctor Who** - something which caused a minor sensation at the time. To actually be able to watch stories you had only ever heard about was literally a dream come true.

Looking back at this time, when the certainties of my parent's generation seemed to be collapsing, it should have been no great surprise that one of the few Target releases of that year was the dark future presented in *The Enemy of the World*. The book was based on a story which was broadcast during a more hopeful time; when the 'white heat of technology' would drive the world toward a brighter, more comfortable future and unemployment would be a thing of the past. It was almost as if this presentation of the future was a reaction against all of this - or perhaps it was a warning. A world divided into zones which were slowly but surely being dominated by a charismatic politician with designs upon dictatorship. Perhaps the story also represented the paranoia of the 1960s, which seemed to exist side by side with the charmingly naïve utopianism.

For a teenager looking for distractions from the world around him, the novelisation was something of a disappointment. The story so reflected what I and others seemed to fear may come to pass, that it was at times an uncomfortable read. There was murder, betrayal, cruelty and even a smattering of bad language – not bad going for a book only 127 pages long. With one of the rebel leaders turning out to be an enemy within, it gave a clear message – be very careful who you trust, especially those who claim to be one of you. Even the Doctor, the ultimate hero, may not actually be *the* Doctor because would-be dictator Salamander was his double. It also made me question who the actual 'Enemy of the World' was supposed to be. Was it Salamander, or was it the invaders that the subterranean people believed they had been attacking through their man-made geological disasters? 'Invaders' who in reality were innocent men, women and children that their underground compatriots were unknowingly slaughtering. Now that to me was really dark storytelling. In the end this story didn't allow me the luxury of turning away from the world I saw around me – it showed me a far worse one. And it made me really think about what exactly I was hiding from.

It always seemed that the more I tried not to notice something, the more it dominated my thoughts. Perhaps I simply thought too deeply about the world and what was wrong with it. Perhaps I did read into things more than I should have done. It turned out that *The Enemy of the World* wasn't actually a science fiction story at all, it was a political thriller. That was the beauty of **Doctor Who** – the programme could turn its hand to anything.

Escapism through **Doctor Who**? Thankfully, not a chance!

The Beauty & Fragility of Memory
The Web of Fear by **Peter Crocker**, 49, Ruislip, Middlesex / 1st story: A Hartnell – parents watched avidly

There are few things in life as fragile, personal, unique and precious as a memory. Shared experiences may be perceived in remarkably varied ways by different people according to their mood, concentration, experience, taste, prejudices and the full cocktail of ingredients that goes to make up that special attribute we call 'personality.'

This is, generally, a good thing. Imagine how boring life would be if everyone's recall and interpretation of events was identical. This would be most useful for historians striving for factual accuracy (if that were possible given the above – a freedom-fighter or an insurgent is a somewhat topical illustration of perspective). In terms of fans' attitudes to **Doctor Who**, this difference of perception is what fuels every aspect of debate, whether it is a quality assessment of the latest episode, theories of continuity such as that old UNIT dating chestnut, or the fan favourite, 'Which missing story would you most like to see?'

As time passes, inevitably our personal recall of our experiences changes. Things we consider insignificant are lost, or at least relegated to some sub-folder in our brains that we seem unable to access – hence that D'Arcy Sarto book you *know* you've read, but still you haven't the slightest idea how it ends. And our memories don't just go AWOL. They atrophy through neglect and, worse, mutate and distort through the overwhelming weight of our subsequent experiences. The more similar experiences we live through, the more our memories become diluted; less distinctive or specific – polluted even. This is why a supporting artist may have clearer and more detailed recall of the rehearsal and recording of a particular episode of **Doctor Who** from half a century ago than the 'regulars' who were there for forty-two weeks each year. As viewers and fans, our memories of television from early childhood are very prone to being conflated. Guy Garvey, lead singer and lyricist of popular Mancunian pop combo Elbow, recently confessed to being spooked by a childhood memory from **Doctor Who** of a man dressed in cricket whites with a face like porridge. Now, the window of opportunity for such 'spooking' is quite narrow for **Doctor Who**, lying in those scant years between the onset of awareness and the development of critical faculties. Garvey was born on March 6th 1974, which suggests that his memory is likely to originate between 1978 and 1983. Could it be the Doctor/Omega running through Amsterdam with Rice Krispies on his face in *Arc of Infinity*? The cricket whites would fit, even if the breakfast cereal is slightly adrift. Or is he remembering George Cranleigh from *Black Orchid*, conflating his face with the cricketing scenes in the story? It turns out that, following a little time with internet resources, Guy positively identified his memory as being of ... you guessed it ... Count Scarlioni removing his face at the end of Part One of *City of Death* to reveal his Jagaroth identity. A viewing experience so vivid and scary that the memory persisted for over thirty years, yet the cricket whites were actually a cream Armani suit and the porridge face, in truth, more a spaghetti carbonara. Garvey's childhood trauma wasn't of a giant, totally convincing snake malevolently subsuming a peaceful race of primitives, which goes to prove that at least he knows his Aris from his Elbow.

Some of my earliest identifiable memories of **Doctor Who** are of *The Web of Fear*. I also remember significant chunks of *The Evil of the Daleks* (doubtless bolstered by the delicious treat of a summer repeat) and, should any more of the great, under-rated Season Four be recovered alongside its current paltry remains, I imagine there'll be quite a few dormant memories to be awakened. I like the idea that I have memories of missing **Doctor Who** episodes in my brain, and the key to unlock them is –

simply and tantalisingly – to see the episodes. But would that always be a good thing?

Probably the most specific and detailed memory I have from *The Web of Fear* in 1968 is of the Yeti advancing through the London Underground tunnels with their web guns. We had recently moved house after my father had been promoted at work and on this particular Saturday the family's usual routine had been thrown out by the need to entertain the boss and his wife, in a situation redolent of many a BBC sitcom of the 1960s and 1970s. I like to imagine that my father's boss was the spitting image of Allan Cuthbertson and the evening progressed, for the adults at least, with hilarious consequences. The disastrous impact for four-year-old me, however, was that I couldn't have my fish fingers and chips on the living room floor in front of the telly, but had to sit in polite silence at the table in the dining room as the grown-ups had their prawn cocktails and Coq au Vin. Eventually the knowledge that I was missing **Doctor Who** despite having finished my food became too much for me to cope with, so I timorously asked whether I could leave the table, 'to see what the Yeti are doing.' Oh no! I hadn't counted on there being a sweet course. But my pleas were heard kindly and I was allowed to go to the living room as long as I returned when the jam roly-poly was served. And it was during that short respite that that image of the yeti in the tunnels etched itself into my memory. And what a fabulous memory it was.

Then, almost thirty years later, a few censor's clips of old **Doctor Who** were uncovered in a collection in New Zealand. Among them was the very shot I remembered so clearly and preciously and – unlike Guy Garvey's porridge face – it was exactly as it was in my memory. And because of that, because it was the same and not in some way different or misremembered, the original memory just vanished into the ether. No longer linked to that kitsch dinner party in 1968, but instead to a much less romantic viewing of a batch of old orphaned clips on a modern television in the mid-1990s, by some bloke in his thirties.

Would I rather the clip had not been found? In some ways, yes. From a selfish perspective I'd much rather a different clip had been recovered, leaving my special, unique, personal memory intact. I wouldn't mind in the slightest, of course, if the whole story was recovered by some miracle, but that's a matter of scale and perspective - and I'm sure we'll all remember where we were and what we were doing when the news of that recovery came through. And all those fragile, exquisite memories will be different, unique and precious. We should try never to lose them, neglect them, or take them for granted.

Educating Peter

Fury From the Deep by **Peter Webber**, 35, Exeter, UK
Earliest memory: **The Five Doctors**

I don't care for *Fury from the Deep*, not really. It's a none-too-original thing about a metal base with some foam in it. It's no *The Abominable Snowmen* or *The Web of Fear* production-wise, and I view it as adequate but overrated water-treading.

So, I hear you cry, why choose to write about it then, you strange idiot? The reasons are surprisingly manifold. For one thing, as a wide-eyed lad of fifteen who listened to this in bed, in the dark, in the early 1990s, this was a serial that *terrified* me as assuredly as the Vervoids and the Haemovores had done years before. Sweaty bottom fear, that sort of thing. I was ten when I first watched **Aliens**, and thanks to a wonderfully daring mother I was not averse to all things fanged and horrible from the video shop. Yet *Fury from the Deep* had this power to chill. So much so, in fact, that I never noticed that nobody actually died in it. My little brain homed in on the atmosphere and the constituent parts – the bits with people getting sucked into pipelines amid lots of hullabaloo, Oak and Quill and their disconcerting plinky-plonky theme tune – and that was enough. As an audio experience, it managed to fill the head and fire the mind. In my *head*, people died. Somewhere. Somehow.

This turned out to be the first audio-only drama I ever heard. Radio comedy I knew and loved, but this was the first time I was invited to immerse myself this way, with a narrative possessed of no visuals. Could such a thing work? Happily it did, and radio would seem a fuller medium to me, because my introduction to radio drama was *Fury from the Deep* and not *The Archers*. Or some over-worthy daytime thing with characters being earnest about Issues, characters probably called Sue and David. But that's not all...

Often with radio drama you can hear actors reading the words from the script. *Fury from the Deep*'s televisual origins showed how to really do it. Perhaps this is why I can find radio drama so hit-and-miss: I can detect when something is read and when something is properly acted. There's the subtlest of differences, and thanks to *Fury from the Deep,* I went on to believe that good radio drama *was* possible, that as a medium it was intimate and captivating when done correctly. I appreciated the good actor, the good delivery, the lack of obvious descriptive exposition from the characters, too.

So, then, how comes I pooh-pooh *Fury from the Deep* as a man? You may well ask, and it is precisely *because* I went off this six-parter that also makes this story special. I wondered why.

As a fifteen year-old, I didn't really get the bigger picture, the wider story, the more mature aspects that can background everything. It's a stodgy, long-winded affair set somewhere decidedly adult called Euro Sea Gas, but the serial marched on and I became absorbed by the inadvertent confusions as well as the deliberate ones. I felt like I was eavesdropping on a solid, adult world which I didn't fully understand, and when things start going wrong there, they really feel as though they're going wrong. An adult world going awry makes the terror seem more palpable. This is, ultimately, atmosphere-building. It is not patronisingly trying to draw me in with knockabout gags, things that I can 'relate' to, things I recognise from elsewhere. It exists and I peek my head in, and curiosity and strangeness suck me in, and I work with it because I want to, I am growing up, and there is enough there already to engage and satisfy the 'simple animal' part of me. I slowly begin to understand it and it rewards.

Atmosphere is so vital for **Doctor Who**, and for all forms of drama. As adults, we truly can forget that we have primal needs, or pretend we're above simpler wants. There can be so much preoccupation with plot, or lack of plot, that we forget that **Doctor Who** really ought to be viewed as being made up of multipurpose moments. Every story has greatnesses – even those stories you hate. In the same way **Doctor Who** is made up of differing serials, so it is made up of differing scenes, moments. When I was listening to *Fury from the Deep*, I remembered and cherished the little moments, and didn't try to assimilate it as a whole in the same way my adult brain might be more inclined to do. Not that a story shouldn't strive to be as full in all areas as possible, but it means, for example, that with *Warriors of the Deep* I don't obsess about the panto-beast made of bad curtains. It is but a part of a still very competent whole. I can love *Revenge of the Cybermen* even though the Cybermen are (likeably) vivacious and the Cyberbombs couldn't blow up a weasel, let alone Voga. I can love *Paradise Towers* because there are *so many* sequences and touches that scream **Doctor Who**, that I feel it's indecent not to see this. So many serials deserve so much more love, because they get so much *right*. I watch it for what it is: a TV show made up of *moments*, rather like how a prog rock track ought to be listened to: lyric by lyric. Perhaps we should be analysing scenes and moments as much as we do the wholes. Provided the show's not messing with the overarching formula too terribly, too repeatedly; that's only when **Doctor Who** gets royally bad, isn't it?

Actually, you know what? I've just now decided I do love *Fury from the Deep* after all. I think of Jamie on the kitchen table amid the naughty foam and Robson on the rig looking like the living dead (oh those happy-making telesnaps) and well, I'm pleased as punch to know that when I love a story from my childhood, I don't have to rely on nostalgia.

Watching Doctor Who With a Three-Year Old

The Wheel in Space by **Mike Morgan**, Kingwood, Houston, Texas, USA / First story: **City of Death**

The parents of any small child will tell you there's a moment when you just can't face another instalment of **Yo Gabba Gabba**. And after a while, the prospect of having to sit through twenty more minutes of **Wow! Wow! Wubbzy!** can cause you to throw up in your mouth.

So imagine my joy when I realised that my three-year-old son, Danny, was old enough to survive watching **Doctor Who** unscathed. Well, the less scary episodes anyway. Probably. Close enough to risk it. And if there is long-term psychological damage? Ha – they'll never trace it back to me!

On hearing my plan of action, my wife, Megan (an astonishingly patient woman), pleaded with me to pre-watch the episodes, just to make sure there was nothing too terrifying in them. But with two small kids in the house, there wasn't sufficient time to pre-screen the prospective episodes, so ... I plunged ahead regardless. Reckless much? We'll circle back to that idea later.

But first, a digression: a year before we started watching **Doctor Who**, Danny found my Dalek-shaped bubble bath bottle and promptly fell deeply in love with it. As a two-year old in Texas, I think he was unique in knowing that Daleks shout, 'Exterminate!' More than that, he was probably the only two-year old in these parts to even *know* the word 'exterminate,' let alone run around the house shouting it out at the top of his lungs.

When Danny and I sat down to watch an entire episode, the first thing I said was, 'Tell me if it's too scary, right? Daddy can put his hand over your eyes for those bits.' The look he gave spoke volumes. *As if*, he seemed to protest, *I am so not missing the good bits*. Careful consideration was given to our first full story. I decided on

The Krotons because I'd seen it recently and didn't remember anything too horrible. Besides, Danny saw the DVD box cover and thought the Krotons were robots, and Danny loves his robots.

Another minor digression: Danny has created a game called Robot. This game involves making me sit on the floor and then running straight at me, full tilt. He pushes me over, clambers all over me, and tries to whack seven shades out of me. 'Is this wrestling?' I ask him. '*No!* Silly Daddy! It Robot!' In reply, I tickle him, but he protests loudly that we are *not* playing tickle, we are playing *Robot* and I am doing it *wrong*. Lately, the rules have changed to require Danny to hop three times before he can run at me. I'm sure next week the rules will be different again. I suspect every version of the rules will require him to pummel me.

Oh, yeah, *The Krotons*. He loved it. Apparently, he's the perfect age for it (I'm not sure that's what the people who made the programme had in mind). Buoyed by this enthusiastic reception, we went on to *The Dalek Invasion of Earth*. The opening sequence of a man drowning himself caused a couple of awkward questions ('What he doin', Daddy?' 'Um, he's going swimming.'). Highlights for my three-year-old fellow viewer were the alligator that threatens Susan in the sewer and *every scene with a Dalek in it*.

We followed the Dalek story with Tom Baker's debut, *Robot* (are you surprised?) and then *Remembrance of the Daleks*. I was exhausting my supply of Dalek stories, so we went onto *The Seeds of Death*. 'Where's the Ice Warr, Daddy?' he said roughly thirty times an episode, not being able to pronounce warrior, 'When they come back?' 'They'll be in the next scene, hang on.' The Doctor floundering in the bubbles was the funniest thing he'd ever seen.

Then Danny saw the DVD box of *The Visitation*. It has a robot on the cover, so of course he wanted to watch it. Nothing bad sprang to mind about the story, so I popped the disc on. And all was well until we got to the very end – and the Terileptil *burns to death*. Never has a father's hand shot over a little boy's eyes so quickly. And I was not appreciative of the production team's decision to show a *second* shot of the alien's skin bubbling in the flames.

That night, as I tucked him in, he told me very seriously, '**Doctor Who** not scary, Daddy.' Silly me for worrying.

At around this point, I agreed to review *The Wheel in Space*. So, I dug out the *Lost in Time* box set and we sat down to watch the Cyberman episodes. They were Danny's first Cyberman stories! He enjoyed certain parts of *The Moonbase*, but all that mucking about trying to repair the Gravitron was tedious for him; and for me if I'm honest. He much preferred *The Wheel in Space*. The cameo of the Dalek in the final episode clinched the deal for him; two monsters in one story? He almost peed himself he was so thrilled (a very real prospect with a three-year-old). Megan took delight in the shot of the Cybermen blatantly *walking* through 'space' to get into the space station's airlock; okay, yeah, that bit is pants.

I asked Danny which monster he likes better, Daleks or Cybermen. Daleks, he said, but he likes Cybermen more than Ice Warriors. At bedtime after watching *The Wheel in Space*, he he was very worried about not all of the episodes existing. 'They were thrown in the trash,' we said. '*Why*?' asked Danny, horrified. We have yet to formulate a good answer.

As an ex-pat living in Houston, I'm glad I can use **Doctor Who** to share a small part of my 'Britishness' with Danny. And it's great to see it all again through his eyes. (But, seriously, did we *really* need that second shot of the Terileptil burning to death, JNT?)

A Dulkis Belies Deep Love
The Dominators by **John Davies**, 40, Manchester, UK
First story: **The Android Invasion**

In this 50th anniversary year, *The Dominators* is doing the rounds on UKTV forming part of the second Doctor's era showcase. However, I doubt this is down to any real affection for the story, more the fact that it ... well ... exists. It's hardly a fan favourite and even the cast, crew and - infamously - writers (real ones not even named on screen) struggle to find kind words to say about it. If *Fury from the Deep*, *The Web of Fear*, *The Power of the Daleks* or *The Evil of the Daleks* resided in the vaults I sincerely doubt that this 'gripping' tale of merciless aliens on a pacifist planet would be gracing TV screens in this way. However, as we all know, due to the mass junking of archive material through the 1970s a lot of black and white **Doctor Who** does not exist; 106 'missing' episodes as I type ... the majority from this very era. So, *The Dominators* it is then. Hu and ... yeah ... rah.

Actually ... scrap that. Yes! Hurrah indeed!

The Dominators may be a tired, pedestrian adventure but it contains something special - something that formed a major part of turning my liking of **Doctor Who** into loving it, something that many actors have cited as a highlight of the show's entire run, something that made Matt Smith's appreciation for the role he inherited in 2010 increase in leaps and bounds. Sorry ... did I say 'something'? I meant some*one*: Patrick Troughton. In every second of every scene that exists showing Troughton in the role there is a magic, a joy, a conviction in everything he says and does that makes his interpretation so perfectly inviting, so exactly The Doctor. My Doctor.

Yes, his version is manic - at the beginning even silly - and yes, it does have its darker side - especially in *The Tomb of the Cybermen* and *The Evil of the Daleks* - but, as a viewer, I always feel instinctively safe with him.

There's a tender and avuncular quality that, while others have had it, he nails superbly and, unlike other Doctors, his hiding of his cleverness behind a lighter façade is actually inclusive to those he travels with and befriends. Sure, the seventh Doctor is affectionate toward Ace and the fourth cares deeply about Sarah, but the former's manipulative streak unsettles and when the latter turns traitor to the Time Lords in *The Invasion of Time* (post Sarah, I know) it is believable because he is so often genuinely unpredictable. With the second, though, that expressive face, the intonation, his endearing fumbling-bumbling manner is all so warm, so encompassing, so constant that I accept the darker side, even admire it, and trust him above all others.

And, I have to admit, my dad helped in this as well. How? Let me take you back...

As a child, I hated football. I still do. Come match day I was not to be found lamenting with my father whenever his team performed badly – as it frequently did. However, there was something we did share a football-esque passion for – **Doctor Who**. In football terms, my dad followed Team Pertwee. As we have always had a friendly mock rivalry it was somewhat inevitable which team I would go on to champion.

Growing up with the Target books, I knew from *The Three Doctors* that the third and second Doctor clashed. Result? I became Team Troughton – long before I had even seen him! Already fiercely loyal, imagine my joy when, on our first date in 1981, I saw *The Krotons* in **The Five Faces of Doctor Who** and fell so hard I had bruises.

As with *The Dominators*, *The Krotons* is not a classic example of **Doctor Who**. It shows the signs of a writer finding his feet with the format and it's hardly Planet of the Gonds-shatteringly exciting – but I was captivated. From the moment Troughton stepped out of the TARDIS and yawned and stretched I had a feeling that this Doctor was going to become *my* Doctor. Love at first sight? I guess so because within minutes, watching his reaction to the destruction of his umbrella, he had me. He still has to this day.

Troughton **Doctor Who** is my mashed potato **Doctor Who**; my Comfort **Doctor Who**. If I want to sit back, relax and just enjoy an adventure with a funny, clever, welcoming Doctor I will sink into the sofa and press play on any of his DVDs. More than the story, it is his company I want and value. So much so that it's not just his complete stories that hook me. When *The Underwater Menace* Episode 2 turned up I was overjoyed. A whole episode! An entire 'new' episode! Although I have still to see it, I know I will ... and I will treat it like another date with the Time Lord of my dreams. And full episode? I will go beyond that. Any clip of Patrick shining as the Doctor that is unearthed should be cheered, cherished, embraced and enjoyed. So yes – show *The Dominators*! Show it with pride.

Put it this way, if I were walking down the street and the TARDIS materialised before me and the fourth Doctor bounded out and offered to show me the Universe I would be tempted. I would, though, have misgivings. However, if the second Doctor landed, sprighted out, yawned, stretched and then offered me the same I would beat Usain Bolt let alone Rose Tyler in my mad dash past him through those blue doors ... even if we ended up on the dullest of planets with the most tedious of locals and bitchy, shoulder-padded invaders who had pet Duracell-powered robots. The opportunity to travel with that incarnation of the Doctor would be a total no brainer for me.

The Fiction Factor
The Mind Robber by **David Agnew** and **Robin Bland**,
The Land of Fiction
Dedicated to the memory of Bernard Horsfall

The Master: As you know, I am retiring - hence your being before me; two writers of repute. This is your audition. One of you will replace me and become Master of The Land of Fiction. That person will be the one that demonstrates more than the other that they have what is required - *The Fiction Factor*! So, David - you're first! I want you to imagine you need to write a story in a series that will capture the minds of the audience. Let's pretend the last story wasn't that good: silly costumes, daft aliens, that sort of thing. The cliffhanger of that one was a lava flow threatening to engulf our heroes... What ... happens ... next?

David Agnew: So... erm, yes. A story that will endure; the kind of story that is adored by children and is rooted in every fibre of their being - that will develop within them a thirst for knowledge that they can take into their adult lives. Right erm ... as the lava rises and engulfs our heroes ensconced within the TARDIS, the fluid links malfunction. The Doctor is forced to use the emergency unit and they are transported into a land entirely comprised of fictional characters and elements. Reference will be made to many great works, ensuring that the viewing children will seek out these stories and expand their literary and historical frames of reference. The stories will then be linked to the show and feel like a continuation of the story of **Doctor Who**. Soon after arriving in the land, they will encounter Lemuel Gulliver. We will need an exceptional character actor for this part. Bernard Horsfall would be superb. Picture it - an eight-year-old boy reading an illustrated version of Jonathan Swift's **Gulliver's Travels**. The story made all the more exciting by knowing that the Doctor knows Gulliver. He will go on to learn about the legend of the Minotaur, and about how Perseus defeated Medusa. He will then go on to read the Brothers Grimm where he will encounter the Princess Rapunzel. All the while, that thread from this episode of **Doctor Who** running through this boy's reading influences. The Doctor's companion Zoe, will recall a cartoon/comic book superhero from the future, introducing this boy to comics. In the last episode, with the Doctor's inevitable showdown with the Master of the Land of Fiction, the Doctor achieves a link-up with the Master Brain to create a narrative of his own. The boy will learn that not only is it fun to be told stories, but it's also fun to tell your own stories too. His imagination running riot at the thought of the endless possibilities. I have a mind for other adventures beyond this one, involving Leonardo Da Vinci and the Mona Lisa, encouraging this ever-growing boy to find out about history and art. Well it is a very pretty painting. He will learn about how the dinosaurs became extinct. There are so many stories to tell. Stories of Shakespeare and the theatre. He will even learn of the dangers of too much caffeine and sugar, when one day I create a monster made purely out of Liquorice Allsorts. Almost everything this boy reads or experiences will remind him of the Doctor and where his enthusiasm for learning began, this next episode of **Doctor Who**. The Doctor will bind the threads of the tapestry of this boy's life, which will continue into adulthood as more adventures are forthcoming. This is the opportunity to influence a nation, to make a groundbreaking episode that will contribute to the development of the people of tomorrow. The Mind Robber? No. Quite the opposite.

The Master: Good. Very good. I really like the twist on the title there. Well done. Now! I want *you*, Robin, to imagine that there is hardly any budget. How might you create a grand televised work of fiction if you haven't got much money to pay for it?

Robin Bland: Before I answer that, hasn't David got a pleasant open face? Hmm. I must remember that line...

Anyway ... interesting question. And one I might struggle to answer were it not for the fact I am here – out of time and with your power to see how the real show tackled this very issue in the weeks following the story you mentioned. Cheating? Not at all! Besides, David's already done it; trying to pass this off as his idea. Hmmm. He's seen it and borrowed from it. Which is how it should be! In this programme borrowing ideas was all part of the mechanics ... as it is here in the Land of Fiction. So it's in keeping. See – I'm fitting in already.

So, low budget? On **Doctor Who** that was nothing new but to answer your question I would use the most powerful thing a human possesses ... something this very show expanded into a vast, impossibly large control room... Hmm. Yes. I like that, too... I would use... My imagination! And that is what demonstrates I have *The Fiction Factor*!

I mean, David, as much as I admire the authority in your voice, how would you tackle having an entire episode added to a four-part story with no sets, no cast bar your regulars and your only prop being the TARDIS? Would you use the opportunity to take a voiceover heard briefly in the written episodes and, using only a white studio and some robot props from another show, write an entire script that actually adds menace to that premise?

See, he can't answer that! Ha! You see? That white set will become the white piece of paper a child watching this will then go on to fill with *their* ideas, their creativity – their hunger to create from nothing – something this show often had to do. Something one of us would have to do on a daily basis!

Further to that, how would you cope with one of your main cast catching chicken pox mid-production? Write the character out for an episode or two? Too easy! Lazy! Use the opportunity to add to the surreal quality of the tale! Re-cast them and keep the character in the narrative. Again, this would be mind expanding to that child watching ... even if on a VHS release of this story years after transmission.

This is what you would get from me, Master. Ingenuity! **Doctor Who**'s ingenuity! If you are borrowing, borrow from the best to turn your crisis into a triumph. No budget? How about no studio! Yes, that happened – many times, but notably twice. Once, there was no way to stop the story being scrapped – no amount of imagination could save a show halted by industrial action occurring during a total production team handover – however much the incoming producer wanted to carry on. It is said that a voice is still heard mourning, 'Shaaaaaaaaaadaaa!' in certain corridors. If chosen I might re-make it here, actually... Anyway! Thankfully, the same producer was able to save the other studio-less serial, this one brought about by asbestos removal – and in so doing actually make it better than it might have been. No studio while filming a story set in a circus? Erect a tent in a car park and film it in there! Seems obvious with hindsight, but it a masterstroke – no pun intended – of imagination.

This ability to turn potential disaster into something good, something *better* is a trait that, just like that white void set linked its way to a child's blank page, would often resonate with viewers as they grew up, got to learn of the more technical demands of turning 'ideas' into 'reality' as they had to do exactly the same in their lives.

And actually, going back to the story we were asked to create and talk about, I think this was where imagination was first really the spotlight of **Doctor Who**'s vision – in terms of storytelling and audience interaction. Yes, the shows before required imagination to go with the premise but this was out of the playing field in more ways than one. Although *The Celestial Toymaker* dabbled with fantasy in **Doctor Who**, this story dated it with a passion ... proposed marriage to it ... and made everyone involved – cast, crew, writers, viewers – take a magical carpet ride into a whole **Who** world.

It is also the tale that took my dream to be a writer and make it my need – my vocation! Write for a living? I want to write for a life time! Any questions? Yes. Just one. Does the green jacket come with the job?

The Master: Both of you are so passionate, so committed to this journey. I believed every word you said. But the winner? The winner? Which of you should inherit this position? Wait ... they want to speak to me...

David Agnew: They?

Robin Bland: What's that head-set for?

The Master: Shhh! Let me listen. I see. Yes. Yes. So. Ohhhhhh!

David Agnew: Ohhhhhh what?

The Master: It's Deadlock.

Robin Bland: What does that mean?

The Master: They want us all. We are all to stay. Trapped! Trapped in **Doctor Who** ... forever!

David Agnew: I can cope with that...

Robin Bland: So can I.

David: So...

The Master: It seems that David and Robin are on their way to *create* new adventures...

Invasion Therapy
The Invasion by **Sebastian Wilcox**, 33, Exeter, UK
First story: **The Sea Devils**

Imagine, if you will, the persona of this story. Not too tall, not too short with a certain roundness, not fat but a roundness that makes people exclaim, 'Blimey he's round.' A person who's hair is untameable, all in all a kind of growth-stunted Yeti. Anyway let's get on with it shall we?

Marching up a particularly uneven street with a gait reminiscent of a cyber-man whose legs belonged to a less fortunate other, our man dodges the rain drops with a singular purpose on his mind ... to buy some **Doctor Who** on DVD. Why? He doesn't quite understand. Where? He has a pretty good idea that the **Doctor Who** shop will have some (yes there was such a place). How? Well let's be fair, if he hadn't worked that one out he'd still be at home staring at the wall. Entering the shop he is confronted by a wall of DVDs. Not knowing which to choose he begins to draw on all the **Doctor Who** knowledge he has to make an informed decision. When this fails to yield anything positive (he doesn't actually know much) he closes his eyes and begins to run his hands over the display hoping one will feel right. One does, almost leaping off the shelf at him. The title inspires: *The Invasion*. Taking it to the checkout, 'Good choice,' says the store owner. 'I've been wanting to see this for a while,' our man replies, hoping the owner doesn't pick up on the trembling undertones in his voice that display a complete lack of knowledge. Purchase complete he heads home through the downpour. Upon arriving at his abode he opens the DVD case and begins to read the inlay card. A sense of nervousness begins to creep over him as he discovers that episodes were missing. This feeling is met with an uncertainty as it is understood that these episodes have been replaced by animation. Uncertainty because he was afraid the animation wouldn't fit and as such would not hang together with the existing episodes. He begins to feel a little wary of having made an uninformed decision. A memory begins to awaken in his mind. For some reason it's the **Antiques Roadshow**. Unbeknownst to him it is connected to the reawakening memories of the Doctor. So with great pomp and ceremony (well he made tea and sandwiches) he embarks on a voyage into the unknown. Sitting in his own personal TARDIS, having the amazing capacity for being roughly the same size on the inside as out, and otherwise known as his room, he watches.

He watches it again.

Fears unfounded he watches it for a third time (I know what you're thinking, 'He has lot of time on his hands').

The animation didn't matter, it was so well presented. In fact he didn't even realise the fourth episode had been animated, so wrapped up in the story was he. Our man is mesmerised by the charisma of Vaughn, amused at the hapless trials of Packer, captivated by the iconic images of the Cybermen emerging in London and safe in the knowledge that good will win the day and the Doctor prevail. A strange feeling begins to well up inside of our hero. A feeling of something shared; despite having watched it alone he knows that others have seen what he has seen and felt the same thing. With a feeling of a young boy at Christmas our man must fall into a restless sleep, so excited and with a need to discuss what he has seen.

The next day he is at work dropping subtle hints about what he has seen. To his surprise a lot of people he talks to are closet fans just itching to have a conversation about classic **Doctor Who**. Meetings are arranged, stories shared and lots of **Doctor Who** watched. He learns of the original fans who recorded and kept the audio of the missing episodes all those years ago and thanks them for preserving what they did.

The next few months are used forging friendships that will last a lifetime, all thanks to a chance meeting of a lonely soul and a man in funny trousers that saved the world.

Yes, okay, the mishmash of words and poor grammar are about me and my sudden urge to buy some **Doctor Who**. The need was raised by my subconscious. I had just moved from everything I knew and needed something to comfort me during a very low point in my life. Thankfully my mind chose the Doctor and an amazing story to boot. Since this time I have made a host of friends and was even asked to write a piece on how a **Doctor Who** story affected my life. Coming full circle, if it hadn't been for *The Invasion* I wouldn't have rediscovered **Doctor Who** after so many years, I would be poorer in the friends department and I wouldn't be writing this now. I owe a lot to the eight episodes of that story. Although I still wake up with an urge to buy checked trousers.

Warning: Spoilers
The Krotons by **Christopher Bryant**, 36, Woking, UK
First story: **Full Circle**

I have seen every **Doctor Who** story. Some, I have seen more often than others. There are only two stories which I have seen just the once. One of these is *The Snowmen*, which aired a couple of weeks ago and is sitting on Sky+ waiting for a re-watch right now. The other is *The Krotons*, which aired in 1969. It's a story with a poor reputation, which may be why I never sought it out. In 1999, UK Gold scheduled a weekend omnibus repeat of *The Krotons*. My mum recorded it for me. Shortly afterwards, I watched it. (As far as I remember, I thought it was okay - certainly better than its reputation.) Then I filed the video away. And not once have I chosen to revisit it.

I am now unwrapping my brand new DVD. I slip the disc into the player. It's time to take another look at Robert Holmes' **Doctor Who** debut and see what I think of it. Warning: spoilers!

Episode One - Well, it starts badly: a hatch sticks in the opening shot and the dialogue ('There's a ramp here.' 'Yes, and there's a door as well.') gives me a sinking feeling. This is Robert Holmes?

06:05 - Oh, it's Philip Madoc! Things just took a turn for the better.

11:00 - I'm really getting into this. Jamie just had a spontaneous scrap with a guy called Axus. It's like a flashback to the Ian Chesterton days. Then the Doctor tore apart these people's society in two minutes and, before anyone starts to believe him, runs off into the wasteland. There's a real sense of something at stake here.

17:00 - Well, that was an hilarious display of outrageously bonkers acting, courtesy of the Custodian of the learning machines, which have big smiley faces. Other actors keep straight faces as this wonderful man boggles at the camera: 'Sometimes ... there is a *voice*!'

20:50 – 'Atomic laser? Is that better than an axe?' Oh, this is Robert Holmes now.

22:11 – And so Episode One ends with the Doctor huffing and whinging (or, indeed, wheezing and groaning) as he's attacked by the offspring of an Exxilon root and Erato. Well, this is fun so far.

Episode Two - The very best cliffhangers must have a good resolve. This one is neat – the Doctor covers his face, thus scuppering the Krotons' pattern recognition – but forces us (and the Doctor) to conclude that this is one stupid machine.

03:55 – I've just noticed: what is Zoe wearing? Has that been fashioned out of a bin bag?

16:10 – Well, I didn't remember that bit! Why isn't everyone talking about that bit? The Krotons are subjecting the Doctor and Zoe to some sort of mind attack. Director David Maloney distorts the perspective, twisting our heroes' faces unnaturally. He cuts quickly between their faces, the light and the breaking chain ... it's tense, stylish and very modern. This is great! One doesn't seem to hear Maloney's name bandied about as much as Camfield or Harper, but look at his pedigree: from *The War Games* to *The Deadly Assassin*. This may be a minor entry on his CV, but he's giving it his best.

20:35 – Must we condemn *The Krotons* because of the Krotons? They have strange voices (so did the Silurians). They are clearly people in boxes (so were the War Machines). They have bizarre appendages (so do the Daleks). The costume designer had to make do with a curtain to cover their legs. But they're still better than the Mara or the Mire Beasts or the Mandrels. And their heads look good.

22:25 – A rather better cliffhanger, because Holmes is using the characteristics of the regular cast to guide the story, something that's all too rare. Alright, so the sets are limited, the story progresses slowly and someone forgot to book Philip Madoc this week. But at the moment, I'm very kindly disposed towards *The Krotons*.

Episode Three - It's hard to defend the gender politics of this story. It acknowledges that women can be clever, but Vana just swoons and clings onto Thara. No other Gond females seem to exist. It seems extraordinary now just how little people thought about this sort of thing in 1969.

11:10 - The episode has become a series of two-man conversations, but it doesn't matter: they're all interesting and progressing the plot. And I do believe everyone's started acting better, too.

14:15 - Okay, the Krotons are becoming very hard to defend. 'Sto-o-op! Sto-o-op!' A shame, because there's something very interesting and original in the concept of a parasitical crystalline alien race, which has unfortunately been turned into something from a 1960s B Movie.

16:15 - Ah yes, the HADS. If there's one thing everyone remembers about *The Krotons*, it's the HADS. I have no idea why that should have caught the imagination so. It was never used again. Mind you, I wouldn't be certain that it won't show up one day. The Macra have proved that - all bets are off!

20:00 - Oh, let their heads spin round more! Have they made a Kroton action figure yet that can do that? [*checks*] No, they haven't. Get on it!

21:30 - Again, I enjoyed that episode, but the revelation that the Dynatrope will exhaust in three hours suggests an easy solution with no adequate explanation. Still, up to now I've liked how everything is relevant in this story. The umbrella, the smell of eggs, now the chemistry ban. It's neat.

Episode Four - I'm having trouble with the scale here. Is that the Dynatrope leaking from its roof? I hadn't previously realised that it was effectively a big Sontaran ship.

09:30 - Oh, look! Thara is out for the count and Vana is conspiring with Selris. Deliciously, the gender issues of which I bellyached earlier have been addressed with a quick reversal!

10:20 – Which of us hasn't had a Chemistry teacher like Beta? 'Let's see what happens! We can only blow ourselves up!' In my day job as a teacher, I never begrudge a fire alarm if it was triggered by a Science experiment. Crucial part of education, that.

12:00 – Everyone goes on about the late Philip Madoc's performance in *The Brain of Morbius* and, yes, it's good. But in each of his other appearances, he makes such a virtue of underplaying that he manages to act everyone else off-screen without appearing to try. See how the War Lord dominates his squabbling underlings. Look at that under-written refinery worker in *The Power of Kroll*, only memorable because of casting. We're lucky the production teams re-used him as often as they did.

14:15 – That's better. The countdown I griped about before is revealed to be bad for the Gonds as well as the Krotons. It's not an easy fix after all. Have faith in Holmes.

18:25 – 'You stand there and I'll stand here...' This scene always reminded me of the intelligence test from *The Dominators*. In fact, these two stories have often been linked together. But with only a few minutes to go, can we all agree now that *The Krotons* is clearly the superior story?

20:55 – 'Come alone, let's get away. I don't like goodbyes.' Surely I can't be the only one who prefers this traditional Troughton/Baker meme to the 'standing around being feted by Ood' approach?

And so, the toy TARDIS dematerialises, leaving Vana, Thara and Bradley Wiggins to deal with Philip Madoc in an unscreened episode five. I switch off the DVD and muse on what I've learned. Our collective memory has consigned this (for so long, the only complete Troughton story) to the turkey pile thanks to memories of wobbly monsters, OTT acting, cheap sets and limited scale. But look how much I found to admire: the regular cast, the guest cast, the direction, the innovation, some choice dialogue, good plotting (every time I moaned about

something, Holmes fixed it an episode later) and spinny heads.
 Revisit *The Krotons* or some other unloved story languishing in the bottom of a drawer somewhere. You will find something to love.

Wendy Padbury's PVC Miniskirt

The Seeds of Death by **John Dorney**, 36, London, UK
First story: **Carnival of Monsters** (Five Faces Repeat)

Sometimes I think *The Seeds of Death* is stalking me.

It's 1985. My ninth birthday. I've been a **Doctor Who** fan for about four years now, the sheer weight of available material allowing this little British TV show to overtake **Star Wars** in my youthful affections. The triple bill of *The Three Doctors* repeat and *The Five Doctors* and *The Two Doctors*' regular transmissions has convinced me of my favourite Doctor, a conviction that hasn't wavered in the intervening decades. I'm a Patrick Troughton man. But I still haven't seen any of his actual stories. Today that is about to change.

Today my mum and dad have bought me *The Seeds of Death*. These things are expensive – over £20 – a lot of money, outside their usual present budget. But they love me and they know it'll make me happy. Which it does.

It's a compilation, it's fuzzy quality, and it's two-and-a-half hours long. But even for an ADD-addled child in the height of summer it is absorbing. The plot is exciting, the characters excellent (oh, poor Fewsham, so like we'd all be in that situation) and Zoe is exceptionally pretty. Sunlight streams through the curtains but I sit silently in the front room all morning, enraptured.

It's 2003. I'm 27. I'm a largely unemployed actor and writer, still with enough time and a small enough collection to watch all the extras on all my DVDs. I'm living with my parents again, glamorously. I'm in their front room watching the commentary on a story called *The Seeds of Death*. And then it happens.

'A fan wrote their thesis on running down corridors in **Doctor Who**,' says Sir Terrance of Dicks. And I have to rewind and listen again, just to check what he said. And it is exactly as I heard it the first time. I can't believe it.

You see, that was me. Okay, it wasn't a thesis, it was a series of fanzine articles, and it was meant to be a joke (a spoof of the more anal factual essays in the **Doctor Who** community), but that doesn't matter. Me and a mate had interviewed the legendary Terrance Dicks for the fanzine and sent him a copy of the finished article ... so he has to be talking about me. One of the **Doctor Who** greats has talked about me in a **Doctor Who** commentary – to Wendy Padbury! My life is complete; what a claim to fame! I play it to my parents excitedly and they nod tolerantly and wonder when I'm going to get a job. My dad wishes I wouldn't waste so much time on this show because he thinks I could do brilliantly if I apply myself. It's a fair point. But still. DVD glory!

It's 2012. I'm 36. I'm a professional actor and writer now. I'm working on the writing team for a project at the National Theatre, I've been a regular in a Radio 4 sitcom and, more importantly, I earn my crust writing **Doctor Who** audio plays. I feel I am neither a failure nor quite yet a success, but generally, life is good.

It's my Dad's birthday. He's 71. We're spending it in a Travelodge in Norwich as they've recently sold their house, but the new purchase has fallen through. I sleep on the sofa, my parents take the double bed.

We don't do much. Dad had his first dose of chemotherapy yesterday, so he's resting. As he sleeps I type away, finishing off the first draft of my current script – *Lords of the Red Planet,* a Big Finish 'Lost Story.' Unproduced storylines written during the classic series run, now being scripted in full and recorded by as many of the original cast as possible. This one is a storyline written by Brian Hayles that was eventually abandoned and replaced by another script called *The Seeds of Death*. I rather like it. I think it's good fun. It's getting released in November 2013, as part of the **Doctor Who** 50th anniversary celebrations. This is a big thing. I'm amazed and proud to be part of it. This silly little series that has given me so much and I get to pay tribute. I'm honoured. And Wendy Padbury's going to be in it. So, bonus.

No one really thinks much about *The Seeds of Death*, do they? No one hates it, but no one really likes it either. It's overlong, the storyline is okay, the acting is variable. It exists and we're glad it does, however it's never going to regularly come up in conversation.

But stories transcend their content. Context is everything. In the same way I enjoy the execrable film version of **The League of Extraordinary Gentleman** rather more than I should because I had a fun time attending the premiere, the actual material can sometimes be the least important part. We cannot divorce the story from the world that surrounds it, from how we experienced it.

For me, *The Seeds of Death* represents more than just six entertaining enough instalments of an old TV show from the 1960s. It represents my parents' love for their child. Their deeply annoying child. Their support and encouragement, their belief and their hope, their aid and their tolerance. Two wonderful people who never stopped believing and never stopped helping and who I hope, in some way, I am now rewarding. When they are gone, it's something I'll keep. So whilst *The Seeds of Death* will never be my favourite **Doctor Who** story, whilst it will never be anyone's favourite **Doctor Who** story, it will always be the one with a place in my heart. Because it isn't a **Doctor Who** story. It is Robert and Suzanne. And that is so very much more.

Zap, Whammo!
The Space Pirates by **Mikael Barnard**, 28, Leighton Buzzard, UK

Life is a continual process of growth and learning. Since the first volume of **You and Who** was published I have learnt many things. I have learnt that the plural of Intonarumori is Intomarumori. I have learnt that Eumig made over one million examples of the P8 film projector and that I hate every single one of them. I have learnt that whilst I like practically everything Lene Lovich has ever written perhaps the reason why I love *Bird Song* quite so totally may have much to do with the fact that my favourite chord, A-flat minor, features heavily. Of course these things are mere trivia and it is to be hoped that we all grow in more meaningful ways over time; that we develop as people.

However, there is one small downside to this growth; to a greater or lesser extent we lose the ability to see things as we did from a child's perspective. To remember in adulthood how one viewed the world as a child can be a highly valuable thing and the ability to recall and see things from this perspective is a very particular skill. Surely one of the most important lessons **Doctor Who** teaches us is that to see things from multiple perspectives is one of the true marks of insight and wisdom.

Which brings us to *The Space Pirates*, a story that is generally considered to be deeply dull and unpopular. Philip Sandifer (he of the wonderful Tardis Eruditorum) essentially puts this down to four things: the surviving episode; the visual nature of the production; comedy voices; and the fact that this spaceship-heavy tale is a product of its time. There is much to be said for this; one common word associated with the majority of the most popular **Doctor Who** stories must surely be timelessness and even I, ardent fan of *The Space Pirates* that I am, would not deny that certain aspects of the story and production have not dated well. The surviving episode also commits the same cardinal sin as the surviving episode of *The Enemy of the World*; in both cases they are probably the most unexciting episode of the whole story.

In the first volume of **You and Who** Mathew Kresal wrote a fabulous essay entitled *Loving the Hated*. The thrust of this essay is that if the viewer cares to look below the surface of certain productions then there might just be something deeper that is worthy of attention. Now obviously this approach just won't work with *The Space Pirates*, there is nothing below the surface; it is just Cowboys and Indians in space, the **Doctor Who** equivalent of Batman.

So how is it then that I can still find *The Space Pirates* totally wonderful? Well, I contend that if we cannot see any merit to the production from an adult perspective then we need to try and look at it in a different way. It seems to me that there are two ways of doing this; the first is to accept it on its own terms, to recognise that the production is mainly surface iconography with little greater meaning or subtext. If, however, you can gain no enjoyment from it in this way then perhaps an alternative method will appeal; to paraphrase the Doctor's words from *Dragonfire*, 'Look at it through a child's eyes, see it as a little child would see it.' The lack of visuals does indeed considerably hinder us at this point but all you really have to do is watch some **Flash Gordon** and follow it with an episode of **Rawhide**, **Destry** or anything with Tom Mix in it. Perhaps I am being a little facetious but the principal remains, thousands of television Westerns have managed to enthral generations of children, and in most cases you don't have to look very far for the occasional dodgy accent or threadbare plot. When I was a child I would barely have known an authentic American accent from Milo Clancey's and I found the character very comical (and continue to do so). Just look at Gordon Gostellow's face when he finishes delivering the line, 'If my old Liz had any speed about her I would have rammed them.' It cracks me up *every single time*. The best thing for me though, as a child, was Jack May. I was then and remain now an avid fan of **Count Duckula**; Milo Clancey, Eckersley and *Igor* all in one room, a dream come true! Lisa Danielly is truly charming as Madeleine Issigri and what I wouldn't give to see Esmond Knight as Dom Issigri. Dudley Foster, the man I knew even as a child from his comedy roles in **Steptoe and Son** just completes this tremendous ensemble.

At this point some of you may be thinking that my argument doesn't hold water, because my main reason for liking *The Space Pirates* is the association I have with the actors based on other productions I've seen them in. Well, I saw Donald Gee in *The Space Pirates* before I owned a copy of *The Monster of Peladon* and I had never seen Lisa Danielly, Esmond Knight or Gordon Gostellow in anything prior to watching the surviving episode. I can assure you that my enjoyment of the show is certainly not limited to Jack May's appearance and whilst I have always had a fascination with astronomy and the space race of the 1960s, I can hardly be culturally drawn to *The Space Pirates* in the way Philip Sandifer suggests children of the time were; I wasn't born until 1984 for a start! No, my enjoyment of *The Space Pirates* is because I do not look at it trying to find meaning or subtext, it is because I try my hardest to look at it now in exactly the same way I did when I first came across it, somewhere around ten years of age, and was hooked by the **Flash Gordon** sets, the pulpy plot, Donald Gee in a futuristic-looking helmet and a whacky old space cowboy trying to keep his battered old ship together. Come to think of it, doesn't that last bit sound just a tad familiar?!

Nothing to Be Scared Of
The War Games by **Alys Hayes**, 50, London, UK
First story: **The War Games** (Episode Ten)

It's funny how one little decision can affect you. Like Gwyneth Paltrow's character in **Sliding Doors** or Donna Noble in the recent **Doctor Who** episode *Turn Left*, I made one small choice in June 1969 that set the course of my life from there on. My choice was to watch **Doctor Who** for the first time.

I'd been aware of the series for some while; indeed my older brother had been watching it himself, but I was then a small child, terrified by the title music alone! I used to run screaming out of the living room every time I heard it. It has to be said that I was an easily frightened toddler – my brother used to crawl around on all fours pretending to be a lion and I still remember how convinced I was that he would bite me. Quite how an eighteen-year-old on his hands and knees crying, 'Raahh!' could look like a big cat, I don't understand, but I *was* only four at the time.

Not surprisingly, my preferred programmes were of the gentle kind, like **The Tinga and Tucker Club** and **Tich and Quackers**, but I did progress on to **Thunderbirds** and **Captain Scarlet and the Mysterons** fairly quickly (the latter becoming my first favourite show). At the same time, I became a voracious reader and found out about strange, grown-up things from the newspapers. One strong memory I have is of finding out about plastic surgery when reading about Cilla Black's 'nose job.' Being a very literal child, I found this most perplexing and was convinced that this meant she had a large piece of hard, white plastic sewn on to her face!

I was also reading the **Radio Times** every week by this time and was intrigued by the regular synopses for **Doctor Who**. They even had an actress in it with a name similar to mine – she was a Padbury and I was then a Bradbury. I knew I should watch this programme, but I was fighting my terror, although I couldn't really articulate what exactly I was frightened of.

So, on this particular Saturday (June 21st 1969, a few days before my seventh birthday), I finally made myself watch the programme. The episode happened to be the last part of *The War Games* - and I was utterly transfixed by it! I don't recall whether I understood all of the story, coming in at such a late stage, but I loved the characters, the ideas and the psychedelic look of the production. Why had I left it so long before watching this wonderful show?

From then on, I decided I would never miss another episode and waited eagerly for the new Doctor to make his appearance the following January. As Jon Pertwee quickly established himself in the role, I became a totally obsessed fan of **Doctor Who** and made a point of tuning in every Saturday. Despite my family's oft-repeated advice that this interest was something I would soon 'grow out of,' more than forty years later I am still waiting for that to happen! I collected all the books, posters, records and any other memorabilia that I could find. I was the only one in my junior class to vote for **Doctor Who** in a favourite TV shows poll - the others all chose **Scooby Doo, Where Are You?**, which was then the current top show for kids. I was teased for being a fan - a female fan, to boot - of such a weird series as **Doctor Who**, but I stuck to my guns. My only regret was missing the earlier stories of Hartnell and Troughton's eras. The **Radio Times** 10th (only the Tenth!) Anniversary Special magazine gave me a chance to see something of what I'd not seen, but it wasn't until the early 1980s and the boom in home video recording that older stories became accessible, albeit illicitly so. Unfortunately, because I had put off watching the series for so long in the 1960s, I had missed seeing stories that have become lost since that time. I could have seen *The Web Of Fear* or *Fury From the Deep* if I hadn't been so terrified of *that* music. Oh well, *c'est la vie*!

Then, in October 1983, I finally got the chance to see the whole of *The War Games* at a special event at the National Film Theatre in London, called **Doctor Who: The Developing Art**. A weekend of episode screenings was promised, and these would include two complete stories – *The Dæmons* and *The War Games* – plus a special symposium on the Sunday featuring guests including Patrick Troughton and Heather Hartnell. Well, I'd been to all the **Doctor Who** Appreciation Society conventions up to this point, but this was something I really couldn't afford to miss – a chance to see the whole of my first story *and* meet the man who was my first Doctor.

It was a wonderful weekend, catching up with friends I'd made through **Doctor Who** fandom and seeing episodes on the big screen. *The War Games* was the last story to be shown, late on the Sunday evening. I sat through the entire show, feeling so pleased that I could finally see it complete. Added to that was the knowledge that Patrick Troughton himself was seated only a couple of rows behind me, enjoying the episodes as one of the audience. I kept looking back and forth, not quite believing it.

Doctor Who has been such a huge part of my life. Today, I have it to thank for introducing me to many of my best friends. It has led me to new interests, expanded my knowledge and influenced my choice of career. Most importantly of all, through the series I came to meet my husband and soul-mate, Alan. Our cat is even named Zoe, in honour of Zoe Heriot. All of this and more leads back to that choice I made one Saturday afternoon in 1969, to watch *The War Games*.

The Third Doctor Who

With viewing figures having fallen to barely more than a quarter of those they'd peaked at earlier in the decade, **Doctor Who** faced cancellation at the end of the 1960s. The fact that it survived was only due to the BBC not being able to think of anything else to make instead. Easy to imagine that the number of episodes of the black and white era that have been recovered today, would never even have been looked for had the programme ceased to be made in 1970.

But with the introduction of Jon Pertwee as the third Doctor Who, the programme rapidly rose to new heights of popularity. Pertwee's decision to play the role (relatively) straight right from the off, having been engaged for the position due to his comic abilities, led in part to the production team's new emphasis on a heightened relevancy, and the programme rapidly grew out of its recent manifestation as 'a bit of fun for the kids.'

Pertwee's producer Barry Letts was perhaps the first true 'showrunner' on **Doctor Who**, a man who, thanks to a shortened broadcast run and thus with more time to concentrate on the wider aspects of the programme's production, was able to bring a vision and a plan to its making. The days of 'as live' recordings came to an end, and although the series was never afforded the budget or the capabilities of the BBC's more prestigious productions, Letts was at least able to make the creation of **Doctor Who** something less stressful and more thoughtful. The days of the programme making it to broadcast by the seat of its pants were left behind.

The early 1970s thus saw **Doctor Who** becoming more the show that all the family really could enjoy than the 'family show' it had been conceived as a decade before. The serials in which Jon Pertwee appeared would often address political and environmental concerns, as well as drawing upon the kind of in-universe continuity that the 1960s show had never been able to tackle, not just in the form of the UNIT stories, but also in connection with Peladon, and Metebelis III, and of course the Master.

The combination of military action-adventure, the monster-of-the-week and ongoing storylines placing the emphasis on more realistically-drawn companions, meant that the third Doctor Who's time at the TARDIS would be one of the general public's most fondly remembered.

For this was the period in which the Home Counties would become a major target for alien invasions, and this down-to-Earth quality really brought the programme home to a nation of viewers.

The Little Boy Who...
Spearhead from Space by **Tony Green**, 38, Oxford, UK
First story: **The Sun Makers**

Nigel was leaning against the wall next to the tennis courts. His eyes blazed from under the hood of his parka jacket, his Clarks Commandos kicked out at a stone on the ground which rolled over the line that marked the area of play which currently was being used for a game of lunchtime football. Nigel looked at it before returning his attention to the game going on in front of him. A game that he was not allowed to take part in. I watched Nigel from where I was sitting, huddled against the November wind within my own parka. I was sullenly watching the game too. I wasn't allowed to play either.

I was nine years old and I loved football. To be honest I wasn't bad at playing it either. It was not, therefore, lack of enthusiasm or skill that had kept me from the game; it was the fact that I had not loaned Gavin my ruler in class. Gavin's outrage at this sleight was enough.

Gavin was part of the clique of three or four boys who controlled the world of lunchtime tennis court football. Gavin had whispered to Phil, Phil to Matt and Matt to Marcus. By the time I joined them in the regular lunchtime game, not one of them passed to me. It became obvious even to my naive nine year-old brain, that I was not welcome. I slowly moved to the edge of the 'pitch' and then, with a hesitant pace, finally off of it and into the terrifying limbo of those who were not playing the game.

I had been sent to Coventry before but, as is the way of these things, it never lasted long and pretty soon (sometimes within hours, sometimes days) another victim would be chosen and I would be kicking a ball again and basking in the warmth of my peer group's acceptance. Today though, it was different. I suddenly became aware that I was utterly and totally sick of being liked one moment and detested the next, and that I tolerated it simply because I wanted to play football. This was why I was watching Nigel.

Outcasts generally kept apart for fear that by grouping together their sins would be multiplied and they would never be allowed back into the sunshine. I saw in his lonely, huddled shape on the opposite side of the court a reflection of myself. Lost and alone, me for the simple refusal of a favour, he for causing Matty's team to concede a goal the day before. He looked pathetic and, as yet unaware of concepts such as empathy or shared misery, my contempt for him knew no bounds. The Tony of a few years later would have gone over and offered friendship. The Tony of that day plunged his hands into his pockets and quietly wanted the ground to swallow him up.

It was then that my hand fell upon the book. We all had these; books that we pretended to read during 'quiet reading time' while actually whispering about **The Dukes of Hazzard**, Action Man or football. I had looked at it a hundred times; a copy of **Doctor Who and the Auton Invasion** purchased for me by my mum from a jumble sale. I occasionally read the back cover or looked at the pictures when the conversation flagged and I needed to look busy. I pulled it out and looked at the cover. A soldier, a monster and someone who was apparently Doctor Who (but looked nothing like the curly haired bloke I had seen that very Saturday). I looked again at Nigel who, with nothing better to do had found another stone to kick. I, however, saw that I did have something else to do. Classrooms were open at lunchtime for those who wanted to do more 'quiet reading.' I could get away from the game in front of me and the bastards who were playing it. I could show them that their little clique was not so strong that I needed it and, love of football or not, it would not control my life. I turned and walked into the school, the sound of the ball being kicked and the laughter of my contemporaries fading away behind me as the entrance door closed.

It was the first time I ever thought I was worth something as an individual. The first time I ever broke free of anything that clearly sucked. It was the first step on the road to 'growing up.'

I read the first chapter that lunchtime and another three that evening. The bitterness turned into an excitement to read more, to fill my mind with this world of monsters and soldiers and this clever, well spoken hero. **The Auton Invasion** was quickly finished and replaced by **The Cybermen** (another different Doctor Who - how the hell does he do that?). I was no longer reading as an escape but purely for pleasure and I was finding it in spades. Even after my return from exile, when football again became my first passion, I kept buying the books. I would always have one in my pocket in readiness for the time when the whispering would start. Now though, I would not stand alone in the playground. I really did have a friend; steadier, braver and far more interesting than those I had in my class, with the added bonus of not having to get cold to spend time in his company. Psychologists today might call it an emotional crutch and they are probably right. It worked though, and what else is a true friend than a crutch to lean on in times of trouble?

I don't think the Doctor would mind if a lonely little boy took comfort from his adventures. In fact, with whatever face he was wearing he'd probably smile.

'Come along with me old chap,' he'd say, opening the TARDIS doors. 'Let's go to Mars.' Being the Doctor he'd probably come back for Nigel too.

Next Week

Doctor Who and the Silurians by **Gary Russell**, freefalling terrifyingly towards 50, Cardiff via Maidenhead and Brockley, UK / First story: **The Tenth Planet**

My love affair with **Doctor Who** started a couple of years after I began watching it. I have no idea when I saw my first episode, but I do know the last episode of *The Tenth Planet* is my earliest memory of the show – three old age pensioners, all of whom looked like my nanna, talking, then one falls over.

I don't recall the regeneration – or why I thought Ben and Polly were pensioners. I suspect it's because at three years old, the most memorable faces in my life were my family, all of whom are (well, were back then – obviously not now) incredibly dark-haired. Thus my Nan was the only white-haired person I knew and on a jittery old black and white TV that took two minutes to warm up, white-hair = old.

But it wasn't until *The Evil of the Daleks* that I became fascinated with the programme. It was probably the Daleks – I loved them so much, fighting with the Emperor, that I ran out into the garden to play Daleks with my friend Jane – and actually missed the last few minutes. Stupid boy!

From that moment on, I watched as often as I could, fighting with one of my brothers over **The Adventures of William Tell** on 'the other side' – my mother resolved our fights by alternating our Saturday nights' viewing. Fine for him, **William Tell** was self-contained. I missed every other episode up until *The Dominators*, by which time my brother was bored of **William Tell**. Or it ended. Or he had Airfix planes to build. Either way, Saturday teatime was finally my own. Had you asked me why I kept watching, I couldn't have told you (well, I was six, what do you expect?). It wasn't until *Doctor Who and the Silurians* that I finally understood why I had to come back week after week.

Ice Warriors I worshipped. *The War Games'* bespectacled Aliens I had been enthralled by. Autons were the greatest thing since the invention of the wheel. But nothing had prepared me for the wonder that were the Silurians, and their pet dinosaur. And caves. And UNIT (oh I loved the Brigadier). And Liz Shaw. And then, I finally 'got it'; I realised with a degree of thrills, and slight early awakenings of cynicism, exactly why I came back week after week.

Episode 4 ends with the Doctor being 'killed' by a Silurian, while locked in a cage. Crash theme music. And I twigged for the first time what I had only subconsciously accepted previously – this was a 'cliffhanger' (I never knew the term until a few more years had gone by) and it was designed to make me come back in seven days.

And so I spent a whole week thinking up ways how the Doctor was not going to be dead. I wrote about them in my 'What I did this weekend' little grey schoolbook. My bestest friend Jonathan and I argued about the Silurians, and whether they were better than Autons and Quarks (well, duh!). And then when Saturday came we watched it together. I honestly can't recall whether we guessed it correctly, or even what our opinion on the resolution was – but I do recall being slightly disappointed that this episode ended with neither the Doctor nor Liz actually under attack. All that changed the following week when the Silurians came through the wall and the Doctor was 'killed' again (for years my six-year-old's memory convinced me they knocked the wall down with their pet dinosaur – when I finally rewatched it, I was most disappointed at the T-Rex's lack of involvement). Maybe this time he'd change face again (I hoped not, I really loved this new Doctor more than the old one because he wasn't silly and didn't clutch his bum when fighting Cybermen).

From this point on, **Doctor Who** was all about the cliffhangers. I would sit through the episodes telling my father or mother or eldest brother, or Jonathan if he was there, how I thought this would end. My parents would say, 'Well if you don't sit quietly, you won't see it,' my brother would just twat me one, and Jonathan would sigh and sensibly ignore me. The next few years were all about vivid cliffhanger moments captured in my mind's eye – Primord hands crashing through a glass door, an Auton policeman, the Doctor strapped to a table with Daleks and old Doctors on a giant telly... I realised very quickly that these cliffhangers made **Doctor Who** both unique and utterly unmissable. Between *The Seeds of Death* and *City of Death*, I only missed two episodes live on transmission – Episode 6 of *The Ambassadors of Death* (why did we go shopping to Tesco on a Saturday afternoon? Why, mummy, why – drive home faster! Drive, drive!) and the final part of *The Monster of Peladon* (the parents realised after that debacle that I didn't give a shit about cub scout camping weekends, they were never costing me another episode of **Doctor Who**, ever. Up yours, Baden-Powell, I needed the Doctor far more than I needed some stupid 'I can boil water over a fire' badge!)

I love modern **Doctor Who** enormously, but there will always be a part of me that thinks a story with three or four cliffhangers really captures the imagination of kids, really creates a 'must-see television' event in a young, impressionable mind in a way a self-contained story never can. Yes, the kids will watch **Doctor Who**, but at their own pace and in this multi-channel, time-shifted TV world we live in, there's a part of me that will forever be sad that no child will ever have that thrill of seeing anything like a Silurian wobbling its third eye at the Doctor and him collapsing against bars in a cage, and then sitting down at school and imagining how he'll get out of that next Saturday.

'There's Been a Murder...'
The Ambassadors of Death by **Jef Hughes**, 43,
Connah's Quay, Wales, UK
First story: **Planet of the Spiders** (almost certainly!)

I have a great deal of time for the stories of the original seventh series of **Doctor Who** – it was this series that was airing when I was born (I made my own debut one week and two days after the third Doctor made his) and when I discovered the four stories of this particular run several years later, I positively adored each and every one of them – this series is most definitely unlike the **Doctor Who** that had gone before (superficial similarities to WOTAN, Yeti and Cybermen stories aside) and *still* markedly different from a lot of what followed.

There's much that can be commented upon about *The Ambassadors of Death* – It saw the debut of the now-legendary cliffhanger 'theme scream,' which, of course, would go on to become part of the public consciousness (and also to serve as my text message tone!); it tries something *very* different with its episode openings and cliffhanger recaps (forerunning the pre-credits sequences of the series post-2005); it uses the character of TV reporter John Wakefield at times as a narrator to elements of the story; it riffs quite shamelessly off **Quatermass** (which doesn't happen quite as often in **Doctor Who** as is sometimes suggested); it takes the unusual step of allowing its dangerously xenophobic villain to concede defeat with his dignity intact – and Episode 2's final scene ('Right, cut it open!') ranks alongside the *great* cliffhangers of **Doctor Who**.

None of this mattered when I finally managed to see this story at the age of seventeen – I was more concerned with the fact that I'd noticed something that nobody in all of the magazines, fanzines and reference books that I'd read seemed to have – that soon-to-be stalwart and steadfast Sergeant Benton, in this only his second appearance, had clearly murdered the terrified traitor Dr. Lennox in Episode 5.

I have watched this episode countless times and I still maintain that Benton *has* to be Lennox's killer - he arrives at UNIT wanting to confess to the Brigadier and *only* him, but the Brig doesn't have the time to speak to him, so Benton is employed to lock the man up until he arrives. *Nobody* else is made privy to Lennox's presence at UNIT HQ, yet soon afterwards a meal is delivered to the prisoner - one containing the radioactive isotope that kills him. We're told that this execution was arranged and carried out by his former paymasters - that's as may be, but once Liz Shaw is forced to tell her captor, Reegan, where Lennox has escaped to, the phone call that he makes subsequently *must* be to a UNIT insider - and I can't see old Benton being persuaded to just hand over the cell key to any old subordinate. It isn't the Brigadier who delivers, unseen, the meal - otherwise Lennox would surely badger him for an interview - so it *has* to be Benton, doesn't it? It sounds a little like him...

For years, I banged on about this to my **Doctor Who**-loving friends. Let's face it, we belong to a group of people who positively *love* to theorise and debate. On this subject, however, *nobody* was particularly interested in my assertion - many just weren't familiar with the story; several thought that I just wasn't following the plot very well; the majority probably just felt that impugning the integrity of that stout fellow Benton was just not on.

I wrote to **Doctor Who Magazine** about it - even *Matrix Data Bank* just weren't interested. Fanzines (you name 'em, I wrote to them!) all ignored my theory too. I asked Benton actor John Levene and Script Editor Terrance Dicks the question at a couple of small conventions - the former just shrugged his shoulders and laughed while the latter gave me the only reply that I ever got to my question - a dismissive, but resounding, 'No - he didn't...'

Then one day, years later, a writer named Tat Wood produced a piece for **Doctor Who Magazine** all about some of the mysteries, plot holes and theories that had been largely overlooked in **Doctor Who** - when I eventually read it, I loved it - it remains in my opinion, one of the finest features ever run in the publication, but initially what grabbed me from the contents page was the article's title - 'Is Benton a Murderer?'

Wood (in much better prose than I can manage) made the *exact same point* that I'd been harping on about for years - it was true, Sergeant Benton really *did* kill Dr. Lennox, and now the whole of fandom would finally see what a visionary I was, *years* ahead of my time - I had called this correctly, and everybody now knew what I had known for years. Oh, this would be a defining moment, one that would rewrite a part of **Doctor Who** history permanently. I waited patiently for the floodgates of opinion and debate to open.

They absolutely *didn't*.

Seriously, though - watch it again. We never do discover who it was that murdered Dr. Lennox, save that it isn't Reegan, who is otherwise engaged sabotaging the Doctor's spacecraft. Of course, we *could* just be dealing with a production oversight here, but I stand by my belief that Sergeant Benton is a killer.

I can see that I'm not really persuading you, am I? Oh, well - never mind, eh? Now - does anyone fancy debating whether or not Benton dies in *The Android Invasion*? As far as I'm concerned, he *does*.

Hello? Where did everybody go?

In Glorious Black and White

Inferno by **Bill Albert**, 50, Amana, IA, USA
First story: Just know it was Pertwee's first season

Doctor Who didn't come to the U.S. until 1973. I was ten and on the weekends I would sometimes stay at my grandparents. At the end of the Lawrence Welk show on PBS, before switching to **Emergency** on NBC, there would be this photo of an oddly-dressed man holding open a cape standing in front of a gun-wielding soldier by a helicopter marked 'UNIT.' It was very OTT but still one of the coolest things I'd seen, but because of the time this show was broadcast I had no way of watching it. Luckily, a few months later, I got my own TV. It was orange, with rabbit ear antennae, and a mighty 12-inch black and white screen. Finally, I could find out what was going on. And this is where my forty-year following of **Doctor Who** began.

It was so different watching **Doctor Who** back then. There were absolutely no spoilers, we didn't even know how long the stories ran, and we had no info on the series' back story. We had to just take it as is and hang on with both hands.

Inferno came along amongst some very highbrow stories in Pertwee's first season. The whole idea of a story taking place in two alternative universes just a few hours apart from one another is quite advanced, and even at that age, I didn't feel like I was being insulted or talked down to as the Doctor tried to explain what was going on. It was a breathtaking adventure with awesome cliffhangers that really kept me going. Luckily, unlike in the UK, we were getting it Monday through Friday nights at 10pm so we didn't have to wait a week for a resolution, but I couldn't wait to get to 10pm to find out what was going to happen next.

The effects, surprisingly, were one of the things that stood out. The series, especially the original, is not known for the quality of its visual effects, but in this case it was the audio effect that was so prominent. As Project Inferno approaches its conclusion in each of the universes, there grows a constant rumbling in the background. As the sound increases, this succeeds in stepping up the danger and sense of urgency and engulfing the viewer in the story and the tragedy that is approaching.

I must point out just how good the performances are. Not only the dual roles for the story's guests, but also the regulars like Caroline John, Nick Courtney and John Levene. At this point they were all still very new to the show and taking familiar characters and throwing them on their sides like that could have meant disaster with a lesser cast. Luckily, they were all good enough actors that they could pitch their performances close enough to keep them familiar to the viewer, but dissimilar enough that you felt uncomfortable with them.

It was an exciting adventure, night after night, and it kept me coming back for more. Despite that I didn't realise until years, or decades, later just what it is that makes the story stand out.

Terrance Dicks talked about the kind of villains they knew the Doctor might face being earthbound. These would have to be either already on Earth or trying to invade the Earth and they were worried the repetition might get tiresome. *Inferno*, however, doesn't fall into either of those categories. It's unique in that, despite the danger and suspense, this story has no villains.

Professor Stahlman doesn't fit such a mould. He has no grand desire to take over the world or defeat anyone. Obsessive, yes, single minded, yes, but his goal is to solve world energy problems. Even in the alternative universe Stahlman has no wicked henchmen at his disposal. He bribes the driver to prevent Gold from reaching the ministry, but not to injure him, and the death is accidental. In both worlds he does have a redeeming moment where he realises just what he's done and there is sympathy for the character.

Even the Primords can't be considered evil. They are, in effect, a version of early man, or animals that act instinctively only to protect themselves. No more villainous than a tiger looking for elk or an owl protecting its young from intrusion.

Some might say Brigade Leader Stewart is the villain. The tough officer in a fascist state who follows orders – which include trying to kill the Doctor. You have to keep in mind that this is his world. He has no grand plan and no 'Nothing can stop me now' moment. Rightly or wrongly we are in his world and, in his eyes, the Doctor is an unknown element who wants to disrupt his normal way of life.

That's what has made this story so memorable, because in just this one instance, the Doctor is the villain. In the alternative world he is the one with the master plan for changing things, and who tries to force his way onto others. He's the intruder.

I've also found over the years that the other stories of the third Doctor's first season include many of the same elements. Take a close look at *The Ambassadors of Death*; again, there is no traditional villain at work, an idea that very few series could try to tackle. Especially children's series in 1970s Britain.

Nothing To See Here
Terror of the Autons by **Simon Brett**, 41, Exeter, UK
First story: **Planet of the Spiders**

'In the beginning, there was nothing. Then God said, "Let there be light." And there was still nothing but you could see it.' - Groucho Marx

Tentacles. Uncle Terry said it had tentacles - along with crab claws and a big eye. For the best part of thirty years, that gruesome yet beautiful painting on the cover of Terrance Dicks' Target novel (possibly only bettered by the *Death To The Daleks* cover) so vividly depicted the physical manifestation of the Nestene Consciousness in my memory. Inside the book, admittedly simple line drawings depicted a slightly less realistic interpretation, yet that cover was so realistic that *surely* this was a representation of what that creature *actually* looked like on screen, quite possibly based on photographic evidence. I'll come back to that. Oh, the innocence of youth...

    Terrance Dicks' novelisation was one of the most exciting and vibrant of the Target books that I'd experienced. Borrowed from the local library, I promised myself that when I had enough of my own money I would buy my own copy if only to own the cover illustration (I was, and still am an aspiring artist). Up to that point, I had only bought the novels that depicted the episodes that I had actually seen, but this was a different beast. Living plastic, killer dolls, Time Lords in bowler hats. This was **Doctor Who** at its comic best and it didn't stop for breath. What a shame that, short of a miracle at BBC headquarters, I would never see the original story on my television.

    The years rolled by. As a reclusive teenager with more hormones than hope, I had gone through a major phase of fascination in the vintage Doctors via the early issues of **Doctor Who Weekly**, which ran a series of basic plots for the series from its birth, and that had literally manifested in an obsessive collecting and reading of the Target novels, especially as they were going through a period of prolific publishing of older stories in the mid-1980s. With the exception of sporadic broadcasting of older stories, such as **The Five Faces of Doctor Who** season on BBC2, I still relied on the books to fill in the gaps in the Doctor's previous adventures. Nevertheless, *Terror Of The Autons* kept a place in my heart as one of the great stories, regardless of the fact that I would never *actually* watch it until nearly thirty years later.

When I admitted to my colleagues on the Blue Box Podcast that I had never watched *Terror Of The Autons* (despite professing it as one of my all-time favourite stories) I was met with utter disbelief. So much so that within two days I had a copy pushed through my letterbox and within a few hours I was sitting matching pictures to the hazy memories. Living plastic, killer dolls, and, oh wow, Time Lords with bowler hats! This really was everything that I'd expected it to be and quite possibly better with the first appearances of not just the Master but Jo Grant too. Like it or not, this story encapsulated much of the Pertwee/Letts template, and although if ever pressurised to name my favourite Doctor, Mr Pertwee rarely makes the top five, it's very hard to deny that this period of **Doctor Who** doesn't deliver fun with a capital F.

Back to the tentacles, the claws and the eye. Sure, the effects in *Terror of the Autons* sustain less scrutiny than a politician's expenses record, but this is standard territory for the dedicated fan. It's no good expecting 1970s visual effects to convince the eye, but convincing the imagination of a dreamy eight-year-old has never been a problem, much like this teenager was convinced that when the Nestene Consciousness finally manifested itself in the finale of the story, it was a hideous sight to behold. I wasn't so naive as to expect anything more than a rubbery puppet with dangling tendrils and clumsy claws. This was the 1980s and the Mara and Myrka were to become current standards. I was under no illusions of what would have been possible in the early 1970s. What I didn't expect was ... well, nothing. Well, when I say 'Nothing,' I mean a big flashy blinky sort of nothing. But still - nothing.

Where the beast should have been, there was a great big sci-fi hole.

Well, I sat back in my chair and laughed. My experience of *Terror Of The Autons* had been based on Uncle Terry's wise decision to 'sex up' some of its visual flaws. When my Blue Box colleagues giggled mischievously behind their hands as I recounted my love for the beautiful cover artwork, little did I know the grim reality. Was I shocked? Mildly. Was I disappointed? Slightly. Does it make the story any less a classic? Of course not.

Doctor Who has a special place in my consciousness. Much like a great book, so much of its beauty lies beneath the surface. It's the gaps between the words, the times between the televised stories, the blank spaces where the missing episodes should be that allow the story to unfold in your own head with no limits. The gap where the hideous monster should be. These are mini-vacuums waiting to suck in our thoughts and dreams. We're not making excuses for our favourite show's failings - we're feeding its life force.

They say absence makes the heart grow fonder - well, a few lost stories and we're all obsessing over them and using our creativity to recreate what should, by rights, still exist. Fan fiction propagates at a rate higher than Gabby Logan's appearances on celebrity quiz shows. This is a format that lives and breathes through the imagination of the viewer. When I became a fan of the show, I didn't just watch it - I became part of it, and it became part of me.

Target Acquired
The Mind of Evil by **Matthew West**, 36, Surrey, UK
First story: **The Keeper of Traken**

Strap yourself in. Buckle up. Brace. I'm about to reveal something that will offend, shock and remain with you for the rest of your life: the first Target book I read was *The Mind of Evil* by Terrance Dicks.

I came to the range late. I was ten but already a precocious reader. I remember struggling to read aloud **Foundation** by Isaac Asimov in junior school because one of the characters spoke with a lisp and I couldn't make out the dialogue. Made me cross at the time because I also had a lisp and when I found out that's what Asimov was writing I felt he was doing it to annoy me.

Because of my reading habits I felt a **Doctor Who** book was a step backward. But my dad came home with it one Friday. We'd not usually see him during the week. He'd be up at 5.30am and on the first train by 6am and didn't come home until a little after 8pm just after we'd gone to bed. But on Fridays he'd often get home early and on this dark November night he handed me an orange hardback with a big neon logo and a bloke I'd never seen before on the front. Bloke in question would turn out to be the Master.

I was expecting large print and pictures. Even at ten years old I considered **Doctor Who** to be a children's programme. I suppose it was by 1987. This was roughly around the time I'd forced my parents to miss **Coronation Street** in favour of *Time and the Rani* and just hung my head in shame as I saw the new Doctor acting the clown without a laugh track or applause. It's not that I disliked it, I mean I could recognise this wasn't great television, but I could tell that my parents didn't like it and that bothered me. I'd watch the rest of that season the following morning at 6.01am on video. Hey kids, videos are what we had before Sky+. I digress.

I was never an obsessive fan. I wasn't familiar with fandom at ten. I hadn't attended a convention, never read a production guide, I'd not seen any documentaries and nobody I knew watched **Doctor Who**. I got the monthly during Davison's run but smaller, more expensive comics took over as **Death's Head** and **Batman** became much more entertaining than Jeremy Bentham's vague recollections of Sensorite designs. So I was never an obsessive fan, but one thing about the cover of that book gave it absolute bona fide credentials: Terrance Dicks. I knew that name. I'd still got an off-air of *The Five Doctors* and he'd written that. If he'd written that, then *The Mind of Evil* must be *amazing*.

And it really was. I started it that night and finished it by lunchtime Saturday. I then hopped on my bike and rode to Hook Library because something else about this book amazed me – it was number *ninety-six!* in the **Doctor Who** Library. There were nearly a hundred of these books out there. The first thing I did when I got to the library was look up Tyburn Tree which was mentioned on page one of the book and I didn't understand the reference. Once familiar with this I headed for 'Science Fiction', my recently returned copy of **Foundation** already sitting back on the top left of the shelf where it belonged. But there was no **Doctor Who**. How annoying. I would've asked at the desk, but I'm a **Doctor Who** fan and we love index files. Following the advice of Tegan's dad I rocketed through the card catalogue of the library (there were no computers!) and looked up Terrance Dicks. I had never seen so many books by one author. They were in the Children's section! How dare they. Oh well, I'd have to dive in. Stepping gingerly (I did everything gingerly, it was unavoidable with my hair) over discarded soft toys and wooden chairs with shapes painted on them I made my way to what was thankfully at least categorised as 'young adult.' There were so many! I grabbed five at random, can't even remember what they were, and read most of them on the Sunday.

Of course there were other authors and over the years I've come to appreciate many of them, not least Ian Marter whose lurid flights of fancy never leave the back of your mind once read. But it was Terrance Dicks who formed a year of solid **Doctor Who** reading for me in 1987. My dad kept bringing books home, sometimes four or five of them in his briefcase on a Friday night. Then Unicorn Books in Epsom started selling Target books for a mere 60p each brand new. My collection was huge.

In 1992 I knocked on the door of a townhouse in London and it was answered by Terrance Dicks. He was expecting me. He led us up several flights of stairs, each floor containing a different room - not unlike the lighthouse in *Horror of Fang Rock* until we reached a huge room (it seemed huge at the time) filled with books, a clapped out old telly and some **Doctor Who** videos, one gnarled with the tape dangling out piled up around it. I sat for nearly three hours and interviewed this man about writing for my English A Level course. He was so welcoming, so tolerant and actually very helpful though I'm sure he'd never believe it. But I behaved myself because I didn't want to be a lovestruck fanboy. I didn't dwell on **Doctor Who** that much at all. I regretted that.

Two weeks ago, November 2012, after some friends made him pass out drunk at a convention, I approached him the following morning, shook his hand and thanked him for those books. I said what I always believed: 'I will never read over sixty books by any one author again, and I doubt many people have. I read them, I loved them, and they made me want to write my own. Thank you, Terrance Dicks. Thank you so, so much.'

'That's Jo – Come On!'
The Claws of Axos by **Benjamin Adams**, 46, Phoenix, Arizona, USA / First story: **The Claws of Axos**

On February 24th, 1976, I met the Doctor for the first time.

KCET Channel 28 in Los Angeles had been showing the Jon Pertwee serials on Tuesday evenings at 7.30pm since July 1st 1975, starting with *Doctor Who and the Silurians*, but I hadn't watched them. This is strange in hindsight, since my parents were big fans of KCET's classy, upscale Public Broadcasting Service (PBS) programming, which was largely sourced from the UK. But at the time, I was still caught up in **Star Trek, Ultraman** and **Space: 1999**, and my dad wouldn't have gone out of his way to let me know about **Doctor Who**, as something that looked so cheap wasn't his cup of tea. (He did finally succumb to the charms of the new series when it premiered in 2005, but that's another story.)

So on that mildly chilly night in February, I'd gone with my parents to the home of another couple for dinner. Bored, restless, fidgety kid that I was, I wound up relegated to the TV room while the adults had a post-dinner drink.

The TV got turned on for me by one of the adults, and I was immediately captivated by what I saw, something which got tattooed on my memory to such an extent that I remembered it exactly decades later, when I saw *The Claws of Axos* on its VHS release.

A pretty girl, screaming, as something – a monster that looks like a mass of spaghetti-like tentacles – materializes through a wall. And then an older man, obviously a take-charge sort, shouting, 'That's Jo – come on!'

By the end of that episode, with Jo, Bill Filer and the Doctor encircled by Axons in the reactor, I was hooked for life. My dad didn't stand a chance. Tuesday nights at

7.30pm, the TV became mine, and I watched the Doctor's exploits religiously.

Part of the attraction was the monsters themselves. I was a huge fan of the Japanese series **Ultraman**, and would rush home to watch it after school, when it was being stripped in reruns Monday through Friday by KBSC Channel 52 out of Corona, California. Although monsters that were men-in-rubber-suits were *de rigueur* on the show, there had been some seriously surreal episodes of **Ultraman,** including one where the monster itself was a sort of tesseract, and judging by *The Claws of Axos*, **Doctor Who** was more of the same ... except better, because there was no outlandish giant silver alien who knew kung-fu. Everything seemed more real, more down-to-earth, but with even greater stakes.

Doctor Who fans like to say that the first Doctor we see is *our* Doctor. That's certainly the case with Jon Pertwee and me. As a bright, socially awkward child, I found his reactions to the often dim-witted and thick people around him to be completely natural expressions of exasperation. But despite his snark, he was also paternal and kind and heroic. In fact, he was just as heroic as another favourite of mine, James Bond, but he fought monsters and an evil Time Lord who kept ... coming ... *back.*

This, on top of my already burgeoning interest in SF, pushed me over the edge. I became an SF and horror geek, and *The Claws of Axos* was one of my most formative influences.

But after eighteen months of broadcasts and several timeslot changes, KCET stopped showing **Doctor Who** on December 31st 1977. In hindsight, it appears obvious they had contracted for exactly eighteen months' worth of rights - no more, no less. So this became my first hiatus as a **Doctor Who** fan ... until good old KBSC Channel 52 began airing the Tom Baker stories in October 1978. Two episodes a night, at 5pm and 6.30pm. This sealed the deal. **Doctor Who** was in my life for good.

So fast-forward to the mid-2000s. As a professional writer, I'd managed to have some modest success, selling quite a few horror short stories to various professional anthologies. Although I'd never been part of any kind of organised fandom previously, I'd found out about the Outpost Gallifrey website and begun posting there. I became intrigued by the **Short Trips** anthologies being published by Big Finish, so I dropped a personal note of enquiry to Paul Cornell, since he had recently edited one. Paul said he'd pass along my information to Big Finish, and a few months later I was contacted by Ian Farrington and asked to contribute to the anthology **Short Trips: The Centenarian.** I was over the moon ... all my previous short story sales were nothing compared to being invited to play in the **Doctor Who** sandbox.

On **The Centenarian**'s publication, I decided to fly to the UK for the book's launch party. I figured this was a good chance to meet some of the folks with whom I'd been corresponding on the Outpost Gallifrey forum.

I met so many wonderful people during that trip who have remained good friends, with whom I am in almost constant contact. I decided to start attending the Gallifrey One conventions in Los Angeles so I could see some of my friends yearly without having to bankrupt myself flying to London.

And as a result of attending the Gallifrey One convention, I met my beautiful, whip-smart wife, Kim. We married at Gallifrey One in Los Angeles on February 27th, 2010 ... almost 34 years to the day since I first met the Doctor on a Los Angeles TV station, and the trajectory of my life was changed forever.

Primitive Culture
Colony in Space by **Steve Roberts**, 47, London, UK
First story: **Terror of the Autons**

'The young Time Lord sat at the side of the old Keeper of the Time Lords' Files at the control console.'

That somewhat clumsily constructed opening sentence was my introduction to the world of **Doctor Who** novelisations. I guess it was also my introduction to TV and movie tie-in books as a whole, which would peak most memorably for me three or four years later with the release of the **Star Wars** novel ... but that's a whole other fandom.

Doctor Who and the Doomsday Weapon was a present from my Mum, returning with her from a shopping trip into Leeds sometime in the mid-1970s. I was already a fan of the show, of course, through the weekly adventures on television and in **TV Action**, and even had a small collection of merchandise, including a colouring book, Sugar Smacks badges and my most prized possession, the **Radio Times** 10th Anniversary issue. I had convinced my auntie to buy me the latter and had devoured the contents from cover to cover many times, quickly becoming an armchair expert in the history of a show that had already been running for two years before I was even born.

Which immediately gave me a problem. There was no story called 'The Doomsday Weapon,' of that I was absolutely certain. Yet there on the front cover were the unmistakable disembodied heads of my Doctor, his arch enemy the Master, and some tubby bloke with an axe, floating in space above a menacing pair of monstrous claws and a single, mysterious word: Achilleos. Once I started reading, it wasn't long before I was able to deduce that this was actually *Colony in Space*. Why change it? That really upset my internal filing system, which wanted everything compartmentalised neatly. And which, a couple of years later, would result in a multi-page hand-written letter to Target listing all of the 'incorrect' names on their

Doctor Who book covers against all of the 'correct' names from my bible, that paragon of precision the 10th Anniversary special, along with a demand for some sort of promise of future accuracy. The letter was returned to me, 'Addressee not known.' I was a bit miffed about that.

But back to the book. It was epic. I must have only been eight or nine, but thanks to my Mum being a librarian I had been encouraged to read at an early age and had already zipped through most of the Famous Five stories and their ilk. I was getting pretty much bored of plucky middle-class British children and had started to explore the American offerings in the library, particularly the slightly more anarchic adventures of Danny Dunn, and the Willard Price zoological 'Adventure' novels with their, erm, plucky middle class American children and exotic locales. A **Doctor Who** adventure was a whole different thing though. It had spaceships, evil miners, plucky colonists, disguised villains and mysterious aliens, not to mention the galaxy destroying potential of the eponymous Doomsday Weapon itself. It had big, bold themes of betrayal, sacrifice, loyalty and the horrors of corporate greed and lust for profit. It had a huge killer robot with a set of false claws. It was bloody brilliant. I must have read it a dozen times over the years, along with the other Target titles that I bought for 20 or 30p of my pocket money or which my Mum set aside for me as soon as the library were sent a new title. Other stories (many with *blatantly incorrect* titles) became favourites but it would always have a very special place in my affections simply because it was my first.

It would be many years until I was finally able to see the story on video. The book was bloody brilliant though.

Still Looking for Devil's End

The Dæmons by **Tony Jones**, 52, Reading, Berkshire, UK
First Story: **The Moonbase**

We all have our favourite things: an old shirt, a certain restaurant, that pair of old slippers long since passed their best; for me, if asked, 'What **Doctor Who** stories would I want on a desert island, one for each Doctor?' (and that's an idea for a survey!) my Jon Pertwee choice always ends up as *The Dæmons*. If you'll bear with me I'll try and explain why. In doing so I will no doubt tell you more about myself than I first expected!

This five-part story written by Barry Letts (who also produced it) and Robert Sloman under the joint nom de plume of Guy Leopold is, if nothing else, a good example of most of the motifs of this period of the show. We have the Doctor and Jo battling against the odds with our UNIT heroes unable to carry the day with neither conventional weapons nor sheer determination. We have a quintessentially English setting – a village, a priest, a church. There are morris men and a maypole. We have the Master and a new all-powerful alien in the form of Azal. Back, then, between the 22nd of May and the 19th of June 1971 we had *The Dæmons* in all its glory. We also had a ten-year-old boy fascinated by **Doctor Who** and science-fiction in general.

Deconstructing my relationship with this story is difficult as so much time has passed and my current sense of the story's context cannot, surely, have been that of me as I was then. The reason why I think this particular story is almost archetypal is that it connects to some of the deeper roots of the programme as a whole; Quatermass and John Wyndham.

The plot of *The Dæmons* has the device of an archaeological dig into a Bronze Age mound in the village of Devil's End. A local white witch wants to stop them but fails, so goes to seek the help of the local vicar – the Rev. Magister who happens to actually be the Master! There is an ancient supernatural power and a small spaceship. These are all artefacts from the Dæmon, a superior, alien entity.

The Doctor tries to enter the village but is initially confounded by mysteriously realigning road signs. Later the Brigadier is unable to enter the village due to an impenetrable barrier that causes anything attempting to cross to burst into flame.

Focussing on the village and the dig the Doctor is confronted by the villagers who are under an alien influence. The Doctor also confronts the Master to no avail. The Doctor is tied to a maypole escapes, challenges the Dæmon and eventually turns the tables thanks to Jo Grant offering to sacrifice herself to save him. There is little assistance from a largely neutered UNIT team. Everything ends with an explosion. En route we are even treated to the Venusian lullaby.

Now compare with **Quatermass and the Pit**; this is a tale of workmen struggling to dig a tube line at Hobbs End (and we later learn that Hobb means Devil so this is Devil's End). There is a spaceship, an ancient power, psychic forces and TV crews. The military try to take control of the situation and fail. The analogies are very strong.

Turn to John Wyndham's **The Midwich Cuckoos**; in this the village of Midwich is sealed off from civilisation by an impenetrable dome, under the protection of which aliens arrive and impregnate the women. The children then proceed to exert a strong mental influence on the villagers.

It is easy, then, to see these influences on the story. In fact all that is missing is the equivalent of the Master; clearly the Doctor is Quatermass, as people have suggested many times in the past and will do again in the future.

What about the influences on the ten-year-old viewer?

I was already interested in science-fiction watching both **Doctor Who** and **Star Trek**. I knew of John Wyndham as my mother had a few of his novels. Knowing I was interested in science-fiction both my mother and grandfather used to tell me of the great BBC programmes of the 1950s including the **Quatermass** serials, and others such as **1984**. As I grew into my teens I devoured everything I could find including all the Wyndham books and, whenever they were on TV, the Quatermass stories. I even attended the 1979 World Science Fiction Convention in Brighton at which the original BBC **Quatermass and the Pit** was shown.

Speaking of the 1970s, you have to remind people that programmes were shown only the once, and if you didn't watch them at the time then you didn't see them. You didn't download, stream, buy the DVD or anything else. Thus *The Dæmons* stayed a memory that I couldn't check. As I absorbed more and more science-fiction I could subconsciously make the associations with *The Dæmons*, building the interconnections. I think they were there to begin with though.

As to me, I do like a quintessential English scene – a village, a pub. I will even stop and watch morris dancers, much to my family's embarrassment. Is this all due to a **Doctor Who** story? I don't know, but we are the sum of our memories and it is possible.

Like life itself I wouldn't claim that *The Dæmons* is without its flaws, but I do believe it tells us something about the deeper values of the show. And do you know what? I may just dig out the DVD one more time!

See you in Devil's End – I'll bring the handkerchiefs and the maypole!

The Bestest, Most Modern, Original Series Doctor Who Story Ever. With Daleks and Everything!

Day of the Daleks by **Richard Dinnick**, 45, Norfolk, UK
First story: **Day of the Daleks**

I don't remember seeing *Day of the Daleks* when it was first broadcast. That's not to say I didn't see it. Indeed, my first **Doctor Who** memory is of that Dalek materialising in the abandoned railway tunnel to menace the Doctor. Except of course, now I can see that it didn't so much materialise as have a spotlight above it turned on! At the time, though, it was about the most terrifying thing I had ever seen.

Some background. I was four in 1972. I celebrated my fourth birthday the day the last episode of the serial was broadcast. This is why I question being able to remember this serial and the end of the first episode (New Years' Day 1972) so well. I was, after all, only three! My brother was nine years older than me and he tells me that I sat on Mum's lap as a baby and toddler watching the end of the Troughton era and the beginning of my beloved Jon Pertwee's. However, I hadn't been born when the Daleks last appeared in 1967.

The point is, I had heard of these mythical creatures, the Daleks, but I had never seen one on screen. So when one appeared, I was beside myself with excitement and possessed of a type of primal fear that must have been built to fever pitch by the ravings of my brother. I guess what I am trying to say is that the Daleks made a massive impression on me. I love them. I know I am not alone in this but I think this story is why I became a **Doctor Who** fan.

You see, I am sure I saw the serial as broadcast, but I think I am remembering the repeat from over a year later in September 1973, by which time I would have been five-and-a-half.

Anyway, no matter which version I am remembering, I loved *Day of the Daleks*. I truly didn't notice that there were only three Daleks. I had no idea they had been added to the story at a late stage because another Dalek story fell by the wayside. How could I? Why would I?

This story has everything. Yes: everything. And so much of what it has makes it a blueprint for New **Doctor Who**. And here are the ten reasons why...

It is about time travel. Amazingly, until this point, **Doctor Who** had concerned itself with the ins and outs of time travel about once before (I'm thinking of *The Space Museum*). This is the story that gave us time paradoxes, the Blinovitch limitation effect, that little glimpse of the future/past that the Doctor and Jo are afforded when fiddling with the TARDIS console. Remind you of anything you've seen lately, Professor Song?

It's got Daleks in it. Did I mention I love Daleks? I have no time for those **Doctor Who** fans who pooh-pooh the Daleks or complain that they are rubbish or couldn't climb stairs or looked silly. The Daleks are the dog's dangly bits. And, what's more, this story has a gold one in it! This was closest the original TV series ever got to the Golden Emperor I was later to discover in the late 1970s Dalek annuals. Russell T Davies knew the Daleks were brilliant. He gave us loads of different Daleks including gold ones (bronze, then, but you're splitting hairs!) as well as a cool Black one and a red one with extra bits, as well as an Emperor! Steven Moffat went further and gave us an officer class.

It's a multi-Doctor story. What do you mean: no it isn't? I count three Doctors on screen (a full eighteen months before they did it again, admittedly with actually moving Doctors, but still...) and that's not including the extra version of the third Doctor who speaks to himself! And he didn't need one of them to be a flesh 'Ganger,' to do it...

If ever there was a relationship between a Doctor and companion that was modern, it was this one. The Doctor and Jo loved each other. There I said it. She definitely loved him and when he left her knowing he could never be with her at the end of *The Green Death*, I would argue it was one of the most emotional scenes for the Doctor until the series returned. And here the regulars are just lovely to watch. Pertwee is on top form as the Doctor resplendent in that maroon smoking jacket, quaffing wine and standing up to quislings, guerrillas, politicians and Daleks alike.

UNIT was great in the old days. Here we have all the key personnel in place. Even though they aren't in the story for a great deal of it, they are all on great form – from Sgt Benton getting his wine and cheese taken away by a knowing Mike Yates to the Brigadier getting shirty with Sir Reginald and scoffing at the Doctor's suggestion of ghosts. No wonder UNIT keeps returning and now we have the Brig's daughter!

Day of the Daleks is a dark, brooding, unnerving piece of **Doctor Who**. The haunted house thing is played well and the first episode would feel quite at home in **Sapphire & Steel** (albeit some eight years later). Not many modern **Doctor Who** stories manage this particular flavour of frightening, although Mark Gatiss's *Night Terrors* is very close.

The future portrayed is a terrifying one. I love the shiny make-up of the controller (I still get excited when I watch **Willy Wonka & the Chocolate Factory** to see Aubrey Woods singing *The Candy Man*); I find the sing-song delivery of the female technicians very creepy and the buildings and life depicted hauntingly stark. *Bad Wolf* had a stab at this type of thing, although with a healthy dose of media savvy.

Day of the Daleks also got a **Radio Times** cover. This was one of only twelve in the whole 27-year run of the original series. The new series had more than doubled that by the end of David Tenant's time. So this was a special event. Part of that is that it marked the return of the Daleks after their longest screen break in the history of the broadcast show (five years). Only their absence of seventeen years between the old series ending and the new series beginning (1988 to 2005) was longer.

How brilliant were the Ogrons? Simple, full-on baddie henchman. No Complications. They even went on to appear later in the third Doctor's run. The Judoon of their day, I think it's a real shame they have not been used on TV since. We did have the very similar pig guards, but I understand the Ogrons were busy appearing as the baddies in a film trilogy about a ring in New Zealand...

Finally, I think of all the original **Doctor Who** stories, this one was most deserving of a Special Edition. I'll admit that the voices weren't the best I've ever heard (although they were the first and *only* voices I'd heard back then) and it is a curious thing that they are now so ably voiced by Nick Briggs who has become an employer and friend. The effects are a wonderful addition to what - for me - is a true classic and elevates it into the pantheon of the best stories ever.

Oh, and did I mention? I love Daleks.

A Voice from the Past
The Curse of Peladon by **Amanda Evans**, Bognor Regis
First story: **The Dæmons**

Deep within the Museum of Antiquities of New Peladon, lay a very precious thing.

A well-manicured hand stroked the glass case which held the object. Something between a computer and a notepad and covered in a strange brown fur material. It was ancient and indecipherable; of archaic technology.

'I trust you understand the seriousness of this undertaking? Do you think you can translate this?' The Chief Curator was worried, staring at the woman standing in front of the display case.

She merely nodded and smiled.

'You have twenty minutes only.'

She nodded again. 'Mum.'

'Doctor Song, this is probably the most valuable relic on the whole of our planet. The Dalek Wars wiped out virtually our whole historical record. If we take this out into our atmosphere for more than twenty minutes it will deteriorate beyond repair.'

'"Found in the ruins of the Citadel of the Ancient Kings of Peladon. Thought to be to be many thousands of years old".' River read the notice on the glass casing out loud. 'Chief Curator, I assure you I will treat this diary the way I treat all treasures.'

He placed the notebook on the desk and bowed. 'Twenty minutes.'

River got to work. She opened her shoulder bag and produced a machine that resembled a small pocket calculator. She pressed a sequence of buttons and placed it on the small furry notebook. Immediately the book started to emit an orange glow.

There was a crackle of energy and a high girlish voice emanated from River's machine.

Alpha Centauri - Honourable Delegate of the Galactic Federation.

Day 3 in the Citadel of Peladon.

Oh how unpleasant this all is! Where are the other delegates? It is terrible weather, and the people here are little more than barbarians. Young King Peladon has given me this as a welcome gift to record my thoughts. A simple voice recorder but the height of Peladonian Technology! The King is charming, but he surrounds himself with the most unpleasant people. And I can't even bring myself to describe my quarters. All stone and hard surfaces. Burgh.

Day 4.

The other delegates arrived today. Ice Warriors really scare me. So big and green. And that Arcturus, what a strange looking creature. He nearly gave me a respiration failure with his laser beam. I feel caution is necessary in my dealings with these disagreeable aliens.

Day 5.

There has been a *murder*...! One of Peladon's aides. He was attacked by a legendary beast! How can this have happened?! Maybe we will be next! Poor King Peladon is so upset! Oh where is the delegation from Earth? There is no way of contacting them in this raging storm.

Update.

Am so relieved. The Earth Delegation has arrived. He said to call him 'The Doctor.' He seems to know just what to do and say, and I am so pleased someone has taken over and is dealing with things. It is all a bit too much for me. And such a pretty companion. Princess Josephine, very regal... But all is not well in the Citadel. We were...

There was a sudden crackle and the light faded.

River smiled as she reset her machine. Alpha Centauri was a legend, it's appearance causing a sensation even in a universe of wonders. Who would have believed it would have gone on to become a decorated war hero?

The diary resumed.

How can this have happened? The Doctor is on trial for his life. He was wandering around the castle and went into some shrine and now that horrible High Priest says he must be executed for sacrilege! This is outrageous... But what can we do? These barbaric alien traditions... Oh I feel ill...
 Update.
 Is this a plot? The Doctor has vanished! Surely he can't be guilty? I thought he was such a nice man. Princess Josephine seems angry at Peladon. We all hoped... Ah well. And that Arcturus thing keeps rolling around in his nasty container acting very suspiciously. And that horrible High Priest... Well even I can see there is more to him than meets the eye; I just want to leave this vile cold place. But the Ice Warriors won't go-go-go-go-go...

River swore loudly and thumped her machine against the priceless artefact. The voice resumed.

- and the Doctor appeared with this huge hairy monster with a horn sticking out of his head! What a dreadful smelly creature and what a terrible noise! And it attacked Hep-Hep-Hep...

Another crackle.

Oh so many deaths. Peladon was heartbroken. He is such a lovely young man. So forgiving.
 Day 6.
 Well a conspiracy has been revealed. I knew it! There are so many rumours going around but Peladon's coronation is a great distraction. I am so worried about how much paperwork there is going to be after that terrible business with Arcturus but I am sure the Doctor will help me sort that out. When he and Princess Josephine

come out of that small blue box. Oh hold on diary I hear loud voices. Will be back soon...

'So many tales Doctor, but this is the last one.' She switched the setting on her machine...

The orange glow turned bright green and there was a loud pop of energy.

'You are now totally free. This tale is now someone else's, my love,' she murmured to herself.

'Did you succeed?' The Chief Curator was standing in the doorway.

'I tried everything. It was beyond my technology.' River shook her head sadly.

She bowed and left the room.

Chief Curator Doctor Manreck Hepesh 16th dropped the axe that he had hidden behind his back, happy that he remained the only living being to have been able to decipher the diary, but sad he had not had a chance to crack the skull of the disgusting alien female, who thought she knew it all. The honour of House Hepesh remained unblemished and he could die taking the secret of the diary with him.

Hepesh picked up the diary, reverently stroking the fur of the Royal Beast of Peladon, and placed it back in its case.

Ah Good, the Sea
The Sea Devils by **Christopher Luxford**, 46, London
First story: **The Sea Devils**

The Sea Devils is my first **Doctor Who** memory, specifically that shot of them coming out of the sea *en masse* in Episode Three. I was five.

Was it the first **Doctor Who** story I ever watched? I don't know; maybe it was, or maybe I'd seen the two previous stories of that season. I definitely remember seeing Alpha Centauri, but can't be sure which of the two Peladon stories that was in. Whether I'd seen them or not, it was that shot of the Sea Devils coming out of the Solent that stuck with me for the best part of forty years between first seeing it and buying the DVD for that all important repeat viewing.

Even if it wasn't the first **Doctor Who** story I ever saw, it is certainly the first **Doctor Who** episode I ever tried to re-enact in the school playground. I also remember pretending to be a Sea Devil when coming out of the sea on holiday, and not just that year either; I remember still being a Sea Devil when coming out of the sea well into the Tom Baker era. Though I can also remember being Moses pretending to part the sea – not sure what that says.

When I finally watched it again as an adult I realised just how little of the story I had actually remembered. Because I hadn't seen the previous year's season I had no prior knowledge of the Master, and because I hadn't seen the season before that I knew nothing of the Silurians. Continuity? I knew nothing of the concept, and probably wouldn't have cared if I did. What I did remember was the lizard men that came out of the sea wearing string vests (well, not really, but that's what my memory told me they were wearing) and carrying disc-shaped ray guns. I think I remembered the sea forts as well. I remember seeing them for real two-and-a-half years later when we went to Southsea for a holiday, and again a couple of years after that when we went to the Isle of Wight. Did I remember them from *The Sea Devils*? I don't know, but I've always been fascinated by them.

That's the thing about **Doctor Who**, it gets into your subconscious. All sorts of things lurk in the long term memory, all but forgotten, only to re-emerge years later. I've often wondered whether my support for Green political causes is down to having seen *The Green Death* at an impressionable age. I'm going to say that it is, whether it's true or not.

But what of *The Sea Devils*? What has it got that has stuck with me all these years?

Hard to say really, it is the only story from Season Nine that I have any definite memory of having watched it the first time around. There must be a reason for that, though I don't know what it is. From *The Three Doctors* on I can remember watching almost everything.

One thing that I didn't appreciate is that is an extremely Jon Pertwee story. The UNIT regulars are missing of course, but some sailors with guns fill part of their role with aplomb. Most of the rest of the Pertwee era is present and correct. There's somebody from the government for the Doctor to disagree with. There's his slightly uneasy relationship with the military top brass, and of course, there's a chase using unusual vehicles (seaborne vehicles in this case) and you can't get much more third Doctor than that. And to cap it all, this is also the only story in which he actually uses the phrase, 'Reverse the polarity of the neutron flow.' There's no Venusian Aikido unfortunately, but there is a sword fight, which is definitely cooler.

So, *The Sea Devils*. An archetypal third Doctor story that stuck in my memory for ever and sowed the seed of **Doctor Who** fandom in my five-year-old mind. Yeah, I think that's a fair description.

Thrills, Chills & Wagon Wheels...

The Mutants by **Philip Newman**, 48, Croydon, UK
First story: **The Invasion** (or *possibly* **Tomb of the Cybermen**)

Funny, isn't it, the things you remember-member-member when you let the years wash over you, transporting you to times and places long past? But I guess that's what comes of having had **Doctor Who** as a defining presence, a continuity, in my life for as long as I can remember. The past, present (and future) intertwined, sometimes so far away and yet always so tangible...

Variously and simultaneously, this extraordinary TV programme has been a source of excitement, inspiration, frustration, passion, curiosity, debate, research, pride, embarrassment, confidence, employment, laughter, fun, romance, friendship and pure, simple, unadulterated joy through the years. At times, it's been a comfort, a refuge even. I've had the opportunity and privilege to write, and have numerous features published, about it; of meeting – and interviewing – some of the many talented people involved in its production; to take part in a DVD commentary – hey, I've even appeared in it (well, if you count *Dimensions in Time* as canon!). No-one else in the Universe can say they've played a large green alien slug in Albert Square on primetime BBC1! Heaven knows how different a person I'd be if my parents had watched ITV on a Saturday night!

Amongst my formative years, 1972 seems somehow to shine brightest; it's not from whence my earliest memories come (that may be dancing around the living room to Sandie Shaw's *Puppet on a String* with a cushion on my head – no, just don't ask...!) but I do have particularly vivid recollections of, and an affection for, that year, not just in terms of **Doctor Who** (though Season Nine remains, for me, the definitive Pertwee series) but of other television shows, music and more personal events.

It was the year the stomping glam harmonies of The Sweet first entered my youthful consciousness (I still love those *ChinniChap* hits to this day), John Ryan's classic **The Adventures of Sir Prancelot** debuted on BBC1 (all 32 episodes of which *still* remain, incredibly, unreleased on DVD), but most significantly, I started Junior School. My form teacher, Mr Webb, was a jovial, rather rotund, flush-faced and flamboyant character – a young Pickwick if ever there was one – who was absolutely obsessed with puppets (especially Pelham Puppets) and Anthony Buckeridge's **Jennings** books, references to which permeated our lessons.

I enjoyed my very first Burton's Wagon Wheel courtesy of him; he would offer two halves of these new biscuit and marshmallow treats as prizes in our end-of-week vocabulary tests. I've loved words and chocolate ever since! I also began learning French, which would become my best and favourite subject at Senior school, so, 'Merci, Mme Parkinson, pour Allouette et Un Petit, d'Un Petit – *je ne les ai pas oubliés*!'

Yet even there, **Doctor Who** was never very far away. At a Book Fair in the school hall one lunch-time, I unexpectedly discovered a copy of Piccolo's **The Making of Doctor Who** amongst the piles of paperbacks we could order. It would be the first book I ever bought myself! I can still recall the excitement as my eyes lighted on the cover photograph of the Doctor and a Sea Devil. What I didn't bargain on, however, was the chilling, gut-wrenching sensation of absolute fear I felt as the pages fell open at a photograph of a group of impassive, gleaming silver Cybermen ... you know, the really scary ones from *The Moonbase.* I was suddenly thrown right back to a Saturday night and my vantage point *under* our black vinyl sofa, from where I watched, transfixed with terror, as a Cyberman emerged slowly from its shapeless cocoon... Of course, I know now that the moment I remembered could only really hail from the climax of the missing Episode Four of *The Invasion*, featuring a different type of Cyberman altogether, but my reaction to that picture was so strong that I must have seen – and been terrified by – the silver giants in one of their earlier appearances.

Other 'moments of terror' spring to mind too: the Auton shop-window dummies coming to life; space-helmeted Ambassadors of Death lying motionless behind a window then a visor being lifted to reveal a distorted mess of a face; the heat-operated Troll Doll of *Terror of the Autons* waking up in the back seat of a car and, later, running across the Doctor's lab bench; *The Mind of Evil's* Keller Machine, with its one-eyed brain and pulsing electronic theme by Dudley Simpson; the squishy brain-faced Guardian; Bok ... all etched forever on my memory, fused with that stomach-churning sense of fear and excitement.

And then, again, there was 1972.

For a seven-year-old, it couldn't have been any more exciting: Daleks, Ogrons, Aubrey Woods' superb Controller, Peladon, Arcturus, Alpha Centauri, the Ice Warriors, James Acheson's beautifully designed Mutts, the Crystal of Kronos, my particular favourites the Sea Devils and their scarily-strange coffin, Roger Delgado's incomparable Master at his suave and sinister best ... what a treat!

And of course, it had begun with *that* cover: 'The Daleks are Back!' the **Radio Times** had exclaimed above Frank Bellamy's sensational comic-strip style illustration. Indeed, for six months every year (yes, *six*!), scouring the pages of the **Radio Times** for the **Doctor Who** listing was a weekly thrill, enhanced whenever there was a photo or illustration to be found, let alone a cover feature! And it reminds me of a moment when my youthful logic completely dumbfounded my parents.

Imagine the scene then, as the next issue of **Radio Times** appeared after the climax of *The Sea Devils*. As usual, I headed straight for the Saturday TV listings.

'Look!' I remember saying, 'it's called *The Mutants*,' reading it in just that way, 'That means we're going we're to get giant ants...!'

'No,' my Dad patiently assured me, 'that's *not* what it means.'

Less than a week later, the Mutts appeared... Result!

Fond and funny memories indeed!

Time Out for The Time Monster

The Time Monster by **Blayne T. Jensen**, 45, Cedar Rapids, IA, USA / First story: **The Ark in Space**

I was eight years old in 1976, when **Logan's Run** was the coolest movie ever for an entire year.

Cut to 1980 and **Clash of the Titans**, with Ray Harryhausen's glorious stop-motion clay-moulded special effects of Medusa with her flickering rattlesnake tail and individual strands of hair, each a slithering viper.

Add in my insatiable diet of science-fiction reading as a teenager and my deep and abiding interest in Classical Mythology and my mind was abundantly primed to fill in the blanks.

So, when I saw *The Time Monster* on Iowa Public Television the first time in around about 1986, I was instantly enthralled by the ambitious storytelling, and **Doctor Who**'s inimitable fashion as a whole for linking the past and present together, by having the Doctor and Jo interact with figures from Greek mythology.

This was an extension of the original mandate of the series a decade earlier, where there was the emphasis on instructive and educational adventures with the Doctor, granddaughter Susan, and schoolteachers Ian and Barbara interacting with historical personages and finding themselves in the middle of key and/or watershed moments in world history, with the resultant drama of how to extricate themselves from the proceedings without becoming a part of the events and thus altering recorded history.

The Doctor and Jo, as a result of the Master's machinations, find themselves interacting with the Royal Court of Atlantis, not as the stuff of myth and legend or the object of derision for being a reluctant king on land, whose superpower is he can talk to fish, but as flesh and blood mortals with all of the complex motivations and yielding to the baser instincts of lust, greed, and the coveting of power which our species is prone to no matter what the age or era.

Many words have been written – quite a few of them by people too young to have known of the genre before the digital CGI jiggery-pokery used as a crutch today, in many instances as a substitute for storytelling – about the dime store ramshackle production values of stories such as *The Time Monster*, but much like Queen Galleia genuinely believed the Master to be a God because she had no frame of reference to think otherwise, so too do I see nothing wrong with the production design of *The Time Monster*, for that minimalist approach is what I was accustomed to and was the height of cutting-edge design for its day.

On one of her commentary tracks, Lalla Ward asserts that the lack of money spent on the series necessitated the production teams responsible for special effects, costume design, and make-up to use their imaginations to create the illusions which would bring the stories to life.

I, as a viewer, already accomplished at using my imagination to fill in the gaps to follow the ambitious and epic storylines which the broad strokes of the framework set out, suspended my disbelief and revelled in the Doctor facing the Minotaur, or King Dalios amusedly chuckling at the Master's futile attempts to hypnotise him.

Rather than be told what to think or what to feel via the overreliance on a digital paint box full of gimmickry, the stories that have always engaged me the most are the ones which place the effects in the service of telling a good story instead of the story being merely a narrative conceit to illustrate how clever computer programmers can be with their new toys.

I Am He And He Is Me
The Three Doctors by **David Guest**, 51, Heathfield, East Sussex, UK / First story: **The War Machines**

When I started joining groups like the **Doctor Who** Appreciation Society, going along to local group meetings, attending conventions and stocking up on poor quality videos in the late 1970s and early 1980s my mum remarked, 'I don't know why you're so into **Doctor Who** now – you never used to enjoy it!'

I was deeply stung by this foul slur: one of my earliest TV memories (along with **Watch With Mother** and **Blue Peter**) was seeing *The War Machines* menacing London; I had had a veritable army of Rolykins Daleks, a Dalek bath sponge, the Chad Valley **Doctor Who** Give-A-Show projector, and other toys; plastic croquet balls had regularly doubled as Yeti control spheres in childhood play; and I would howl with anguish at the thought of missing any episodes – many a time I would be dragged to my aunt and uncle's to watch a second Doctor story on their TV with a record player on the top as they were closer to where we were on a Saturday afternoon!

So I approached the tenth anniversary story *The Three Doctors* with some excitement – though to be honest I can't particularly recall being aware that it *was* the tenth anniversary. Jon Pertwee's UNIT era had kept me glued to the screen, Patrick Troughton seemed like an old friend, and William Hartnell might have been a dim memory to this eleven-year-old just after Christmas in 1972, but he was certainly not a stranger.

When you read reviews of *The Three Doctors* nowadays, it's a sure bet that someone will say, 'Ah, but it's not actually very good!' That might be the view of those who never saw the original broadcast and are watching it through those rose-tinted glasses of hindsight (even those who saw it for the first time less than ten years later during **The Five Faces of Doctor Who** season in 1981) but for those of us who did, watching on dark winter evenings at the end of 1972 and beginning of 1973, it was thrilling and tremendous fun.

I had proudly purchased a copy of Piccolo's **The Making of Doctor Who** book in the summer and had devoured all the information contained within. In these days of guides galore about the series, it is hard to put across just how treasured this book was to fans in the early 1970s. Not only was it a factual run-down of stories but there was also the extra detail of the Doctor's trial and hints of much more mystery surrounding this enigmatic Time Lord. It really set the scene for *The Three Doctors*: many of the articles and photos jogged happy memories of previous adventures and we could only guess at how and why they would meet.

I seem to remember the story coming along almost without fanfare – no surprise, when you think about it, given that the series had only just celebrated its *ninth* anniversary! I certainly recall getting very excited when upon opening the Christmas edition of the **Radio Times** there was a teaser for the New Year issue and its iconic 'Which Doctor is Who?' cover.

I was very much into my stride with the Pertwee era. We had enjoyed three seasons of his stories already and there was no hint that the coming year would see the departure of a much-loved companion, the last appearance of a perfect villainous actor, and the arrival of an even greater-loved companion. Even the **Radio Times** Tenth Anniversary Special wasn't around to distract me just yet. The only warning of what was to come – and it led to much urgent discussion with friends – was the trailer with its jingly version of the theme music, which didn't seem quite right somehow.

As I sat with my cheese sandwich and mini roll (bound to have been – that was my usual fare for a Saturday evening), having tittered my way through **Basil Brush**, *The Three Doctors* initially seemed a very cosy way to end one year and begin another. There was something that made me a bit nervous of the Gel Guards – I think it was memories of **Marianne Dreams** and those moving rocks - though once they started 'speaking' they became quite sweet, and many a school dinner was peppered with cries of, 'They're forcing us to eat Gel creatures!' when jelly was served.

There can be little doubt that the relationship between the second and third Doctors was a highlight - their bickering was enough to amuse any child - but even then there seemed to be something serious and a bit sad about 'the old man Doctor' having so little to do and being trapped in the time eddy. I remember being told, 'Of course he's *very* old, dear,' as though that explained it all. And I explained knowledgably to any who would listen who those men in the flowing robes were - I knew it all from *The War Games*.

I loved Omega. It was a great performance, and you felt really sorry for him; and he was the character I always wanted to be in school playground recreations of the story. The cry of despair at the end chills me to this day. I do remember anxious glances from my mum to see if Omega being all anti-mattered out was going to give me nightmares, but she needn't have worried.

As I write this, I have before me the new action figures of Jo, the Brigadier, and a Gel Guard. And I have a warm comfortable feeling inside of childhood innocent pleasures. This was, after all, the *original* Doctors' reunion and even to me then it felt like something truly significant. In retrospect I just wish the Brig had uttered his infamous line from ten years later on January 20th 1973 - 'Wonderful chap, both of him,' *just* misses the poignancy of the historic moment.

Intellectual Silliness
Carnival of Monsters by **Tom Jordan**, 21, Northampton
First story: **Planet of the Daleks**

Doctor Who teaches us many things: the powers of friendship, the importance of knowledge over strength and to never, ever trust a shop window dummy. But something I often feel is overlooked, especially in light of the Serious and Important science fiction and fantasy, is the sense of silliness.

Not silliness in a true sense of the term. Anything that is truly silly tends to also be bit rubbish. Proper silliness can't carry the weight of candyfloss, let alone something as magnificently weighty as **Doctor Who** occasionally can be, when it puts the effort in. Take the collected works of **Monty Python** for example, widely regarded as both very good and also very silly. There are those sketches that everyone remembers, and everyone has their favourite film. The attraction of it, at least the surface detail, is that it seems all deliciously lightweight and fluffy and ever so silly. It really isn't. Beneath that feathered exterior lies something with a bit of intellectual heft, or satire, or insane logic that carries the silliness. That's what makes it enjoyable. It stimulates far more than something that is simply unrelentingly grim.

Carnival of Monsters falls under that example of deceitful silliness so easily that there are some who do take it simply at face value. Vorg, in a line I'm sure everyone reading this is familiar with, says, 'Our purpose is to amuse, simply to amuse. Nothing serious, nothing political.' But of *course* it's serious. Of *course* it's political. Why else would Robert Holmes even insert that into the script if he didn't know what he was doing? It may well be said by a man who has a plastic hat that must make his head extremely hot, but anyone who takes Vorg's line at face value is very much denying themselves a richer experience of all the silliness therein.

I can't really express quite how clever the silliness is to *Carnival of Monsters*. It works, like all good children's drama, in stages. For the grown-ups, there's the blustering political plot constantly working in the wings. For the industry types, there's the satire with Vorg and Shirna being the type of BBC light entertainment duo that nowadays would probably appear on **Britain's Got Talent**. For those paying attention, it's a brilliantly constructed plot that works on several layers, literally, thematically and metaphorically. But on top of all that, the kids get to enjoy the Doctor and his companion being chased by the hideous, terrifying and anagrammatic Drashigs throughout the Miniscope.

Bob Holmes was a very, very clever man.

There aren't many other shows that could do the kind of intricate and bizarre plotting that **Doctor Who** can get away with. Most other shows don't revel in the silliness that **Doctor Who** does, and that's exactly what I love about it. Showrunners of the programme have talked in the past about the great strengths of the show, and any number of fans could come up with any number of reasons for its continued success, whether that be the Daleks, the concept of regeneration, or the 'flexible format' (a concept I don't think is as true as is made out to be, but that's another essay), but I reckon they all boil down to the same thing, really. It is the silliness we fall in love with.

But I've said before, pure silliness doesn't work. Silliness needs to be strait-laced. It needs to treat itself with the utter conviction of intelligence that a show, any show, deserves. Sure, the Doctor may be fighting tax collectors on Pluto, or an absorbing creature from Clom, or blue vampires from the future, but he does it with conviction. The moment he doesn't, the silliness is insurmountable. Thank goodness Tom Baker was never allowed to turn to the screen to reassure the kids that it's pretend. How else are we supposed to take blood-sucking rocks seriously?

Of course, I'm applying this all retroactively but there could be no better version of the Doctor to tackle this story than Jon Pertwee. Jon is the straight man with a wealth of comedic acting in his background. He knows exactly how to pitch his performance to make sure that everything comes off. His interactions with Jo are rarely bettered than they are here, and his utter confusion with Vorg and his indignant anger at the Miniscope's existence make sense of the colourful costumes, the dog-headed worm-things, the plesiosaurus attacking the SS Bernice. The Doctor is the intellectual heft that keeps our silliness grounded, even in the face of Jo's awful pink jumper. I can't imagine for one second that any other actor would put in quite the same sedate commanding performance as Jon gives.

He's intellectual in the face of silliness, but silly in the face of intelligence. Like the best of **Doctor Who**, and this is some of very best of **Doctor Who**, it constantly plays with your expectations of how it should work. It's definitely silly. But it's as silly as *Gridlock* is, and that's the best intelligent rumination on the nature of faith to feature giant crabs ever written. *Carnival of Monsters* is a rumination on entertainment and the many variations of it, from the ethics, the purpose, the effect – it's practically a commentary on itself, without ever feeling preachy about it. Should you want, you can access all of that, it's there for the taking. But there's still a cracking adventure story about monsters and dinosaurs and space aliens, and all the silly fun of it all as well, and I love it for everything it does. This is what makes it the Best Show Ever. This is **Doctor Who**.

Losing the Space War
Frontier in Space by **Jon Cooper**, 31, London, UK
First story: **Remembrance of the Daleks**

It's an afternoon in early January, and the colour has been leached from the rural landscape by a low sun in a cloudy sky. Everything looks deader than it really is, with the horizon washed out like a watercolour. I'm on a train back home, heading into London.

This, like the muted look of the fields outside the windows, isn't quite the reality. I'm not heading home because technically, I don't have a home (I've taken to telling friends I'm not homeless, just 'Domestically Challenged').

If I do have a home, a true one, I've just left it. In the basement of that home there is something I left behind fifteen years ago. Something that's been rotting for quite a while now, and that didn't really deserve that treatment.

The basement is very damp. From time to time, frogs live there. The walls are covered in repurposed bookcases but they are useless – useless in as much as they contain only useless things, bric-a-brac, old bottles and broken things, and useless in that the other detritus piled around them makes them impossible to actually get at.

Like the land outside the window, everything here is in muted shades – mustard yellows, mud browns, the dry-blood red of pitted bricks. In the corner, hidden by a stepladder and a bed sheet spattered with emulsion is a bookcase with the word JONATHAN carved into the top. It holds on its shelves, like so much else here, something discarded, forgotten, no longer cared for; perhaps eighty **Doctor Who** VHS cassettes that are slowly growing mouldy.

For me, collecting the BBC's VHS releases was what my fandom was all about. Is there are purer way of showing your devotion to the show than owning the show itself? Sure I had books, t-shirts and the Dapol toys with the limbs fallen off, but these were always somehow less special to me than those magic boxes. Much like the TARDIS, their name was an acronym, they were bigger on the inside, and dammit if they didn't make you travel back in time.

I loved the uniform design, too. When that shelf still saw the light of day and my collection slowly grew, that section of my room's wall began to slowly fill with black, the titles picked out below the iconic diamond logo. And then there was the artwork – to this day I love Alister Pearson's covers, and would take them any day over the characterless Photoshop collages that adorn the DVDs. A show with so much character deserves something more than what looks, you have to admit, just a bit like a Sixth Form art project. The show, to me, was art. Quite right that the cover should be true art too.

But then the covers changed, and so did I.

It was *The Green Death* that did it, with its gaudy foil title and the cover on the spine. Sure, there had been different covers before, but this was radical. It just didn't sit, it looked out of place and overcomplicated between *Frontier in Space* and *The Time Warrior*. I'd say it nagged me, but at this point other things had begun to command my attention. Up until then, my general daily routine had been School-Homework-**Doctor Who** VHS. But the latter was dropping out out of favour for other sci-fi and horror (more often chosen on their obscurity than their quality), nervous phone calls with girls, illicit dope smoking and even my own first tentative attempts at writing. I'd found other things to fill my time – I was growing up. I don't think I bought another VHS after that.

The dust settled on the boxes and I'd wave away the collection to cooler friends and girls as *just something I did when I was a kid*. I moved out, relinquished any right to a room in my family home. My parent's taste in decoration – William Morris prints and upmarket chintz – tended to clash with a looming black cliff-face of classic science fiction. It was basement time.

Every time I go back I find myself in the cellar, and not strictly because it's cool enough to keep my beer at a perfectly drinkable temperature. Like the affection I have for **Doctor Who**, those tapes will always be there. They're no longer worth selling, probably aren't even watchable, and yet they haven't been binned and neither are they going to be. On my sporadic visits home I'll pull that paint-sullied bed sheet aside and look at them, run my fingers across the spines until the tips are covered in condensation and grit. Pull one out and admire the artwork. Read the back blurb. Remember.

Like old memories, these old tapes aren't on show. They're buried, neglected ... maybe even a source of embarrassment. But like memories they're *still there*. They'll always be there. I like to think that when I've found myself a true home they'll travel with me, a reminder of a part of myself and the boy I used to be – a boy that sometimes, thanks to age and cynicism, depression and over-thinking, I desperately feel the need to reconnect to. The boy that could just enjoy hours of his old tapes, revelling in one story while plotting which to watch next, and next after that. Losing himself in adventures.

Right now though, I just don't know how to do that. Perhaps the tapes will help me get there, someday.

And as for *Frontier in Space*, well, as some of you may know, the Target novelisation of that Season Ten gem was titled **Doctor Who and the Space War**. Well, Jon Cooper had a Space War too, a battle for the space in a life that was really only just beginning. As the sad tale of the old tapes tells, literally and figuratively, this was one battle that the good Doctor lost.

Defining Courage
Planet of the Daleks by **Jack Dexter**, 43, London, UK
First story: **Full Circle**

Behind the sofa...? I'm not too sure. I remember retreating to the kitchen, though – terrified! Of course, retrospectively it was a pretty futile gesture: peeping through the crack of an ajar door, awestruck at the kaleidoscope of sound and vision emanating from the telly in the front room, too scared to stay and watch and too entranced not to. This was how I spent countless Saturday afternoons in 1973 when the **Doctor Who** title sequence began. I probably missed more than I saw – but then that's fear for you.

A well-read edition of the **Doctor Who and the Planet of the Daleks** Target novelisation sat proudly amidst at least two-dozen other **Doctor Who** paperbacks on the shelves of an oak-panelled bookcase in the school library. 1982 was my first term at a new prep school and last year I had learnt about regeneration – this year my attention had turned to the novelisations. The thing about the **Doctor Who** novels was that the reader didn't have their suspension of disbelief punctured by wobbly sets and men in rubber suits. In an era where it was rare to see an out-of-season repeat, the novels painted the scenes of the scripts across the landscape of a young mind with panoramic vastness.

After a very long wait that followed a staggeringly climactic end of season story I was eager to gather whatever information on the series' past I could glean, and in 1982 this primarily meant books (or the **Doctor Who Monthly** magazine – regular VHS releases were still a few years away). I knew the Doctor was a Time Lord and that he'd regenerated before – several times, apparently – and that once he'd looked like *him*: a white-haired man in a velvet jacket, one of two men wrestling with a Dalek on the cover of the Target book. It was nearly a decade on since I'd hidden in the kitchen from a haunting title sequence and there wasn't much I recalled about the Jon Pertwee era, but I was fascinated.

My first clear memory of actually watching *Planet of the Daleks* was in 1987. By this stage of my fanaticism I'd amassed a small collection of **Doctor Who** stories on VHS from fellow fans I'd met at conventions who had been kind enough to provide pirated copies. They were primarily episodes from the 1960s and 1970s. In the case of *Planet of the Daleks* I was disappointed when I received it to discover that some of the episodes were in black and white (and assumed that there had been some fault in the recording process).

1973 seemed particularly dated by the late 1980s, but I had learned to appreciate the series on a level beyond the shortcomings of its production values and - as productions go - *Planet of the Daleks* fared rather well. There are extensive interior TARDIS scenes, which was uncommon throughout the 1970s; the colour separation overlay was seamless; it has a strong supporting cast, and is an enjoyable and epic tale of courage and survival against the odds.

Terry Nation's script effectively toasts the tenth anniversary of the original Dalek story and feels reassuringly reminiscent of it, with several scenarios echoing many of Nation's previous Dalek scripts as well as some touching and rare examples of inter-series continuity. From Rebec hiding in the Dalek casing and only just escaping in the nick of time to Jo forming a romantic bond with a Thal, the revisited story elements work just as well ten years on from its progenitor and besides, the children of 1973 would never have seen the original in 1963.

I was fortunate enough to meet Jon Pertwee in 1989. He was appearing at the Bristol Hippodrome in a stage production called **The Ultimate Adventure**. I managed to corner him outside and he posed for a photograph with me - what a wonderful man.

I love this series, its spirit, its very concept - a police box, larger on the inside than on the outside that can travel anywhere in time and space. I love the way that, over the years, it has encouraged me to think outside the box, to see things from others' points of view, to consider the seemingly impossible.

I remember 1973 - glam rock, the Osmonds, David Cassidy, the Jackson Five, and a frightened child who hides in a kitchen, trying to muster the courage to watch a science fiction television programme; in 2013, forty years later, and a day after the sad demise of one of the serial's principal supporting cast members, Bernard Horsfall, I remember something else, something I'd completely forgotten - *Planet of the Daleks* contains one of my favourite lines of the entire series of that programme:

'Courage isn't just a matter of not being frightened, you know. It's being afraid and doing what you have to do anyway...'

Jon Pertwee, 1973

'I'm Up On the Slag Heap With the Professor'
The Green Death by **Brad Jones**, 35, York, UK
First story: **The Dæmons**

It started out of curiosity.

I didn't intend to become a fan of **Doctor Who** at all. I was already some three years later to the party. The classic series had ended in 1989 and here I was, aged fifteen in 1992, having never really seen the show at all. It wasn't on in our house. I was scared fairly easily so never really wanted to watch it. I do recall the starfield title sequence, but other than that it was standard Saturday night ITV fare. We're talking the mid-1980s here when the show returned to Saturdays. So while most of you had the Rani, the Borad and a brightly coloured coat, the Jones family had **Blind Date**, **Beadle's About** and Les Dennis ... in a brightly coloured coat.

I'd read somewhere about the re-colourised *The Dæmons* and was curious to see how a programme could have had its coloured returned. At this stage, I wasn't aware of the extent of all the junkings. So, I sat down to watch Episode One. I couldn't understand a word of it. Where's the TARDIS? Where are the Daleks? The Daleks are in every single episode aren't they? Who's the evil-looking chap with the goatee? Why are the army involved? Why isn't it set in space? I knew nothing of exile, the Master, and UNIT. I switched it off, rather annoyed with myself for not understanding it.

I tried again the following year. *Genesis of the Daleks*. This was better. It seemed to fit my idea of what **Doctor Who** was. It was a long time before I tried a Pertwee again. I read up on the history of the show. Ah! Got it! It put *The Dæmons* totally in context. In that first year I managed to buy quite a few videos of the series, so to see a terrestrial repeat was quite a rare occurrence. We had *Planet of the Daleks* in late 1993 (can you imagine a twenty-five minute black and white episode being shown on prime time BBC1 now?) and then we had this. *The Green Death*. Instead of nicely slotted in on a Friday evening, this was placed on a Sunday around midday. An odd slot perhaps, but we'd often had vintage programmes shown at that time.

The Green Death is one of the few serials I've watched as it was originally intended, that is one episode per week as opposed an omnibus on UK Gold (usually hacked to shreds) or all in one go on a video or DVD. It's also a serial I'd describe as part of my 'comfort zone.' I get a lot of those with Pertwee episodes. *The Sea Devils, Inferno*; they're just familiar to the extent that you can almost have them on as background noise and still know what's going on.

If you can actually have a 'favourite' TARDIS materialisation scene, then this is it for me. The TARDIS materialises in the UNIT office as the Doctor rushes to answer the telephone. Just love it. It's seamless. And *The Green Death* itself is comforting in the sense that you just want to sit round and eat high protein fungus and drink wine with them all, maybe doing some sculpture between glasses. It is dare I say, cosy. Yes, the colour separation overlay is awful, we know that. But that's its charm. The way the credits are upside down on a couple of episodes, the switch between studio and VT for the scenes with Bessie. And I haven't even mentioned the word maggot yet. The pure delight of Pertwee dressed as a milkman and cleaning woman. It shows that he doesn't have to play it straight all the time.

It's the second time I saw a companion leave too. The first was *The Chase* with Ian and Barbara. This of course was Jo. You can't help feel a tear and, unlike in the new series, you know full well you won't see them again.

I never bought the serial on video. So my copies were those early 1994 repeats from BBC2. There's a fair amount crammed onto the DVD, being a relatively early release. The *Global Conspiracy* short is very odd but it's great to see how the actors have aged since, particularly

Stewart Bevan. What would have been nice I guess, is a *Now and Then* featurette. I have no idea if the pit is still there or what happened to it, but these are always the highlights of the range to me.

I do have something to admit. I haven't read the Target novelisation of *The Green Death*. Or *any* Target novelisation. I never saw the point as I have access to the episodes. The one thing about **Doctor Who** that I like, in fact what got me into it in the first place, is that each era is tied to just that, an era. They look the part, they feel the part. Special effects, music, all help place it in a timeframe in my mind. Which I guess is why I'm not that fussed with the new series. It's too shiny, fast, loud. I like my stories to plod (unless they're *The Web Planet, The Mutants* or the *The Monster of Peladon*!). Yes, you could have *Inferno* without all the parallel universe stuff in, but would it be as good? No. Probably why I've never been into Big Finish either. They sound *new*. It's a funny philosophy I know, but as a vintage television fan, it's what matters. The joys of seeing an old **Nationwide** or **Blue Peter** clip; I love it.

Anyway, next time I get my hair cut and I'm asked if I'd like 'something for the weekend,' I'll ask for a few extra. I'll only be making maggots out of them after all...

The Time Warrior and Sarah Jane Smith

The Time Warrior by **Tony Kenealy**, 47, San Diego
First story: **Spearhead from Space**

It was 1973, Saturday 15th December, and just ten days before Christmas. I was eight years old and the excitement was building, but it had nothing to do with the coming holidays. A glance at my Timex watch (the one with the luminous numbers that could be seen under the bed covers at night) showed me that it was nearly five o'clock and time to get a move on. I had a very important date that I could not be late for. Rushing into the front room, I jumped onto the sofa, eyes glued to the small black and white TV in the corner.

It was the start of the new series of **Doctor Who**, with a brand new story: *The Time Warrior*. What was the new monster? What horrifying sight would greet me this time as I battled side by side with the Doctor to save the world from another alien menace? Over the past four years I had already survived shop dummies that came to life with guns in their hands, monsters coming out of the sea with flashlights that could kill you, a demon that looked like a church statue, and giant maggots. I had even survived the Daleks!

I was getting nervous now and the programme hadn't even started yet. I edged my way to the end of the sofa (not behind it because that would be too silly) where I could still see the TV screen, but near the door - just in case...

The programme started and the titles rolled. They looked different, but the Doctor was there, still the same, still 'my' Doctor. I knew Jo Grant had left the Doctor after the giant maggots and I had guessed he would have someone new to travel with him (deep down I was hoping for the call, but it never came). I was not prepared for someone as amazing as Sarah Jane Smith and as soon as she appeared, I was smitten. She was different: she was brave, and wasn't going to be pushed around by anyone; she even demanded to go back into the enemy castle with Hal to capture the Doctor. I watched her every scene with my eyes glued to the TV. I had even forgotten to be worried about the new monster!

But how could Sarah Jane not trust the Doctor? How could she think he was transporting all the scientists back in time and that he was the one helping Irongron and his men? He was the Doctor, he was the good guy, and he always helped people. If they were on opposite sides, was I going to have to decide between Sarah Jane and the Doctor? I was confused. How could I ever choose? Luckily, it all worked out in the end. It was a great relief when Sarah Jane realised that the Doctor was not the bad guy after all and they began working together to defeat Lynx and Irongron.

Over the coming weeks, I could hardly wait for the next episode and by the end of the season, I was hooked. Every Saturday night, I was there, not only to see the Doctor, but to see Sarah Jane Smith and to share in their adventures. Even the shock of my Doctor changing into a new Doctor was lessened by the fact that Sarah Jane was still there beside him.

1973 was definitely a turning point in my relationship with **Doctor Who.** It was already a part of my regular routine on a Saturday night, but from that moment on it became a major part of my life. I can still remember walking through the arcade in Bedford and there in the window of a newspaper shop was a magazine with my Doctor on the cover. I dragged my Mum in to take a look and there it was – the **Radio Times Doctor Who** Special with details of all the old stories plus the new ones still to come for the season. There was a picture of Sarah Jane looking terrified pressed up against a wall with Lynx in the background (I never did find that scene in the actual episodes). It also contained a plan to build a real Dalek and all for only thirty pence! I read the magazine from cover to cover, devouring everything I saw. This was the start of my **Doctor Who** collection which I have continued adding to over the years and which has travelled with me all over the world.

But good things don't last forever, and on the 23rd of October 1976, the TARDIS disappeared and the Doctor left Sarah Jane Smith behind to travel back to Gallifrey. I didn't want the Doctor to leave her behind or Sarah Jane to leave me behind, but time moves on.

But I have never forgotten my first love and 33 years later the same feelings returned when Sarah Jane Smith met up with the Doctor once again. I knew how he felt when he saw her as the same lump was in my throat. And when the new series of **The Sarah Jane Adventures** started, I was eight years old all over again.

Sadly, after the death of Elizabeth Sladen in April 2011, there will be no more Sarah Jane Smith, but I will never forget her. The Doctors may change, but there will always only be one Sarah Jane Smith, and she will always be my Sarah.

Walking With (Rubber) Dinosaurs

Invasion of the Dinosaurs by **Ion Williams**, 45, London
First story: **Invasion of the Dinosaurs**

As a kid, *Invasion of the Dinosaurs* was responsible for fuelling my rather worrying obsession with prehistoric monsters, one which lasted for most of the remainder of the1970s. I'd get ridiculously hyper if anything even vaguely dinosaury came on the television. I remember the film **Gorgo** unexpectedly being shown one school holiday afternoon. I was so excited I rushed into the kitchen to let my mother know the good news and I can still picture now the way she looked at me in slightly bemused puzzlement, happy at my joy yet not quite sure if it was all that healthy for her son to be so ecstatic about a big wobbly lizard on ITV. Around about the same time my Auntie Maud bought me a dinosaur encyclopaedia, which was chock-full of illustrations of every dinosaur imaginable, roaming about in their natural habitats. I'd stare at the pages for hours and hours, trying to imagine myself wandering around amongst a herd of Brontosaurus as they waded through their swamp, or running away from a Tyrannosaurus, just like the Doctor and Sarah had done in modern day London. In 1975 a new comic came out called **Monster Fun** and one of the strips featured the ongoing story of two children, John and Jenny, battling a load of electronic film-set dinosaurs that had escaped into the countryside after having miraculously come to life during a freak thunder storm. Scenarios included John riding a triceratops pillion as it charged towards an intercity train (I wonder if Chris Chibnall had a subscription to this too?), a load of cavemen ransacking a supermarket, and one of the kids falling off the end of a pier into the sea and being attacked by an Ichthyosaurus. I bought the comics again off eBay recently, the originals having fallen to pieces more years ago than I care to remember. It cost a bloody arm and a leg. But as you get older, nostalgia seems to become more and more important.

Then along came the 1980s and as a sulky, overtly hormonal teenager, I'd shut myself away in my bedroom reading my Target collection (and no, that's not a euphemism!); **The Dinosaur Invasion** was *always* a favourite. Apart from anything else it had the best cover ever. You know ... the one that taught us all that the sound a Pterodactyl makes is 'KKLAK!'; although I also had the one with the T-Rex sight-seeing in front of St Paul's (but I always thought that owed more to **The Valley of the Gwangi** than to **Doctor Who**). In the late 1980s/early 1990s I went to live with a bunch of hippies (well, it seemed like a good idea at the time). This marked the point in my life when I first became politicised. Before I knew it, I found myself empathising with Adam and Ruth and the rest of the 'People' aboard the spaceship. I joined Greenpeace and CND and went on demonstrations against the Poll Tax and the Iraqi War. It was the first time I'd really thought about the story in terms of it being anything other than a runaround featuring charmingly ropey prehistoric monsters. All of a sudden I 'got' what it was all about, and I found myself hoping that the government evacuated to Harrogate was a Tory one, and that they were having to slum in it some awful, rundown, northern B&B, with polyester sheets on the bed and an outside loo. Post-hippy period I discovered clubbing. I'd go out at a weekend and get absolutely trashed, and, on the occasions when I actually made it back home, I'd fall asleep (or pass out) as a copy of *Invasion of the Dinosaurs* that I'd made my mum tape off satellite television and post down to me in London, comfortingly played on the video.

In 2012 the DVD came out at last. Again, I was ridiculously excited. For one thing, I couldn't wait to show my partner, William. Even though he never really 'got' the whole **Doctor Who** thing, because he loved me, he attempted to love the show. Sadly, I never got the chance to share my favourite story with him. Will was suddenly taken ill at the beginning of July 2012 and died a month later after a mercifully short illness. He was only fifty. The same age as **Doctor Who** is now. How ironic. My world fell apart. In the immediate aftermath I couldn't eat and I couldn't sleep. During the long hours, as I waited for my parents to make the journey down from Wales, I again turned to *Invasion of the Dinosaurs*. This time I watched it as I cried my eyes out, desperately wanting its comforting familiarity to wash over me and restore the childhood innocence I possessed when I first saw it as a seven-year-old, hoping against all hope it would somehow miraculously return me – just like the passengers on the spaceship – to a simpler, more innocent time … one before I knew what it was like to lose someone I loved.

As I watch the story again now, I swear I can hear Will chortling in my ear as the Doctor and Sarah are attacked by a rather nippy pterodactyl, sniggering as the radioactively green stegosaurus uninterestedly hangs around the back of a warehouse looking for all the world as if it's trying to have a crafty fag, and unashamedly laughing out loud (and probably pointing) as the most unferocious Tyrannosaurus rex in the history of television has a bit of a growl at Pertwee's equally unconvincing stunt double.

Unfortunately, we all have to grow up. Life forces us to. But while I've got *Invasion of the Dinosaurs*, I know I'll always have some kind of an escape.

The First Time
Death to the Daleks by **Andy Davidson**, 42, Surrey, UK
First story: **The Sea Devils**

I watched *Pyramids of Mars* with my three children recently. We browsed through the vast collection of classic **Doctor Who** stories on Netflix, debating the relative merits of Mummies, Daleks and Voords before highlighting the episode we (oh, alright then, I) had agreed upon and pressed play. As we were plunged into the time vortex, I tried explaining that such luxuries as on-demand media were as much a fantasy as the TARDIS when I was their age.

Their reaction was much the same as mine when my parents talked of satsumas and chalk for Christmas and their 'Shut up Dad, **Doctor Who**'s on,' was met with a mixture of resignation and fatherly geek pride. But spare a little sympathy for those of us who grew up in an age when the only chance we had to watch **Doctor Who** was when the BBC permitted. There's a good reason why **The Five Faces of Doctor Who** repeats are still talked about; it's all we had back then and the idea of owning episodes was the stuff of fantasy.

The advent of home video meant unlimited rice pudding for many of us, but there was a small, increasingly furtive group who bought the wrong machine. While some were basking in the glory of *The Brain of Morbius*, others had to make do with the possibility of tracking down one of the four copies of *Revenge of the Cybermen* available on Betamax, or persuading a friendly shopkeep that, yes, my grandmother was perfectly prepared to be sold on in exchange for an L750 of *Day of the Daleks*. As VHS swept the world, those of us who chose the format that dare not speak its name were increasingly left out in the cold and I had to content myself with my off-air recordings of *The Trial of a Time Lord*. Don't talk to me about the catharsis of spurious morality.

Then, one day, my dad came home with a VHS recorder. He hadn't even unboxed it before I was on my bike, speeding into town as fast as my spindly teenage legs would go. I'm not even sure that I took the time to climb off the thing when I made it to Woolworths and instead rode up to the counter brandishing my life savings and demanding their entire stock of **Doctor Who** videos. They had, I think, three.

I was sixteen years old, I'd known the pleasures of a woman, the intoxication of alcohol, the satisfaction of fine food and basked on exotic beaches. I should add that I now have a life, but back then none of those things came close to what I was about to do. After a spectacular teenage tantrum I managed to clear the house. **Doctor Who** was a solitary pleasure in those days. That's another thing today's youngsters no longer have to contend with.

I knew every word of every Target novelisation, but to finally hold in my hand a capsule that contained such power; to actually watch those hallowed adventures... My head was filled with vast spacescapes, impossibly beautiful craft and hideous aliens. With trembling hands I loaded *Death to the Daleks* into the machine.

And, minutes later, I stopped. Where was the desolate landscape? The legendary city of the Exxilons? This was just a bunch of people mucking about in a quarry to the occasional tuneful fart of an off-camera quartet. I was crushed. Now, bear in mind that by this point *Time and the Rani* hadn't aired, but it was the single biggest televisual disappointment of my young life.

I now realise that the reason for that disappointment was that I had no context by which to judge the classics. The memory may well cheat but all I had to go on was a decade of reading and rereading Terrance Dicks' novelisation with its spectacular cover of fiery Dalek destruction and the occasional tantalising picture in the pages of **DWM** and the hallowed **Doctor Who Monster Book**. It was inevitable that my expectations would far exceed the reality of a 1970s BBC budget but I hadn't even considered the possibility until then. I don't know quite what I was expecting, but it certainly wasn't *that*.

With the scales well and truly dropped from my eyes, I hesitantly tried again and tried to appreciate what the BBC had managed to achieve all those years ago with £2.89, some old rags from War on Want and a nearby quarry. And the more I watched, the more I enjoyed.

Okay, so the city of the Exxilons may not be quite up to the standards of the other 699 Wonders of the Universe, but Bellal really is a delightful little chap. The Daleks have rarely been this much fun, with their strap-on machine guns and blind panic every time one of them falls foul of the local wildlife (and Bellal aside, it's all pretty wild). And Joy is ... well, she's lovely.

The *Death to the Daleks* I watched bore no more than a passing resemblance to the one I'd read about. It wasn't as grand, glossy or action packed as I had fantasised, but it was somehow all the more fun for it. How could I fail to love a story where the Daleks are defeated by nothing more than a grumpy Scotsman in a bag of mud? Watch the scene where a Dalek overseer is destroyed by the creature in the lake ... one of its friends turns nervously to its neighbour, whose eyestalk droops slowly to the ground. Any story where the greatest evil in the universe has a Laurel & Hardy moment or another self destructs through the sheer guilt of losing a prisoner is all right with me.

No amount of special effects could replace Jon Pertwee at his patronising best and Daleks on the verge of a nervous breakdown. *Death to the Daleks* is quite simply magnificent.

The Power of The Doctor
The Monster of Peladon by **Steven Dieter**, 42, Ottawa, Canada / First story: **The Monster of Peladon**

My very first introduction to **Doctor Who** came through the last part of *The Monster of Peladon,* although my first entire story was *Planet of the Spiders.* At that time – it was 1981 or 1982 – viewers in the Canadian province of Ontario were limited in the television outlets on which the series was available. The primary source was TVOntario, the province's television education channel, which would broadcast one episode each week on Saturday night, with a re-broadcast on Thursday nights. Of course, the time lag of seven years between original broadcast and re-transmission was both fortuitous and painful: by the time fans finally had the chance to see a regeneration on-screen, we were already aware of the next, new regeneration occurring in the United Kingdom.

So, what was it about this series that captured the attention and imagination of a pre-teen in small-town Canada? After all, wasn't this an environment of hockey and lacrosse? These were all very well, but they weren't for me – and perhaps that was what intrigued me about **Doctor Who**. But why did this particular episode appeal to me? I watched the DVD prior to taking pen in hand, to see if anything was triggered deep within my synapses.

Overall, the serial itself didn't spark any specific memory or feeling. I mean, it's a decent story – and I still think the Ice Warriors, although clumsy and cumbersome, are pretty neat. (Dan Abnett's **The Silent Stars Go By** was a very quick read). Elisabeth Sladen hit a nice chord, and Jon Pertwee struck me as the kind of grandfather I might like to have if he had a British accent. The workers in the mines struggling for their rights, working for their Queen – I guess this resonated in me as a Canadian whose families had been workers their entire lives, loyal to the Crown. But it wasn't just this cool storyline with a neat fuzzy monster which captured my attention.

To me, the attraction to the series was, in part, escapism. The power of this weekly event, the ability to commandeer the television for the Thursday evening repeat broadcast was the true appeal. My personal world was turbulent at that time, and those thirty minutes opened up a world into which I could escape. It was also about the only time when my step-father was out of the house, and not able to control the remote.

And boy, did I escape. Between broadcasts of new (and old) stories on the nearest Public Broadcasting Service affiliate, buying every Target novel I could find, and ordering items from the UK, I had my fill of material. I also found solace in the **Doctor Who** Information Network (the Canadian fan club) where I made pen pals across North America, was a member of the local fan group, and inadvertently began a career in writing and reviewing with FASA's version of the role-playing game as my fodder, and DWIN's fanzine as my medium.

Now, over thirty years later, my life is richer and in many ways more complete because of the series. Technology has broadened the base of new friends made, and increased both outlets for my writing, and sources for the books, audios, and toys that are now filling my many bookshelves. The friends made and stories shared have been a bonus. In fact, one friend (a fellow RPGer) commented how my initial writings on **Doctor Who** role-playing games filled a void and helped introduce people to the hobby.

I always saw the early columns in context to my current writing – that is, elementary, crude and simple. I forgot that, at one point, someone thought enough of my suggestion to write on the RPG to give me column space. That's the beauty of this series, the power of the Doctor. The fanzines, and now podcasts, the new role-playing games, and the multitudes of websites allow anyone the chance to express themselves – and their version of the Doctor's song.

And that, in a word, is fantastic!

Little Miss Muffet Sat On Her Tuffet Slurping Down Cherryade

Planet of the Spiders by **Colleen Hawkins**, 44, Cullompton, Devon / First story: **Planet of the Spiders**

I'm quite certain that I never watched **Doctor Who** from behind the sofa when I was small. Not because the show didn't terrify me back then because it most definitely did! I simply seem to have always lived in houses with rooms so tiny that the sofa had to be jammed right up against the wall, leaving no space for a child to run behind and cower. Clearly that's another of the many advantages of coming from a higher socio-economic group; middle class children were fortunate enough to be provided with a specific place to hide from **Doctor Who** monsters. There was none of that namby-pamby pampering for us working class kids!

I watched *Planet of the Spiders* at my granddad's house in Southend-on-Sea, which was also the family home at the time. My parents were still saving for their own place and granddad's rather rough-and-ready abode came rent free. The price was right, even if – according to mum – everything else about it was not. Her misgivings were baffling to me as I *adored* every aspect of living there. Granddad doted on me and I never minded the stench of raw onions and tobacco that always clung to him. I revelled in the imaginative possibilities provided by the overgrown back garden and the fact that the kitchen – despite my mum's best efforts – was constantly overrun with mice, as if my favourite nursery rhyme had miraculously come to life just for my personal entertainment. Nor did I realise until much later that my asthma was acutely exacerbated by the house's lack of heating. Only the front room had a *real* fire; every other room was usually as chilly as a butcher's meat store and my breath was often visible in my box-room bedroom. To me though all of this was perfectly normal and I always felt completely safe and secure there; except, of course, whilst watching **Doctor Who**.

Planet of the Spiders is the first **Doctor Who** story I can *remember* watching when it was first broadcast. It's also the story which has probably had the most profound impact on me. Unfortunately that impact was arguably somewhat negative and precisely the sort of thing batty Mrs Whitehouse was banging on about for most of her life. Thankfully she's not around to pour cold water on the near universal love currently engendered by the relaunched series. Mind you, she'd probably have hated practically every aspect of contemporary British culture, so 21st century **Doctor Who** might not - even with Captain Jack, Weeping Angels, inter-species lesbianism and all the other good stuff - have been at the top of her hate parade in quite the same way that the classic series always was.

Spiders - especially *giant* ones - were an almost inevitable choice for **Doctor Who** monsters. Even normal-sized spiders are deeply unsettling and the writers were exploiting a primal human distrust of these unpleasant, scuttling creatures. Or is this personal retcon? Before *Planet of the Spiders* engendered my latent Miss Muffet, perhaps spiders were merely Itsy and Bitsy and the Incy-Wincy Spider to me and therefore entirely unthreatening. Maybe those irresponsible makers of a children's television show callously produced a story so terrifying to impressionable minds that it stole a portion of my innocence. Maybe, but we'll never know for sure, so - as much as it pains me to admit it - I doubt there's a viable claim for damages to be trumped up.

Watching *Planet of the Spiders* tore me away from the cosy sanctuary provided by my granddad's cold and horrible house. The dark walls simply seemed to melt away as I sat transfixed by the horrors unfolding onscreen. Nothing, not the cherryade that I knew had been delivered that morning by our chirpy Unigate milkman and which was my beverage of choice while watching **Doctor Who**, nor the fact that I was sitting on my mum's lap - the safest *available* place in the world, short of doing the impossible and returning to the womb – could drag me back to my normal reality for the duration of the scariest episodes. The iconic image of the story – lovely Sarah Jane Smith with an Eight Legs on her back – was indelibly seared on my consciousness from the moment I first saw it and, for me, it remains the most potently horrific image that the show has ever conjured up. Afterwards, giant arachnids frequently squatted in my nightmares and many an anxious hour was spent fretting that maybe *my* back had an unwanted passenger on it too. Not that I found the courage to check. I was probably jolly lucky that my parents allowed me to watch **Doctor Who** ever again, but a sustained campaign of whining and wheedling wore down their resistance in time for the arrival of *Robot*.

Watching it again, it is difficult to comprehend how it had exercised such sway over the imagination of my younger self. It was still great fun – albeit over-stretched at six episodes and somebody really should have read Pertwee the Riot Act over that episode-long chase scene – but a bit too creaky to be scary to today's generation of children. Still, modern **Doctor Who** provides plenty to keep them scared and *Planet of the Spiders* was heady stuff for those of us who saw it at just the right age back in 1974. I credit it with expanding my mind and imagination enormously and also with burdening me with a lifetime of arachnophobia and epic spider-themed nightmares. Perhaps a little perversely, I offer my heartfelt gratitude for *all* of those things.

The Fourth Doctor Who

When Tom Baker was engaged to become the fourth Doctor Who, he was a relatively unknown actor who was currently out of a job. In all likelihood it was his unpredictable personality that made him an unlikely leading man and therefore someone who was seldom employed as such, but it was just this quality that made him perfect for the lead in **Doctor Who**.

Coming out of the Barry Letts/Jon Pertwee era, a time when the programme had firmly established itself as a regular fixture on the television screens of a nation, the casting of such an unknown might have led to a downturn in popularity and the eventual fall of a series that ought to have been well past its prime and that had so very nearly been cancelled before. But in Elisabeth Sladen and Tom Baker, incoming producer Philip Hinchcliffe struck gold. The pair became what is perhaps the series' quintessential Doctor/companion team, and the stories in which they appeared very soon became the stuff of legend, producing some of the most memorable imagery **Doctor Who** has ever generated. Mummified robots stalking the English countryside, the pot-pourri man with his head no more than a brain in a jar, and the half-man/half-Dalek cycloptic evil genius – these unforgettable sights are what made the series an institution in the mid-1970s.

Indeed, such was the love for the show at this time, and particularly in regards to a watching audience who had grown up with the series and were now heading off to university, that it was during the early Tom Baker tenure that organisations like the **Doctor Who** Appreciation Society began to spring up, and the fandom that we nowadays take for granted was born.

But the fourth Doctor Who outlived his companion Sarah Jane, his producer Philip Hinchcliffe and even the willingness of the actor who portrayed him to play it straight. As real-term budgets fell thanks to spiralling inflation (a situation that saw all three of the series finales of the late 1970s become troubled productions, one of them irrevocably so), and with the post-Mary Whitehouse BBC eager for the show to tone down its scaring-the-kiddies manifesto, Tom Baker's performances became ever larger as the sets became cheaper and the plots and monsters less inspired and more ludicrous.

By the time of his departure, Tom Baker had become one of the most famous actors in the country in one of the most universally familiar parts, and his Doctor Who was the longest-lived of them all. But a change in the production regime finally gave him the impetus to relinquish the role, and the stage was set for a change of actor and a change of tone, in what would perhaps be **Doctor Who**'s most difficult transformation since 1969.

A Winter's Night in 1981
Robot by **Bob Furnell**, Vancouver, British Columbia, Canada / First story: **Robot**

It's time to go back in time, way back, to a wintery night in 1981. I was living in Edmonton, Alberta and the PBS station we got via cable had been airing this strange British series called **Doctor Who** for several months. I'd seen bits and pieces of various episodes and couldn't really fathom what this weird programme was about. I basically shook my head and thought the show looked interesting but it just didn't grab my full attention. But as fate would have it, one cold winter night as I flicked through the TV channels, I came across this odd show again. Something caught my attention. This looked interesting. Intrigued, I curled up on the couch. By the end of the episode I was hooked. I had to know what was going to happen next.

The next night I tuned in to Part Two; it was the same all over again. The same the night after that. The show became a ritual. Every weeknight at 7.30pm I tuned in; (hey, they even had full stories running Saturday nights at midnight!). I couldn't miss the next instalment. I loved every minute. This show captured my heart and imagination in a way that no other show had ever done before. I was becoming obsessed.

Over the next few weeks I sought to find out more about this show. A little bookstore had opened up down the street from where I lived. One day on my way home from work I stopped off to have a look around. I was browsing the various shelves and tables when something on the table in front of me caught my eye. I couldn't believe it. Oh my God. There in front of me were dozens of **Doctor Who** books. My excitement levels went off the scale and I'm sure I just about wet myself. I felt like I'd found my own secret cache of these books. I grabbed five novels, rushed to the till to pay for them and practically ran all the way home. That night I read three of the books and the next day I was back in that bookstore buying more.

A week after that I discovered **A Celebration** by Peter Haining and purchased a copy. In the back of the book was an entry for the **Doctor Who** Information Network of Canada. I couldn't believe it. There was a fan club for the show here in Canada! Again my excitement level jumped off the scale. Right then and there I wrote a letter to the club's organiser and within two weeks I was a full card-carrying member. The club published their own fanzine and when the editor was looking for articles, I was soon writing for it.

I then discovered that a female co-worker was also a fan of the show and we struck up a friendship. We were forever talking about the previous night's episode or some aspect of the show. Because of our friendship I started wondering if there were other people out there that were fans too. I don't know why or how but I got the idea to start up my own **Doctor Who** club. I got creative, made up some posters and put them up in the bookstore where I'd bought those novels and before I knew it, was playing host one Saturday afternoon to ten strangers in my living room - well they weren't that strange; they were all **Doctor Who** fans.

My obsession with this show didn't stop there. Over the next several years it grew and developed. I moved to Vancouver and started another fan club. From there I began organising small **Doctor Who**-related events, building up in time to full scale conventions. I began reaching out to other fans. I began trading videos with fellow fans around the world. I rediscovered other British television series I grew up with and grew to love British series I'd never heard of. I started writing more and more and began writing, publishing and editing my own fanzines; I even started my own long-running fanfiction series. I became involved in the search for lost episodes. I met, interviewed and worked with stars from not only **Doctor Who** but other television series. This show I had become obsessed with started opening doors, and opportunities, for me.

And all the while, without quite realising it, I was developing skills and qualities I could use in real life. Supervision. Organisation. Working with others. Writing and editing. These skills I learned because of my involvement in fandom and eventually led me into my work field as an executive assistant.

Since that night back in 1981, **Doctor Who** has been a big part of my life. It has made me who and what I am as a person. It has influenced me in so many ways, some I'm sure I'm not even aware of. Over the past thirty-odd years this show has given me so much. If I hadn't tuned into that episode of *Robot* back then, I don't honestly think I'd be where, or who, I am today, and for that I'm thankful. It's really amazing when you think about it how one little television show has done a world of good for some many.

Not Scary? Nonsense!
The Ark in Space by **Stuart Douglas**, 43, Edinburgh
First story: **Invasion of the Dinosaurs**

It's fashionable, amongst fans now in their forties, to claim that **Doctor Who** was never *really* scary, that hiding behind the sofa is as much a fictitious construct of bored newspaper writers as wobbly sets and the idea that **The Tomorrow People** was ever a serious rival to the BBC's greatest ever TV show. 'Creepy, yes,' they say, and, 'Occasionally a bit spooky,' but not actually scary. Not the sort of thing to send any but the most weak-minded of fans scurrying for the security of the space between sofa and living room wall.

To which I say ... nonsense!

For me, there is a triumvirate of television scares from the 1970s and early 1980s, back when I was a kid, which even now have me reaching for the light switch before I go to sleep. That episode of **Space: 1999** where they discover a civilisation straight out of Wells' **The Time Machine** is one, the early **Blakes 7** story where Gan and Jenna are attacked by alien assassins woken from cryogenic sleep is another – and *The Ark in Space* is the third.

Actually, *The Ark in Space* is the first, both in terms of when I saw it and in how scared it made me. In early 1975 I would have been five years old and I can still vividly recall sitting on our (predictably) beige and brown living room carpet, nose about a foot from the glass of the screen, holding my breath as Harry and the Doctor fought a laser-firing robot using only Harry's shoes, and Sarah Jane (the great love of my five-year-old life) was rendered unconscious by some horrible machine. *This* was my kind of **Doctor Who** – clever, funny, exciting, loud and full of incident.

And it's scary. So, so scary. Body horror wasn't a phrase my five-year-old self would recognise, but the concept was one which even a pre-schooler could understand. What could be more horrifying than turning into an insect? I'd never seen bubble-wrap at that point, so watching one of the good guys slowly turn into a green, bubbling mess sent me into nightmare territory.

Slowly is important, actually. If it'd been a quick change – some sort of primitive shimmering effect, say, like a regeneration – it'd have been far less terrifying. That sort of thing belongs to science fiction, but seeing a man metamorphose in stages, a limb at a time, so that you can almost smell the gangrenous, mutated flesh? That's the stuff of horror right there.

So don't tell me that **Doctor Who** isn't scary. There's a five-year-old in 1975 who quickly shifted from his spot on the carpet to a safer one behind the sofa who begs to differ...

Not the Face! Not the Face!

The Sontaran Experiment by **Alister Davison**, 42, Sunderland, UK / First story: **The Ark In Space**

As a child, **Doctor Who** filled my mind with vivid images: green slime creeping through the white corridors of space station Nerva in *The Ark in Space*; the embryo room in *Genesis of the Daleks*; the glowing Rutan ascending the lighthouse in *Horror of Fang Rock*. The latter stuck with me so much, that the boxes of my dad's after shave gift sets – the ones with big transparent fronts – became TVs with that image hastily sketched and coloured onto a sheet of paper and slotted inside. Never good at drawing, it was simple, and effective, to paint a green blob on a black column.

All green, all glowing, all alien, they fired a young boy's imagination, keeping me tuning in every week to be thrilled. Yet, it would be the grey that had the most profound effect on me.

I remember it well, if not entirely accurately. Sitting in my grandma's house – 300 miles away, visits to her were rarer than we'd have liked – wedged between my mum and dad on a high, stiff-backed sofa on which I couldn't settle (never did, for nights after), dog at my feet, my favourite TV show about to start. I think it was midweek, so it would have been a repeat (they weren't called re-runs back then) but definitely after tea, a deck of cards ready to be played in half an hour or so.

Back then, the joke was that us kids watched **Doctor Who** from behind the sofa, but I never knew anyone who did. Where was the fun in that? Besides, even that young, the very alien-ness of the creatures and their studio settings meant we knew they were special effects. Nothing to worry about (although, seeing a Dalek close-up a few years ago gave me an involuntary shudder), nothing at all.

Then came *The Sontaran Experiment*, and suddenly everything became real.

The key was filming using video cameras on location – unashamedly so, with long slow tracking shots across windy vistas as far as the eye can see – far from the safety of a studio or that stone quarry we were all getting used to. Here was a landscape so familiar, so real, that anything occurring on it just had to be true, like the normal TV shows.

A re-watch shows me how much I'd missed; astronauts with dodgy accents, a robot more amusing than those that used to sing, 'For mash, get Smash,' the apparent uselessness of Harry Sullivan. The golf ball space ship was exactly as I'd remembered, as was Sarah Jane's yellow cagoule.

And, three-and-a-half decades later, that reveal still gets me.

Sarah Jane knows what to expect – as would any older regular viewer, given the unsubtle title – but my young eyes had never been clapped on a Sontaran before. Here comes a bloke in a padded suit, wearing what looks like a stone helmet. His hands go up, the helmet is taken off and ... behold, a Sontaran. He isn't green, isn't shaped like a pepperpot, doesn't have ears like the handles of grandma's sugar bowl. No; our new friend is grey, ugly and flipping scary. Then, as if that's not enough, there's that scream of music just before the end credits roll. Job done – I'm terrified.

So, I never hid behind the sofa, but – in accordance with the beliefs of Mary Whitehouse – I did have nightmares. Whenever I closed my eyes (not easy, out of the comfort of my own room and bed) that gargoyle face was in front of me, beady eyes seeking me out. I got to sleep eventually, waking the next morning, the daylight enabling me to laugh off my fear. I was safe, at least for those precious hours of daylight until bedtime that night.

I was fine, of course, and the Sontaran was defeated a week later, enabling me to lie safely in my bed. Yet, for those long nights between episodes, I couldn't help wondering if the Doctor would actually succeed this time. Had he not met his match with this grotesque creature?

Following this, there were occasional reminders of the Sontaran, shelved in the back of my mind, but always waiting to be brought to the fore. One I recall is from a children's school programme, a character called Wordy who floated in the air and helped kids with their letters. All very innocent, but there was something unsettling about the way his mouth moved; was he testing us, seeing how educated we were before the rest of his race arrived?

Only one other **Doctor Who** has ever come close. In *City of Death*, we've seen Scaroth of the Jagaroth before, we know what to expect, yet when that rubber face is pulled off to reveal the green Cyclops beneath, it sent a chill up my spine.

Still does. Like the Sontaran reveal, the effects have severely dated, but the emotional response remains much the same. It's the same with much of 1970s **Doctor Who**; never perfect, but the scripts are filled with moments that resonate, scenes that have captured my mind for over three-and-a-half decades.

I'm older now, but still a fan of the show that was essential viewing all those years ago. Much has changed - the latest Sontaran is a comedy sidekick - but the heart and soul remains the same. New memories, for a new generation.

The Genesis of Whovianism

Genesis of the Daleks by **Daniel J McLaughlin**, 18, Salford, UK / First story: **Genesis of the Daleks**

'Dan! You've had a shave!' exclaimed my girlfriend.

Indeed, this was correct. My face could no longer be used as sandpaper. But I ignored the remark, and carried on with inserting the DVD into the disc drive. You see, this was a very important moment for me. More important than being accepted into university; more important than being the best man at my friend's wedding; more important than accidentally bumping into Russell T Davies in Manchester and squealing, 'Hello!' in the most high-pitched voice I could muster. If Jenna-Louise Coleman knocked on the door wearing nothing but a smile whilst carrying massage oils, I would ignore her. Yeah, *that* important.

This was the day I introduced my girlfriend to *Genesis of the Daleks*.

She enquired: 'Why have you had a shave?'

The genesis of my Whovianism (is that a real word? It is now) started in the seemingly most unlikely of places: Myerscough Car Boot Sale. Every Sunday, I would be dragged along to this Aladdin's Cave of bric-a-brac in the hope of finding a treasure; mainly, an Action Man with clothes (I was confused as a child why Action Man was a man, because at a closer inspection he seemed not to have the necessary components).

And there it was! Shining in the Lancastrian sunlight were three video cassettes: *The Five Doctors*, *Castrovalva* (which didn't work – the cassette, not the episode; I don't want Christopher H Bidmead chasing after me) and the Terry Nation epic. I gave the seller my pieces of silver and ran back to my haggard parents arguing that a second-hand spanner will make their lives significantly better. Soon after eating salmonella-flavoured chips, we embarked upon the journey back to Oswaldtwistle: famous for the world's biggest pear drop, that girl from **Britain's Got Talent** who cried a few years back and putting the bricks on the Empire State Building backwards.

I responded to my girlfriend's earlier question (keep up): 'I thought I would make an effort for you. You don't want to be holding hands with a short, chubby, hairy Northerner; a short, chubby Northerner is acceptable, but not a hairy one.'

She gave me an enquiring look. All women have the in-built sceptical look that can reduce fifteen men to tears simultaneously; and I mean fifteen tough men who probably go to the gym and kick puppies for fun.

'Is there somebody else, Dan?'

The thing is, dear reader, there is. Please do not judge me. As much as I think my girlfriend is great and I slightly fear her, she cannot match the love of my life. I am going to offer you advice, because I am a kind, benevolent soul who is seeking your acceptance: never ever ask your girlfriend or boyfriend who their celebrity crush is. If you like your ego intact, avoid it at all costs. They do not say one, they list *thousands* – and none of them is someone along the lines of Johnny Vegas. From David Tennant to John Barrowman, from Matt Smith to Arthur Darvill. All of them have bigger sideburns, muscles, chins and noses than me; I never thought I would experience sideburn envy before.

'I'm sorry.'

'Who?'

I was first introduced to Sarah Jane Smith at the tender age of ten when viewing *Genesis of the Daleks* for the first time. The companion is there so that the viewer can familiarise themselves with someone who is not a crazy alien with a fixation for long scarves. During this first viewing, Sarah Jane Smith made me feel the tension when the Doctor stepped on the mine; she made me feel desperation when the prisoners attempted to escape; and fear when confronted with the Daleks, to whom this was my introduction.

This was a strictly platonic relationship. But Elisabeth Sladen helped me through my life. When faced with the fat mutant kid who ate glue at school, who sadistically enjoyed aiming footballs at my genitals, I would find comfort in knowing that Sarah Jane Smith had faced greater threats than me: the Kaleds, the Mutos and Davros – whom she would meet again in *The Stolen Earth*, causing a spine-tingling sensation for Whovians. When I was embarking upon the excruciating process of puberty with teenage girls laughing me off when I suggested the possibility of a relationship, I knew that no one could beat my Sarah Jane Smith. When I left my friends behind to go to university, I was reminded of Sarah Jane being separated from the Doctor and Harry only to be reunited later.

I have a somewhat rebellious streak. I chuckle to myself whenever I hear the term 'hipster' used, as in the person who follows an independent fashion. No, they don't. They wear the same clothes, they listen to the same music and they have the same haircuts. One would mistake them for a clone race. I am eighteen, and I listen to the blues, wear clothing which my girlfriend describes as, 'a farmer going on a date,' and I – like Sir Bradley Wiggins – think sideburns are cool. I suppose this influence came from Sarah Jane Smith herself. **Doctor Who** writer Toby Whithouse described her thus:

'She changed the companion from being a rather helpless hysteric to being a feisty, opinionated, strong equal to the Doctor. And, at the time, you know that was quite an extraordinary thing to do.'

And so we return to my girlfriend. We have finished watching *Genesis of the Daleks* and we are supping cheap vinegar-flavoured cider. Naturally, I am giving a post-mortem examination of the episode including interesting but useless facts. She remains unimpressed.

'It wasn't bad.'

But being Lancastrian, there is a natural pessimism in our language. 'It was alreight' would qualify as, 'It was good,' and, 'It wasn't bad,' qualifies as, 'Amazing.'

As Sarah Jane Smith told the Doctor in *The Hand of Fear*: 'Don't forget me.'

Oh, my dear Sarah Jane, I don't think you will ever be forgotten.

The Most Wonderful Bunch of Tin Soldiers Ever!

Revenge of the Cybermen by **Tony Green**, 38, Oxford
First story: **The Sun Makers**

I had a car once ... and it was terrible! Bought from a work colleague who was delighted to see the back of it, it had been stripped for a re-spray that had never actually happened. At some stage a previous owner had shorted out the electrics and so it had neither a working dashboard nor a functioning heater. It reeked of petrol from a mysterious leak and in some places you could actually see the world outside through vast holes rusted through the bodywork. It smelt, it was dangerous but it was the first car I ever bought with my own money. It was terrible but it was mine - and I loved it. Even thinking about it today makes me smile!

I had a cat once ... and he was terrible! He just came and lived with us one day. He had poor personal hygiene, was unpredictably aggressive and seemed to have a permanent eye infection. He could neither meow nor purr, was boss-eyed and bit you if you ignored him. He was the complete antithesis of anything good about cats but he could make you laugh just by the way he looked at you with that phoney cat dignity. He was terrible but he was mine - and I loved him. Even thinking about him today makes me smile!

I had a videotape once and it was terrible! A Betamax tape in an oversized box which featured images on the front cover which were almost wholly unlike what was actually on the tape. It cost the rough equivalent of two months' paper round money and in fact took significantly longer than two months to save for. Purchased from a video shop in Oxford which required special parental dispensation to even visit. The story,

Revenge of the Cybermen, still ranks as one of the worst of the era it came from and every criticism of it is justified. It looks cheap, it has plot holes you could drive a bus through and the Cybermen, making what should have been a triumphant return to the series, are at best, ciphers of their former selves. It was terrible but it was mine – and I loved it! Even thinking about it today makes me smile!

As with many things that mark a significant point in our lives we are prepared to overlook a great many shortcomings in favour of the broader picture. A much-loved car, relationship or pet may seem to be far more wonderful than it actually was as the mythos of one's own life evolves. Even if these shortcomings were obvious at the time some things are always special. To a **Doctor Who** fan that can be as simple as an obsolete videotape gathering dust on a shelf.

Revenge of the Cybermen was the first of its kind. The first story ever on video!

I still remember the money, more than I had ever carried before, weighing heavy in my pocket. I remember approaching the shop with an understanding of the financial commitment I was about to make. Excitement mixed with doubt. Joy mixed with terror at the most significant purchase I was ever likely to make. I was about to own a piece of **Doctor Who** history. It would be mine forever and if there was never again another repeat I would always have this one story to remind me of a bygone age.

I never really noticed that the story wasn't that great because to me *Revenge of the Cybermen* was never just another story. It was one of those handful of stories that most fans can point to which mean so much more than ninety minutes of BBC sci-fi. If you watch a story, any story, with the eyes of a child it tends to be wonderful. If you watch it with the eyes of a child that has bankrupted himself to own it it's even better; if you watch it as an example of the only classic **Doctor Who** that will and may ever exist in your possession it becomes sublime!

The video of *Revenge of the Cybermen* is, for those of us of a certain age, the epitome of being a fan. It wasn't the beginning of the whole series being at our fingertips, it was a once-only moment. The only story from the series' past we might ever own. But owning it had a price. It was a commitment to being in love with a television series which took both emotion and money. You would never reasonably spend fifty quid on anything aged ten if you didn't love it - or were prepared to admit that this was about to be your reality. It was more than I should have been willing to spend but to be honest the cost never even crossed my mind. Even after it was joined on my shelf by scores of other episodes on video I would always reach to my first ever purchase, and give an appreciative nod.

I still have it today. Even after my other VHS tapes had been recycled or replaced by DVDs my Betamax *Revenge of the Cybermen* was never thrown away. Even as I am typing this I can see it, poking its over-sized head over the top of my book shelf. And looking at it now, I am aware that I am writing this confession to the only people in the world who would understand why one would keep a dusty Betamax video purchased in 1984 of a story almost nobody likes - and still hold it as one of their most prized possessions. It was terrible but it was mine - and I loved it! Even thinking about it today makes me smile!

Doctor Who and the Loch Ness Monster
Terror of the Zygons by **Al No**, UK
First story: **The Invisible Enemy**

Thousands of years ago, which can't be right, I lived on top of a hill and next to a park. The park ran down the side of the hill and was filled with the sort of things you'd expect: trees, flowers, grass, pensioners and garlic. The base of the hill, the end of the park, are represented in this story by a road. On this road there was a newsagents and it was here my Loch Ness adventure began.

For some long-forgotten reason probably connected with newspapers, I was in this newsagents on a Friday afternoon. My memories are definitely manufactured, but I can recall that the shop's owner used to wear plastic bags over his hands, that it smelled of pear drops and I was bought the second issue of **Scream!** there – the one with the Ron Smith cover showing an alarmed gentleman trapped in a giant cobweb. Back at the dawn of time, newsagents would sell books rather than scratch-cards, and one such caught my eye: the promisingly-named **Doctor Who and the Loch Ness Monster**.

I haven't been able to place the year exactly but the following probably took place in, at the latest, 1979. That's mostly going on which issues of crayon-vandalised **2000AD** were brought out to distract us when trapped in tropical classrooms because it was too monsoony to play outside. It can't be much earlier than that because the logo was green. The colour of monsters.

I hadn't been reading for very long, largely because I hadn't been alive for very long; prior to that, I wasn't trying anything much more challenging than **Rupert** – and even then, only the rhyming couplets under the panels with any consistency, because the paragraphs were still a bit daunting. I got an odd echo of these days a few centuries later when the style was referenced in the sixth Doctor's comic adventure *Once Upon a Time Lord*.

Let's start with the Achilleos cover, then. The Doctor's head floating in the centre of a **Looney Tunes** backdrop, held up only by his scarf; the leathery long-necked dog monster stretching up and shouting in the Time Lord's ear; the tiny bubbling baby-thing in the other corner, hemmed in by the frame but still escaping. All of that grabbed me firmly by the aesthetic and I managed to leave the shop with this object of wonder clenched in my tiny hands.

It took me the whole weekend – with breaks to go and climb, and fall off, things – but I'd read the whole book by Sunday.

Being a child, I was already familiar with **Doctor Who** (I still maintain that my earliest confirmable memory is Tom Baker banging a ganglion to annoy a prawn) but this book was set in, and a relic of, an unreachable past. I'd never seen *Terror of the Zygons*, had no idea who Sarah or Harry were, no concept of the UNIT dating controversy and only a hazy understanding of where Scotland was. And none of that mattered.

The 'cold, dark sea' closing over Jock Munro's head was what hooked me. Up to that point I'd struggled a bit, trying to come to terms with how this whole reading lark was going to work. Once I stopped making such an effort everything was fine and I was soon ploughing through the rest, carried along by the excitement of the imagery unleashed and unfolding in my imagination.

From this initial interaction I followed a path that, whilst unique, still took in a lot of landmarks that other fans will find familiar. To begin with, the Target collection grew until the shelves started to vanish; **Doctor Who Magazine** back issues filled up other available spaces; then there was Longleat. After this, I developed a steady, and erroneous, dissatisfaction with the series that turned out to be more hormonal than I would ever have guessed, but by then I'd drifted off onto other things. Even later, a return and rediscovery of something that was never really lost ties in with a sort of renaissance and eventually leads to the inevitable fan-pilgrimage of watching every story in broadcast order – complete with accompanying blog.

Other things happened on the journey, providing a counterpoint to all these calendar pages we're shuffling through now. Civilisations rose and fell, science and magic started arguing again and superhero movies unexpectedly achieved a respectability of sorts. Also, I became a parent, the world kept not ending and the internet arrived in time to distract us all from the gardening.

Rereading **The Loch Ness Monster** in preparation for writing this, I was surprised by how much I remembered from childhood: the stag's head of stealth, the Duke's library, the Doctor desperately attempting to release the calling device as Nessie galumphs inexorably closer... It's all still in there.

It was interesting to find that Terrace Dicks had continued acting as a script editor by refining, ironing and smoothing Robert Banks Stewart's original script. The adaptation to prose also allowed for character motivation to be highlighted, and Broton's constant attempts to impress the Doctor with superior Zygon technology are particularly entertaining, although the words 'Ma'am' and 'tentacle' were noticeable by their absences.

I suppose I was lucky enough to find **Doctor Who and the Loch Ness Monster** at a point in life when I was still forming – that mix of slow crawl and mad headlong rush toward adolescence. The encoded messages wrapped within the text blueprinted themselves into the glowing magma of malleable personality, grafting behavioural signifiers into the molten core of who I'd eventually become all those thousands of years later.

Well, it's the only explanation that fits all the facts.

Spaceship Models and Jungle Planets

Planet of Evil by **Christine Grit,** 46, The Hague, The Netherlands / First story: **Genesis of the Daleks**

Doctor Who has only been on Dutch television for a very short time, but luckily for me when I was eight to ten years old, my family lived in a location lying in the southwest of the country where we could actually watch the episodes on the BBC. It was also lucky that our family had been living in an English-speaking country for a few years, so the language spoken was easy for my brother and me to follow even without translations underneath.

The main impact **Doctor Who**, and in particular *Planet of Evil*, has made on my life is that for years and years I truly believed I was going to become an astronaut. I was mostly influenced by the events on the space ship (actually within the studio) and I felt that – despite the fact that quite a few crew members were killed off, and there was a maniac on the loose who was turning into a monster having taken samples of a forbidden substance on board – life in space would be very interesting. One would be able to visit such lovely creepy planets as shown in *Planet of Evil*, or go for a trip to Mars – for which I also had an enormous fascination. Besides, it disturbed me no end that there were no female spacers aboard this particular ship. I firmly set myself to the objective of becoming perhaps the first one of those.

I read a lot of science fiction at the time (not understanding even half of the concepts involved, but as long as the stories were about people in space that was no problem). I also read serious non-fiction books regarding the Solar System, the Universe as a whole and the role humanity plays (or rather doesn't play!) within it. Both **Star Wars** and **Star Trek** strengthened my resolve to in the future become one of the select few to truly be an astronaut, even though I might not be the first woman after all, as there were female characters present. It was only when I realised that, although quite successful in gaining my A-levels, I would never be that comfortable with physics and technical subjects. I may have theoretically 'developed' an atomic bomb on the drawing table together with a friend, but the actual technicalities would forever be beyond me. And in all those non-fiction books, and some of the hard-core science fiction books as well, it appeared necessary to be either a medic or a technical expert. So, I decided to study Nutrition and Dietetics as well as Political Science at university, and decided to let my dream of flying into space go. Furthermore, another hindrance was the obvious fact that the real life space programmes just weren't as far advanced as I had originally expected them to to be. No sentient extraterrestrial life found whatsoever!

However, science fiction still fascinates me. I enjoy watching films and serials (**Doctor Who** is again one of my favourites), reading various novels (from **Star Wars** to the original **Dune** novels and whatever lies between), and even buying toy Daleks to showcase in my living room, as they are so wonderfully alien-looking. No other monster has ever been able to promote the general feeling of alienness as Daleks can.

Even imperfect memories still allow for the renewed enjoyment of watching such a serial after approximately 35 years, but *Planet of Evil* also had some more, shall we say secondary impacts. The TARDIS was a Police Box, and what that exactly was didn't register that well with me at the time, but the fact that it was blue and, more importantly, bigger on the inside than the outside obviously did. That led me to making a kind of TARDIS for myself from a former cardboard wrap of a Punch and Judy booth with a height of about five feet. Obviously this thing (the inside of which was strung up with all kinds of fake Doctory tools, and there was even a kind of console) was rather smallish on the inside but with a bit of imagination one could always pretend and make believe that the inside was bigger for real.

My brother and I made up all kinds of adventures using that big cardboard box, like rescuing Anne Frank from the 'Achterhuis' by sweeping the whole Frank family away in the TARDIS during the German occupation in WWII before they got sent off to concentration camps, or pretending that the infamous Professor Sorenson from the story under discussion actually tested the dangerous crystals on monkeys, and we would be confronted by loads and loads of anti-matter 'ribbed' or lighted apes. The fantasy world of children can sometimes take morbid turns! We really don't need television programmes to make us have bad dreams and nightmares; we can do that very well ourselves in what we make up!

Which immediately touches upon another secondary impact: the imagination. I don't recall how many stories I wrote at the time, featuring the fantastic Jungle Planet as well as the endlessly deep black hole out of which climbed the anti-matter monster on its killing sprees, but there must have been a great many of them. I know now that I blatantly plagiarised all kinds of other books and tales in existence, from **Peter Pan** to **The Wizard of Oz**, but the one thing the stories I wrote had in common was the magnificent setting of the swampy, jungle planet of Zeta Minor. And it was absolutely wonderful that when I eventually saw *Planet of Evil* again on DVD, the jungle was exactly as I remembered it. Sometimes memories don't cheat.

A pity that I didn't keep the stories though.

Clocks, Telephones and Granda's Tale

Pyramids of Mars by **Robert Morrison**, 30, Ellon, Aberdeenshire, UK / First story: **The Chase** (I think!)

I don't particularly like the telephone. I've never felt completely comfortable using it. I don't know the mood of the person at the other end, so I have *no idea* how I'm supposed to react. I can't see their facial expression, or their body language or even interpret their tone of voice. I admit it! I'm fearful of the humble phone. Yet ... one of my fondest recollections could never have happened without it. It is a memory most close to my heart, and whilst the majority of the exact details have faded, the essence is etched into my soul.

The telephone, the television, and the clock, were the catalysts for one of the greatest adventures of my life. If I already owe plenty thanks to John Logie Baird for my love of **Doctor Who**, then I owe much the same to Alexander Graham Bell, for a very *specific* **Doctor Who** event. Humanity achieves true greatness *together,* joining hands gives us the best in life, and one of the earliest, most precious, moments I have is in joining hands with someone close over the telephone. I experienced something quite wonderful, and quite unique. Not just a precious **Doctor Who** moment, but a precious moment in my life. Something transcending the mere television programme. A lot, lot bigger than that - the reason why **Doctor Who** means so much to me.

Memory. When you think about it, a human being's life is the sum of their memories. Besides your memory of the actual story, there's your memory of *where* and *how* you saw a **Doctor Who** adventure. What was going on in your life? I remember a certain occasion in *my* life, that happened during a repeat in 1994. It involved the telephone, my granda and *Pyramids of Mars*...

My earliest reminiscences of **Doctor Who** are sporadic. They include a jungle planet, with the Daleks' army frozen deep within; a disused mine, infested by green slime and Giant Maggots; a man being crushed to death between Robot Mummies; and, most of all, the terrifying voice of Sutekh! Those are the images and sounds that I recall most. I vividly remember rushing out of bed on Sunday at midday, to catch the twenty-five minutes of **Doctor Who** on BBC2 - the repeats of *The Green Death* and *Pyramids of Mars*. I didn't notice any dodgy effects - just excitement and pure entertainment. Recalling those childhood times has a valuable poignancy; you can never relive those precise feelings again, or experience the story in precisely the same way again, but you *can* remember...

I do remember, and one reminiscence in particular is more powerful than *any* other. It has always stayed with me. I have never lost it. It's made *Pyramids of Mars* a very special story to me - not just for the plot (which is very good indeed!), but the life's tale that it inspired. Everything started out in the most normal way, then it became peculiar. I rushed to the television set as usual, to see Part Four, and I pressed the large 'on' button firmly. The screen burst into life ... and into the black and white picture of **The Fugitive**! I was perplexed. Where was **Doctor Who**? Had there been some dreadful mistake? There simply must have been. I didn't understand it. My parents didn't understand it. Then realisation finally, disappointingly, dawned. The clocks had gone forward! It wasn't 12pm. It was 1pm, and I had missed **Doctor Who**! I was crushed, and I was dreadfully upset. If ever there was a time I needed a time machine (a TARDIS!), to go back an hour, then this was it. But I couldn't. My mum came up with the perfect alternative solution (as mums so often do!). My granda was an avid fan of the show too (he had been since my mum was young), and she thought of phoning him, to ask him if he'd watched it or not. He had!

I was promptly, and timidly, put on the phone and my adorable granda related the exciting conclusion of

Pyramids of Mars to me, in that wise and comforting voice of his. He recapped the cliffhanger from the previous week, asking me if I'd seen it. I had, and could still visualise it. He then launched into the narrative, a master storyteller, recounting the words, 'Kneel before the might of Sutekh!' and launching into the present tense - 'The Doctor (the mighty Tom Baker!) has his mind taken over, and is forced to help Sutekh, by taking Laurence Scarman to Mars in the TARDIS. Once there, he faces fiendish traps and tricks, threatening himself and Sarah Jane. For a heartbreaking moment, we believe the Doctor is dead, whilst the evil Scarman sends a radio signal, to free the imprisoned Sutekh ... it's all a ruse! The Doctor lives! He is able to reach Earth before the signal, trapping the escaping Sutekh in a time tunnel, ageing him to death. Then, as the ancient priory burns to the ground, the Doctor and Sarah quickly leave ... The End!' Our conversation must have lasted thirty minutes. A telephone adventure with my beloved granda - the *best* conversation of my life! Tense and exciting, it really made up for having missed the episode that day.

Years later, I purchased the story on VHS, and I came to this final part with much anticipation. And it disappointed me. So for me, *my* initial version is definitely the better one! Part Four is by no means bad (it's brilliant!) but anticipation can always be too high. More than anything, I actually missed the sheer *joy* of my original experience. So my lesson is this - don't just think about the plot, good or bad. Always remember that *first* experience of *yours*. And cherish that moment. For that is what *truly* makes an adventure, not just entertaining, but very special.

Face-Off

The Android Invasion by **Richard McGinlay**, 42, Ilford
First story: **The Android Invasion**

29th November, 1975: five-year-old Richard McGinlay watches *The Android Invasion* Part Two on BBC1. That's my earliest memory of a specific episode of **Doctor Who**. Oh, I'm sure I'd seen the show before that. I had some vague knowledge that prior to Tom Baker, the Doctor had been played by Jon Pertwee. I might even have retained a memory of watching Pertwee's Doctor ... in a large chamber or cave ... in *Planet of the Spiders*, perhaps? Or maybe I just imagined that, a bit of retroactive continuity in my mind. Anyway, the earliest identifiable **Doctor Who** transmission I can recall is the second episode of *The Android Invasion* - specifically, its cliffhanger ending:

The Doctor realises that something is wrong with his companion. She's not the real Sarah. The Doctor throws the impostor against a tree. The front of its face falls away, revealing electronic circuitry beneath, human-like eyes poking out from the workings. The Doctor looks on in disgust.

That's all I remembered about the entire serial. I didn't remember the Kraals, the men in spacesuits, or the chap with the eye patch. I have since reacquainted myself with the story, courtesy of Target Books and BBC Video - but in terms of the transmission, all I took away was Sarah's face falling off.

I didn't even remember that bit entirely accurately. The android Sarah is not thrown against a tree, but falls to the ground. Tom Baker looks disappointed rather than disgusted. JNT was right when he said the memory cheats. I enhanced the experience in my mind - though the gist of it was there.

Why that scene in particular?

Well, it's a cliffhanger, and they're often the most memorable parts. Not only are they the dramatic climax to an episode, but they are repeated at the start of the next one, which always helps to embed the experience in the old noggin. Other cliffhangers that stood out include the Doctor being buried in sand at the end of Part One of *The Robots of Death* (I remember being confused when this became merely the halfway point of a fifty-minute repeat several months later); the Doctor shouting something about a black star at the climax to Part Five of *The Invasion of Time*; Davros coming back to life at the conclusion of Episode Two of *Destiny of the Daleks*; and Scaroth removing his false face to reveal his true, one-eyed spaghettiness in *City of Death*.

There's a lot of dramatic mask removal in **Doctor Who**, but I don't think that's the reason why *The Android Invasion* made such an impression on me. A similar cliffhanger in *The Talons of Weng-Chiang* failed to register at all. It's probably the whole android thing. There was a lot of it about on TV at the time, probably inspired by the movie **Westworld** (1973). The main culprits were **The Six Million Dollar Man** and its sister show **The Bionic Woman**. Humanoid robots with detachable faces first appeared in **The Six Million Dollar Man** in 1974. They didn't have creepy human eyeballs among their circuitry, though - **Doctor Who** did that first. The more familiar Fembots, complete with human eyes, appeared later, in **The Bionic Woman** in 1976.

As the years passed, I continued watching **Doctor Who**, remembering more and understanding better. To begin with, my comprehension was little more than a random collection of spectacular events. My earliest memories after *The Android Invasion* are from *The Hand of Fear*: Sarah being buried in rubble; finding the stone hand; the female Eldrad being replaced by some strange shouty bloke; said shouty bloke falling down a big hole. I remember being thrilled by the Doctor's journey inside his own body in *The Invisible Enemy*, though my seven-year-old self would not have been able to tell you how he could be there. I recall a number of scenes from *The Invasion of Time*, though at the time I failed to grasp that it was set on the Doctor's home planet, and I thought the Vardans and the Sontarans were the same thing (I didn't remember the humanoid Vardans at all).

During the 1970s, **Doctor Who** was something I found frightening. Even the stories that I now perceive as explicitly comical seemed scary to the young me. The music helped, I am sure. The opening titles set the tone, and Dudley Simpson's incidental music was seldom light-hearted. The production values were never an issue, even though in retrospect I can see that many of them are less than convincing. Like JNT said, the memory cheats.

By the time the 1980s came along, I was comprehending the stories better (apart from *Warriors' Gate*, obviously). While watching *State of Decay*, I noticed a bad special effect for the first time (the rubbish scout ship impaling the not so Great Vampire). I began to appreciate the programme in terms of concepts rather than because of the fear factor. I was becoming ... a fan.

19th January, 1982: twelve-year-old Richard McGinlay watches *Four to Doomsday* Part Two on BBC1. Bigon lifts his artificial face, revealing the circuitry beneath. It's another cliffhanging moment that sticks in my memory, probably because it reminds me of that other android face-off all those years ago. That was probably the last time I viewed **Doctor Who** as a frightened child. From that point on, I watched as a thrilled teenager and finally an adult. I still enjoyed the show, but I wasn't really scared by it any more.

The Android Invasion and *Four to Doomsday* – not classics in anyone's book (not even this one), but those two Part Twos were pivotal points in my development as a viewer.

The Brain of Morbius and the Mind of a Child

The Brain of Morbius by **Paul Driscoll**, 43, Leigh Lancs, UK / First story: **The Time Warrior**

1976 was a memorable year for children's Television on the BBC. This was the year that **Rentaghost** and **Swap Shop** made their debuts. In the BBC's flagship children's show **Blue Peter**, we were treated to Leslie Judd interviewing Otto Frank; a real coup especially since it was the first time Anne Frank's original diaries had been shown in public. The opposition upped their game too, with **Chorlton and the Wheelies**, **The Muppet Show** and **Jamie and the Magic Torch** each making their entrance into my six/seven-year-old imagination. This new variety of shows did not include any direct competition for the Doctor, but the next year was to signal a change to that with a certain George Lucas film the catalyst for live action shows such as **Buck Rogers**, **Blakes 7** and **Battlestar Galactica**. But for now **Doctor Who** still ruled family entertainment, despite Mary Whitehouse's increasingly vociferous criticisms.

In the **Doctor Who** world *The Brain of Morbius* bookended the year; originally transmitted in January it was then repeated, albeit in a cut-down omnibus version, in December. In between, from *The Seeds of Doom* to *The Deadly Assassin* we had an unforgettable run of magical TV. Moments etched on my mind forever, the departure of Sarah Jane and the return of the Master among them. But of course this was the period the show supposedly went 'gothic' as Hinchcliffe and Holmes cranked up the horror. For a six-year-old the most horrific moments invariably involved body parts – Morbius' brain falling on the floor, a stone hand coming alive, another one turning green.

A keen reader from a young age, I remember flicking through the **Radio Times** looking for **Doctor Who**. What a joy it was to discover over Christmas 1975 that a new story was coming. It was a good Christmas to be six; my parents might have replayed *Bohemian Rhapsody* endlessly, but thanks to John Peel, we also 'rocked' to the sound of staple school holiday TV entertainers Laurel and Hardy singing *Trail of the Lonesome Pine*. My brother and I would imitate Stan, believing it was his voice all the way through.

We liked to do impersonations back in the day (inspired by a recurring act on **The Generation Game**). Some were cruel – we mimicked the local 'oddball' who would stand for hours on our street corner and grunt at passersby. Condo was very much like him and his treatment by Solon actually pricked my conscience. Others were less offensive (except to the ear) and I certainly mastered the Dalek voice, though Tom Baker's remained a challenge. Naturally then, upon hearing Morbius speak off camera I was expecting a Dalek to be revealed.

My six-year-old self watched The *Brain of Morbius* in a way I hadn't previously. Using association and memory I attempted to predict the plot. I was convinced that Solon would be revealed to be the Master, even though I would have only been a toddler when Delgado was in the show. My recollections of watching Pertwee as a child are limited to the odd image from *The Time Warrior* and *Planet of the Spiders*, but I certainly remember *remembering* the Master. The appearance of the Mutt however, brought no recollections of *The Mutants*, whilst Solon's hybrid allowed more recent memories of the Clawrantulars to surface (from the stage play *The Seven Keys To Doomsday*, which I had seen the previous Christmas). In the infamous mind battle I had no trouble believing that the faces were all of previous Doctors, but I was somewhat confused by the absence of Trevor Martin in the montage. On first viewing I decided that I had simply missed it. It wasn't until the Davison era that my family owned a VHS recorder so I was delighted to discover the story was to be repeated. It meant I would be able to look more closely at each face.

After not trusting the fourth Doctor throughout Season 12, by January 1976 I was starting to believe that this Doctor was someone worth looking up to. As a toddler you place 100% trust in those who are in authority, but by the age of six you start to challenge that a little more, especially when teachers and parents give conflicting views. I was starting to think for myself. In the Doctor's opening scene there are echoes of *Genesis of the Daleks* as he confronts the Time Lords. Back in 1975 the Doctor's attitude went straight over my head. But this time, as the Doctor shouts, 'I won't do it!' I knew exactly what he meant. I wanted to shout with him, to share that confident defiance towards my parents or teachers (in particular that sadistic PE teacher who commanded me to run *away* from the football). At a more basic level, seeing the Doctor play with a yo-yo in that same scene, did much to endear the character to my young mind. The yo-yo I received in my Christmas 1975 stocking was transformed from an object of frustration to a treasured prop in my dressing up game, alongside the dressing gown, hat and scarf.

The summer of 1976 brought to the UK a heat wave that was to have a devastating impact on parts of the countryside. My family's annual holiday in Snowdonia gave us a firsthand view of forest fires, so much so that the abridged rerun of *The Brain of Morbius* seemed all the more frightening with its heavy use of fire throughout, including the attempt by the Sisterhood to set the Doctor alight. I do recall struggling with the paradoxical concept of keeping the sacred flame alive. Like many young children I had been disturbed by the many public safety announcements in the 1970s, including the one of the girl touching a hot sparkler (voiced by Ray Brooks) and 'Charlie Says Don't Play With Matches.' I certainly developed a healthy fear of fire. That year we had a 'Castle Pass' so our holiday was a tour of as many castles as my parents could fit into two weeks. I would go into my imaginary Doctor mode inside the grounds of these castles, encountering Morbius at the end of a passageway using a twig as my sonic screwdriver (it didn't matter that the screwdriver was virtually absent from this story).

Two years later, on our annual pilgrimage to North Wales I purchased my first Target novelisations, amongst them *The Brain of Morbius*. It was the first novel I had read at my local library and later I was rather proud of the fact that I did not need a 'junior' edition. Repeated readings meant that my imagination supplemented and ultimately supplanted what was originally transmitted. So much so that when I finally did get to see it again over thirty years later, I feared it would not live up to expectations. How wrong I was. The story still feels as claustrophobic as it did in 1976 with the limited studio space, but the performances of the cast are without exception astonishing. This story has grown up with me unlike any other, from the original transmission to its repeat, from the Target novelisation to the detailed production notes of **The Fourth Doctor Handbook**, and finally back to the story itself, beautifully restored on DVD.

Whitehouse's dogmatic assertion that the show was damaging young children, could not have been further from my experience. Stories such as *The Brain of Morbius* helped to instil within me values such as tolerance and respect. I may have wet the bed on the odd occasion but I learnt to fear what should be feared and respect what should be respected. To pinch a line from Dick's novelisation, I can honestly say that on occasion when faced with one of life's dilemmas the example of the Doctor has indeed 'forced the solution on (me) in a way that challenged (my) most precious beliefs.' As devout Christians my parents supported much of Mary Whitehouse's campaign; I even suffered the ignominy of having **Rentaghost** banned. Strangely though, whilst alarmed by some aspects of **Doctor Who** they always allowed us to watch it (for this story the religion of the Sisterhood was of more concern than the horror aspects – they later detected a trend and a finger would hover over the off-button during *The Masque of Mandragora* and *The Stones of Blood*, and as for *K9 and Company* ... well that sent my Mum catatonic). I like to think I am a better person because of their inability to switch off what was after all a national treasure.

Aged eight I took ownership of my bookshelf, gradually replacing the **Noddy** and **Secret Seven** books with my own choices, predominantly **Doctor Who** novelisations. It might sound a little incongruous, but in 1978 next to my copy of *The Brain of Morbius* I slotted in **The Secret Diary of Anne Frank**.

Floriana Requiem
The Seeds of Doom by **Al No**, UK
First story: **The Invisible Enemy**

There are two buildings in Cardiff that were later converted into Henrick's. My son and I were born in one of them, and a fisherman named Rawlins White was burned as a heretic in what is now the menswear section of the other. Public executions also took place outside the old city walls. The condemned would be trussed and carted along a short path – where A. J.'s Coffee Shop would one day be found – to the field where the gallows stood. This miserable site was known as Plwcca Halog, which translates as either 'unhallowed plot' or 'unhallowed pool,' depending on who you ask. Today, it's the meeting point for five roads and looks like a weird star-shaped sigil from the air. Locally, it carries the nickname of 'Death Junction' and in the autumn of 2004 I was living on one of its arms.

In the centuries since I was young, life had turned out to be sharper-toothed than I'd expected. I had drifted across several countries, pursuing different types of success and arriving slightly after they'd sunk forever. Eventually the tides of time washed me up in the city that spawned me, like a confused salmon. I tried digging the black soil of my garden – it only yielded worryingly long bones, carrier bags and screechingly-coloured polaroids. I opted to lose myself in the past instead.

Cardiff Central Library (long-gone now) had only a small area devoted to local history. I consumed this in much the same way I had the children's section of the library located at the base of the hill on which I used to live. With my disaffected frame of mind, I found nothing truly diverting in Cardiff's biography beyond the dog-faced men, the dung-heaps, the bear-baiting, the lepers of Queen Street and the seam of piracy and corruption that seemed braided to its soul.

I strolled toward home through the coldly ubiquitous rain, imagining how the shapes of the modern buildings might fade to reveal the landscape's truthful contours. The path of the forgotten canal that I trod would one day run beneath Mr Saxon's pixillated face, though I could not know that then. I also remained unaware and uncaring that the cluster of lorries gathered by the museum and the film-crew that were bustling about the Temple of Peace were in fact fixing Platform One in my future. My introspection was too fierce and all-consuming to be distracted by such fripperies.

At the top of Crwys Road, near the eventually resting place of Clara Oswald, I turned more or less south, strode down the hill and onto Death Junction itself. I crossed at the lights and, facing a cave made of records, took a decision that changed my life.

I turned right.

Walking through the strange miasma of decay that came and went, I entered the nearest charity shop. I can admit of no real reason other than a desire to browse – it was not as though I had ever found anything in this particular shop that had caught my eye. I had long-since drained this suburb of the records that interested me; I had no desire to add another tier to the library wall; the clothes of the recently deceased held no real interest either. In all, I expected nothing.

Nestled innocuously on a shelf with seven other videos, was a relic – paired, like policemen. Instantly, I was drawn back to my initial literary devourings. I had read an over-sized hardback translation of this long-lost and thus forbidden tale so many years before that the details, beyond the peeling plastic laminate cover (the hero in pointillist black and white, brandishing a sword, the heroine a plank; above them a towering eldritch nightmare crushed a stately home whilst shrugging off the ineffectual pin-pricks of air-bombardment) had faded like a gargoyle's face.

A sudden, desperate passion enveloped me. My heart pulsed and my skin was too tight. I purchased the video and rushed along the conjoined star-fish arm to my flat. Here I shut out the world and prepared to immerse myself in a long-rumoured experience of perfection.

This was an unalloyed masterpiece, germinated in the astounding stories of the 1930s and earlier. For this story, and perhaps this story only, every single strand of production hit the correct note: the direction, editing, acting, design, writing, makeup, music and – yes – effects, created something greater than they had any right to. In many ways an atypical example of the series – the violence and the seriousness almost venture beyond the brief – it was, to my mind, the first time that the stakes were so high, that the trick had gone wrong and the magician couldn't tell for certain which was the correct card.

For many years my melancholy had led to a sneering, affected ironic dismissal of a thing that I had once loved. Here was true evidence that my path had been misguided. The story built, beautifully, from a sneaky prologue that subtly carries me up a mounting madness that became an exhilarating roller-coaster in which smiles never quite reached the eyes, until the very final shot of two friends sharing a genuine, life-affirming moment. I slowed to a halt as, with a radiophonic scream, *The Seeds of Doom* flowered into something totally unexpected.

A future.

Dance of Death
The Masque of Mandragora by **Mietek Padowicz**, 52, Newcastle, UK / First story: **The Green Death**

Having learned to fear potted plants in *The Seeds of Doom*, we now move on to politics, intrigue and the search for the wettest, creepiest, oldest corridor to run around in, while being stalked or stalking.

As stories go, *The Masque of Mandragora* is typical of the era in as much as however you slice it, it still centres on the age old struggle between those of the ruling classes who wish to retain power through brute force and intellectual darkness, and those who would risk the questioning of ancient, long unquestioned dogmatic positions, despite the natural fear of the masses and bureaucratic classes, in order to drag the world a decade or two into the future. As a person who has been active in politics for more years than I care to admit, this suits me down to my toes. But the real appeal for me is the fact that our family does come from Northern Italy originally and we were amongst the ones actively trying to outwit each other in a deadly game of brinkmanship, power politics and the genuine pursuit of science and philosophy, something our family has never tired of to this day. The fact that the genteel version of the game we play today no longer carries the risk of being poisoned, beheaded or stabbed in the dark by a disloyal bodyguard just makes the story all the more delicious for me. Every time I watch it I imagine that perhaps I would have made slightly better choices and frankly would have had my treacherous uncle killed off long before he would have tried to have *me* eliminated first. The real fun then becomes the many different ways I could do it; poison comes to mind, a slow painful one, but he could escape and hurt me, no... Torture, torture with hot pokers in all the places he was cruel to the innocents, yes, that would be just the thing. But then the pleasure of sending him out into glorious, hopeless, pointless, brave but ultimately fatal battle, affording him a hero's funeral and disposing of an enemy all in one gesture would be lost. I would even then have the chance to write the epic poem and song forever immortalising him in convenient fiction, which brings us nicely to the music and the dancing in the piece.

Unlike most people, I learned from an early age the fine art of courtly dance, idle chit chat and flirting that is an essential tool of survival in business and politics. *The Masque of Mandragora* again gets it right; a party at the height of peril isn't a frivolity, is not a jejune gesture in the face of certain death, it is in fact strategically a wise move. Getting the social advantage on your rivals by spinning a good yarn or being a good listener will always weigh in your favour when a new ally from out of nowhere pretends to be the leader of the rebellious hordes, religious sect or court faction that was trying to kill you five minutes ago. But a word of warning about the jugglers and the servers, they are never what they seem and they will eventually get you if you let your guard down. That is why you need a good private secretary/second for duels; it is his job to take the lesser risks while you inspire the rest of the troops and followers to save your skin and that of their own long term positions rather than, you know ... run away like snivelling cowards.

The Masque of Mandragora does something a modern story hasn't done in a long time, it assumes I know the major lines of history and conflict involved in the late 15th century and all the residue of the Roman Empire and later periods that I already knew about by the time I was twelve. In fact, for a children's story, **Doctor Who** raised a lot more questions than it answered. Even now, after not having seen this story in over ten years, I feel the need to pop into Newcastle Central Library to do a little digging about astronomy, Demnos, costumes and where San Martino really is.

Tom Baker (and the people putting the words in his mouth) also does this fun thing that drops us into a chapter of **The Three Musketeers**. He would never dream of psychic paper when a good dropkick or feint followed by stealing a horse will do. Tom Baker is my favourite Doctor, not just because he's my first, but because he is a Musketeer. His Doctor in this story, as in most of his other stories, is brash, says things like 'I don't know why I like you humans, you're so irrational,' or, 'I am not a peasant!' At the start of the story, we even get a prolonged tour of the TARDIS interior during which he, much like Aramis, is flippant, secretive and yet very revealing without meaning to be about even things like his old control room.

I approach and leave *The Masque of Mandragora* every time with the same wistful feeling of seeing an old friend I never tire of. The story, like Tom Baker and his Harpo Marx face, lingers like a fine meal you look forward to having again and again, except you know you can't on account of familiarity breeding indifference and God forbid ... letting it become just another story you see in your head five seconds after the opening credits have rolled.

How Dark Rings Have Lured Me to Epic Mythologies

The Hand of Fear by **Anthony S. Burdge**, 41, Staten Island, New York, USA / First story: **The Hand of Fear**

It all began with a ring. Again. On a grey overcast day in the mid-1980s I got caught in the rain on my way home from Intermediate School. I sat quietly in dry clothes and towel in the living room of my family's Staten Island, New York home. My father was looking for something for me to watch on TV. As he clicked away at the remote, I scanned the passing images.

A picture of a young girl in colourful overalls, holding what looked like a Tupperware box with her fist clutching a ring, surfaced but disappeared as the channel was changed. 'What was that?' I asked my father. 'Go back, please.' My throat was a little hoarse and weak from an oncoming cold.

My father flipped the channel back quickly, and a light blue glow now filled the screen from a square dark ring. The young girl in colourful overalls, a villainous look upon her face, thrust her palm out bearing that ring which had, I discovered, zapped a guard from the Nunton Complex. Instantly drawn into the story of this girl continuing into a nuclear facility with her Tupperware dish, I would later find out I was halfway through the first of a four part story.

My father sat back, smiling. My parents had already introduced me to another story featuring a dark, evil ring. While in-utero, they claimed, they read me Tolkien's **The Hobbit** and **The Lord of the Rings**. As a child, I began to read at an early age and just a few years before finding this mysterious girl with her own ring, I had been given the books containing Tolkien's epic stories of Middle-earth. This story, with the girl, the ring, and the

Tupperware dish, was *The Hand of Fear*, the girl was the beloved Sarah Jane Smith.

Both *The Hand of Fear* and Tolkien's stories have antagonists, Eldrad and Sauron, without physical form; yet their force of will exists to manipulate the ring-bearer. The One Ring was forged by Sauron in order to gain dominion over the other rings of Middle-earth and enslave the Free People. Much of Sauron's own power was bound into the One Ring and as long as it existed, so did the will of Sauron. Therefore those who found and bore the Ring – Gollum, Bilbo, and Frodo – slowly became corrupted and twisted under Sauron's watchful influence. The Ring of Eldrad completely took over the mind of Sarah Jane, leading her to the Nunton Complex nuclear reactor. Exposure to the glow of Eldrad's Ring yoked the ring-bearer beneath Eldrad's influence.

Intently following Sarah Jane into the nuclear facility – where she locked herself into a radiation chamber, opened the Tupperware box, and exposed a severed stone hand – I was enthralled as the episode ended with the hand animating to flex its fingers.

With rolling credits, the WLIW phone operators appeared, to take donations. The telethon host introduced them as the Gallifreyan Embassy: the Long Island **Doctor Who** Fan Club, who wore multi-coloured scarves and wide brimmed fedoras. I questioned why these kids were wearing Indiana Jones hats? And why the host announced an interview with the 'new Doctor' Sylvester McCoy? My child-brain was confused: who was the Doctor and why was there a new one? I hoped for answers after the telethon intermission. My father asked if I wished to continue watching and I exclaimed a loud, '*Yes!*'

Soon enough, I recognised the elements seen during the intermission: the long multi-coloured scarf flailing about a curly-haired Doctor, the blue police box and the fedora. Who was this Doctor? I sat grounded on the floor for the next two hours. I laughed at the Doctor's quips and pantomime. I hoped in earnest that Sarah Jane would be released from the effects of the Ring. I was reminded that the fate of Eldrad wasn't dissimilar to that of Gollum; both characters fall into a pit with their respective rings;, Eldrad trips over the Doctor's scarf and falls; while Gollum loses his balance after biting off Frodo's ring finger, plummeting into the Crack of Doom.

Between each episode, I learned more and more about **Doctor Who**. In a childhood afternoon, I firmly thought of myself among the group of **Doctor Who** fans so I could learn more about the Doctor and his exploits.

Once *The Hand of Fear* ended, I asked my Dad to find more. I was devastated to discover this was Sarah Jane Smith's final episode. Dad checked the TV Guide each week, and would find more WLIW **Doctor Who** telethons. The next featured the black and white, second Doctor classic *The War Games* along with the Gallifreyan Embassy Fan Club manning the phones during intermission. I would soon learn that *The Hand of Fear* had already been a ten-year-old story by the time I saw it, and *The War Games* was older. During the mid-1980s **Doctor Who** was not as readily transmitted from the BBC as it is today, and it had already been cancelled when I came aboard the TARDIS.

In the years that followed, I would sketch police boxes in my high school notebooks, pretend my father's screwdrivers were sonic and found myself landing the TARDIS in Middle-earth in my mind's eye. By 2008, three years after the relaunch of **Doctor Who** my wife and I began developing a book, **The Mythological Dimensions of Doctor Who**, which gained the support of two members of the Gallifreyan Embassy – Louis Trapani and Ken Deep. Not only did I show my love and support for **Doctor Who** through my book, but it was promoted and discussed amongst the very same fan group I had wished myself to be amongst more than two decades earlier.

And all this, was due to an evil ring ... a girl in bright overalls, a Tupperware dish, and a long technicolour scarf.

The Deadly Assassin
(Or, How I Learned to Stop Worrying About My Curfew and Just Watch Dr Who)
The Deadly Assassin by **David Busch**, 40, Iowa City, IA
First story: **Revenge of the Cybermen**

It was a magical time, that summer of 1982. Being a ten-year-old science fiction fan that year was like having Christmas, Halloween, and my birthday happen every week. **Star Wars** was at the height of its popularity, and partly because of that, the movie theatres were filled with such amazing sci-fi/fantasy films as **E.T. The Extraterrestrial**, **Star Trek 2: The Wrath of Khan**, **Poltergeist**, **Tron**, **The Thing** and **Blade Runner**. Television was not quite as rich for such offerings, but if you had patience and knew where to look, there were some gems to be found.

It just so happens that this was the summer when I unearthed the diamond in the rough known as **Doctor Who**. Even to my pre-adolescent eyes, it was obvious that the series was not as polished as its bigger-budgeted competitors; the effects were crude, it was shot on video (a pretty big stigma, even in those days!), and in my area, it was consigned to the graveyard shift of 11pm on Sunday nights. But since it was summertime, the late night airings were not a problem for my brother and I, as our parents let us stay up and watch it. I became addicted to the show, and could not wait until each week's episode, filling the time between Sundays by scouring bookshops and comic stores for any **Doctor Who**-related items.

Alas, as any fan of science fiction or fantasy knows, all forms of good magic have a darker counterpoint, and this particular dark side hit me like a ton of bricks in September. School was back in session, and suddenly I was not allowed to stay up past 10pm on

Sunday nights! 'But, but... That's the only time **Doctor Who** is on! I have to stay up to watch it!' I pleaded, but my protestations fell on deaf ears. To my parents, **Doctor Who** was just a TV show – they didn't understand that it was much, *much* more than that! It was what I lived for, craved, and thought about all day long. It wasn't a TV show – it was a way of life!

Unfortunately, my parents felt that ten years of age was too young to declare that one is following a new life style, and off to bed it was, at 10pm. I would lie in bed angrily, staring at the clock, knowing that the theme music and time vortex were appearing *right now* on television for those lucky enough to have been born six or seven years earlier. The first story that I missed was *The Masque of Mandragora,* and since I had read the novelisation, I was especially miffed at losing out on the chance to see the Doctor and Sarah Jane travel back in time to Renaissance Italy.

I had a brief reprieve from my cruel and unusual sentence the following week, due to the Labor Day Holiday – there was no school on Monday, so I was able to stay up again! This week's adventure was *The Hand of Fear,* a pivotal story which ends with the Doctor being recalled to his home planet by his own people, and thus having to leave Sarah Jane behind on Earth. I was crushed to see Sarah leave, but also captivated by the notion that next week, we would be going to the Doctor's home, and we'd get to see Gallifrey and the Time Lords! Oh no, I was not willing to miss this, not for anything!

My plan for the following Sunday was a simple one in theory, yet complicated in execution: I would go to bed early to throw my parents off the trail, then wait until they had gone to bed too. Then I would sneak out of bed (tricky, as we had a small house, and my parents' bedroom was right across the hall from mine), tip-toe down the stairs as silently as possible, close the door, and turn on the television with the sound turned down to a minimum. (Crafty as I am, I had already turned the volume knob down to '1' before going to bed!) I needed to sit about a foot away from the TV to actually hear what was going on, but that was just fine with me – it only served to immerse me more fully into the story, entitled *The Deadly Assassin,* which was one of the most exciting things I'd ever seen. The Doctor, sans companion for the first time ever, arrives on his home planet, to be immediately struck with a psychic vision of the President's assassination. He tries to warn the authorities, but in true **Doctor Who**-style, they ignore him and seek to imprison him. He of course eludes them, and in attempting to prevent the assassination, actually seems to have caused it himself. The Doctor is put on trial by his own people, and escapes immediate execution by declaring himself a candidate for the new President himself! (Gallifreyan law is apparently a strange and murky thing, subject to the whims of plot-necessity...)

The deliciously evil icing on the cake was when it was revealed that the Time Lord pulling the strings behind this plot was none other than the Doctor's arch-enemy, the Master! The Master is a character who I had read about in books, but had never seen on-screen before. In this story, he has reached the end of his regenerations, and thus has the gruesome appearance of a walking corpse, the very figure of Death Incarnate. Of course, I delighted in every second of it! My plan had succeeded marvellously, magic had returned to my world, and I vowed never to miss an episode of **Doctor Who** again.

The next day, I confided in my older brother what I had accomplished, and he decided to sneak up with me the next week. As my brother was not quite as sneaky as I was (and because his room was even closer to our parents' room than mine), we got caught, and were sent to bed without being able to see Leela's debut in *The Face of Evil*. But much like the Master himself, I refused to give up after just one defeat, and the next Sunday I was downstairs by myself, enjoying the Agatha Christie-inspired whodunit *The Robots of Death*. This behaviour continued for a few more weeks, before my parents finally understood that this obsession of mine was not going to fade away. This led them to the most brilliant idea they had ever had – the purchase of our family's first ever VCR! Now, the best of all worlds was suddenly mine. I could tape the show while I slept, which made my parents happy, and could also watch it any time I wanted, throughout the week! I soon built up a huge library of **Doctor Who** on Betamax tapes, all carefully labelled and stored in chronological order. It took quite a while before *The Deadly Assassin* came around to be repeated again, but as I finished writing its label on the tape and punching out the 'do-not-erase' tab, I smiled, knowing that it was the story that started it all.

Her Name Was Leela, She Was A Who Girl
The Face of Evil by **Andrew Stark**, 45, Cardiff, UK
First story: **The Green Death**

At first, I really didn't plan on liking her at all.

And why should I? She wasn't the Doctor's proper companion. That was Sarah Jane Smith. The Doctor was going to go back and pick her up exactly from where he'd left her, on the streets of some stupid place called Croydon - wherever that was - and the adventures of the Doctor and Sarah would continue in time and space just the way they always had.

Or almost always had. True, I had a vague memory of this young, leggy girl with the long blonde hair and the silly clothes who had helped the Doctor in that story with the maggots. But then that wasn't this Doctor - that was the other one who was a bit too old and too serious and didn't even have a long scarf like the real Doctor did. I'd even seen pictures of other companions in **The Doctor Who Monster Book** which Mum and Dad had bought me (two copies - one to cut out and one to keep) but I wasn't really sure about them as I'd never seen them on the telly, so they didn't count either.

And none of those was Sarah Jane Smith, the real companion. The Doctor's true and bestest friend who was plucky and beautiful and determined and funny and just, just brilliant in every possible way. Even if she did get stuck in ducts an awful lot.

No, this was all just the Doctor pretending and next Saturday I'd sit down with my Mum and my Dad and my little brother in front of the telly with my banana sandwich and my slice of Battenberg cake just like every Saturday since ever and the TARDIS doors would open, Sarah Jane would walk back into the control room, and she and the Doctor would make up and everything would be alright once again. There was really no need to worry. Was there?

But the following Saturday came and there was no sign of Sarah Jane at all. Just some old men in fancy robes with ridiculous collars and a scary man with googly eyes in not fancy robes and lots of boring stuff that didn't make any sense to my nine-year-old brain and it was all wrong, wrong, wrong. The next Saturday came and went and no Sarah Jane and the next and the next and still no Sarah Jane and I wasn't liking this one little bit. The Doctor needs his best friend, I thought. I was, to put it mildly, not happy.

Christmas arrived, and with it lots of parties and presents and cake, and my mood lifted and, with my fickle butterfly-like child mind, for a while I put aside my feelings of loss and partied like it was 1976. Which, fortunately, it was.

Then, suddenly, it wasn't and it was New Year's Day and it was Saturday and it was **Doctor Who** and my mood deteriorated once more and for the first time in ever such a long time I wasn't looking forward to it. Because by now I knew. I'd worked it out and I knew. Sarah Jane wasn't coming back and **Doctor Who** was never going to be the same again.

However, tradition is a hard thing to break free from, so at the appointed hour I sat down with my Mum and my Dad and my little brother in front of the telly with my banana sandwich and my slice of cake (though Christmas cake this time because, you know, there was still such an awful lot to get through) and I began to watch. As the familiar music faded and the words *The Face of Evil* disappeared from view, the first thing I saw was this young woman, a young woman who very definitely wasn't Sarah Jane, saying things that Sarah Jane definitely wouldn't say and wearing clothes that Sarah Jane most positively, *definitely* wouldn't wear.

And her name was Leela.

And she was fantastic. Fantastic, and yet very different to Sarah. She was stronger for sure, but then she wasn't as smart either, at least not clever smart but maybe she was cunning smart. And she killed people! How great was that? Sarah Jane never killed people, not even once. So, I thought to myself, maybe I'll give her a chance, this savage girl. Perhaps I'll just give her a week or so to see how she turns out. She's no Sarah, but maybe she'll do.

So that week and for the next three weeks I sat and watched a story of savages and techs, of mad computers and invisible monsters and a crazy priest who wore a glove as a hat. And by the time those four weeks were over it was as if Leela had always been there so when she ran past the Doctor into the TARDIS at the end of Part Four I hoped she would travel with the Doctor forever.

But of course, nothing is forever, and the following year when it was Leela's turn to say farewell, once more I was distraught. This time however, with the new-found wisdom of a ten-year-old, I realised that a new companion would soon be along to continue the adventures and provide companionship for the Doctor again.

So it has continued. For each Sarah Jane or Romana or Martha who has left me forlorn and temporarily bereft, there has always been a Leela or another Romana or a Donna who I have liked and loved just as much, and sometimes a little bit more.

And to be quite honest, I wouldn't have it any other way.

The Robots of Death Effect

The Robots of Death by **Paul Mount**, 53, Cardiff, UK
First story: **The Tenth Planet**

It was *The Robots of Death* wot did it. I'd been watching **Doctor Who** since about 1966 – In a serious, can't-miss-this sort of way since 1970 (in colour!) – and I don't think it had ever much crossed my mind to wonder if the show had other 'fans,' people who'd watched it for years, people with a thirst for its canon and its history, people with an authoritative knowledge of **Doctor Who** and what made it tick. I probably felt I had access to all I needed regarding the show's history – I'd never see any of it, after all, buried away in some dusty TV Archive and the BBC were hardly likely to start selling copies of their old shows to the public! – courtesy of the Pan 1972 paperback **The Making of Doctor Who** (what a revelation!) and its 1976 Target Book rerelease. Then there was that well-thumbed 30p **Radio Times Doctor Who** Tenth Anniversary special, a glossy, all-colour magazine packed with 1960s story titles (mostly wrong, as it turned out) of adventures I'd scarcely been able to dream about, and modern pictures of companions I vaguely remembered or had never heard of. And a preview of the next series! Story previews and titles! That new girl, Sarah Jane Smith looks a bit ferocious ... not sure I'm going to like her much...

Those three books were pretty much the 'Holy Trinity' for the mid-1970s **Doctor Who** buff and they had already given us more backstage access to our favourite show than most other more mundane TV series. I was happy, watching **Doctor Who** every week and swapping opinions with the few friends who watched it a bit less avidly than I did. But other fans? *Fans as fanatics*? No, surely not... Then along came *The Robots of Death*, Season Fourteen resuming in January 1978 after a short Christmas break and there was something about that first episode which got me thinking; there must be some sort of **Doctor Who** ... fan club, surely? By chance a bi-monthly British Sci-Fi poster magazine had just, in the middle of its usual fawning **Star Trek** coverage, printed the address of the **Doctor Who** Appreciation Society. Why not? Part One of *The Robots of Death* had captivated me to the extent that I really needed to find an outlet for my enthusiasm for the show beyond just chatting about it for a few minutes with family and friends.

For Part One of Chris Boucher's *The Robots of Death* is just packed with *ideas*, big bold concepts and images guaranteed to pique the imagination of a viewer who was already probably just beyond the show's target audience. Moody model work showing the great clunking Sandminer crunching across the surface of a storm-swept alien world, the TARDIS spinning through Space, the Doctor lecturing Leela on the TARDIS' dimensional-transcendentalism (it's bigger on the inside than the out), elegant robots, their boots trimmed with silver Kit Kat wrappers, ominously sweeping about the Sandminer corridors. Add to all this Boucher's crisp, rich dialogue, economically evoking the pampered lifestyle of the miner's crew, the all-Doctor and Leela relationship fumbling its way out of the shadow of Sarah Jane Smith (she turned out okay in the end), a real sense of adventure as the travellers realise they're trapped and in danger of being ripped to shreds by sand being collected through the mine's open vents. At the time I still missed the simple military-versus-monsters spectacle of the Pertwee era (Hell, I was missing the *monsters* after the paucity of beasties in the latest season so far ... would an Axon or two *really* be too much to ask for?) and whilst I was aware that **Doctor Who** was growing up even as I was, it seemed to have become a little smaller-screen than it had been in the early 1970s, the stories a bit more intense and a bit less action-packed. And I liked action-packed, dammit. Suddenly and wonderfully, this was to change... *The Robots of Death* seemed to crack open my preconceptions and my expectations; this was **Doctor**

Who, I finally understood, freed from the fetters of modern-day Earth and UNIT's five-man army, and launching itself out into the darkest corners of space where huge machines clanked and whirred, humanoids wore odd make-up and 'art deco' robots plotted a sinister revolution. Part One suddenly woke me up to the endless possibilities of the show again; the TARDIS can go *anywhere* (it was the spinning-through-space bit; always been a sucker for those), deep inside alien machinery on desolate planets and, inevitably, the Doctor and his chum will arrive just at a time of crisis and find themselves accused of murder.

In truth Part One was as good as *The Robots of Death* got. The script remained witty and intriguing but the Agatha Christie-style mystery fizzled out into the usual gubbins about a hooded megalomaniac (whose voice wasn't *radiophoniced* enough to make his identity a mystery) with a grudge manipulating the robots for his own purposes, but by the end it didn't seem to matter. Part One had done its job and sent me scurrying into the arms of a **Doctor Who** fandom I had no idea existed, and before long I was embroiled in an ongoing war of words about the recently-screened *The Deadly Assassin* (which had, apparently destroyed the magic of the Time Lords forever!) and scratching my head at worrying popular opinion that **Doctor Who** just wasn't as good as it used to be. *You fools! Can't you see that...* No. Arguing vociferously with total strangers about the merits of a TV show? Not for me. That way lies madness, surely?

Ultimately then, I owe it all – whatever *it* is – to Part One of *The Robots of Death*. Through that one episode I not only discovered fandom, I became a part of it; I edited a fanzine, wrote some fiction, sent monthly letters to the Appreciation Society's **TARDIS** fanzine. Eventually some of those early-days fans started to drift into the professional arena and, somehow, I found myself hanging onto their coat tails and the rest is ... well, if not exactly *history* then it's *my* history. *The Robots of Death* is very clearly a special **Doctor Who** adventure; it was the title chosen to properly launch the BBC DVD range, after all, and yet despite what it means to me and what it did to me, it's not a story I revisit all that often because of everything that's come since, the good and the bad. But whenever I come across the title, or see a photo of a Voc or even see the TARDIS spinning through space in a glitzy new episode, I can't help but think of that first episode of *The Robots of Death* and the wild, crazy, unpredictable creative journey it launched me on, a journey which, I hope, is only just beginning...

The Curse of Talons

The Talons of Weng-Chiang by **Rob Irwin**, 37, Sydney, Australia / First story: **Revenge of the Cybermen**

Victorian London. All you have to do is read those two words, or hear them spoken, and I can guarantee it won't be long before most people are thinking of pea soup fogs, Sherlock Holmes, the East End, Jack the Ripper, lonely Bobbies wandering through the night, and bodies being pulled out of the River Thames.

Funnily enough, all of those things are present (or are at least mentioned), in *The Talons of Weng-Chiang*. So if we can put aside, for the moment, the sparkling Robert Holmes script and above-average acting for 1970s **Doctor Who** in general, I'm of the belief that story means quite a lot to me and (if countless fan polls are to be believed), quite a few of you reading this essay, because it hits multiple bulls-eyes on all the tropes the audience is looking for in a Victorian London-based story.

And yet it goes much further than that. When I find myself working on story ideas for (non-**Doctor Who**) novels that I never have any time to write, I often have to stop myself from setting at least half of them in Victorian London. Why? I think there's something a little intoxicating about all those tropes I mentioned in the first paragraph and, if you're a **Doctor Who** fan, throw *The Talons of Weng-Chiang* on top of that and, *voilà*, you have a creepy, cold, gritty, yet strangely colourful kind of setting for crime fiction or an adventure story in general. Who *wouldn't* want their characters walking down those streets if you had half a chance for them to be your backdrop?

Indeed, the more I've thought about it while preparing to write this essay, the more I've come to the conclusion that *The Talons of Weng-Chiang* has been massively influential on the way I think about the era in general. When I try and visualise, for example, how a police station or mortuary from the era might look, I end up visualising scenes from this story. When I try and conjure up a music hall impresario of the era, who else but Henry Gordon Jago appears in my head? Ditto for a man of science from the era. If not Holmes, then Litefoot it is. I'm going to call it the Curse of *Talons*. A story that hits its marks so well, it's almost impossible to not invoke it when you're thinking, reading or writing about the era in general. That's some achievement!

Thankfully, I know I'm not the only one afflicted by the curse. I mentioned the combination of that Robert Holmes script and some above-average acting a moment ago and I think they also play a massive role in why this story is such a winner. This isn't one of those stories where you have to play the role of a fan apologist with remarks to your pals like, 'What I think the writer was trying to do was...' or, 'This is actually a great story and, if you read the Target novel, you can see the real storyline and just forget all about the acting...' because both the script and the acting are spot-on, too. It's no accident that this story falls in a season that also includes *The Deadly Assassin*, *The Robots of Death* and others of that ilk. This was a golden age not just for Tom Baker in the lead role, but the series in general.

Besides, who can forget lines like, 'Never trust a man with dirty fingernails...' or one of my favourites, delivered by the Doctor to Leela with a warm smile, 'If you're very good, I'll buy you an orange...'? Yes, this is a solid-gold example of **Doctor Who** writing that is light-hearted and fun to watch, without ever being OTT or slapstick. Robert Holmes truly was a master wordsmith.

Hammering home that this is not only a good, but an incredibly influential story for many **Doctor Who** fans, besides myself, is a quote I found from Russell T Davies regarding *The Talons of Weng-Chiang*: 'Watch episode one. It's the best dialogue ever written. It's up there with Dennis Potter. By a man called Robert Holmes. When the history of television drama comes to be written, Robert Holmes won't be remembered at all because he only wrote genre stuff. And that, I reckon, is a real tragedy.'

When I look back on this era of **Doctor Who** in general, I'm struck by how many stories I genuinely like without the need for rose-tinted glasses. And *The Talons of Weng-Chiang,* in particular, is not only very likeable but also plays a key role in cementing the way in which I think most of us view the mid-Tom Baker era. It's well written, it's well acted, the sets are great and the music is entirely appropriate to the action.

This is a classic for the ages.

The Incomprehensible Doctor

Horror of Fang Rock by **Jenny Shirt**, 41, Manchester
First story: **Horror of Fang Rock**

The eerie, claustrophobic feel of a stormy night at sea and a group of people trapped in a lighthouse, still scares me to this day. The unknown enemy, the rolling sea mist and the constant sound of the fog horn are what made *Horror of Fang Rock* so chilling. The worst part for me was seeing the creepy smile on the possessed lighthouse keeper Reuben's face, which had me hiding in my mum's arms. The alien Rutan had gone on a killing spree and the body of the dead lighthouse keeper had being taken over and reanimated by this creature, something I can never forgot seeing. Watching now it doesn't have as much impact, as the Rutan looks a bit like a cabbage mixed with a jelly to my grown-up eyes, but at the time it was absolutely terrifying.

My whole love of **Doctor Who**, and the fourth Doctor in particular, stems from *Horror of Fang Rock*. I grew up with Tom Baker's Doctor and this was the adventure that has always remained with me. Leela's decision to slap the very annoying Adelaide, the snobby secretary who had been shipwrecked and was screaming far too much and far too loudly, was one of the story's best moments, but I'll never forget the chill that ran down my spine when the Doctor locked the Rutan inside the lighthouse, instead of shutting it out.

There is another brilliant Leela moment as she asks the Doctor to use her own knife to kill her when she thinks she has been blinded, after witnessing the intense flash of the Rutan Mothership – which Leela looks at despite being told not to by the Doctor, and which transforms the colour of her eyes from brown to blue. He takes the knife but laughs at her and tells her the effects will pass. Leela and the Doctor were a brilliant team, and her savagery, together with his complex nature, made the pairing feel particularly special; they worked so well together.

I can remember watching this Gothic, Agatha Christie-style **Doctor Who** story at the age of six sitting next to my mum, whilst tightly holding onto her for reassurance. *Horror of Fang Rock* really lived up to the 'horror' aspect of its name, so in addition I decided that it was safer to keep a cushion nearby, as a secondary backup for hiding behind – just in case. I had seen **Doctor Who** before, in fact I'd been watching it for the previous couple of years, but this was the first time I really took notice of it and saw how special it could be. I loved the whole concept of the show and wondered just who this mysterious man, the Doctor, really was? He was complex, moody and blunt. Tom Baker played him so alien and so unsympathetic towards most of the people trapped in the lighthouse, and this really confused me. I now see as an adult, of course, and understood later why he didn't empathise with them as much as I wanted him to when I was little. It was the greed of the shipwrecked aristocrats trapped on Fang Rock, only really thinking of themselves and having no regard for the well-being and safety of their fellow travellers or anyone else in the lighthouse, that made the Doctor treat them with the contempt he did. It was a more serious fourth Doctor who made an appearance in this tale, and this was the one occasion where he failed in his quest to save anyone, and that left me wondering what had happened and why he had got it so wrong? (Based on a poem called *Flannan Isle* by Wilfred Gibson, where everyone in the lighthouse did die, I now understand why this had to happen.) The Doctor was also dealing with Reuben's story of the Beast of Fang Rock, which he explained to Leela did not exist, whilst at the same time trying to understand what was happening in the lighthouse. And from that point forwards, I couldn't stop watching; I needed to know more to try and understand the Doctor, something I have constantly failed to do – he is such an unpredictable character.

I was determined to go on more adventures, though, and so *Horror of Fang Rock* became the trigger for my love of the show to this day. I have gone on to watch every episode from the age of six to the present, and have met some lovely people through conventions and social networking, people who have become friends for life - and all through my love of this wonderful television programme. Every incarnation of the Doctor has his own quirkiness, and I hope the series continues on for many more generations to discover and enjoy. It's fantastic and brilliant, and the world of television wouldn't be the same without **Doctor Who** in it.

So in spite of the fact that I will never truly understand him, I am so glad I found the Doctor and his wonderful adventures.

Prawnography
The Invisible Enemy by **Alan Hayes**, 47, Enfield, UK
First story: **The Sea Devils** (Omnibus Repeat)

'I was a late developer,' the Doctor admitted in *Terror of the Autons*, referring to his academic performance when compared to that of the Master. This statement could so easily be applied to how I came to **Doctor Who** as an eleven-year-old, having spent the previous five years living in fear of watching the programme. Other than the fact that I'd seen and enjoyed a couple of the Jon Pertwee feature-length repeats (or omnibuses as they were quaintly called in those days), my trepidation was based almost entirely upon hearsay - tales which had spread like wildfire in the school playground, or the line that my parents would regularly throw me, that **Doctor Who** was simply too scary for kids. One factor, however, dominated, striking terror into my very soul - and that factor was, believe it or not, Tom Baker. Whenever I had caught glimpses of the programme, it wasn't the aliens or the tense situations that had me engaging in my own particular variation of the 'behind the sofa' routine (nervous child that I was, it was 'behind the house' in my case!), it was the Doctor himself. Maybe I just walked in - and ran out! - during the wrong scenes, the ones in which he was displaying the cold, detached streak of his early episodes, serving only to amplify the terror? Whatever the cause, it wasn't until Saturday 23rd October 1976 that I summoned up the courage to sit myself down in front of the programme. Watching the fourth episode of *The Hand of Fear*, suddenly I realised how foolish I'd been for all those years. Twenty-five minutes of television changed my life in an instant and suddenly, **Doctor Who** was *the* fascination in my life, surpassing football and even the joyous European game-show, **Jeux Sans Frontières**! I must have been insufferable - everything, *everything* on my mind was **Doctor Who**. Practically overnight, I went from being a normal kid to an obsessive with stuck record syndrome who lived and breathed the series. Nothing else mattered.

Little over a week later, I found myself so completely entranced by Peter Pratt's sublime portrayal of the Master in *The Deadly Assassin* that I embarked upon my first artistic endeavour related to the series, to make a life-size bust of this devilish good-looker. I grabbed one of my mother's polystyrene wig stands, melted red and green candles all over it and then cut a table-tennis ball in half to make the eyes, finishing it all off with some torn fabric that just about passed for a cowl. Looking back, I'm staggered that I didn't set fire to the house, and just like Corgi and Dinky, who could never get the colours right on their TV tie-in toy cars, I got the colour scheme an impressive 100% wrong. If only I'd been watching **Doctor Who** in colour, instead of on the black and white portable telly in my bedroom, things might have been different. Regardless, for the next couple of years I awoke every morning faced with that nightmarish vision. That might explain a thing or two!

The remainder of that series sped past and, by its end, my now voracious appetite for all things **Doctor Who** had been treated to such wonders as the Time Lords, Leela of the Sevateem, Taren Capel and his robot killers and the incomparable Jago, Litefoot and Li H'sen Chang. It had been wonderful, but during the next year I was to learn an invaluable lesson in my **Doctor Who** education: *The Invisible Enemy* would prove to me that it was possible to love something that most people derided.

There are many things not quite right with *The Invisible Enemy*: the story is hardly the most original to grace the series, its effects and camera tricks are highly variable, and, where it really matters, its alien threat is ... well ... less convincing than Larry Grayson as Rambo. As a thoroughly uncritical and easily pleased fan tuning in in 1977, even I could see that this wasn't exactly of the same high standard as *The Talons of Weng-Chiang* or *Horror of Fang Rock*, but that really made no odds. I loved it to bits and was drawn in right from the opening model shots, complemented so gloriously by Dudley Simpson's incidentals. Could I be put off by the wild eyebrow make-up that would have embarrassed even Denis Healey into reaching for his clippers? Would I collapse laughing at the Doctor's microcosm meeting with what looked like a black plastic bin liner? Would my suspension of disbelief be stretched to breaking point by the revelation that the Nucleus of the Swarm was, in actual fact, a giant prawn that could do little more than quiver agitatedly on a trolley? Would that robot dog I'd heard about irritate the hell out of me by the end of the serial? On all counts, the answer was an unequivocal, 'No.'

Thirty-five years later, would I give the same answers? Much to my surprise, yes, I honestly would. *The Invisible Enemy* is a gloriously ambitious story, full of invention, humour and thrills. The fact the production underachieves in some areas is really neither here nor there for me. This was the story that taught me that a **Doctor Who** story didn't have to be perfect for me to fall completely in love with it, and that it was possible to look beyond production limitations and still find something very special, even when others might swear blind that there is simply nothing to find.

The Invisible Enemy is the mangy, three-legged cat with the dodgy ear that most people can't bring themselves to love, but for me it's the ultimate comfort watch – an absolute joy. There's no denying that there are a hundred stories better than it, but I regard few with the same fondness, black plastic bags, glittery eyebrows, maniacal prawns and all. Contact *has* been made.

Things That Go Bump in the Night

Image of the Fendahl by **Tony Eccles**, 43, Liverpool
First story:**The Green Death**

My earliest memories of **Doctor Who** include the maggots, giant spiders and a robot; I was five years old. I remember the third Doctor well but it was Tom Baker's portrayal that left an impression on me. The show had a unique flavour and I was particularly taken by its iconic theme which evoked fear and mystery. However, as a young boy, I wasn't captured by the wonders of the TARDIS or the complex nature of space-time flight; I was too young to appreciate such ideas. I was, on the other hand, rather captivated by the monsters the Doctor encountered each week. I loved monsters because they were scary.

For Christmas and birthdays my dad bought me various horror film books whose pages were filled with black and white photos of Lon Chaney, Jr., and Boris Karloff in their various monster guises. Of course this small book collection included four **Doctor Who** books; two of which were the monster books produced by Target in 1975 and 1977. They are cherished today but are battered and bruised. These wonderful publications gave me great pleasure and I revelled in the variety of fiends the Doctor faced. I was in awe of their frightening countenance; the Sea Devils remain one of my favourites with their large sinister staring fish eyes that never blinked. It was these very images that had a profound effect on my imagination to the extent that as an older boy I had the desire to be a writer of spooky tales.

During the 1970s I also watched **Sapphire and Steel**, **Armchair Thriller**, and Nigel Kneale's **Quatermass** with John Mills. The world of fear had been introduced to me at a young age. Around the age of nine I remember waking up in the middle of the night to see

Dracula standing beside my bed with a big sinister grin on his face. In his hands he held a birthday cake. I screamed and suddenly my mind's projection disappeared. Such frights were not common but they were very memorable; perhaps I ought to make a suggestion: parents should be mindful of what toys they buy for their children. Dracula was one of a number of action figures I regularly played with.

Growing up, of course I realised that monsters were opportunities for storytellers to reflect on the darker side of human nature, they were metaphors for human flaws. Monsters also reflect the very things we fear, for example, isolation, fragility of life, death, the hidden and the unknown. It's these very elements that help to make great stories and **Doctor Who** in some ways reminded me of Grimm's fairy tales.

As a teenager in the 1980s I gradually left **Doctor Who** behind and spent my time with friends playing role-playing games or trying to watch horror films that one could only access via the video store with a fake ID. It was at this time that I became witness to a new era of films being made that pushed the boundaries in special effects; costly technical processes that were lost on many television shows at the time.

I watched **Psycho** when I was thirteen and **The Exorcist** when I was fifteen and this made me think about the scarier tales of classic **Doctor Who**. Stories like *The Dæmons*, *The Talons of Weng-Chiang* and *Horror of Fang Rock* which were not being produced any more; a shame as they each contained great atmosphere that was amazingly maintained throughout four episodes ... grrr, Mary Whitehouse, you just didn't get it did you? It's my humblest opinion that with the exception of *Blink* there aren't many modern **Doctor Who** stories that would be considered frightening. Atmosphere requires landscape, characters and time, which is difficult to achieve in singular episodes.

During my teen years an older cousin of mine introduced me to the works of H. P. Lovecraft. Lovecraft was one of the earliest writers to bring the science fiction and horror genres together and my discovery reacquainted me with **Doctor Who**, as I could see where a number of his ideas may have influenced some of the classic stories such as *Image of the Fendahl*. *Image of the Fendahl* has a priory that sits close to a haunted wood, occupied by a group of scientists using futuristic equipment to study human evolution. Strange buildings, weird landscapes, scientists and alien creatures were the tenet of Lovecraft's worlds. Often the influence for many horror writers of the 20th century and I wonder if he will ever influence **Doctor Who** again.

In the last twenty years I've honed my writing skills and learned how to write screenplays. As a child I always wanted to be a writer of spooky tales and last year that ambition came true. My first short story was published in an American anthology called **After Dark**. *The Empty House* features monsters of a bygone era and they are able to cross the boundaries between their world and our own. In the same way that *Image of the Fendahl* conveys the idea that an alien race came to Earth many millions of years ago and influenced human evolution, my own monsters were also primal inhabitants of this world and only now are they claiming back what is rightfully theirs.

In the back of my mind monsters are trying to scratch their way onto the page and into our world and some succeed causing utter terror. Unfortunately the Doctor isn't there to save the world but that's okay because the **Doctor Who** of my childhood opened those very doors of fear for me, showing me how to make monsters go bump in the night. Since then I've kept him firmly in my pocket.

The Warm Glow of Hazy Withdean Days

The Sun Makers by **Matt Hills**, 41, Aberystwyth, UK
First story: **Robot**

When I was a young boy, we used to visit my Gran and Grandad in Brighton every few months. These trips were sometimes on a Saturday, which meant I'd be allowed to settle into my Grandad's big armchair to watch that week's **Doctor Who**. One of the most exciting things about this change in family routine was that Gran got the **Radio Times**, so I could read all the **Doctor Who** material, going back through old copies stacked under the kettle, looking for features and interviews and devouring previews of episodes I'd watched weeks ago.

I saw Part Three of *The Sun Makers* on a pre-Christmas trip to Gran and Grandad's; I recall being horrified by the fact that Leela was going to be gassed. (As a six-year-old, I didn't quite get the steaming part of the storyline, let alone all the tax and economics.) Gran happened to mention that she knew one of the actors in that Saturday's **Doctor Who**; he lived a few doors down from them, in Brighton's leafy Withdean area, and she said hallo to him sometimes when she popped out to the Matlock Road Post Office.

This was a radical new concept for my six-year-old self: **Doctor Who** characters were also actual people who I might bump into at the local store, or meet walking along the road. A few years later – between *Logopolis* and *Castrovalva* – I recognised Peter Davison whilst out shoe shopping in Woking (I asked for his autograph, which he kindly gave me before immediately exiting the shop). But back in 1977, I'd never met someone who'd actually been in **Doctor Who**. And here was Gran, saying that one of her neighbours on the other side of the street was a real-life actor, and he'd played Bisham in *The Sun Makers*.

Enquiries must have been made behind the scenes, plans concocted, and schemes hatched. And so it transpired that on our next weekend visit the following year I was asked if I'd like to meet that actor from **Doctor Who**. I was a rather shy child, and the thought filled me with excitement and dread in equal measure. What could I possibly say to someone off the telly? To someone who'd spent time with Doctor Who himself, and Leela, and K-9?

Mum, Gran and I headed over the road to visit the man who'd been Bisham. I vividly recall walking past the flowers, fences and hedgerows of this well-to-do Brighton suburb. I recall walking up an alien, unknown driveway that seemed vast, and set such a long, long way back from the pavement. I remember feeling scared, and not the enjoyable kind of fear that accompanied watching **Doctor Who**. No, this was a whole different strain of social unease, topped off by edgy fanboy anticipation.

And here's the strangest thing. My memories of meeting David Rowlands are hazy in the extreme, perhaps whited-out by all that childhood anxiety. I'm afraid to say that I really can't remember much. Looking back now, I guess he was a jobbing actor, and so there were no glossy, signed pictures to be had, and no, 'Here I am with a celebrity,' photo opportunities. After all, this was simply a local man giving up half an hour of his Saturday to indulge a neighbour's grandson.

Rather than recalling much detail about the meeting itself, what stayed with me was the fact that Mum and Gran had arranged this outing on my behalf, recognising and validating my **Doctor Who** obsession. The programme occupied my imagination on a constant basis, dominating all my schoolbook stories and drawings, and now I'd had the chance to meet one of the stars of *The Sun Makers*, all thanks to my family. Later on, whenever I read the novelisation, saw photos from the story, watched it on video or DVD, I remembered with a warm glow of nostalgia the actor who'd lived down the street from my Brighton Gran, and the brief chance I'd had to wander into the glamorous, exciting, unearthly world of People Who'd

Been In **Doctor Who** (which, confusingly, proved also to be a domestic, ordinary and everyday world). Although my fuzzy memories of that day undoubtedly cheat, *The Sun Makers* will always be special to me.

Nowadays I'm lucky enough that I can afford to fleetingly meet actors at conventions, photo shoots and signings; a domain where commercial imperialism has surely made itself felt. However, *The Sun Makers* pre-dated both my understanding of capitalism and the growing commercialisation of corporate-style conventions. I don't know whether it was Marxism or a Withdean weekender, but the story stayed with me over the years. To my impressionable young self, aged six-and-a-bit, it was an absolute epic. Truth be told, I've never been able to get to grips with the anti-Graham Williams sentiment which flourished in sectors of fandom; I was simply too young for it at the time. For me, this era of **Doctor Who** was vibrant, imaginative and utterly thrilling.

And perhaps I was also too young to properly appreciate meeting professional actors back in 1978. But, as a **Doctor Who** fan born in the early 1970s rather than the late 1950s, my timing was always going to be slightly off in one way or another.

It's Not That Bad...
Underworld by **Felix Dembinski**, 17, Derbyshire, UK
First story: **Rose**

I was born in the 1990s, and came to **Doctor Who** through the Christopher Eccleston series. I had heard of the series before but probably only through the Dalek Kit Kat adverts. I knew very little about the 1963 to 1989 series (I have never called it the 'classic' series or 'old' series; to me it is all one long ongoing story), having only seen brief clips of it on **Doctor Who Confidential**. My exposure to the stories of the first eight doctors came between Series Two and Three of Russell T Davies' reign as producer, when broadband internet became available to me. On a site called YouTube, not as well known back then, someone had uploaded all of the stories from 1963 to 1989, each episode split into three segments (given the ten-minute limit was still in place then). I watched all of them. In order. Over six months. Which averages at just fewer than four episodes a day, which is very worrying.

But because of this incredibly fast exposure to the series and going into it with very little foreknowledge, I never had the experience of disappointment when a story turned out not to be as good as I had been told or remembered it was. It also (and importantly for this essay) made me immune to 'fan-wisdom.' Having enjoyed stories like *The Mutants* and *The Creature from the Pit*, I was very disappointed to see how low they had ranked in the 2009 poll of 200 best **Doctor Who** stories made by **Doctor Who Magazine**. I was also surprised to see that *The Tomb of the Cybermen* was a fan favourite, a story that I had found as slow and dull as parts two to four of *The Space Museum*. The greatest irritation, however was that *Underworld*, one of my favourite stories, by my favourite writers, had come fourth from last. 'Why?' I asked myself. 'Why all this hate for *Underworld*?' At first I thought that having the word 'Under' somewhere in your title was something that most fans must hate, but a short time searching the internet I found that people disliked *Underworld* because of the amount of CSO in it. 'CSO?' I asked myself. 'I can't recall it being that bad.' I re-watched it on YouTube and again found nothing wrong with it. It was only when I saw the 625-line 50fps version on the DVD that I realised what everyone was talking about. It was also when buying and watching the rest of the series on DVD that I realised why everyone had been moaning about **Doctor Who**'s special effects. Having watched the series first on YouTube, and a YouTube in its earliest days, I hadn't been seeing the series in its fullest quality. YouTube back then had a rate of 25 frames-per-second and a resolution of 240 lines. So I had experienced the 1963 to 1989 series at about a quarter of its original quality. In hindsight, this was the best possible way I could have watched it. It made *Frontier in Space* look like **Star Wars** and *Snakedance* look like **Blade Runner**.

Fans hating a story because its special effects aren't particularly good is a bit rich given the series that they are watching. If effects mattered to them they should have moved to a different series. By the same logic they should also dislike *Terror of the Autons* just as much, it's probably got the same amount of CSO in it!

All in all, what *Underworld* taught me was to never judge something based on what other people think, always make up your own mind and if you don't enjoy something experience it again in a lower frame rate – and those three lessons can sum up what **Doctor Who** as a whole has taught me.

Attacked by Blurry Bacofoil

The Invasion of Time by **Nicholas Hollands**, 37, Glasgow, UK / First story: **Destiny of the Daleks**

As a child, I was never really 'crafty.' I don't mean sneaking chunks of cheese out of the fridge ... I was good at that. I mean that I can't really *make* things. To this day, my creative outlets are limited to playing with Lego, making origami models, and creating weird and wonderful contraptions on my computer using a physics simulator. But the one thing I *could* create as a child was computer programs.

My sister and I got a computer between us when I was nine. It was an Acorn Electron, a cheaper version of the then ubiquitous BBC Micro... A staple of comprehensive schools throughout the UK. After a brief period of using it solely for games, I discovered BBC BASIC, and I was set for life. I can still remember the first 'proper' computer program I wrote. You gave the computer a letter, and it would print a limerick whose subject matter started with that letter. But I was nine, so they weren't very good limericks.

I got interested in graphics fairly early on, and I was probably the only kid at primary school who had a working knowledge of basic trigonometry (you needed cosines to draw circles). And one of the first *graphics* programs I wrote emulated some of the graphics screens on the new TARDIS console. The squiggly coloured lines, the white curved diamond, and the Doctor's 'Progress bar' stars towards the Dark Tower in the death zone.

BBC Micro graphics were everywhere at the time. Instead of having an in-vision continuity announcer, children's programmes were introduced by a disembodied voice over some simple graphic display ... the one I clearly remember is a green dancing robot with bouncing eyes. There were competitions for children to enter to design new ones, but I never went for those. I was too busy recreating and improving on the ones already on-screen.

The bloopy noises and the blocky graphics are extremely primitive by today's standards, but they were state of the art then. And like any cutting-edge technology, sometimes it worked and sometimes it didn't. Looking back through **Doctor Who** history, there's a fair few special effects that went a little wide of the mark. We laugh at them these days, but in and of their time they were extremely innovative.

I sometimes wonder what went through the heads of the special effects team when they saw some of the **Doctor Who** scripts. I suspect it was along the lines of, 'How the *hell* are we going to do *that*!?' on numerous occasions. What I *am* certain of is that they worked hard to try and achieve what the writers wanted us to see.

(Side note: Having said that, it's also fairly clear that they didn't necessarily always talk to each other. The script for *Shada* sees the instruction, 'Chris is enveloped by a spinning cube of white light and disappears.' I'm fairly sure Douglas wanted a 'laser cage' to surround the actor, before he faded, like something out of **Tron**. What he got was a cross-fade to a spinning plastic cube painted white, with a bright light shone on it. Not quite as spectacular, but I can see where they were coming from.)

So given the hard work these innovators put in, what place do we have to blot out their art with our modern computer-based trickery on the DVDs? Should we mess about with the classics?

It's a tough call, and it's one where my partner and I fall into different camps. And I take the opportunity to needle him about it whenever the situation arises.

I like the new CGI, particularly where it has been used to 'tidy up' existing effects. I love that there are people who still care enough about the old show to want to try and make it better, from the simple case of a prettier laser beam, to a spectacular shuttle crash that would never have been possible with the old technology.

My partner is the purist. Initially he would refuse to switch the CGI on, considering it (and I'm allowed to quote him on this), 'Painting a new smile on the Mona Lisa.' I had to wait until he wasn't around to see them. I finally managed to convince him to at least watch them together with *The Invisible Enemy*, showing him where they've repaired the crack in the wall for K9's shoot-out. Now at least he'll sit and watch them, but when we get a new DVD, it's got to be the unmodified version first. And there's still the occasional complaint that it looks, 'Too new.'

For me, *The Invasion of Time* is a production that shows how well these new effects can be integrated into the old programme, and *why* they get to be done. The original realisation of the Vardans as blurry blue-fringed Bacofoil never really lived up to the pictures I had in my head from reading the novelisations; of shimmering, not-quite-there people. The new Vardans are admittedly a little flashy, but they do look how I imagined them. For me, that's a firm case that you *can* mess about with the classics.

That said, I notice that the 'Next Generation' version of Jeff Wayne's *The War of the Worlds* has disappeared from my Christmas wish-list. There's a possibility that the new year will see me and him indoors grumpily listening to the old version, and complaining about 'kids today'...

Promised Lands
The Key to Time by **Naomi Padowicz**, 27, Newcastle
First story: **Genesis of the Daleks**

I grew up and discovered **Doctor Who** in the Dark Times when there were no new episodes. However, because my family had moved to Cincinnati Ohio from New York City, I was introduced to the Doctor through PBS. Public Broadcasting in the United States differs from the BBC in a key aspect: rather than having a licence fee which everyone must pay every year, while PBS stations receive a certain percentage of funding from the government, the rest must be raised from the viewers themselves. **Doctor Who**, as one of the most popular programmes, is key to the local broadcaster's very survival. So when it was announced that the show had been cancelled, my local PBS station decided to continue playing omnibus weekly stories every Saturday at 10.35pm. In fact, they were kind enough between episodes, to remind us that they were not responsible for the cancellation, directing everyone to the correct names and addresses of the people who were and giving a direct line to the BBC complaints department. In fact, depending on who was working on the day of broadcast, sometimes they would even scrawl the addresses at the bottom of the screen during the show to give you as many opportunities as possible to write them down correctly. You weren't considered a proper fan until you had sent at least one anonymous death threat to Michael Grade; some people I knew would even send one in on a regular basis, just so they had something to do on a Sunday after the **New York Times** had been read.

When it became glaringly obvious that a lack of funds was in danger of crippling the station, they would take to desperate measures and over the course of a weekend, play through the entire Key to Time series, interspersed with segments begging for money. When the 2005 series was announced, PBS stations all over the United States kicked into gear to raise the money to buy it, a goal that would never be achieved as the BBC turned on its American equivalent and went to the Sci Fi channel instead. This decision actually shut down the state of Kentucky's last public broadcasting channel, who were counting on the series as a last chance to rejuvenate their failing station due to economic conditions that kept the state in perpetual depression.

The group that was most hurt by the move to cable were the oldest and most loyal fans. Many of the people who had been watching **Doctor Who** since William Hartnell were old age pensioners, who could never afford a monthly bill for cable as it would mean choosing between the new series and insignificant things like eating. And while the average fan is part of the 20% of the United States population with at least a Bachelor's degree – and who hold positions such as doctors and lawyers – the over-35 intellectual classes loathe television in general and have to be coerced to take on cable for one show. Even without this natural loathing of television, the period in which **Doctor Who** returned was during the malevolent reign of George W. Bush, when many **Doctor Who** fans who happened to be left-leaning politically, were being hunted down and were having their careers and lives destroyed under the Patriot Act, forcing many to flee the country in a trail of financial ruin.

I, however, watched classic **Doctor Who** as escapism – from a dreary upper middle class life in a foreign area, as I went through the pain of my parents' divorce (which took ten years to finalise), and suffered silently from the physical and emotional abuse and neglect of a stepmother and father who shared a mutual addiction to alcohol. The first Romana appealed to me for her clothes, many of which I actually owned, and her intelligence and rebuttals of the Doctor. My friends all watched **Doctor Who** as it was the only show that actually challenged our intelligence. The Key to Time was very special as every aspect and type of science fiction gets a look in. From the Swampies' struggle against the unwanted refinery of the Dryfoots – a clear questioning of

Western attitudes towards developing nations – to the allegory of European history seen on Tara through the deeds of the evil Count Grendel, our minds as viewers are challenged to think beyond just the story and of better, deeper and more noble aspects in our own lives, regardless of which aspects of the show were our favourites. Conversations could go on for hours; everyone would agree on one thing. We all loved Gallifrey. Gallifrey was so far removed and so exotic that we were obsessed with the Doctor's home planet. We loved the politics, and the strange etiquette. It was proper science fiction that didn't have any of the bluster and touchy-feely elements of other popular shows in the 1990s. We loved the cold logic of K9 and Romana and the Doctor during the Key to Time which helped to assess every situation, from the disappearance of Calufrax, to how Jethryk appeared in the case with the crown jewels. And the sarcasm and quick one-liners we repeated at school to one another, along with that other favourite, **Monty Python**.

Yes it was upper class twittage at its best, and yes we were hardened nerds with pimples and coke-bottle glasses. But **Doctor Who** was as much a part of being one of the uncool as **Star Wars**, and **Star Trek**, and Isaac Asimov novels. The Doctor was an integral part of our pantheon of superheroes, and was a finisher to a Saturday evening of **Dungeons and Dragons**. American nerds deserve an intelligent charismatic hero not afraid to discuss interplanetary coordinates and advanced particle physics, because at the end of the day, since **Star Trek** went off the air he is the only thing we have left.

The Colour of Ribos
The Ribos Operation by **Mark Trevor Owen**, 41,
Douglas, Isle of Man / First story: **Robot**

A friend and I used to play a game. We had to do something to pass the time. **Doctor Who** was off the air, and the internet ran on telephone wires, rumour and hope. Inspired, like so much of modern culture by **Smash Hits** magazine, the game was called 'What Colour Is This **Doctor Who** Story?' Some stories provided general consensus – *Time-Flight* is certainly pale blue. Others led to heated and charmingly pointless debate. *The Sontaran Experiment* – beige or green? *Time and the Rani* – obviously pink, but what shade – Barbie, neon or slutty? *The Ribos Operation* offers no argument in this respect. It's a rich, reddy-brown. As rich and brown as Tom Baker's voice. Or Robert Holmes' writing. Or Dudley Simpson's music.

From a personal point of view, *The Ribos Operation* is my jumping-on point. I'd watched **Doctor Who** before, inasmuch as I'd sat in front of the television and observed thrilling, bewildering and endearingly terrifying fragments of an intriguing story. My very first memory of the programme is what I now know to be the end of the first episode of *Robot*. When I watch it now, I still see the cliffhanger as I originally saw it; a jumble of distorted images, as an unknown 'something' looms towards 'the girl.' But the beginning of the search for the Key to Time is where I reached the age when the fragments coalesce into narrative, plot and characterisation. With that level of understanding, I became a regular viewer.

We've known each other for a couple of paragraphs now, so I'll share a confidence with you: I don't like science fiction. As a genre, from Jules Verne to **Star Trek**, there's a coldness about it that leaves me (if you will) alienated. Many a time a well-meaning pal has declared, 'If you like **Doctor Who**, you'll love this,' and presented me with a DVD full of uniforms, brushed metal and dialogue untroubled by wit. This would be greeted with one of those, 'Thanks!' with the tell-tale squeak of insincerity in the middle letters. It might be a touch deceiving, but trust me, it is so much easier than the instinctive true response – that I don't see **Doctor Who** as science fiction. And that opinion is really the only common ground that fans of 'proper' SF and I share. Sure, there are spaceships, aliens and lasers aplenty in any phase of **Doctor Who** up to the present day, but there's a witty warmth, a love of characterisation, and a tradition of storytelling that seems amicably divorced from the world of 'hard' science fiction. And it can't be too much of a coincidence that the story that turned me into a regular viewer of **Doctor Who** is one where the lasers and aliens could barely be treated in a more cursory way. *The Ribos Operation* is an adventure for the Doctor, disguised like a segment of the Key to Time, in the trappings of theatre, cinema and folklore.

Watching *The Ribos Operation* as an adult, the beauty of the dialogue shines brightly, reflecting the neatness of the plotting. Even though the cleverness of the words being spoken would have largely flown over my little Manx head on first viewing, I like to imagine that it was material like this that stimulated my love of words and their meanings. 'It would seem that providence has placed in my hand a weapon already forged,' declares the lip-smackingly villainous Graff Vynda-K, in one of my favourite lines. In his hand is a 'weapon' – the mineral survey of Ribos – that has indeed been 'forged' in a rather different way. To write lyrical, rhythmic cod-Shakespearean dialogue is talent enough in itself. To then use that dialogue in wordplay that informs the viewers' knowledge of both plot and character is just breathtaking. Of all his scripts for **Doctor Who**, *The Ribos Operation* plays to the strengths of Robert Holmes most satisfyingly in my opinion. Here we have the richness of an historical setting, but by being set in another planet's medieval period, Holmes is free to place imagination before research, with quite beautiful results. For a writer who placed his dislike of historical settings in **Doctor Who** scripts on record, it's the perfect compromise.

As the start of the linked Key to Time season, *The Ribos Operation* had to be designed to draw in an audience who would stay loyal for the whole 26-episode-long quest. For me, it had the desired effect and more. The Key to Time has been found (sorry if that's a spoiler for you), but more than thirty years later, I'm still following these adventures whose wit and warmth could coddle even Ribos in the Ice Time. (It would be fun to see Ribos in the Sun Time. Presumably the Shrieves swap their fur hats and cloaks for shades and shorts, and Binro the Heretic pongs to high heaven.)

If you want to play my game, you might find your **Doctor Who** stories to be all sorts of colours – I certainly hope you do. The rich reddy-brown of *The Ribos Operation* has never faded. It's a story that has matured with me, revealing new facets each time I've returned to it over the years. This sumptuous tale, with Tom Baker at the peak of his power and Mary Tamm making a delightful debut, sits among my very favourite **Doctor Who** stories. It's a treasure among the reliquaries, awaiting discovery; one of those wonderful times when all aspects of the production are revelling in their storytelling possibilities. Seek it out.

Better Than to Receive
The Pirate Planet by **Peter Nolan**, 38, Wexford, Ireland
First story: **The Robots of Death**

Wisdom isn't something that's generally thought of negatively. We don't usually wish we'd been a lit bit less wise, a bit more ignorant and uninformed, and whole civilisations have built themselves around the accumulation of it.

Yet, for all that, people are rightly suspicious of wisdom freely given on a silver platter, of wisdom *received*. With a history as long as **Doctor Who**'s, for decades there have inevitably been new generations joining the party, and older generations eager to sit them down by the fireside and tell them the Way of Things.

I was four years old when *The Pirate Planet* went out, though I may well have seen it. But when I first got my proper, grown up Fan Card (issued, as you know, only after the elite have sniffed you over to see if it's okay for you to like the same TV show as them) I was almost entirely dependent on others for so much information. From the day I arrived on the scene and blinking, stepped into the sun, there was more to be seen than can ever be seen and more to learn than can ever be learned (no, wait, that's **The Lion King**...) ... anyway, I learned what 'everybody knows' about *The Pirate Planet* and about the work of Douglas Adams in general. A lot of this down to Adams' successor, Christopher H Bidmead who's been admirably successful in dictating the terms of the debate down the years. Conventional wisdom dictates that this was a time of silliness, humour and fun that eschewed basic science and sensible plotting and was replaced, rightly or wrongly, by a more serious, less jokey, era of 'hard science.'

Naturally, what everybody knows is wrong.

Sitting down to watch Douglas Adams' work on **Doctor Who** for myself was a personal revelation. It's not even that its humour and outrageously charismatic performances outweigh supposed scientific illiteracy. On the contrary, it's that few other writers bristle with such a love of science and knowledge or so blithely assume that love is shared by the audience. And few have been so explicitly writing for children while so explicitly holding that kids are as smart, or smarter, than grownups. I guffawed at the brilliance and daring of a joke about neutron particle accelerators in a children's television show. I boggled at the audacity and verve of the scene where the Doctor and the Captain sketch out, literally in perfect miniature, the way balancing gravitational forces of planetary bodies allows for stable systems. You've got the Doctor making jokes about how he, 'always thought conservation of momentum was one of the more important laws of physics,' and giving pithy, short, easy to understand explanations of the principles of singularity. And even though it's not spelt out, it's a story driven by the observation that if E no longer equal MC^2 (as travel through the vortex insists) then, well, anything could be moved through the vortex, with mass no longer a limiting factor to speed.

Adams' script is so packed with these brilliant, brain-melting, wonderfully barking ideas that it's the equivalent of lighting the blue touch paper on kids' brains and standing well back as their imaginations explode. It certainly blew and expanded my mind simultaneously and, as someone who'd never been exposed to much Adams before, prompted me to immediately run out and buy everything else he'd ever written.

Plus, there's a robot dog in a laser battle with a robot parrot dropping what looks like deadly radioactive bird poo. What more could I want?

But it's about more than just *The Pirate Planet*. *The Gunfighters* is to me one of the wildest, funniest stories of all time. *Inferno* is, in fact, not one of the all time great **Doctor Who** stories but one of the worst pieces of television I've ever seen. You may disagree. In fact, you probably do. But the important thing is that, whoever you are, there are things that 'everybody knows,' that you'd think were completely wrong once you find out for yourself.

We're gifted with an age where, more than ever before, almost every moment of **Doctor Who** can be easily located and experienced by anyone. We've even found four more missing episodes in the time since I first became a grown-up fan; where even seeking out fan reconstructions of those episodes still missing doesn't require the dedication to trade in blank VHS tapes and brown envelopes but simply an internet connection.

So, there's really no excuse. Order *The Pirate Planet* if you haven't already done so; and *The Gunfighters*; and *Inferno*. Track down recons of those old black and white tales that only survive on audio that sound like such hard work. Subject yourself to what everyone tells you are the terrible episodes. Because your favourite **Doctor Who** story may well be out there, sitting on a shelf somewhere, made decades ago and just waiting for you to catch up.

Because with wisdom, what's better than to receive, is to decide for yourself. So put 1.795 and 2.205 together and get your own version of four.

For me, that story is Douglas Adams' mad, supremely intelligent story of a boy playing pirates and his vortex-hopping planet. It's a story to come back to time and again. So, excuse me as I settle down, a glass of wine in one hand and a sonic screwdriver remote in the other and lose myself in a world of plank-walking, bone-bleaching, physics-based madness. And, by the Great Parrot of Hades, and Newton's Third Law, I'm going enjoy every second of it.

The Wind Hissed, 'Ogriiiiiiiiii...'

The Stones of Blood by **Michael Russell**, 40, Portland, ME, USA / First story: **Robot**

Yes, I grew up within walking distance of an abandoned quarry. Even the landscape told me to love **Doctor Who** and imagine its magic happening anywhere. I was in the middle of rural Arkansas, where anything or nothing would happen, depending on where your mind could go. I already had a loopy imagination, and my favourite show greatly encouraged me.

Apart from a very brief period in which Tom Baker's Doctor was considered intriguing, my classmates didn't care for **Doctor Who**, but my mom and brothers loved it. **Doctor Who** almost felt like a secret family tradition. What, PBS only started airing it when I was eleven? Well, that was forever to a twelve-year-old. With my family, it was more of a casual love. The only truly devoted nutter was me. I didn't know anything about organised fandom, so naturally, it didn't exist, and I didn't miss it.

The Stones of Blood was one of many stories that I loved as it kept multiplying in my mind after I watched it. It was both gothic and silly, and I saw nothing contradictory about that combination. I didn't get all the jokes and meanings at the time, especially not the lesbian subtext. The Doctor's claim that John Aubrey invented druidism as a joke inspired me to look up Aubrey in the family encyclopaedia, and there he was. See, everybody, **Doctor Who** was real! My favourite show pointed me in many directions I wouldn't have noticed otherwise, even with a delightfully breezy remark. It was a beautiful improvisation, probably.

The Doctor fought evil with wit and silliness, which made perfect sense to me, surrounded by neighbours who believed in guns, and I mean really believed in them, upholding weapons and macho preening as something to be admired. By contrast, the fourth Doctor's celebratory but unbending inquisitiveness showed me a huge world of more fun possibilities. Tom Baker made it seem that keeping a barrister's wig in his pocket was the most natural thing in the world. It seemed right that such a remarkable being would battle humourless posh sparkles capable of destroying galaxies.

The monsters never looked silly when I was a boy, not even Erato or Kroll. Now, I can see their technical limitations, but then and now, the joy, imagination and perseverance of the show steamrollers over such boring, literal-minded adult concerns. Stone circle rocks that were actually vampires – that thrilled me much more than Dracula ever could. And that hypnotic theme music sent me the sound of a thousand suns rising.

My boyhood home was in an agricultural experiment station, next to a forest. A bumpy, twisted dirt road led to a long-abandoned quarry. The tall pine trees blocked most of the sun, and the walk seemed dark even at noon. Potholes and lumps let me pretend the road was the moon's surface. Shadows of tall pine trees looked like rockets, or tall, stern silent aliens nodding their heads in the breeze.

In those years before cell phones, I could wander off by myself for hours, and nobody in the world knew where I was. The quarry was small, barely more than a gravel pit, but to my eyes, it was enormous and epic, full of thrilling possibilities. I never knew what had been mined there, as it was desolate and abandoned before I moved to the experiment station. Nobody else went there, so that made it mine.

In the sunset shadows in the quarry were several tall, weathered rocks. I convinced myself that the Ogri moved toward me. The sun threw shadows across the quarry and gave each looming stone a CSO fringe fire. I was old enough to think I was too old to be childlike, but fortunately, I was wrong. The rock monsters were comfortably scary. They didn't judge me. It never crossed my mind that being by myself in the woods was anything but safe. Going to school seemed more dangerous.

After enjoying my alone time outdoors, I always felt reinvigorated for my walk back home. I'd walk fast and then run to get back in time to watch another episode of **Doctor Who** at 6.30pm. With each step, I could hear the Ogri's loud heartbeat in my chest.

Within a one-year span, I got to see most of Tom Baker's stories, and I don't remember having a single, 'Ewww, it's awful!' cringe moment that many other fans speak of. In my mind, if anyone had asked K9 to compute the odds that **Doctor Who** could be anything but wonderful, he would have made a sputtering noise and spun around from the impossibility of the question. The Doctor was on TV, and my own private alien planet was just a few minutes' walk away. Whatever else was going on in my life could wait until later.

When Young Meets Old
The Androids of Tara by **May Norwood**, 12, Sheffield
First Story: **The Christmas Invasion**

The first episode of **Doctor Who** I ever saw was *The Christmas Invasion*. I was gripped immediately. It was terrifying at times; after I watched the tenth Doctor story, *The Idiot's Lantern*, I wouldn't watch television for a month. I was convinced that the telly was going to suck my face off and eat my brains! But I also found it amazing. **Doctor Who** was my favourite television show.

My dad shortly introduced me to classic **Doctor Who**. I found these less fast-paced and quieter than new **Doctor Who**, but I liked them none the less. Some of the classic stories that stuck in my head were: *The Green Death*, *The War Games*, *Castrovalva*, and, possibly most of all, The Key to Time series (borrowed from the boy next door). It is about one of these stories, *The Androids of Tara,* that I am writing now.

We had just finished *The Stones of Blood,* when I said to my dad: 'Wouldn't it be great if, in one story, instead of them searching for the segment the whole time and only finding it at the end, Romana found it straight away and it got taken off her? They could spend the story trying to get it back.'

And, to my delight, that was what happened! The first time I watched that serial I was really struck by it. I'm not quite sure why; maybe because I guessed the start. I enjoyed the whole of The Key to Time series, but, joint with *The Pirate Planet, The Androids of Tara* is the one that I remember most.

The series also introduced me to K9. I really like animals, and the fact that they had a dog that wasn't a dog in the TARDIS as a long-term companion was great. In fact, the first time that I ever saved up a lot of pocket money was to buy a remote control K9! I used my Christmas money, all my pocket money up until my birthday in April, and some of my birthday money.

Everyone was impressed. I still get it out sometimes. When my brother bought a remote control Dalek, we discovered that the controls operated on the same frequency; we played about with using K9's control for the Dalek and the Dalek's control for K9. We used to make them dance!

When Mary Tamm died in the summer of 2012 I decided to do a Key to Time marathon. Sadly this was interrupted by the beginning of the school term - funnily enough, this was in the middle of *The Androids of Tara.* I didn't notice it at the time, but looking back, whenever I watch The Key to Time, something happens around *The Androids of Tara*. That's creepy!

Kroll! (dumdumdumdum!)
The Power of Kroll by **Gareth Kavanagh**, 40, Manchester, UK / First story: **The Deadly Assassin**

Obsession. It's probably the only thing we truly have in common as fans, whether we care to admit it or not. Many obsess about continuity, others about episode titles. I've even seen people descend into a foaming rage about the sudden appearance of a 2|entertain logo on the DVD spines.

Not me, I hear you scoff. We're the cool kids. **Doctor Who** is just part of our balanced diet of culty goodness, indie music and nights down the pub. And I would have considered myself right there with you my cool brothers and sisters, right down to my non-alphabetically collated DVD shelves and retro-ironic T shirts. And yet, under all the camouflage, we're such hypocrites.

Do you remember how difficult it was to be a **Doctor Who** fan (especially in the darks days of 1986 to 1995 when it was positively sub-normal in the eyes of many)? I'm sure we all have our own 'Peter in the Olive Grove moments,' where we've denied being fans. Paul Magrs memorably tells of a dinner he and Russell T Davies shared while working for Granada in the 1990s, where they talked for hours without ever daring admit they were fans. Mine came in 1999 when, despite my protestations I was outed as a fan by a sniggering, piggy-eyed web design agency director in a meeting and made to feel, in front of his team, like a grown man who'd just been caught chatting to his **Star Wars** toys in work (the agency in question went bust a few years later, *schadenfreude* fans amongst us will be pleased to note).

Of course, the very notion that being a devotee of the Doctor could be detrimental to your career or personal standing seems outlandish nowadays. **Doctor Who** is so loved and so popular, and as such is now a very acceptable thing to obsess over. A little like football, music and celebrity culture and other things we all take for granted as being safe to know too much about.

I suppose what I'm trying to say is that obsession and fandom walk hand in hand. We're all obsessed with the thing we love to a certain degree. I also think the sixteen-year hiatus did us good on that score, broadening our palettes. I started watching other shows (and not just ones that had **Doctor Who** links), reading new genres and trying new things. The old pattern of new programmes every year, learning everything about the past via **DWM** and buying the Targets and rudely expensive videos was well and truly broken.

The hiatus was our rehab, and looking back absolutely vital to the health of fans and programme alike. It also helped detoxify our obsession, to find the playfulness in our love again. To a time when we weren't all calling for JNT's head and slavishly following **DWB**'s mantra on classics and duds. A more innocent time when Target novels were the ultimate must-have for any fledgling **Doctor Who** obsessive worth his salt.

I used to tell people my hobby as a kid was reading. Which was true, except I missed off the rest of the sentence, '**Doctor Who** books.' I read as many as I could, voraciously and often. They punctuated my life and were all that kept me sane on the boring swimming galas that would fill my Saturdays in the late 1970s and early 1980s. *The Ark in Space*? Leonard's Newsagent on Madoc Street. *The Brain of Morbius* – found that in Largs in a tiny bookshop on a swimming trip. *The Green Death* – that was Menzies in Lytham St Annes, while Southampton and her majestic WH Smiths (*truly* the Real Madrid of **Doctor Who** book purveyors) will forever belong to *Carnival of Monsters*.

Years later, I learned from Dez Skinn how print distribution worked. Not every title would be distributed evenly, but would often cluster around regional depots. It's why Humberside ended up with all the Yellow Dalek **Radio Times** covers a few years back, and why the hardest Target to find in North Wales in this distributor-devised maze of shops was *The Power of Kroll*.

Usually, our WH Smiths in Llandudno was on the money, so pretty much every time I had assembled 85p there would be a new book for me to pick up. But not *The Power of Kroll*. I looked in every WH Smiths I could, we enquired in small book shops and I even asked for a cheque off my Mum so I could order from Star Books. The answer was no. The months rolled on, *The Power of Kroll* began to dominate my imagination. What a great name, I'd think. What could it mean? It's even by Terrance Dicks and he's *the best*!

Eventually, after what seemed like an age but was probably no more than six months, I found it. Not in the shops that had served me so well, but in Colwyn Bay Library, five miles up the coast. Not that they made it easy for you. You had to find the index card in the Junior Library, take it to the desk and ask for an inter-Library loan that took up to four weeks to complete.

I waited and waited and finally, it arrived. It's difficult to accurately sum up the excitement of picking that book up, of running home, smelling that library smell and reading it on my bed. But it was wonderful and for me, was the great victory just to hold it in my hands. And, y'know; it's not a bad read looking back. The flashback to the devoured priest is great, as is the world-building that goes into Delta Magnus. The Dame Nellie Melba escape is thrilling and Kroll is so much better on the page. Even Kroll's demise as he's blown into a million squidlets seems just right.

I never watch *The Power of Kroll* nowadays because I don't need to. It's all there in my head, beautifully carved from the purest, loving obsession and that's where I'd like to keep it. Past perfect.

Relative Safety

The Armageddon Factor by **Dean Hempstead**, 38, Chelmsford, UK / First story: **The State Of Decay**

Saturday 22nd November 1980. The day I met the Doctor for the first time. I remember those days of my childhood with much fondness. The summer was long and warm, and winter was bitterly cold. The excitement of another birthday looming and soon a visit from Father Christmas ever tangible in the air. Previously I remember many evenings lying in front of the TV with my Granddad, watching episodes of **Rolf Harris's Cartoon Time**. It was upon this date, three days before my sixth birthday that my Granddad decided that I was ready to watch **Doctor Who.** Saturdays were always very exciting at my Nana and Granddad's house. There was always the promise of sweets, fizzy drinks and burger and chips for tea.

My Granddad watched the horse racing on TV, and as the afternoon shifted into evening he watched the football results come in. All afternoon he promised that soon we would watch **Doctor Who** together for the first time.

So there I sat in my grandparents' living room, with my small table in front of me that I used every Saturday teatime. My Nana brought in my much anticipated dinner and a small glass of fizzy pop. Just in time for **Doctor Who.** The football results had finished, and the man on the TV announced, 'So now we begin a new four part series with **Doctor Who**, *State Of Decay*.'

I was fascinated by the theme music as soon as it started. It was upbeat and eerie at the same time. It was from here that I realised that **Doctor Who** was something special, it was magical. I was captivated. The more I watched, it just kept on giving. There was a brave man with crazy hair, big eyes and huge smile. He wore the longest scarf and was really rather funny. There was a huge console in the middle of his ship with a central column that went up and down. It was always going wrong. A robot dog that spoke, and all these things fitted inside a police telephone box. There were monsters and villains to fight every week. When he got hurt he changed into a new man. Pure magic. All from the safety of my grandparents' house. Safety. Safe. I think that is why I still love it so much to this day. Whenever I watch, read or listen to another story, I feel that safety that I felt as a young boy. This busy, fast and quite stressful 21st century life that I lead requires me to be an adult. This is fine, I can cope with that because I know that I always have the relative safety of **Doctor Who** to return to whenever I need it.

All through my childhood, I realised that nothing else excited me quite as much as **Doctor Who.** The weekly episode however, wasn't enough to keep my expanding mind satisfied. I wanted more. At school one day we received a brochure to take home to our parents with exciting books that could be ordered for children to read. There were two titles available that interested me. **Doctor Who and the Horror Of Fang Rock** and **Doctor Who and the Armageddon Factor**. Being a very lucky little boy who was enthusiastic about reading (I always enjoyed Roald Dahl) my Mum ordered both books. I remember the day they arrived, in a brown paper bag. I can still remember the smell of the paper, and the excitement of knowing what it contained. After school, I ran home and couldn't wait to open the parcel. When I arrived, I said, 'Hi,' to my mum and ran straight to my room where I tore open the bag. There they were, all shiny and beautiful. Two brand new adventures with the Doctor. I opened **The Horror Of Fang Rock** and I think I devoured the story in about two hours. After this, I always saved up my pocket money and looked forward to a trip to the second-hand bookshop in Maldon, where I would always buy a few more. I always remember the smell of old books, it reminds me of **Doctor Who** still. I adore second-hand bookshops.

It was eight years later, that my fandom of **Doctor Who** was fuelled by another of my grandparents.

Christmas Day 1988. It was a traditional family day, all exchanging presents and looking forward to the much-anticipated Christmas dinner that was always lovingly prepared by my Mum. As usual I was very lucky, the presents even to this day are always never-ending. My Mum passed me a present from my grandma from under the tree. I opened it to reveal my very first **Doctor Who** video, *Death To The Daleks*. I think even now, that it is still my most-watched story. This was very quickly followed up the year after by *Pyramids Of Mars*. In the 1980s, past adventures of the Doctor were not as readily available as they are today, so this was something truly special. Both of them had the lovely Elisabeth Sladen in them. As a teenage boy I fell in love with Sarah Jane.

That Christmas of 1988 is the day I believe the creation of my **Doctor Who** collection started. As the years have progressed, more **Doctor Who** has been produced in many different formats. These days it is everywhere. I love it. I always look forward to the next story with much excitement. I become a six-year-old boy once again.

Doctor Who has always been a big part of my life. It still retains that magic, that special element that no other show seems to have. These days many of the faces that I adored as a child have sadly passed away. They will never know the true legacy that they have left behind in the minds of all those children that are now, or will one day become, adults.

And the same is undoubtedly true of the new faces appearing in the modern series, shaping and affecting the next generation of fans.

Fear of the Daleks
Destiny of the Daleks by **Nicholas Hollands**, 37, Glasgow, UK / First story: **Destiny of the Daleks**

Often when I talk to friends about **Doctor Who**, the subject of the Daleks comes up. Being of the **Doctor Who** tribe (as opposed to a Not-We), I can be quite talky on the matter. Like David Banks with his marvellous Cyber-histories, I've got the various timelines of the Daleks in my head, and have worked out my own little stories as to how all of the inevitable incongruities fit together. I firmly believe that Tom fudged one of the first shots in the Time War, back in that Skaro bunker corridor with Sarah Jane.

And in the talk of Daleks themselves, regular themes creep in. There's talk of protective sofas and cuddled cushions, but eventually I'll hear, 'Of course, I wasn't really *scared* of the Daleks...'

I was. Petrified.

Picture a four-year-old boy, huddled in his dressing gown on the floor at the foot of the stairs. He's drunk his Ovaltine extra slowly to try and stay up past bed time, but it was a mistake.

Beside him the half-glazed front room door is closed, but it's not thick enough to muffle the evil grating voices or the screams. It goes quiet. Small hands hold the bottom of the window frame, as the young face rises and looks through the glass. They widen. There on the screen is a horrible burned old man; a blue eye blazes brightly in his forehead as he's pushed down a corridor in his Dalek-chair, waving his claw-like hand madly and shouting.

The face ducks quickly out of sight again and there's the repetitive thud of his feet as he runs upstairs.

Terrifying. Thus was my introduction to **Doctor Who**. As far as I can recall, I didn't see a Dalek on-screen again until I was nine. But I still have a clear memory of the cold of the wall against my back as I listened to the harsh tones and exterminator blasts.

I wasn't allowed to see more for some time. I suspect I had nightmares. I have no recollection of the rest of Season 17, which is probably a good thing as I reckon Scaroth would have scarred me for life. I've got vague memories of an episode involving the Marshmen, but a healthy fear of spiders probably put paid to seeing more. But by *The Keeper of Traken* I was hooked. I drew a picture of Melkur flying through space for 'What I did on my weekend' at primary school.

From there, I can fit **Doctor Who** in as part of my life pretty much constantly. The first book I read that didn't have pictures was **Revenge of the Cybermen**. (It was also my first video, and I remember being peeved that the Cyberleader said, 'Hostile to our function,' rather than, 'Inimical...' when talking about gold. I was always destined to be a ming-mong about *something*.)

Every novelisation that turned up at the local county library was claimed. Once I took the same book from the school library as well to check them for differences. Then I got a demand letter from county because I'd given the wrong book back to the wrong library. I started buying the books myself, and after a while started a lending library of my own. 10p (or two ice pops) got you one of my books for two weeks. I remember proudly reading aloud out of the first pages of **The Five Doctors** to my class, and then utterly failing to know what an obelisk was when questioned. Although I *could* recreate the TARDIS display screens on my Acorn Electron.

My older sister needed a video recorder because the programmes she required for college were on late at night. I could start rewatching the shows! No more sitting in front of the telly with a tape recorder, shushing my dad while praying I'd fit all of Part Four of *The Twin Dilemma* onto one side of a C60 audio cassette.

From there, I'd reckon my story is the same as most **Doctor Who** fans. I didn't miss an episode. I had my

VHS collection to fall back on during the dead years. I loved it when McGann's shoes fitted. I went back to the novelisations, old and new. And then ... 2005.

Rose had happened, and I was round my sister's for tea and *Aliens of London*, along with Mum, Dad, brother-in-law, and the nieces. We'd had burping wheelie bins, a plastic Mickey, and now farting politicians. But I didn't care. For the first time in probably ten years, we had, as a family, chosen to sit and watch the same programme. No talking, no commentary; the telly was the centre of attention. As the episode drew to a close, and Jackie sat screaming in her kitchen, the round Os formed by my youngest niece's eyes and mouth took me straight back to that cold stairwell. As the credits howled in, I looked at her and smiled. 'Don't worry. They'll be alright.' I'm pleased to say, she's hooked.

And so, to the present day. After a couple of years of watching new **Doctor Who** solo, I joined an online forum, as I felt that I'd need to talk to someone about *The Doctor's Daughter*. I joined in with the community, started talking to some like-minded people and finally, in 2008 met the man with who I now know I'm going to spend the rest of my life. I've moved to the other end of country, I'm currently jobless... But I couldn't be happier.

And *Destiny of the Daleks*... That's where it all started.

A Tale of Two City of Deaths

City of Death by **Mark Cockram**, 40, Exeter, UK
First story: **City of Death**

My earliest memory of **Doctor Who** is of the insane machine (in *City of Death*, I later discovered) that turned an egg into a chicken to the point of death and then back to an egg again. I also remembered a thrilling high speed bicycle chase through bustling city streets (which never actually happened!). Which just goes to show how our young minds remember fragments of information and simply fill in the gaps in order to try and make sense of it.

Now, at the age of six my mind was probably more occupied with playing with Lego, and rather tellingly, it wasn't long before I was making a Lego TARDIS (never could get the hang of making it bigger on the inside).

By the time *The Horns Of Nimon* began its run I was hooked. Of course these days it's looked upon as a campy, over the top piece of fluff, but at that young age it was an incredibly exciting story with some clever ideas, like the constantly changing configuration of the walls within the power complex. I still have the Target novelisation knocking around somewhere, which took my new obsession to a whole new level. I think the tie-in novelisations did more than anything else to encourage me to take up reading; my appetite for these books was voracious. As well as giving me the chance to catch up on the previous stories involving my new hero Tom Baker, they opened my eyes to the realisation that there had been three previous Doctors, which fuelled my burgeoning interest even further.

I remember when Peter Davison took over the role, I got my hands on a copy of Jean-Marc Lofficier's **Programme Guide**, which I must have read from cover to cover many, many times over. I can remember wondering why the BBC hadn't shown *The Evil Of The Daleks*? This had sounded like a much more exciting story than *The Krotons* which had been shown as part of **The Five Faces Of Doctor Who** collection of stories chosen to lead up to Season 19. I was sure that there must have been a perfectly good reason; still, I was convinced that they would probably show it again at a later date...

These days with all the existing stories available on beautifully restored DVDs you have the entire series at your fingertips; back then however, VHS was only just starting to make its way into people's homes, and the BBC took a long time to release any **Doctor Who** stories for public consumption. That void was very pleasantly filled by those wonderful Target books, but eventually the fan gene kicks in and you want to *see* the stories not just read them.

We got our VHS recorder (complete with new fangled remote control, attached by a cord!) in 1985, just too late to record Peter Davison's thrilling swansong. My parents knew the extent of my **Doctor Who** obsession and kindly forked out what would have been a small fortune in those days for a copy of *Revenge Of The Cybermen* on VHS for what must have been my twelfth birthday.

I watched it countless times, and this was my introduction to Harry Sullivan and Sarah Jane Smith. I was immediately smitten with this 'time team'; I mean, how could you not be? Sarah Jane, the plucky, feisty female companion and Harry, the brave if somewhat daft male companion. 'Harry Sullivan is an imbecile!' and the Doctor, my Doctor up against the deadly Cybermen.

So **Doctor Who** became a very important part of my childhood. I remember being absolutely inconsolable when my older brother, who liked **Doctor Who** but wasn't as into it as I was, got to meet my hero Tom Baker in full fourth Doctor get-up, at a design-a-monster competition being held locally, but I wasn't allowed to go! I must have been six or seven at the time. Still, I can laugh about it now.*

I also have a vague recollection of going on a trip organised by our primary school to see a theatre production of *Treasure Island*, with Matthew Waterhouse playing ~~Adric~~ Jim Hawkins. I remember being very excited about this, although looking back, maybe I can see why some of my friends weren't quite so thrilled...

But that first, albeit wonky memory from *City Of Death* stuck with me. For a very long time I just thought that I must have dreamt it, so imagine my surprise many years later, when watching old reruns of **Doctor Who** on UK Gold the 'chicken machine' appeared on screen and I was joyously transported back to the autumn of 1979.

That feeling of dawning realisation was wonderful; watching the story back as an adult I could appreciate the real-life romance between Tom and Lalla making itself apparent on screen, Tom's effortless delivery of some classic one-liners courtesy of another of my heroes, the late great Douglas Adams, and a really memorable score by Dudley Simpson. This story achieved some the highest ratings in the show's history, thanks in part to a strike by the only other broadcaster at the time, but there is something truly magical about *City Of Death*, it encapsulates everything I love about **Doctor Who** and it's a perfect example of why the programme has endured for fifty years and hopefully will continue to do so for many more to come.

[* Gritting my teeth as I type.]

The Seven Ages of Fan
The Creature From the Pit by **Hugh Haggerty**, Glasgow, UK / First story: **The Invisible Enemy**

Poor *The Creature from the Pit*. Just like its eponymous character, Erato, it's lonely, misunderstood and unloved. When it came in at a lowly 184 out of 200 in a poll taken by **Doctor Who Magazine** a few years ago I was sad and dismayed, because if I were to select a fun, scary, enjoyable romp I'd happily pop this into the DVD player and be entertained from the bones out. Why do fans dislike the story so much?

Let's drag ourselves back to the dark days of 1979 to when I first viewed it. Six years old, and by now **Doctor Who** had established itself as my favourite thing in the world ever, which, of course is absolutely correct and proper for a primary school chap with excellent taste. There was no one above Tom Baker in my eyes – no one! Even good old, magic-trick-performing dad would have to do something *spectacular* to even come close, and even if he did where was his metal dog with a laser for a nose?

The seventeenth series had been a blast: it had given me my first Dalek story, and the bellowing menaces were just as terrifying as my big cousin had told me they were; then Romana and the Doctor had gone to Paris in France – proper France too with all those French buildings and French cars and grumpy French artists in cafes throwing ruined portraits about. Amazing!

What the heck was next? Oh, that was the best one yet. Nothing prepared me for this new adventure. One minute, K9 is reading **The Tale of Peter Rabbit** to a clearly enthralled Doctor, the next they're on a real, live jungle planet with a mystery to solve, giant pulsating space eggshells sending distress signals... My little eyes soaked in every pixel from our luxurious 21-inch television set. Then the story went and traumatised me.

In a moment of peril, K9 steps in to save the day. Here comes the laser nose – yay! He zaps one of the nasty wolf-weeds, but no! He's been overwhelmed by the rolling nasties. He lets out a worrying burble as Lady Adrasta snootily informs me, 'He's Dead.' I'm devastated – and Romana agrees, clasping her hands together, lamenting her faithful doggy companion. I don't even get time to mourn as the Doctor grabs the rope above the pit – and jumps in! That was just Part One. The rest of the story pins me down to the worn-out spot in the carpet thirteen inches away from the cathode-ray tube, glassy-eyed, wide-mouthed and thoroughly entertained.

So vworp vworp, as they say, and back in current time (being all relative and stuff) I have to ask, is it just my joyful nostalgia that keeps *The Creature from the Pit* from languishing on the shelf of rarely-watched stories or is it still worthy of my undying love? Nostalgia does play a part, but as a recent re-watch confirmed, I was delighted to find I still love this story. I've changed massively since my pre-pubescent years, but older me still adores the wonderful energy that sizzles throughout. Even in its quieter moments, it has a sense of fun that only miserable, sour-faced *Warrior's Gate* fans can deny.

The cast love it too. Tom Baker is a gleeful swaggering joy, sweating profusely through the filmed jungles scenes and adding to the hot, exotic feel of the planet Chloris. Thrust down the pit he actually reaches out to the mass of grotesque, seething monster monster we think is malevolent and once more sends out that beautifully uncomplicated message **Doctor Who** has often come back to: don't judge anyone (or anything) too quickly. A simple truth always worth repeating. Lots of fans have stated that they picked up their early ideas of morality from **Doctor Who** and I wouldn't be surprised if this was one of those stories where those values were formed. Here, confronted by an enormous monster with hideous skin, the Doctor is unconditionally *kind*.

Elsewhere, Adrasta and Romana fight it out to see who can be the snootiest and it's a tough call. Romana's put-downs are delicious, but Adrasta's acidic sneering villainy and awesome Kate Bush shapes see her just swipe the lead over the Time Lord to claim the crown of most alluring vixen.

Best of all is David Brierley as K9's new voice – he's just so tetchy. Brierley adds a new sarcastic edge to the robot dog and it's great fun listening to the bitching between Adrasta and K9.

You see we *all* loved K9 once but then we get too stuffy and intellectual and pretend we don't. How we react to the computer pooch shows us where we are in our lifecycle as fans, and if we use Shakespeare's 'Seven Ages of Man' analogy, it might go something like this:

- The Infant: 'Oh look! *A robot doggy*!'
- The Whining Schoolboy: 'K9 is my favourite character!'
- The Lover: 'It's well-written this dialogue between the Doctor and K9.'
- A Soldier: 'That tin-dog is getting in the way of the stories.'
- The Justice: 'Oh Christ, I'm so glad to see the back of that bloody thing.'
- Old Age: 'Oh, there's K9, I used to love him. Nice to see him in action again.'
- Second Childishness and Mere Oblivion: 'Oh look! *A robot doggy*!'

Well, as an analogy it's not a perfect and neither is *The Creature from the Pit*. But there is no denying it's a thoroughly Tom Baker adventure worthy of another view. Go on, watch it through eyes that want a fun romp and stop being such a grouch about it.

The Unlimited Potential of Saturdays

Nightmare of Eden by **Terry Cooper**, 43, Pontypridd, South Wales / First story: **The Monster of Peladon**

For me, science fiction and Saturdays were always inseparable. Growing up in London in the early 1970s, I was raised on a televisual diet of cartoons like **Scooby Doo** and **The Fantastic Four**, and exciting live-action American shows such as **Planet of the Apes**, **Logan's Run**, **The Fantastic Journey** and **Project UFO**. These kept me interested in all things fantastical and otherworldly, but **Doctor Who** was the high point of the week for me and my brothers. My Mum worked during the day, so Dad would take command of the living room, subjecting us to hours of **World of Sport** and **Grandstand**. Often, we'd escape into the streets to play. But as soon as the late football results came in, we'd all race back into the house, and impatiently sit there buzzing with excitement for the next programme. There was no setting the video recorder or Sky+ back then.

Often, we'd read in **The Sun** some tale about the upcoming story or a new monster, and that would only add fuel to the fire. One week, I'd read about 'The scariest monsters ever seen in **Doctor Who**!' accompanied by a fuzzy black and white photo. The story was *Nightmare of Eden* and these terrifying new monsters that were certain to get Mary Whitehouse on the phone again, were called the Mandrels. Or Mendrals. Both spellings appeared in the article so I had to wait and see.

I had become accustomed to the monsters of **Doctor Who** looking somewhat home-made, as if Lesley Judd had slapped them together with sticky-backed plastic and cotton reels on string, but when the Mandrels appeared, I had to admit, they looked pretty impressive! Bear in mind, this was my ten-year-old self appraising them, not (sigh) a slightly more cynical 43-year-old professional designer. They were giant, hulking things, with fluorescent green eyes, shaggy hair, claws and scales. Like Yeti that had quit the pies and gotten down to the gym. They also had this odd clam-beak-thing instead of a mouth, so they looked a little cute, like a doe-eyed platypus. What do I think of them today? Well, not as ridiculous as I thought they'd be after all this time. Sure, they stagger around, waving their immobile limbs as these creatures are wont to do, but they're certainly not the worst things to come out of a **Blue Peter** scratch-building session. I think the Slitheen might hold that title, where tens of thousands of pounds on animatronic suits and CGI enhancement still can't sell a flatulent green blob. And anyway, the Zygons did the same thing only a million times more terrifyingly.

The story had two major weak points for me, even then. One was that Lalla Ward had replaced the divine Mary Tamm as Romana - haughty, smug and too 'public school' for me. Then the inconsistent and lacklustre voice of K9 from David Brierley. More John Inman than John Leeson. But Tom Baker's beloved Doctor was always the focal point - to this day he seems to be having fun with it (having Douglas Adams as a script editor helped here, methinks), playing the detective always one step ahead of the rest and often snappy and impatient with his co-stars. I'm aware that this was not always just an act.

What totally passed us all by was the fact that the story was all about smuggling illegal drugs. The Mandrels are effectively drug mules and the narcotic here - 'Vraxoin' - never struck me as a thinly-veiled version of heroin. Life (and people) were much simpler then; to the Cooper family, it was just, 'Doctor fights escaping scary monsters.' Again.

One of many typical families sitting around the telly on a Saturday evening, I recall, while sandwiched between my brothers, my mother yelling at us for sitting far too close to the screen. No cowering behind the sofa for us - we didn't want to miss a thing! My experiences of **Doctor Who** in the 1970s are closely linked to memories of dinner time – home-made burger and chips, ketchup, bread and butter, salt and vinegar, and a sticky vinyl tablecloth. I can still look at a sauce-drenched chip on a fork and think *The Creature from the Pit* because my Dad came up with the name 'Erato Tomato' for that story's eponymous monster.

I suppose the advancement of my teenage years, the discovery of freedom, cinema, **Star Wars** and the opposite sex led to the demise of my Saturday nights as they then were. In addition, the show moved from its Saturday slot and although I very much enjoyed Peter Davison's youthful, exasperated take on the Doctor, there was no real reason to get home by five o'clock on a Saturday any more. We'd already seen the Daleks and the Cybermen take on Tom, and these more generic stories were getting a little samey.

Now that it's returned to its familiar Saturday evening slot, **Doctor Who** is, I'm sure, making new mental connections for the country's children, ensuring that Saturday tea-time is once again synonymous with time travel and the TARDIS. Although the skateboard, Chopper bike and flared jeans have also made comebacks of a sort, it's not quite the same. But then I've travelled in time too – forward another 32 years. But for ten-year-olds living through it today, I hope the magic is just beginning. In fact, I've been to the future, and I can say for sure that it is. Did. Oh, you know what I mean.

Nimons Are Forever
The Horns of Nimon by **Tony Cross**, 42, Cricklewood
First Story: **The Talons of Weng-Chiang**

I spent a lot of my time as a teenager and adult defending **Doctor Who**. It was often an uphill task as the BBC did their best to let the show die a slow death. I fought battles with **Coronation Street** fans at University over what to watch in the TV Room, which I normally lost. I argued long and hard that despite what they might think, **Doctor Who** was one of the greatest TV programmes ever made and that if only someone would give it the tender, loving care it so obviously needed then by Jove they'd soon see. People mocked me.

When New **Doctor Who** arrived in 2005 a lot of friends and colleagues came to me admitting humble pie. You were right. We were wrong. Our kids love it. I love it. It's nice to be right.

But when I think of the **Doctor Who** that I adored it is to *The Horns of Nimon* and the rest of poor, battered and beleaguered Season 17 that I go. This is my idea of perfect **Doctor Who** and I don't care if it looks tatty or that it sometimes gets very silly indeed - *Nightmare of Eden*, I'm looking at you - because none of that matters. To me.

The Horns of Nimon is my comfort **Doctor Who** story. It's made glorious by the fact that I was I was eight and about to be nine when it was first shown, possibly the ideal time for **Doctor Who** before real life and girls come along to distract us from the path of true virtue.

I am aware that there are people out there that do not like Tom Baker's portrayal of the Doctor and I feel sorry for them. For me Tom Baker is, was and always will be *The Doctor*. The costume, the eyes, the huge smile and above all that voice. Yes, he can over-act and sometimes he's very silly indeed, but you know, that's what I love about Tom Baker's Doctor. He can be the smartest, most frightening man in the room and then he's the biggest, sulkiest child. If there's a motto for the fourth Doctor it must be his own words: 'There's no point in being grown up if you can't be childish sometimes.'

Then there's Lalla Ward. In her hunting outfit. Now I love the second Romana. I like the fact that with the fourth Doctor and K9 she combines to form one of the smartest and wittiest TARDIS crews that the programme will ever see, and that none of them ever showed the slightest discomfort about being clever and witty. It's what the good guys were. The bad guys were pompous, humourless and dressed in dowdy uniforms. The good guys were bright, silly and wore fantastically baroque outfits. They had a teaspoon and an open mind.

The Horns of Nimon pits the pair against a particularly pathetic bunch of imperialists on the wane: the Skonnon Empire. Once their spaceships caused fear and terror wherever they went. Now they're barely functional rust buckets crewed by aging over-weight men who shout a lot and don't have adequate trousers. Their home planet isn't much to write home about either. But there's the prospect of a return to greatness that seems to keep them all going.

They are led by Soldeed, the last decent Skonnon scientist left. I like to think Soldeed specialised in something esoteric and impractical before the Nimon came, and that, shocked to find himself in cahoots with a large, bull-headed, platform-booted creature, he completely and utterly lost his marbles. He keeps himself together only with the prospect of the Second Skonnon Empire and a bit of bullying. Soldeed is played by a gloriously over-the-top Graham Crowden. He gives some of the most bizarre line readings ever but – and I know some of you reading this are going to disagree – he is magnificent. Imagine how tedious *The Horns of Nimon* would have been if Crowden had been playing it straight. Or if there was some other, undoubtedly fine, British character actor going through the motions in the part. Now, Graham Crowden's hamtastic performance is one of the great glories of this story. Soldeed is a mad as a box of frogs and we know it.

There's an argument that this is the best **Doctor Who** Christmas story ever. It's a proper pantomime, in all the best senses of the word. There are villains to boo, heroes to cheer. There are catch-phrases, like 'Weakling Scum.' Gather friends together, ply them with drink and put on *The Horns of Nimon* and scenes of joyfulness will follow. Add a dash of Christmas to that and what more do you want? *The Horns of Nimon* is meant to be watched with big groups of people, like **The Rocky Horror Picture Show**, so we can shout out the best lines, and boo and cheer to our childish heart's content.

And that is why I love *The Horns of Nimon*. Of course there are better **Doctor Who** stories out there, if you analyse this with your head. But *The Horns of Nimon* wants your heart. It is as joyous a representation of **Doctor Who** as is unlikely to ever be seen again. At a time when inflation ate into the budget, when lights were turned off at 10pm in the studio whether one wanted them to or not, **Doctor Who** could still tell good stories and terrify children.

And I love the *Horns of Nimon* because it is a part of me. A reminder of a time when I didn't have a care in the world, a time when I had nothing to be afraid of and if **Doctor Who** scared me and I ran to watch through the crack in the door my Mum would say, 'Don't be scared. It's only a television programme.' But it was so much more than that.

The Best Ever Episode of Jackanory
Shada by **Isobel Tolley**, 30, Birmingham, West Midlands
First story: **Remembrance of the Daleks**

I was born in 1982 and my younger brother in 1984, but most of our cultural references come from the 1970s or earlier. We spent our childhood reading **The Goodies** annuals, listening to *The Best of Queen Volume 1* and fighting over a handheld Tetris game, all inherited from older brothers who had left to work in care homes. Our family seemed to move house on a biannual basis, so on return visits our brothers made up for the fact that they weren't returning to their actual childhood home by perfectly preserving their childhood television schedules. We watched everything they'd watched as children that was still on: **Top of the Pops**, **Tomorrow's World**, **Record Breakers** ... the rest we caught up on through videotapes. This meant almost constant **Doctor Who**-watching, occasionally interrupted by a compilation tape of **TISWAS**.

My memories of **Doctor Who**'s original run were either of being scared, of the Daleks or the thought of Sophie from **Itsa Bitsa** drowning, or of everyone being disappointed that it wasn't scary enough and had an alien that looked like Bertie Bassett. It's while watching **Doctor Who** with my older brothers, who had years' worth of nostalgic affection for the show, that I realised the show could actually be enjoyable. Fear was part of it, but tea and crackers and student choirs singing *Chattanooga Choo Choo* can be part of it too. It was these parts that gave the scary parts meaning.

A TV appearance by Tom Baker was a guaranteed moment of shared warmth and happiness in our household. I imagine you already feel the same way if you're reading this, but I should at least try and say why or there's not much point writing it. A good place to start is to describe the Doctor, the mad unknowable genius, the interplanetary warrior for goodness, the fun-loving adult child ... and then say that the fourth Doctor's Doctor is the most Doctor-like of the Doctors. He's the one with the scarf and the jelly babies and the beaming smile, the one brave enough to be silly in front of a people with the power to do something horrible like suck every mind in the universe into a small plastic ball. In the *Shada* video you get a double whammy of Tomness, Tom as the Doctor and Tom as Tom. Tom gives his all to those linking scenes he should never have had to film; they are a showcase for his acting, storytelling and emotional commitment to the show. He greets his old enemies like old friends, before the sight of a Kraal sends him howling with anguish. The sound of him mournfully declaiming the name 'Victoria Burgoyne!' lingers in the memory like a haunting chorus. It's like the best ever episode of **Jackanory. Jackanory** would have been improved no end by having clips of **Doctor Who** in it.

Of course **Doctor Who** can't just consist of Tom Baker talking to some old masks in an empty room. **Doctor Who** writers were probably the first TV writers we knew enough about to appreciate their particular traits. Douglas Adams was first and foremost the funny one. This is probably unfair on Robert Holmes, but it was years before we realised Robert Holmes was funny. We thought he was just disturbed. Brilliant, obviously, but also badly in need of help. Douglas Adams is funny when you're seven and stays funny for the rest of your life. He treated humour as much more important than light relief. The invisible spaceship makes for an amusing scene in a field but it's also an amazing way of showing how advanced and brilliant the villain is. (It also made for an easy spaceship to build on a **Doctor Who** budget.) The Doctor and Romana's conversation in the punt is clever, witty, inventive and teaches you physics without you even noticing. And all that, 'Crackers? Sometimes,' stuff in Professor Chronotis' rooms tells us all we need to know about his damaged mind and the way he sort of blends in on Earth but sort of doesn't. It is lovely, and the Doctor should be the defender of that which is lovely. *Shada*, *City of Death* and **The Hitchhikers' Guide to the Galaxy** showed me what a fine thing it is to be able to write, and to do so many things simply with words and ideas. Learning more about Adams' life taught me something else: writing is very hard, especially if you're hoping to actually finish anything.

Before this page makes a whooshing sound, I'd better try and mention everything else that's great about *Shada*; all those actors for a start. Daniel Hill is touching as Chris, suddenly confronted with scientific discoveries that leave him having to rearrange his entire mental universe. Christopher Neame makes a marvellous blank-eyed psychopath as Skagra; the man with utter belief in his own rightness and no self-awareness whatsoever. And of course there's Romana. Romana managed to be an independent **Doctor Who** girl without being saddled with a lot of clunky speeches designed to tell us how independent she was. She just quietly got on with being brilliant; she could cope without the Doctor around just fine. She has a career away from him, as an historian, and it's dealt with in one line. It's like the writers just trusted her.

I don't really know what everyone roughly my age was watching while I was watching *Shada*. Still, if I did know, what would I do with this information? I don't like nostalgia, looking back on what a certain era was like and wishing it was still that era. I had **Doctor Who** on tap; my brothers had to wait months on end for it. In between times they were at the mercy of schedulers. God knows what else they had to watch. They passed on to me the bits of the 1970s that were worth preserving.

Unconditional Love
The Leisure Hive by **Simon Hart**, 37, Bracknell, UK
First story: **Destiny of the Daleks**

It was the trailer that did it.

Swap Shop finished and as I jumped down from the battered orange sofa to turn off the TV, a trailer began with the promise of new bizarre adventures for the Doctor, Romana and K9. I can remember it vividly even now, the startling images it contained: a strange world filled with screens that were round like balls hanging from the ceiling, and the Doctor and Romana creeping around exploring, but most excitingly of all a man who's head detached from his body *while he was still talking!* Those fantastic images immediately etched themselves into my mind. This was something I *had* to see.

I talked about nothing else all day. How could these things be happening? What was it all going to be about? Where was K9? Suddenly **Doctor Who** was coming back! This was just about *the* most exciting thing I could imagine! This one little trailer had captured my imagination and sent it spiralling, but that was nothing compared to the effect the story itself had on me.

I think it's the strangeness of it that got to me back in 1980. There was nothing else quite like *The Leisure Hive* on TV that I'd seen before. This story provided me with a gorgeously weird collection of images that embedded themselves in my head for years to come: K9 exploding in the seawater on Brighton Beach, Pangol's head floating in the screen, the glimpses of the Foamasi eyes, their claws ripping through the fibre optic cables, and most of all the Doctor screaming while being pulled apart for the cliffhanger of Part One. I was scared and thrilled, and I couldn't wait to find out if the Doctor was still alive the following week.

This was it - the moment where my liking for **Doctor Who** turned into love. I was obsessed but in a good way. I'd found something that was mine. This was my story.

But as the Doctor likes to tell us, time marches on and other stories came along that captured my imagination in different ways. There were stories that I absolutely adored, stories that made me think, stories that excited me and took my imagination flying off in weird tangents and gradually I forgot just how important *The Leisure Hive* was in the formative stages of my becoming a **Doctor Who** fan. Other stories took on more importance as I met other fans - what was your first story or which story was your first Target book, those became the more significant ones (for those interested, the answer to both is *Destiny of the Daleks*) but I'd never really thought about what had made me a fan. I just was.

Then, one day in late 1990 I was given the opportunity to see any **Doctor Who** story I wanted. I was taking a tentative step into the world of pirate **Doctor Who** videos and thanks to a contact via a friend at school, I suddenly had a long list to choose from, all available for a small price.

My week's paper round wages ran to two stories. What to choose? So much I had never seen. So obviously, *Shada,* as I might never get the opportunity to see that again, but what else? Without thinking I wrote *The Leisure Hive*. My friend was bemused by the choice, wondering why I'd chosen that one when there were so many classics to be seen. I could see his point of view, why had I chosen *The Leisure Hive*? I explained that I wasn't sure why, I'd just had this urge to see it again.

Eventually my parcel of videos arrived. I put on *The Leisure Hive* and I remembered. I watched with rapt attention, transported back to 1980, absolutely delighted that I'd chosen this story. As Part One headed towards the cliffhanger, I sat forward in my seat, and had a shiver down my spine, as I knew what was about to happen; it had been etched in my mind almost shot for shot all those years, I just hadn't realised how far it had burrowed into my head.

I don't really think I'll ever quite be able to adequately explain how much I love this story. So much has been written about it down the years, from the JNT effect on the show, through the 'style over substance' argument, the subdued Tom to how the Foamasi couldn't possibly fit in those human bodies, but what none of these have ever mentioned is the effect that it had on one rather tall, shy five-year-old boy who sat watching this story in Weymouth in August and September 1980.

Sometimes you can't adequately explain why you love something, you just do. That's me and *The Leisure Hive*.

Saving the Best...
Meglos by **Alun Harris**, 37, Hebden Bridge, UK
First story: **Nightmare of Eden**

I eat my food in order. This isn't an OCD thing, it's a matter of personal preference. You might even do it yourself. Some of you may even wonder how food can have an order, but it's quite simple. I eat my food in the order of least favourite first. If I'm having, for example, steak, salad, coleslaw and a baked potato, I'll eat the salad first, mix the coleslaw and the baked potato, and save the steak for last. I always save the best for last because that way (in my mind at least) I'll have something nice to finish with. I enjoy the meal more that way. As I say, it's not an OCD thing (if I'm eating a chilli, for instance, I don't feel that I have to pick out the onion first, followed by the rice, the tomato, kidney beans and beef, because that would be insane), although I will admit to liking certain things to be ordered (my DVD/BD collection, for instance, has its own system which I find very easy to use. Some people don't need any order at all, but once you own more than a hundred discs I think some sort of order is imperative. I own a lot more than a hundred discs).

Collecting things is something nearly all **Doctor Who** fans do. I remember the day I completed my Target book collection. I'd been taken to the dentist by my parents and we were wandering around town when we saw a charity shop with some **Doctor Who** books in the window. Naturally we went in, and within five minutes I had found the elusive fifteen books I had never been able to find before.

This was the worst day of my life.

Rather than feeling elation, the prevailing emotion was one of abject horror. I'd spent eight years amassing this collection, and suddenly something which had made every bookshop a place of great mystery and excitement was over. I was finished. What should I do now? I look back to that day and sometimes blame it for my ever-increasing DVD collection.

On the plus side, given that this was around 1989, I knew that there were still a few Target books to be released, so I could at least keep on collecting them, and the videos were just about to reach a sensible release rate, meaning I had something else to collect.

After I'd joined fandom, been to conventions and met other fans, a new type of collecting started: watching every **Doctor Who** story that existed. Prior to fandom the only chance I had was BBC video, but then I met people with off-air copies and suddenly I had access to every episode that existed. Naturally, the truth of the situation became clear to me around 1992, at a Panopticon. They were showing stories on one of the hotel's TV channels and, despite a shocking hangover, I woke up at 5.30 to watch *Planet of Evil* (annoying an equally hung-over Colin Brockhurst who was sharing a room with me). I'd never seen *Planet of Evil* before, you see, so this was something very exciting. (Colin was the more sensible one. He'd brought his VCR with him and was just taping everything off the TV.) As I watched the story (which, in all honesty, wasn't quite as exciting as I thought it was going to be, although that could just have been the result of the cider) I had an epiphany. I had seen nearly every surviving story. Which meant yet another collection would soon be completed. And unless something as exciting as the *Tomb of the Cybermen* recovery happened again (which seemed unlikely, even then) I had a very limited number of choices of what would be the last story I saw for the first time. My preference would have been something black and white, but I'd already seen everything. (Oh, if only I'd not seen a terrible copy of *The Romans*.) I didn't like Pertwee then as much as I do now, and I'd seen everything from Davison onwards. That left Tom. But which one? I'd already seen most of them, the field was narrowing quickly. So I made a logical choice (or so it seemed; in hindsight it wasn't the wisest of moves). I liked Season 18 a lot. I liked Lalla Ward. I'd seen *Full Circle*, so didn't really see the point of not watching the rest of the E-space trilogy as soon as possible. I remembered *The Keeper of Traken* from the repeat in 1981. I had a pirated *Leisure Hive* on VHS and *Logopolis* had been released that year.

This left *Meglos*.

On paper *Meglos* sounded perfect. Tom, Lalla, K9, Paddy Kingsland and Peter Howell, Season 18, a time loop (the only thing I remembered from the novelisation. The fact that I remembered nothing else should have been a bit of a hint, really) and Jacqueline Hill (who, to this very day, I believe to have been the best thing to have ever happened to **Doctor Who**. But only when she was Barbara). How could this not be the best story ever?

I waited for years. Patiently. Pretty much like the ridiculously stupid villain at the centre of the story. I rejected offers of copies for the one story I hadn't seen, knowing full well that it would be eventually released on VHS. I waited eleven years to experience this story, knowing that it would remain the only **Doctor Who** story I hadn't seen (I nearly didn't watch the McGann film, but then realised I was being silly. Besides, with everything that *Meglos* had going for it, how could it not be better?) and that I was going to finish on a high. I was saving the best for last.

I have never been so disappointed in my whole life.

Be careful what you wish for. Sometimes that steak you save is overdone, tasteless and very chewy.

The Quantum Duality of Andrew Smith!
Full Circle by **Tony Green**, 38, Oxford, UK
First story: **The Sun Makers**

When Mistfall Comes...
    The swirling grey vapours caused the dark of the early winter morning to seem like the beginning of dawn. It clung to, and caressed the trees and grass with a million icy fingers which never quite withdrew their grip. The world was like a ghost of itself in the fog which covered everything and held it in silence.
    As the dark, anorak-clad figure moved through it though, it seemed to part around him as if respectful of his presence. The gesture was ignored as the boy walked on, quietly muttering to himself...

One of the finest lines ever written in British cinema appears in the film **Clockwise**. Faced with the final realisation that his dreams may not be fulfilled John Cleese's character finally succumbs to despair and rages:
    'It's not the failure, I can live with the failure ... it's the hope!'
    I have never had my life summed up better. The torture of any situation, be it failing exams, looking for the perfect partner or even searching for a job does not lie in the certainty of failing but in the glimmer of hope that success might just be possible with a little more effort, a little more luck or many more tears. It's what keeps us going as a species, and what also keeps us miserable! That is the true cruelty of the world we live in ... and that is why Andrew Smith tortures me even today for one simple reason – he was a fan who'd written a **Doctor Who** story – and it had been actually made!
    Thus it was that I began every morning in the winter of 1989 working on my script. The 45-minute paper round was a time to entirely focus my mind on my great

project. I barely noticed the freezing fog or the weight of the bag. All this was lost on me because, as the mornings got darker and colder I had better things to do - I was writing a **Doctor Who** story like Andrew Smith did - it was going to be perfect and it was going to be *made*!

It drove and obsessed me because Andrew Smith was living proof that everything I wanted to achieve was possible; you just needed a good idea, a receptive production team, and a little hard work. It was that simple and, at the same time, infinitely complex. Both reachable and so far beyond me it could make you weep.

At one time or another most fans have written **Doctor Who** stories. Be it as scribbled drivel in a childhood exercise book or as a professionally presented and typed manuscript. It's something we fans 'do.' Even those who never put pen to paper probably have had at least one good 'idea' in their time. Maybe they forgot it almost immediately, maybe getting it on paper was just pushed to the back of their minds ahead of other priorities such as children, jobs, or the pub. Maybe they even typed it up lovingly and sent it to the production office only to receive a polite and encouraging 'Sod off' letter... Whatever the manifestation or the level of action - we've done it, you can bet your last river fruit on it!

This is why the Andrew Smith Conundrum was and is, so devastating. He was the one who did it all. It suddenly became a possibility while at exactly the same time it was as close to impossible as it could be. It was a physicist's nightmare! The impossible dancing a quantum tango with the possible - and blowing the mind in the process! He is the **X Factor** winner of **Doctor Who** fandom. And thus, regardless of lack of talent, ability or understanding of our own limitations we continue to chase the dream.

This was why I spent so many of my teenage years muttering to myself. I was running scenes, dialogue and plot twists through my mind in order to make of my own script another *Full Circle*. I just needed to work a little harder, tweak a bit here and there, trim this and expand on that and it would be ready.

And I was so nearly there ... and at the same time not even close.

Andrew Smith got his story made because it was *good*. It was a bright idea with a good plot and well worth the time and investment spent by the production office. My story was not made because it sucked, and was essentially a remake of ...

The War Games!

And all those years of perfecting had come to nothing. All the hope was fruitless, all the work wasted. And all the time Andrew Smith, in his castle of evil, felt my pain through the ages, and, like Mr Sin in a comfy jumper, he gave a smile. Even knowing this though, I can't bring myself to fully resent him. I mean at least trying to achieve what he did gave me something to do all those years ago on those cold mornings when the Mistfall came.

State of Play
State of Decay by **Andrew Clancy**, 40, London, UK
First story: **The Stones of Blood** (I think)

'The Doctor and his two companions, Romana and K9 were lost. It wasn't the first time this had happened of course. The steering mechanism of the Doctor's Time And Relative Dimensions In Space machine, the TARDIS for short, was erratic to say the least. The battered old Police Box had often taken him to the wrong planet in the wrong century; but this time it was worse, for the Doctor and his travelling companions were actually in the wrong universe...'

I could go on ... no really, I could!
    For anyone who doesn't recognise the above passage, it is an extract from the audiobook of *State of Decay* which was released in 1981. There are many **Doctor Who** audiobooks around today; what's so special about this one?
    I'm fairly certain that this was the first audio cassette I ever owned. I remember that I was very excited to have a version of a **Doctor Who** story which I could say was mine. I was a huge fan of Tom Baker and so the thought of the fourth Doctor reading a story exclusively to me (because the cassette was mine after all) was just too much for my over-excited mind. So, what do I remember about it? For anyone under the age of twenty who cannot remember cassette tapes, you used to get a bit of tape at the start and end of each side (yes, there were two sides) which was silent, kind of like the audio equivalent of the black screen that you would see for a few seconds at the start of a videotape (what do you mean, what's a videotape)? Anyway, this bit of tape was florescent green, which I'd never seen before (I used to get excited by the silliest of things)! The audio started with a strange sound effect and then Tom Baker's unique and fabulous voice kicked in. It was magical; my brothers and I were hooked.

We listened to it many times over the next few weeks, or was it years? It really held my attention, perhaps because in addition to being very exciting it wasn't actually all that long at around 55 minutes.

So, what effect did this audio story have on me?

Well, I don't think it's too much of an exaggeration to say that it improved my vocabulary immensely. I worked out the meaning of words that I hadn't really noticed before such as seldom, appalled, toil, urgency and ducklings ... okay, I might have made that last one up!

It also educated me; I'd never heard of the party game Chinese Whispers, which is described in the story (I was obviously going to the wrong parties).

I wasn't much of a book reader and so this was the first **Doctor Who** I'd experienced that wasn't visual. Perhaps because of this I took much more of an interest in the storyline rather than just looking out for monsters and laser guns. I loved the scenes with Ivo and Habris where the former is arguing with the latter about there needing to be an increase in the food rations for the workers to work harder; I was also fond of the scene with Kalmar and the rebels where the Doctor reacts angrily when hearing that reading and knowledge are forbidden.

I think possibly the biggest influence to come from my listening to *State of Decay* was that it may well have started another fascination of mine; that being the thrill of audio. I was, and still am to a certain extent, pretty obsessed with listening to things, to the point of missing great TV or going out. I loved to hide in the bedroom and listen endlessly to audio cassettes. Many were of **Doctor Who** (mostly off-air recordings of the TV show), some were TV or film theme compilations and the rest were either songs recorded off the radio or silly tapes of me and my brothers messing about with the cassette recorder's in-built microphone.

Did listening to *State of Decay* help to shape my career or any hobbies of mine? Probably not if I'm honest, although the interest in audio that perhaps stemmed from it may have got me interested in incidental music, which I have recently started messing about with. I'm also a jazz musician but I can't really pin that on an audiobook, although perhaps the words 'State of Decay' may describe my piano playing ability as I get older!

Some things just work very well in certain media. How often do we hear comments like the book is better than the film; the film is better than the book or the stage show is better than both the film and the book?

As it happens I do really like the TV serial of *State of Decay* too; mind you I'm a big fan of the whole of that season. The TV show has great performances and a great atmosphere, due quite a lot to the excellent incidental music score by Paddy Kingsland; however, maybe it's pure nostalgia, but there's something about the audiobook that just does it for me. My original cassette tape broke or melted or something many years ago. I purchased a later release of it during the 1990s I think, which was released on two cassettes, with weird music added to the start and end of each side which I didn't really care for. Thankfully I do now have a recording of the original version, so when I get some time to myself it is often this I choose to listen to.

A Gateway to Other Universes...

Warriors' Gate by **Matt Hills**, 41, Aberystwyth, UK
First story: **Robot**

Received wisdom tells us a few things about *Warriors' Gate*:

- Firstly, its visuals are more cinematic, more surreal and more striking than those belonging to most other 'classic' **Doctor Who** stories.
- Secondly, it's overly complicated, compressed and cryptic, and not at all suitable for **Doctor Who**'s younger fans: it's been condemned as symptomatic of a show trying to reach a slightly older audience, and losing its way in the process.
- Thirdly, it was one of **Doctor Who**'s textbook troubled productions, all rewrites and over-runs, disputes and sackings.

Well, I was nine when I first saw *Warriors' Gate*, and speaking metaphorically it opened the door into another universe for me. Because for the first time, I could re-experience brand new **Doctor Who** over and over again. This was on-demand **Doctor Who**, years ahead of VHS releases that were painfully outside my pocket-money budget, and probably an idea planted by the *Genesis of the Daleks* LP that I'd already listened to far too many times.

I'd realised that I could use our chunky cassette recorder to tape **Doctor Who**'s off-air audio. I'm still not quite sure why the Hills family owned this silver slatted brick of a tape recorder; I have no recollection of it being used for anything other than my attempts at recording TV theme tunes (**Knight Rider** and **The A-Team** in particular, along with **Bergerac**). And then **Doctor Who**, of course. Was it Mum's or Dad's, the tape recorder? No idea. And at this point, I didn't really know any other fans, so my taping activity wasn't an expression of fan belonging. It was just a personal, emotional necessity that I'd worked out by myself.

So it was that I settled down to enjoy my BASF cassette tape of *Warriors' Gate*. The fabled black-and-white images, the cobwebbed Gundans, the white void and tumbling TARDIS graphic... It was all in my mind's eye, sure, but for me *Warriors' Gate* had to be about the sound. Paul Joyce would've been so annoyed. Stunning visuals, all sorts of dissolves and unusual camera shots... No, for me, *Warriors' Gate* was radiophonic ambience and enticing dialogue all the way. So much for the received wisdom.

And that other thing – that *Warriors' Gate* is too grown-up? Well, I adored Season 18 at age nine, but especially *Warriors' Gate* and *Logopolis*. What I most loved about them was their impenetrability. Full of enigmatic signifiers, they promised meaning that I couldn't quite get a hold of. But I was energized and fascinated by them. Here was **Doctor Who** talking about E-space and N-space, and CVEs and causality and dwarf star alloy – things that sounded hugely important and scientific, and things that I really ought to know about, I decided. Soon I enjoyed looking them up in the **Programme Guide** I'd been bought. So, no, *Warriors' Gate* didn't give me what I should have wanted in demographic terms – that was **Knight Rider** or **The A-Team**. Instead, it gave me what I didn't even know I wanted; to be inspired, and to feel another world – of concepts and ideas – brushing up against my suburban existence, like time striations jolting across the screen (though I couldn't see them, not me with my BASF C90s, an episode per side with plenty of tape to spare). When I studied science in my teens, when I applied to King's College to read Natural Science – even when I eventually read **Doctor Who: The Unfolding Text** and grew up to be a TV Studies Professor – I suspect that the after-image of Season 18 was hiding under there somewhere, making difficult words an exciting, thrilling challenge rather than a drudge. Charged Vacuum Emboitment. Chronic Hysteresis. Block Transfer Computation.

But *Warriors' Gate* was the pinnacle, the high point of alluring incomprehensibility. Never mind the idea that it was too grown-up, I adored its philosophical verbosity and scientific veneer. Or even its philosophical veneer and scientific verbosity. Above all, I just loved its esoteric *words*. So much for that received wisdom.

Oh, and that third thing – the troubled production? As a nine-year-old I knew nothing about any of that; all I had was the small start of an audio collection. Even the departures of K9 and Romana didn't greatly trouble me. I liked both characters, but Romana stepping out of the Doctor's shadow felt about right. That so much was left unsaid simply meant there was even more of an elliptical, enigmatic charge to my wheezing, hissing tape recording.

For me, *Warriors' Gate* was resolutely a thing of grandeur. And I knew the name of its writer: Steve or Stephen Gallagher. So when, on a visit to Fleet Bookshop some time later, I found a book called **Valley of Lights**, I bought it and read it in one sitting simply because it had to be brilliant. How could it not be? It was by Stephen Gallagher, whose work I had replayed on a crumby old cassette player with a tiny little 'ext.mic' so many, many times. *Warriors' Gate* opened up yet another universe for me as a result. It paved my way into a new English library of British horror fiction: Gallagher and Peter James and Stephen Laws and Christopher Fowler. The Greats.

So much for received wisdom.

Perhaps fan knowledge represents a sort of N-space where we all know our co-ordinates and feel comfortable with shared understandings. By contrast, I was trapped in the E-Space of commuter-belt Hampshire; fandom's negatives were my positives. In any case, I transformed the story into a gateway. A gateway to intently re-experiencing and studying **Doctor Who** for the first time; a gateway to enjoying jargon rather than fearing it; a gateway to other stories, genres and darkly beautiful British things.

The Boy Who Waited
The Keeper of Traken by **Robert Day-Webb**, 39, Dursley, UK / First story: **The Keeper of Traken**

On a cold, dark, wintry night in the old spa town of Cheltenham, situated on the edge of the Cotswolds, a small seven-year-old boy quietly crawls out from under his bed sheets, making a supreme effort to be as silent as possible so as not to arouse the attention of his parents located directly beneath him in the living room.

The boy tiptoes across his room with trepidation. He pauses as he reaches the bedroom window. Tentatively, the boy pulls the curtains apart and presses his inquisitive little face up against the window pane. Peering out and up into the dark, starry night sky above him, the little boy desperately tries to spy a strange little flying blue box, hoping beyond hope that the strange and mysterious, yet heroic, owner of the box – a man simply known as the Doctor – will come and take him away for an adventure beyond the stars...

...Fast forward thirty-odd years and a fully grown 39-year-old man gazes excitedly out of his bedroom window at the night sky, his four-year-old son nestled snugly in his arms. The young boy turns to his father and asks him where the blue box is and when is the Doctor coming to take them both away to fight the Weeping Angels. The father hugs his son tightly, relishing this shared moment, reliving his childhood dreams with his own child. 'Soon,' the father reassures his son, 'very soon.' Then suddenly, just at that moment, a strange groaning and wheezing sound from afar disturbs this tender moment. Father and child stare at each other in disbelief, broad smiles appearing on both of their faces at the same time...

...This is my **Doctor Who** story.

Well, unfortunately, that strange groaning and wheezing sound wasn't the sound of the TARDIS dematerialising to take me and my son off for a far flung adventure battling Weeping Angels, but rather the more earthly sound of air bubbles in our water pipes. Nonetheless, my son and I continue to live in hope that one day that funny little blue police box, bigger on the inside than on the outside, and its mysterious pilot, the one known as the Doctor, will come and whisk us away!

So when did my obsession with **Doctor Who** begin? Well, to answer that question, we must travel back in time to the winter of early 1981 and visit again that small seven-year-old boy living in Cheltenham. Already aware of a certain person, 'all teeth and curls,' and called the Doctor, the very first episode that lodged itself entirely in the boy's memory, and hence instigated the obsession, was *The Keeper of Traken*. This was the first story in that holy trinity more recently known via DVD as **New Beginnings**, the other two stories being, of course, *Logopolis* and *Castrovalva*. I don't think I need to go into too much detail, but this collection of episodes is essentially where Tom Baker morphed into Peter Davison due to a confrontation with my favourite ever **Doctor Who** villain, the Master.

So what was it that so attracted me to **Doctor Who**? Well, er, everything! I was already a sci-fi buff thanks to **Star Wars** and **Star Trek** but for me, **Doctor Who** offered something more real. Here was a time traveller who visited Earth, a lot, and liked to take on young human companions. As a very young boy, I could connect more with this and hold a belief that I could one day become the Doctor's companion – far more likely I thought than ending up in a galaxy far, far away with Han and Luke or visiting the final frontier with Kirk and company. Conveniently, there was also a phone box, albeit a red one, just down the road from my house which served as an admirable TARDIS, and local clothes shops with Auton shop dummies in their windows to shoot at ... ah, halcyon days! Time travel also fascinated me greatly, not only as a child, but even now as a (supposed) grown-up. And as for being able to regenerate! Wow! This was just such an utterly and brilliantly magical concept for a young boy like me. And again, even today, I still get ridiculously over-excited about regeneration scenes. So how could I not fall in love with a time-travelling, regenerating Time Lord?

And so I stayed loyal to *my* Doctor, Peter Davison, for his entire duration. When, in 1984, he regenerated into Colin Baker, I was fairly traumatised. Who was this chubby buffoon in his nightmarish technicolour outfit?! I must quickly point out that as an adult I am now actually a *huge* fan of Colin's Doctor but back then, as a young whippersnapper, I was left largely unimpressed. I tried hanging in there but soon found my loyalty failing as I was drawn away to other TV delights like **Manimal**, **Knightrider**, **The A-Team** and, later, **Star Trek: TNG**. In 1987, with the whiff of regeneration in the air, I avidly took to my sofa once again to watch *Time and the Rani* in the hope of seeing some improvement. Oh dear. To say I was a tad disappointed would be a, ahem, slight understatement. I subsequently decided to abandon the TARDIS altogether and take up with Captain Picard and the crew of the Enterprise...

...Until 1996 that is, when my old pal turned up once more in the wonderful guise of Paul McGann. Throw in a regeneration scene, my favourite old enemy, and a wonderful new TARDIS interior, and I was smitten once again. However, the powers that be deemed that a new series would not be forthcoming, and I found myself boarding the USS Voyager instead with the rather perky Captain Kathryn Janeway.

And I thought that that, as they say, was that. Work, marriage, kids, divorce, another marriage, another kid followed. The Doctor was out of sight and out of mind. Then of course, in 2005, nearly a decade after the McGann movie, the Doctor reappeared. And how! The new series has been utterly brilliant. From the actors to the writers to the amazing production values, new **Doctor Who** has grabbed my old hero by the, ahem, bits and blasted him well and truly into the 21st century. A different beast, at least in some ways, to classic **Doctor Who** but none the worse for that. And so I find myself today just as infatuated, if not more so, with the good Doctor as I was all those many years ago after I first watched *The Keeper of Traken*. And this time, I have companions of my own on this journey – my three wonderful sons.

We salute you Doctor!

'21st March 1981'

Logopolis by **Chris Orton**, 36, Durham, UK
First story: **Logopolis**

It's strange how tiny fragments of time can have long-lasting repercussions on somebody's life. My initial exposure to **Doctor Who** was odd in that it came right at the very end of an era. Glimpsing a snippet of a programme that I had never seen before magically resulted in a life-long love and devotion. How could such a short piece of television cause somebody to become such an all-consuming fan of the series it came from? Just what is it about **Doctor Who** that causes it to have this effect on people?

The first story I remember seeing on its original UK transmission was *Logopolis*. More specifically, *Logopolis* Part Four. Even more specifically than that, the very end of *Logopolis* Part Four. The regeneration scene. It's true, my earliest memories of television consist of the aftermath of our hero falling off a radio telescope. Tom Baker later become my favourite Doctor and without realising it I had just gone and missed seeing his *entire seven years*, a few minutes. Despite being only four years old at the time I can vividly remember the scene in question, the mysterious Watcher appearing, merging with the Doctor and being mysteriously reborn as the 'pleasant, open-faced' Tristan Farnon from **All Creatures Great and Small**. What was it about this pivotal moment that lodged itself as my first memory of the show? Anything before 21st March 1981 was an unknown, but something about the programme somehow caught my attention; from that moment on I was hooked.

Missing out on the fourth Doctor is rather typical of my luck, although I couldn't have done anything about it: **Doctor Who** experienced its thirteenth birthday the day after I was born and that was that. Apparently a whole galaxy of stuff had already happened, which I had missed. *Three* other Doctors! Just how many stories had there been? The really frustrating thing was there was no way that I could get to see any of it. Back then television was more of an ephemeral affair and more often than not, the first showing was also the final showing. Video recorders hadn't yet made inroads into most homes and repeats were few and far between. Short of owning my own TARDIS I couldn't have appreciated Tom as the Doctor in his original place in time and space. I was destined to discover the fourth Doctor properly way in the future: after Peter Davison's, after Colin Baker's and after even Sylvester McCoy. I still find it strange that I saw the Doctors completely out of order.

We never owned a video recorder until 1989 and so I couldn't even see any of the stories that had been released during the 1980s. It became frustrating to know that there were whole other worlds out there waiting to be explored and yet not being able to do so. So I was really excited to finally have a video machine – I would be able to buy the tapes and record all future episodes of **Doctor Who** to watch time and time again! Bad luck struck again however, as unbeknownst to me 1989 would provide viewers with the very last series of **Doctor Who** ever (or so we thought...). After *Survival* everything just sort of went quiet. The lack of reassurance from an announcement over the end credits of the final episode probably made fans realise that something was up. There was to be no more taping, and the show looked over and done with. Perhaps it was time to start putting things from childhood away anyway... But in the case of **Doctor Who** I just couldn't.

I'd soon read plenty of the Target books and found out something of what happened to the earlier Doctors. The series of books seemed endless, and somebody called Terrance Dicks, I noted, wrote most of them. Our local library wasn't much good on Tom though as they only had three **Doctor Who** books: **Doctor Who and the Cybermen**, **Doctor Who and the Zarbi** and **Meglos**, the cover of which terrified me, so I relied on pocket money to keep up. After the VCR arrived my younger brother and I began to collect the tapes in earnest. The BBC had realised they had a cash cow and ramped up the release schedule. Having saved up our pocket money we would trek to Woolworths or WH Smiths in order to see whether there were any new stories out or not. Tapes cost £9.99 then and we would sometimes go halves on a story. When we couldn't afford one we would borrow them from a cousin and generally got most of the new stuff. Trips to our grandparents - where all of us cousins met up every other Sunday - often resulted in carrier bags full of **Doctor Who** stuff being carted home to devour over the next couple of weeks.

Tom Baker quickly became my favourite Doctor. He completely nailed the part and you could almost believe that the actor himself was somehow alien. Quirky, clever, wistful and brave the fourth Doctor was *the* Doctor. I would go on to appreciate and enjoy the performances of the rest of the actors who played the part, of course, but none of them could quite match Tom. Everything seems to have been in more or less perfect alignment for his time on the show. The other Doctors are all indeed 'splendid chaps,' but for many fans the persona created by Baker the First is the definitive one. Even today if you ask someone for a general impression of what the Doctor looks like, there is a good chance that they will mention the curly hair and a ridiculously long scarf. That image of him burned its way into the public consciousness like no other before or since. Actors doing spoofs of the Doctor even today often go along these lines still, dressing themselves in an outfit approximating that worn by the fourth Doctor. Tom is primarily known to people of a certain age as 'Doctor Who' and it is a testament to his brilliance in the role that he is still remembered so fondly today by so many.

Logopolis clearly isn't the show's finest hour but nor is it the worst and I don't quite hold it in the same esteem that I do with certain other adventures. Other than featuring that momentous regeneration scene it isn't a particularly iconic instalment. Changes were afoot all over the programme and despite it being Tom's final season the new producer John Nathan-Turner made his mark on the show by giving it a radical overhaul. After getting to see *Logopolis* in full following the VHS release I finally discovered what had gone on prior to that fateful fall from atop the Pharos Project radio telescope: why the Doctor had travelled to Logopolis, that he had gained some new helpers, that an old enemy called the Master had returned with a vengeance and a little more about the enigmatic Watcher and the mysterious process of regeneration. Viewed from a more analytical perspective *Logopolis* does have some rather odd twists of logic and plot, whilst falling off a metal structure isn't perhaps the most heroic way to depart, but for me it will always hold a special place in my affections as it was the point at which I came in.

This was the story that set the ball rolling for a life-long love of a magical, fascinating, complicated, frustrating and entertaining television show. The end of an era for a Doctor was the beginning of something for me. Lots of time and money has been spent following the show, even down to contributing to books such as this one. No other show has ever done this to me and it is difficult to put a finger on quite why it can draw people in in the way that it does. Through thick and thin, through stories good and bad, and during the long, bleak period when the show was in television's wilderness I have remained a fan. When people mocked the supposed deficiencies of the show I would valiantly attempt to defend it ('Sigh ... yes they *can* go upstairs ... no, the sets didn't wobble any more than on any other BBC show of the time...') and never wavered in my support. All because of a scene in *Logopolis*. This little lad's attention was grabbed on 21st March 1981 and resulted in a devotion to the strange series that began almost exactly thirteen years to the day before he made his own debut. What's not to like about a scene where a man lies on some Astroturf beneath a model of a steel structure whilst strange faces float around his head just before he turns into somebody else?

Hopefully the programme will continue to work its magic on young fans of the current series in the way that it did for us. Will **Doctor Who** still be running in another thirty years' time on some new-fangled Time-Space Visualiser type system when I am getting on in years, and will my little boy end up a fan just like his dad did?

Despite *Logopolis* having such an effect, it's odd I can't remember a single thing about *Castrovalva*. Surely I wasn't watching the other side was I...?

The Fifth Doctor Who

1982 was the year in which **Doctor Who** underwent its most significant changes since colour and a six month broadcast run established themselves in 1970. For the first time, the series relinquished its early Saturday evening transmission slot, having shed viewers like a cat sheds fur during the previous series. The move to a twice-weekly screening and a later time meant that the programme was now being watched by a new audience, one more accustomed to a slightly different – and perhaps more involving – kind of entertainment. **Doctor Who** was no longer a mainstay of the kind of light entertainment line-up that also included **Jukebox Jury** and **The Generation Game**, but was now finding its home in what would become the domain of the soaps.

On screen, this was reflected in the way the series focussed its attentions on the regular characters; this wasn't the first time the Doctor had travelled with multiple companions, but whereas previously characters like Vicki and Steven and Jamie had simply been passengers on the journey, now Adric and Tegan and Turlough seemed to be included with a purpose, and the stories devoted more time to exploring their function within the fiction.

As the public face of the show, nowhere was the change in emphasis more clear than in the choice of Doctor Who. Gone were the patrician, eccentric and unpredictable characteristics that had so come to define the nature of Doctor Who, to be replaced instead by a gentler, younger, more human character. The actor chosen to represent all this was Peter Davison, a talent whose star was currently very much on the rise. It says a lot about Davison that, in spite of the ways in which the series was changing in the early 1980s, drifting further from the inspiration for its previous successes, he is still so very well remembered among both fans and public alike.

Something else was happening in the early 1980s as well, something that would irrevocably alter our perception of the programme, and would ultimately lead to a fundamental change in the way we experienced it. The video recorder was making its way into the homes of a watching nation, and now we could not only record programmes we might otherwise miss in order to watch them later, but we could also rewatch those programmes we had recorded time and time again, absorbing all the little details that made up their production that we might have missed on first viewing.

The video recorder was to prove a vital component in both the on- and off-screen fate of **Doctor Who** over the next few years, but for now, it was enough that we could catch up with the Doctor's exploits even if we had a scout meeting or family engagement on the night of its actual broadcast...

Castrovalva, How Do I Love Thee?

Castrovalva by **Neil Thomas**, 34, West Sussex, UK
First story: **Warriors Of The Deep**

I dream about Castrovalva. Quite a lot actually. Not the story but the city and its surrounding woods. It's (literally) my idea of heaven. If I could visit any planet or city from the **Doctor Who** universe, it would be Castrovalva.

Just imagine it; my day would begin with a lovely stroll through the forest, before joining up with the masked hunting parting and spearing myself a giant pig. Then I would climb up the rocks via rope ladder and explore the city. It always disappointed me that we never actually got to see inside Shardovan's library, so I'd go in there and see if they had any Christopher H Bidmead books. Doubtful. After a wonderful supper of roast pork and celery, I'd hang out with Ruther and Mergrave all evening and we'd get the Portreeve hammered and talk him into declaring a holiday for the women. Finally I'd make a start on a tapestry. Sorry. I'm talking nonsense.

Castrovalva. A gorgeous word. One of my favourite words ever probably. And certainly one of my favourite **Doctor Who** stories. I first watched it in 1992. I was thirteen and I bought the video. I hadn't seen it when it aired as I had only just turned three years old (I didn't start watching **Doctor Who** until I hit the big five!).

Castrovalva features two adventures in one story. After a nice bit of location filming, we are in the TARDIS. For ages. I do like seeing new areas of the TARDIS and the cricket room is just brilliant. It even has its own little theme music as we see into it! A fantastic bit of design. After an episode-and-a-half, the TARDIS lands (on its side) and the next chapter begins. Bliss.

From this point onwards the locations, sets, music and performances give *Castrovalva* a dreamy quality that I simply adore. There's something about **Doctor Who** being set in the woods or the countryside that really pleases me. I love it when the stories feature a lush green location. *Castrovalva* features a beautiful sequence in which Tegan and Nyssa push the Doctor in his Zero cabinet through the woods towards the city. The music is gorgeous and I have hummed it frequently over the last twenty years. I really need to get the soundtrack but I never have any luck tracking it down online. I'll keep trying.

With the possible exception of *Enlightenment*, no other **Doctor Who** story comes close to making me feel as warm and childlike as *Castrovalva* does. One day I will own a house and I shall call it Castrovalva. Every night I will go to sleep in my very own Zero Room and life, like *Castrovalva*, will be absolutely splendid.

Don't You (Forget About Me)

Four to Doomsday by **Kevin Stayner**, 36, East Sheen
First story: **Logopolis**

This is my confession: there was a period in my life when I forgot to love **Doctor Who**. I don't mean that I grew tired of it or disliked a specific period in the show's history, I just forgot to love it. There were all those passionate fans who did everything they could to keep the show alive after its cancellation and then there was me, moving on to new shallow empty relationships with **Star Trek: TNG** and **The X-Files**, all without so much as a cursory glance back. Even though I never missed an episode when it was on TV I didn't have a single VHS of the show, I had no copies of **DWM** cluttering up my cupboard and I didn't even know the Virgin New Adventures existed. How can that be? How can a programme that so defined my childhood be so casually forgotten just because it wasn't on TV anymore? Had the Master placed a perception filter around the show making it invisible to me? Probably not and even if he had I wouldn't have got the reference at the time anyway. Quite simply, **Doctor Who** left me, so like a jilted lover who burns all his old photographs I cut my ties and pretended it didn't mean anything to me anyway.

I think some perspective might be required here. Perhaps the reason it was so easy to forget my love for the show was actually a side effect of the very thing that enabled me to love it as much as I did. Namely that my affection has always been somewhat fickle and for that I lay the blame squarely at one concept: regeneration. Yes, arguably the one concept in the show above all others that has enabled it to endure for fifty years is the very reason I found it so easy to move on when the show went away. I had been trained by it not to get too attached. When I was five years old I watched my first **Doctor Who** story, *Logopolis*. Over the course of my first few weeks in the company of this character I fell for him completely. He became my first hero, I followed his adventures perched on the edge of my sofa, eyes open wide in wonder, wondering where we would go next ... and then he died. What the...? You can imagine the wailing, the screaming, the floods of tears, can't you? Well don't because there weren't any. I simply accepted that he had become someone else and that was fine, especially as the someone else was that nice man I liked from **All Creatures Great and Small**.

I suspect most fans consider the first Doctor they saw to be the definitive incarnation but my time with my first Doctor was so brief that the fifth Doctor became my Doctor. The distance of time has led to me appreciating that there have been incarnations that are more iconic and I can almost even admit there may have been incarnations that have been more 'Doctory' but love isn't objective. Peter Davison is my favourite Doctor, no, more than that. To me Peter Davison was (and judging by the thrill I got when watching *Time Crash* still is) The Doctor. He was my first and ultimately it was he that would bring me back in from the wilderness some twenty years later. Well, maybe not literally him, but when the show started to creep back into my consciousness, it was his Doctor that I saw in my mind. Actually, to be specific, it was an image of his Doctor watching a tribal dance. I couldn't place exactly what the memory was and I certainly couldn't piece together any kind of narrative but I could picture that scene perfectly and I knew that I needed to revisit it, whatever it was. The more I thought about it and its inherent strangeness the more I thought I may have made it up. Perhaps it was something from a dream? Although I instinctively felt that the fifth Doctor was my Doctor, his stories were hazy in my memory. It seemed that my brain had wiped them in order to deal with his leaving me only to be replaced by an angry bloke that tried to strangle his busty friend. Apart from this one memory of him watching a tribal dance, what the heck was that?

In 2001 I became friends with someone that it soon became clear had a vast knowledge of **Doctor Who** and what's more had several off-air recordings on video. Talking to him made me feel silly and frankly a little guilty for the ease with which I had allowed my love for the show to dwindle. Eventually I broached the subject of my hazy memory, not thinking for a second it would mean anything to him, but he simply exclaimed, '*Four to Doomsday*, I'll chuck a copy your way.' So there we have it. Within a few days I found myself popping a VHS tape into my video recorder and pressing play. From the first note of the theme I became a time traveller myself, transported back to the sofa in my parent's house shushing my Dad for eating his Monster Munch too loudly. As for the first appearance of Davison, well that really opened the floodgates. There he was, my Doctor ... and he was wonderful. An old man in a young man's body clearly wondering why the other guy had left him saddled with the Maths kid. Yes, the plot doesn't quite sustain the four episodes and yes, the science is a little off but I didn't care, my love was well and truly rekindled. **Doctor Who** was back in my life and this time it was going to stay. I had been given a second chance with my first love and I've happily dived back in. Looking back over the full fifty years of **Doctor Who** there are plenty of stories that I've enjoyed more and to be honest there have even been eras of the show that I've preferred, but there can be no doubt that the fifth Doctor is my Doctor and *Four to Doomsday* is my story.

Welcome to the Jungle...
Kinda by **Simon Fernandes**, 43, Cambridge, UK
First story: **Planet of the Daleks**

Last night, I dreamt I went to Deva Loka again.
 It seemed to me that I walked spellbound through its jungles, treading their strangely flat floors and pushing aside the plastic foliage as the suspiciously bright and even light glared from above. I raised a hand in greeting at the plaster cave of the Wise Woman, and skirted a wide berth around the crime against the Forest built by the Not-We from another world. I stopped a moment to savour the calming whisper of the Wind Chimes that are the gateway to Dreaming, before pressing on to a clearing where there stood a strange object, not of the Forest. Tall it stood, and blue, with a strange legend inscribed above its door – 'Police Box'...

Even now, thirty-odd years later, *Kinda* has that sort of power for me. As a bright twelve-year-old who'd loved **Doctor Who** all his life, it was a revelation to see a story of such depth, with so many layers, so many levels of meaning. I didn't understand them all, of course – I wasn't *that* bright a twelve-year-old – but even the references I didn't understand had a deep resonance, like the haunting sound created by Peter Howell for the Deva Lokan Wind Chimes.
 Yes, if you look at it afresh in this far distant future of 2013, it looks a little ... cheap. It's overlit (like all 1980s **Doctor Who**), which shows all too obviously that the Forest of Deva Loka is plainly a BBC studio, and at the end, there is what we have all come to know as, 'that snake.' But to an imaginative twelve-year-old in 1982, none of that mattered. I was caught up in a story, like nothing I'd seen on **Doctor Who** before, that entwined Buddhist mysticism with hardcore sci-fi and colonial allegory, its two plot strands – the mystic danger of the

Mara, and the unhinged madness of the colonialists – cunningly feeding into each other.

What really sells it is the performances. Everyone plays the material with utter conviction, regardless of the production. Having Nerys Hughes as the female lead might have seemed like typical stunt casting, but she actually gives a believable, serious performance. Richard Todd shows a versatility **The Dam Busters** only hinted at as he descends from gruff colonial stereotype to sanity-shattered childhood.

But the performance that still hits you hard is Simon Rouse (later to be sentenced to years in **The Bill** as DCI Meadows) as Hindle. **Doctor Who** had shown us madness before; Davros, Magnus Greel and the Master could never be said to be entirely sane. But Hindle was the first time we saw the show consider madness as it really is – as an illness. Hindle wasn't a megalomaniac, intent on ruling the galaxy for no clearly defined reason. He was a poor sensitive young man unsuited to a harsh life in an overbearing militaristic Empire.

Rouse's performance totally sells his breakdown, which, together with the aptly named Sanders, has more than a shade of Conrad's **Heart of Darkness** in its depiction of unprepared colonisers driven to insanity by an environment that mesmerises and breaks them. Just like poor deranged Mr Kurtz, Hindle co-opts the natives to his madness, only to find them uncooperative at the last.

Kinda is full of that kind of allusion – literary, religious, psychological – which is why it still stands up today (if you can overlook the production values). It's such a dense piece of writing that it inspired an unfathomably pseudy Media Studies treatise, **Doctor Who: The Unfolding Text**, which focussed in inaccessible psychological jargon on the complexities of the tale. I tried reading it, aged thirteen, and gave up on its incomprehensible line diagrams of how the various psychological archetypes related to each other. Looked at now, it seems unbearably pretentious. Because like a good theatre piece, *Kinda* has the depth to inspire that kind of pretension.

And indeed, theatre is what Tegan's unsettling dream under the Chimes still seems like, with the eerie appearance of Anna Wing (**EastEnders**' Lou Beale) and the frankly terrifying Jeff Stewart as the sneering Dukkha.

The sheer minimalism of those dream sequences gives them the feel of nightmares; the blank, black backgrounds with just that one weird tumbledown structure. Not for the only time in this story, it's like stepping into that other paragon of terror, **Sapphire and Steel**. As is the nightmarish, hallucinatory vision the Doctor and Todd step into from Panna's cave, the whirling, screaming faces in the blackness, fading into an obviously allegorical depiction of Doomsday as the Kinda tribe dance obliviously in a circle of clocks ticking down to Armageddon.

Then there was the sex. Yes, really. We'd seen chaste romance in **Doctor Who** before, with Leela taking the hand of Andred, or Jo Grant's innocent kiss with Cliff Jones. But never had we seen anything so boldly lascivious as the possessed Tegan, dropping from a tree to tempt Adrian Mills with an apple.

As a family show, there was no mention of actual sex. But one look at Janet's lecherous sneer, together with her open blouse, was enough to see what was going on. As a twelve-year-old, I was just hitting puberty, and suffice it to say, Janet's sinister, dominatrix-style sensuality made a big impression. Though given my eventual sexual preference, so did all those shirtless men in the jungle...

This was **Doctor Who** as it had never been seen before, even in Tom Baker's newly serious final season. It was allegory, it was theatre, it was anthropology and religion all examined in a story whose complexity had more to do with the human condition than Chris Bidmead's dry obsession with maths. There's so much going on, played with such conviction, that even a decidedly ropey giant snake can't spoil it. Back in 1982, those newfangled videotapes were so expensive that I could only afford to keep one story from each season of **Doctor Who**; despite the conundrum of *Castrovalva* and the grim body count of *Earthshock*, *Kinda* was the one I kept. I liked it that much, because it made me think *and* feel – and still does today.

Forty-Five Pence

The Visitation by **Richie J Haworth**, 30-something, Cardiff, UK / First story: **The Keeper of Traken**

As an earlier regeneration of mine gazed longingly out of our bay window on a June Sunday morning in 1982, eagerly anticipating an impending arrival, my vision was suddenly impaired – well, disturbed at least – by a flash of lights. This, however, was no spaceship crashing to Earth, but the twinkling of the reflectors (free with Kellogg's Frosties) from the paperboy's Raleigh Burner BMX. It was here! I listened intently for the clatter of the letterbox and as soon as I saw the paperboy cycle away, I rushed to the door. Amidst the black and white of the strewn Sunday papers, was the terrifying visage of a green hooded monster – a Terileptil – staring back at me!

Of course, this wasn't an actual escapee from the tinclavic mines on Raaga, but **Doctor Who Monthly** issue 65, said Terileptil on the cover. I was in a near state of apoplexy, a frenzy probably not bettered until the one that caused me to fall down the stairs in anticipation of *Dragonfire* Part One. I had first spotted this particular issue of **DWM** the previous day, whilst walking home with my Dad from Splott swimming pool. He had decided to pop into the Newsbox (other newsagents are available) and as he chatted to the proprietor I had spotted the aforementioned edition of **Doctor Who Monthly**, nestled between copies of **Look-In** and **Buttons**. It was the Terileptil staring out at me that caught my attention. I'd remembered it from **Doctor Who** a few months previously, and had even co-opted a school friend to be a Terileptil, to my fifth Doctor, when playing **Doctor Who** in the yard one playtime. To say I nagged my Dad to buy it is probably an understatement; alas I was soon told in no uncertain terms that I'd already had a treat that day – a packet of Skydivers (maize snacks in the shape of skydivers, for those too young to know) from the vending machine at the pool. As I started giving up hope that I would ever posses a copy of the enthralling-looking journal, my Dad asked the newsagent to deliver it the following day with his papers! My excitement was stoked!

I devoured issue 65. The free poster, featuring the Doctor, Tegan, Nyssa, Richard Mace and Adric's hair was soon white-tacked to my bedroom wall (Blu-tack was too expensive). Holding **DWM** in my hands was my first step into the world of **Doctor Who** – outside of the TV show. Until now, **Doctor Who** had been like any other TV programme – better of course, but just TV.

Growing up during this period in **Doctor Who** wasn't about the usual related clichés. It wasn't about Saturdays, football results, **Basil Brush** or **Juke Box Jury**. It was part of a world that included **Juliet Bravo** (best theme tune ever?), **Angels** and a lurid blue and green (or yellow, depending on how high your contrast was turned up) BBC1 globe. The one that was sliding towards the edge of the screen like some LSD-fuelled vision of what a flat Earth might look like. BBC1 was all flying records, adventure games, Sarah Greene and Jan Leeming. *The Visitation* and Terileptils take me right back to this world.

Watching **Doctor Who** most often with my Dad, sometimes with Mum, I adored everything about it. From Peter Howell's dynamic theme, to the starfield opening, the Doctor's face appearing out of the stars (now to be immortalised as a stamp) and the team of companions ably (or not so ably) assisting the Doctor on his adventures.

The experience of having my first **DWM** was so important to me that the next day at school (Baden Powell Primary School, fact fans), when asked to write about something we did on the weekend I chose to write about getting my **DWM**. I also drew a picture of the cover to accompany it. I later discovered that (thanks to the excellent **Vworp Vworp** publication) the very cover that first attracted my eye, nearly never was. It turns out John Nathan-Turner thought it offensive and could be open to crude interpretation – perhaps he thought the Terileptil looked like a flasher, pulling back his cloak to reveal his scaly body!

It's funny, of all the hundreds of **Doctor Who** books, video cassettes, magazines and DVDs I've collected, I can only really recollect where and when I bought a handful of them. But when thinking about this piece I realised I can account for all the versions of *The Visitation* I own, whether it be the novel (Carousel '90 convention in Cardiff), the video (a double pack with *Black Orchid* – a family holiday in North Yorkshire; I bought it on the first day of the holiday, then had to wait a week to watch it; the rest of the family were enjoying the holiday but all I wanted was access to a VHS!) or the DVD (MVC Cardiff, with grey membership card for a discount). It can only be because of the impact of having my first **DWM** with its Terileptil connections that I remember all this. I even once wrote to Dapol asking if they were planning a Terileptil action figure; they replied with a 'Maybe' and sent me a green K9.

The Visitation is by no means my favourite story, but perhaps it should be: it is the first story that gripped my imagination; its historical setting is perfect for **Doctor Who**. Its Disco android, Nyssa's ear muffs, Adric doing a Susan and tripping over nothing much. I loved Season 19, I wanted to be part of this TARDIS crew. *The Visitation* was a memorable adventure, it is the start of my love for **Doctor Who**, all thanks to spotting that Terileptil on the cover of **Doctor Who Monthly** issue 65 (45 pence). Perhaps I should pay my Dad the 45 pence back – for me it is the best money he ever spent.

Missing Episodes
Black Orchid by **Robert Hammond**, 44 (and not bitter. Not at all), Surrey, UK / First story: **Planet of the Daleks**

You'll have to excuse me. This is not so much an essay as a rant; an exercise in listing and venting - possibly even a therapy session. With a message.

On the face of it I have two strands that interweave. Firstly - family holidays. Family holidays that were spent with relatives. Family holidays that were spent with relatives who didn't watch (or care for) **Doctor Who**. See where this is heading?

Secondly, there was also the perfect, very real threat my parents wielded to draw me back into line if I was misbehaving at home, if school reports weren't all that were expected - there was no, 'If you're not good, Santa won't bring you any presents,' in our house, the threat made was far, far worse - my sword of Damocles was the removal of **Doctor Who** as my one true viewing pleasure.

And while writing this, I kept thinking of all the 21st century converts to the series, and hope they will be the ones to take special heed (and show some pity) at the end of my ramblings. They live in a golden age, no matter what they think. If it's proof you need then here, in order, I present the list of episodes of **Doctor Who** I missed on original transmission and the reasons why I missed them.

The Time Warrior (Parts Two to Four)
Invasion of the Dinosaurs (Parts One to Six)
A *nine* episode ban on the series following the nightmares suffered after the final shot of *The Time Warrior*, where Linx was unveiled and unmasked. *Nine* episodes *missed*. Harsh. Okay, so I was only four and I *was* terrified, but I think the ban had a greater effect on me than the actual Sontaran ever did.

The Masque of Mandragora (Part One)

Ah, the curse of the family holiday with relatives rears its ugly head for the first time. I was seen by many at school as a **Doctor Who** oracle - a lot of the other children weren't allowed to watch the programme because many of their parents considered it too frightening. So I would be there on a Monday, an expectant group gathered around me in the playground during morning break, explaining the episode that had aired over the weekend, (and probably exaggerating it somewhat as no-one else would truly know what had happened). It was great as my circle of friends was (still is) quite small, and it proved a good popularity booster for me - and suddenly that was taken away from me (albeit for one episode), and with the awful flipside that I had no-one at school to ask what had happened. The set-up of the story, the new console room, the execution-by-beheading cliffhanger - all unknown to me.

I must have made one *hell* of a fuss about this (although I really don't remember), but other season openers - *Horror of Fang Rock*, *The Leisure Hive*, all made their debut while on family holidays, and yet were seen.

Destiny of the Daleks (Episode Two)
Okay, so neither family holiday or a ban; worse in many regards - my first camping trip away with the Cub Scouts. Cold nights, even colder mornings, dragging great plastic containers of water from a standpipe half a mile away, and yes - most terrible of all - **Doctor Who** on the television but not being at home to watch it. However, things were now slightly different. My family had bought a Philips radio and cassette recorder, so despite missing the episode I could at least listen to the soundtrack later, complete with all of the background noise, including my Mum ssshhing my sister into silence as the theme tune started, and the occasional clatter of tea plates and cups audible beneath Tom's dialogue. Some 33 years later I still know this episode off by heart, thanks to repeated plays of that cassette, and the visuals I created for the episode

were only washed away by the eventually BBC Video release.

The tape-recorded episode technique also came into play for Part Three of *City of Death*, when I attended the birthday party of a school friend (we had mint birthday cake, and I was told off for asking for a second piece. It was good cake). As luck would have it, we *did* watch the episode as part of the celebration, and just as well – the cassette tape used to record it in my absence mangled in the player, and only the first fifteen minutes were listenable after salvaging and respooling the cassette.

The Horns of Nimon (Part Two)
A trip to a pantomime meant that I missed this episode, and developed in me an utter disdain for the Christmas theatre trip – compounded two years later when the same annual event came around and I missed the final episode of **Blakes 7** (my Dad didn't attend that panto with us. He had seen the episode though, and told me upon my return, 'The whole cast were shot and it ended.' This was met with a, 'Yeah, right...' kind of reply from me, but was all horrifyingly confirmed as real by a friend on the return to school a few weeks later).

Which brings me to *Black Orchid*. Screened over one week on original transmission, and coinciding with my younger cousin staying for a week – my younger cousin who stabbed a felt-tip pen through the back seat of the reasonably-new family car and for which, despite a ton of protestation, I was wrongly blamed, and which in turn led to another ban of the programme.

But this was bigger than previous bans. The twice-weekly slot of the show and the fact it was only two episodes meant I missed the whole story – not one piffling episode; *the whole story*. Alright, so on reflection I didn't miss much. But at the time it was *devastating*. Fellow schoolmates were now old enough to watch the programme but none of them did – they were too busy getting girlfriends and buying Ultravox records. I had a couple of months waiting for the **DWM** review to eventually put me out of my misery.

A handful of weeks later I missed the first fifteen minutes of *Time-Flight* Part Four, due to the transmission schedule suddenly changing for that week and that week only.

I started to feel doomed. But only a handful of years after that, the BBC made sure I would never miss an episode again with first the hiatus, and then the cancellation of the series.

Some of this probably seems very strange and archaic to 'the modern fan,' the concept of missing an episode completely. In this day and age you get DVD releases of the episodes mere months (rather than years) after the original broadcast. The show is now regularly repeated on other satellite channels, where a lot of the 'classic series' never had second screenings. **DWM** and the BBC website give you big photos, teaser hints, clips, prequels, a ton of stuff before an episode has even been screened. We sometimes only found out the name of the next story at the tail-end of the previous adventure, and occasionally on the day of broadcast within the TV listings of the Saturday paper.

So should you still be reading this, dear 21st century convert; if you have come to love the series in all of its forms, old and new, then please - don't bemoan a mere eight episodes a year; or having to wait a week to watch an episode on BBC Three; or, heaven forbid, not seeing location filming photographs on the same day as the filming took place - as you really, *really* have never had it so good. Among the many things you now have that us old guard didn't, you will never have that true terror and pain of missing episodes.

A Spoonful of Cybermen

Earthshock by **Stuart Flanagan**, 36, Belfast, UK
First story: **City Of Death**

If Eliot's J Alfred Prufrock measured out his life with coffee spoons, then surely **Doctor Who** fans have measured out theirs in 25-minute episodes. Let me qualify that – if you're in your mid-twenties or older, there's the original-run episode nearest your birth. Maybe you can lay claim to a *Pyramids Of Mars* instalment being nearest your arrival on Planet Earth. For the younger fanbase perhaps a *Paradise Of Death* or Big Finish release is nearer the mark, and if you're reading this in ten years' time you might be genealogically shackled to *Fear Her* (unlucky!). Other landmark life events will be tied in with a temporally paralleled episode – reminding you of the first day at school, a new job, friends, parties and weddings. Episodes of **Doctor Who** are a special, magical thread weaving their way through the tapestry of our lives.

Some of these episodes will of course go on to become personal classics – those lasting instalments that conjure up a certain nostalgia for many times and places over the years, joining us on our life journey to provide intrigue, thrills and especially comfort at various stages. With the advent of video and DVD releases, as well as repeats, particular stories keep on tapping into our nostalgia gland (we do have one, I'm determined to find it someday) and bring new layers of happiness every time we see them.

So it is for me and *Earthshock*. Yes, we all know about the shock ending to Part One, the shock ending to Part Four and the nation's shock at having to endure *Time-Flight* a mere six days later. But *Earthshock* holds a special place as my first classic tale, one I'll often go back to when I need a hit of good old **Doctor Who** love.

I was six when *Earthshock* was transmitted. In amongst my daily TV diet of **Rentaghost**, **Mighty Mouse** and **Blue Peter**, a regular teatime dose of **Doctor Who** had wormed its way into my brain in the winter of 1981. I'd already been addicted to the Saturday prescription of course, but by the time **The Five Faces of Doctor Who** rolled around on 2nd November 1981, I was a whole five years old, and had already laid claim to the TV channel squatting rights. Every Monday to Thursday at 5pm belonged to BBC2 for the now legendary repeats season. As I became terrified by the Troughton title sequence, and curious about how Worzel Gummidge could pilot the TARDIS, I became utterly enamoured with the show. Those five weeks became a pivotal moment in my life - having been cocooned in the history of **Doctor Who** for a month I was emerging as a full blown fan.

So as Season 19 rolled around I enjoyed the first series I could call my own. And by the time those silver marauders arrived on screen their impact couldn't have been greater. They were simply the most terrifyingly relentless foes I could ever imagine, and their ability to take out one of my heroes (hey, I was six!) made them even more impressive. Looking back now, I realise this was one of my first encounters with true drama, and even though those silent credits look slightly hokey now, back then I was being taught to respect the power of great televisual moments.

But the really interesting thing is that the story started to take on a life of its own for me - I became somewhat obsessed with Cybermen and particularly *Earthshock*. I wanted to experience it again, and fortunately the Beeb agreed, selecting it as the first Peter Davison story to be repeated as part of BBC2's **Doctor Who And The Monsters** season that summer. Finally I could sate my appetite for Cyber-menacing!

JNT and Eric Saward clearly also loved *Earthshock*, as they tried to repeat it a few times over the years, resulting only in diminishing returns. By the time I was ten I was depending on the excellent Ian Marter novelisation to massage my memory gland. As the years went by, I hit my teens and joined a local DWAS group, with the ultimate fan-rush on hand thanks to dodgy VHS copies of old stories. I expect not many younger fans have had the opportunity to 'enjoy' *Earthshock* as a fifth generation monochrome story, but I think that version brought me as many delights as the original transmission. I watched and rewatched that tape until the tracking finally gave up and died, and those memories are amongst the happiest I have in my love affair with **Doctor Who**.

By the time the VHS release rolled around in 1992, I'd hit my mid-teens, and music was taking up more of my interest than a defunct show. Incredibly ten years had passed since Season 19, so more out of loyalty than love, I picked up the official BBC VHS and suddenly found myself questioning why the plot holes were so gaping you could drive a Starliner through them. Suddenly the story had lost its shine, and for some years I found myself in the Saward-bashing brigade, struck down by the cynicism that comes with over-familiarity.

Then something interesting happened – **Doctor Who** came back (for one night only) and I was hooked again. By the time of *Earthshock*'s DVD release I still had my doubts: could this story really stand up to the scrutiny of a commentary, documentary and production notes? More importantly, could I really enjoy it, knowing just how flabby the plotting was?

Well, we're all here for happy endings, and I got mine. Watching *Earthshock* again, spruced up and lovingly presented, I was back to being six years old. The plot holes were more than excusable for a claustrophobic atmosphere. The silent credits were poignant and moving. Hell, even Beryl Reid was fun! *Earthshock* had kept on giving, kept on delivering something new, for over twenty years. The true classics are the stories you grow up with, measure out your life with. And the biggest **Who**-spoon for me has been *Earthshock*. Anyone for coffee?

Flight of Fancy
Time-Flight by **Ian Wheeler**, 39, Harrogate, UK
First story: **Destiny of the Daleks**

These days the perceived wisdom is that *Time-Flight* was crap. Which may well be true. But I was nine years old when it went out for the first time and when you're a kid you don't think like that. *Time-Flight* was just as good as any other **Doctor Who** story and it was such a joy to watch the continuing adventures of the heroic, breathless fifth Doctor that the pop-eyed man with the hat and the scarf seemed like a very distant memory.

Nowadays, *Time-Flight* is mainly known for featuring the bloke who became Colin in **Eastenders** and some rather awful monsters called the Plasmatons. But when I was little, the story was notable for one other key thing - it had Concorde. A plane admired by every schoolboy in the land and one that seemed glamorous and futuristic. I never got the chance to go on Concorde but my grandmother and auntie did. There was a photo of them on my grandmother's living room wall sitting in Concorde raising a glass of champagne. It was a fond memory for them - something special they had done.

They weren't alone in their love of Concorde. I remember reading about producer John Nathan-Turner's delight that he had been able to include the plane in the series and how the people who ran Concorde had been keen to help with what they termed the BBC's 'project.' Concorde was cool and everyone from the man in the street who had never been on it to celebrities like Joan Collins who used it regularly knew that.

When there was a 40th anniversary Panopticon in London in 2003, the organisers played a long video with clips from the series and associated news footage and other interesting items. Forty years of memories. Certain things provoked a cheer from the audience. Patrick Troughton brought the roof down. But later, there was a clip from *Time-Flight* showing Concorde and that got a cheer too! This was around the time the plane was being de-commissioned. People may not like *Time-Flight* but boy they love that plane!

And you know, there are other good things about *Time-Flight*, things which I appreciated as a child. Okay, so the series' regulars were back on Earth again (what was it about the fifth Doctor and Earth?) but Heathrow was a cool place to set a story. And UNIT got a mention! Prior to **The Five Faces of Doctor Who** season being shown on BBC2 in 1981, UNIT was just something I'd heard about or seen on Target book covers or collectable cards from Weetabix! When *The Three Doctors* was repeated I got the chance to see it for real. And now here it was being mentioned in a contemporary episode. As the years would roll by, UNIT would be something I'd come to know and love.

Talking of Target book covers, the *Time-Flight* one was a gem. Normally, the Davison covers were rubbish. The Doctor standing next to the TARDIS on *The Visitation* cover – boring. But the *Time-Flight* cover was brilliant – the Doctor with Concorde looming behind him. Possibly the best (the only good?) photographic Target cover.

Other aspects of the story stimulated my nine-year-old mind. There was the desolate, prehistoric landscape. Yes, it looked stagy and obviously shot in the studio but as a kid you accept these things. Maybe adults should try and use their imaginations more and go along with it. When you go and watch a play at the theatre, you don't shout out, 'This is obviously just a load of actors standing on a set!' so why worry when a cheap 1980s BBC programme shot in the studio *looks* like a cheap 1980s BBC programme shot in the studio?

Then we had the Master. At this point, it was still something of a pleasant surprise when Anthony Ainley used to crop up for one of his regular appearances. 'Wow, it's the Master!' we would say. Later, it would get just a little more predictable (Sir Gilles anyone?) but here it was still fun. It was great seeing Kalid's mask fall away with all that gunk to reveal the Master's face. And, as would become traditional, there was no explanation as to how the renegade Time Lord had survived his last encounter with the Doctor!

We also had lovely little cameos from Adric (for someone who was dead he seemed to have remarkable resilience when it came to making cameos in the series!), the Melkur and a Terileptil. These little touches of continuity were something the Davison stories did so well, like when we saw the Android mask and the Kinda helix in *Terminus*.

Finally, we had the Plasmatons. And yes, they are not the most popular **Doctor Who** monsters by any means but I for one could see nothing wrong with them! They were big blobby things which is what **Doctor Who** monsters should be and they were fun. They reminded me of the Gel Guards from the Pertwee era and my nine-year-old self had no problem with them.

Overall, Season 19 was a pretty wonderful thing for a nine-year-old. We had a terrific new Doctor, a team of young and (largely) enthusiastic companions and everything from giant frogs to Cybermen and the Grim Reaper. Happy, happy days!

So there you go. *Time-Flight* is good. Ignore the perceived wisdom and enjoy!

Who, Me, My Dad and When I Regenerated

Arc of Infinity by **Giles Milner**, 35, New Forest, UK
First story: **Logopolis**

It's the 3rd of January 2013, and we're waiting for the first episode in the fiftieth anniversary year of **Doctor Who**. Thirty years ago today, the first episode of the twentieth anniversary year, Part One of *Arc of Infinity*, was broadcast for the first time, so I'm watching the DVD again tonight. In 1983 I was five, had only been at school for three months, still had stabilisers and enjoyed watching **Doctor Who** with no idea of its history and future, and with no critical analysis.

My dad was 35, the same age I am now, and had a mane of curly black hair, worked in something to do with science, fixed things a lot, had a long green knitted scarf and took us on adventures. When he got a Walkman, he adapted it to run off three C batteries instead of two AA batteries so that they would last longer. The doctor I first saw on TV was a lot like my dad, and I was like his companion.

The next doctor was a lot younger, blonde (like me), seemed to get into trouble for running down corridors, and was continually hunted by some unseen malevolent entity – just like me. Which brings me to *Arc of Infinity*. You don't question the story when you're five, you just enjoy it. You don't look back to the tenth anniversary story when Omega made his first appearance, see the significance in his return in the twentieth season or pick up on the Doctor's reference that he has only been summoned to Gallifrey twice before. Neither do you notice the sixth Doctor has assumed the identity of Commander Maxil to ensure the Doctor returns to Gallifrey, or see the first Weeping Angel to be killed in **Doctor Who** by the Ergon (it's in Part One, it's thirteen minutes in; blink and you'll miss it). You just enjoy the thrill of the Doctor running away from people with guns and getting all excited because the Time Lords have grounded him; he even gets sent to his room.

Now we get to see the DVD, we find out the cast and crew didn't think much of the design of the Ergon. But you know what? It worked; I didn't forget the first time I saw the Ergon, and I didn't forget the scenes on Gallifrey and Maxil. What *did* I forget? The cast running around Amsterdam, for what seemed like half the story, just to fill time.

Who do I relate to now when I watch it again? It's not just the Doctor and the injustice he faces from the authority of the Time Lords, a cold authority who care nothing for his welfare and safety, it's Omega too. For the last few years I've had ME and can relate to the anger and frustration of wanting to be whole and well again, feeling let down and abandoned by society and feeling invisible like Omega. Of course I don't want to destroy the universe, watch Punch and Judy or run around Amsterdam being chased by Janet Fielding. That's one of the joys of **Doctor Who**; in a well written story - and in this case a mediocre story - the characters are not black and white. We can comprehend their motivations and we can empathise with them, even if we don't agree with their choices and decisions. Do we do that when we're five? Probably not in a conscious way, but I think it's there on some level.

Omega hasn't made another appearance in any TV episodes since *Arc of Infinity*, although the Hand of Omega featured in the Season 25 story *Remembrance of the Daleks,* set in 1963. So maybe Omega will make a comeback for the fiftieth anniversary? If so I hope he retains that element of frustration and injustice that makes the character work so well.

Thankfully, unlike the Doctor, my dad isn't fictional. He hasn't got his scarf or his Walkman anymore, but he still fixes things, has darker hair than Tom Baker and still goes on adventures. In fact, he's going for an adventure with my wife next Friday to a deserted church in the wilds of Somerset whilst I'm busy working. I still get told off for running down corridors, and the malevolent entity that haunts me is still there, but now it's the bank and civil servants instead of ancient beings made of anti-matter. But I get to go out on my own adventures with my daughter. On Boxing Day we found a lost puppy and reunited it with its owner; not exactly saving the universe but you never know who that puppy will grow up to be.

When I was five or six my hair turned from blonde to dark brown; without question I quietly assumed I'd regenerated, just like the Doctor. You don't question things like that when you're young, but last year I had a car accident. A couple of months after I recovered I raised concerns whilst at hospital. My feet now fitted size 8½ shoes (previously I had been a size 10), I was three stone lighter than I had been a year before and I was at least an inch taller. They checked my height against their records and found I had grown by over an inch. They couldn't explain it.

It seems I've regenerated again.

Mother's VHS Ate My Doctor Who Stash!

Snakedance by **Colleen Hawkins**, 44, Cullompton, Devon, UK / First story: **Planet of the Spiders**

Christmas 1981 was unremarkable apart from one momentous event: my family acquired its first video recorder. I would like to tell you my working hypothesis was that collectively we – me, my mum and my brothers – had been especially good that year and warranted such munificence from Santa, but he'd been unmasked as a drag king several years before. Not that mum went to the bother of donning the full Coca-Cola trademarked gay apparel, but I'd long known she was the true architect of our Christmases and that they were an expensive, long-term undertaking for her. Without her there'd be no gifts, boxes of those disgusting 'Eat Me' dates that granddad loved so much, tins of Quality Street or any of the other treats that we innocently took for granted. Back then we truly did wish it could be Christmas every day, except – ironically, perhaps – when creepy Uncle Roy was on telly expressing that same sentiment via the medium of popular song.

My mum had in fact bought our VHS on 'tick' and would still be paying for it by the time next Christmas rolled around and beyond, but this knowledge (assuming I even understood its ramifications) did nothing to dampen my enthusiasm for our shiny new box of delights. All I could think about was the wonderful vista of opportunity that it had opened up for me: I could record every new episode of **Doctor Who** as it was broadcast and *rewatch it whenever (and as often) as I wanted!* Up until then I'd recorded the show's soundtrack with my trusty cassette recorder and thought myself extremely fortunate. I'd start it running next to the speaker of my tiny black and white telly and then hurtle downstairs to watch the episode in colour. Bribery or pleading was required to prevent my brothers from attempting to ruin the recording by either shouting '**Doctor Who** is crap!' (or some equally stinging piece of Wildean wit) through the keyhole or from deliberately flushing the toilet with the door open (my bedroom being right next to it). I know better now, but at the time I genuinely believed that I was the only person who had ever formulated this idea and somehow felt I was performing a vital service for posterity. I hoarded my collection of C60s with a creepy, Gollumesque fervour.

Weirdly, the first thing I recorded with a **Doctor Who** connection was **K9 and Company**, unlikely to be the foundation of anyone's collection nowadays, but I had to start it somewhere, so (thanks to JN-T) it started ... there! When I bought it on DVD 27 years later I watched it just once and after (figuratively speaking) tearing it a new one, haven't watched it since, but back in the early part of 1982 I watched it more times than could possibly be healthy for an impressionable young mind. This was simply a consequence of this young Mother Hubbard's cupboard being rather bare! It played a diminishing role in my **Doctor Who** rotation once my collection of 'proper' episodes expanded and was all but forgotten once **The Five Faces of Doctor Who** season gave me access to five additional stories (and four additional Doctors). Soon I was fantasising about owning a complete collection of episodes, not even slightly deterred by the realisation (gleaned from **Doctor Who Magazine**) that a great many were missing from the archives. I'm guessing around 140 episodes were AWOL in December 1981 and I fervently believed that every one of those 140-plus holy grails were out there somewhere, just waiting to be rescued from the vaults of foreign TV stations or liberated from the greasy clutches of selfish private collectors. A part of me still half-believes this if I'm being completely honest.

My collection of home recordings steadily grew and I was even given the first official BBC VHS release, *Revenge of the Cybermen*, as a present. My passion for **Doctor Who** remained undimmed by anything the travails of adolescence could chuck at me. Everything from

Logopolis onwards – plus the small cache of earlier stories I'd amassed – were mine for the watching. Then part way through Season 21 (what seemed like) disaster struck!

I should perhaps explain that my mum, bless her, has always been somewhat mystified by my devotion to the show, especially as it had spent much of the mid-1970s scaring the pants off me with its Giant Spiders, Wirrn, Krynoids and all the rest. Not that she hadn't been a fan herself. She often mentions that she watched religiously during the 1960s and although she can't remember much about those episodes – except for vivid memories of the first story – she is adamant she rarely missed a Saturday during the black and white era. I still sometimes rue that fact that she was fortunate enough to watch most of the episodes I will almost certainly never get to see. Episode 4 of *The Tenth Planet* is perfectly preserved in her memory somewhere, as are the hundred-odd other lost episodes. So near and yet so far away!

So imagine my horror when one day I came home from school to find a pile of clearly unwell E240s – *my* E240s! – in front of the family VHS. Spewing out of the back of each of those tapes – like a cloud of black smoke from a dodgy exhaust – was a ribbon of magnetic tape that the VHS – my *mother's* VHS! – had decided to feast on. Om nom nom!

I never did a get a satisfactory explanation of why she fed so many of my precious tapes into the machine once it had already chewed up and spat out the family tape! Perhaps she viewed the problem as a sceptical scientist would and was only willing to extrapolate a working hypothesis once she'd demonstrated that the results of her experiments were repeatable. Eight mangled tapes was apparently the required threshold for her theory's vindication, allowing her to conclude (without fear of contradiction) that our video recorder was *indeed* broken!

When I encountered that pile of ailing tapes I started to sob uncontrollably and that reaction *really* mystified mum. She viewed them merely as blank tapes and obviously it made no sense to weep over something so easily replaced. When the promise of new tapes produced, not the expected cessation of my grizzling, but an increase in the volume – both in the sense of loudness and quantity of liquid produced – she lost all patience with my irrational behaviour and sent me to my room. I don't mean to make her sound harsh (because she wasn't and isn't); she simply failed to understand the intensity of emotion that I'd invested in the integrity of my collection. Even I find it amazing to recall that I blubbed for several hours because I thought I'd lost a few tapes containing a children's television show that I really ought to have grown out of by the age of fifteen (and inexplicably still haven't several decades later!). It perhaps goes without saying that **K9 and Company** was not on one of the damaged tapes.

    I was so upset that for several weeks those tapes languished untouched on my bedside cabinet; I merely glared at them balefully whenever they caught my eye. My resolve eventually crumbled though and I grudgingly inspected the damage more closely. The tapes were, in fact, quite capable of being patched up and it slowly dawned on me that I'd been a massive drama queen about the whole affair; not that I ever admitted this to mum. I cut away the concertinaed bits of magnetic tape and spliced the ends together with sticky tape. Playback tended to stop at the repaired point in the tape – although not always – and I would push play again to find the story had leapt forward by maybe twenty or thirty seconds. It was nothing terminal – with only eight episodes affected in all – but it seemed earth-shattering to me at the time and I never felt *quite* the same again about any of those damaged tapes.

    Snakedance was one of the casualties and I was painfully aware when I watched it that it no longer contained the part where the fifth Doctor shows Ambril up as a prat over the Six Faces of Delusion. Nowadays I'd be too busy wondering how someone so dense could hold such an important academic position to worry that the scene was partially missing, but back then it distressed me every time I watched the episode. This distress instilled in me a resolve never to be caught napping again: once I'd finished watching one of my tapes, I would immediately return it to my bedroom and lock the door to ensure that mum's gluttonous video recorder would never have the chance to get its teeth into it. Eight times bitten, nine times shy!

Mawdryn and Me

Mawdryn Undead by **Susan L Coleman**, 40, Chandler, Arizona USA / First story: **Four to Doomsday**

When I was a little girl, my dad came to me one day and said, 'There's a TV show I think you might like. It's about a guy who travels in time and space.' Little did he know what an incredible gift he was giving me. My Doctor, Peter Davison. You never forget your first. As Steven Moffat has said, 'The one with the two hearts, always!' But the fifth is my Doctor.

Back then, on our local PBS station, Channel 8, **Doctor Who** began at noon on Sundays. Our house was very long and narrow. I forbade my parents to even walk through the room when the Doctor was on; they had to go around through the living room, or choose where they would be until it was over. The stories were broadcast in one block of 90 or 120 minutes, or however long it took. I can't believe my parents actually did this for me, but they were supportive in my **Doctor Who** obsession.

Four to Doomsday was my first story, but *Mawdryn Undead* is my favourite. I re-read my Target novelisation and re-watched it, for the first time in a few years, for this essay.

Looking back, don't we all want to escape school? To have a Mad Man with a Box come get us out of the banality of day-to-day lessons and bullying? To be honest, my love of *Mawdryn Undead* is so ingrained within my being that I cannot even tell you why I was so drawn to it, but I'm guessing Turlough's escape from school, from this planet, was a big part of it. I, too, wanted to get away from this planet, this life, to run away with the Doctor into danger and adventure.

And the Brigadier, oh, Nicholas Courtney, how I miss you! (I had the great honour of meeting him a few times; he was as consummate a gentleman as he was onscreen.) Whilst the Doctor was helping him recover his memory, I was being drawn ever more into this wonderful show, finding that there was so much to discover; meeting the Doctor could last me a lifetime! As, indeed, it has. You see, I was new to **Doctor Who**, so these flashbacks were a glimpse into my future, the wonderful world of **Doctor Who** which I had not yet seen.

The scenes in which the Doctor realises that, although he can leave Mawdryn and his companions to their endless lives, but will not do the same to Nyssa and Tegan, also touched me deeply. Friendship (along with the Doctor) is the touchstone of my life. The concept of sacrifice for those whom you love is deeply entrenched within me. I knew I had found someone who would never let me down, and the Doctor never did. Never has. Never will. I found a Hero who would/will always be there for me/us. Because he never leaves anyone behind. And it's personal. The Doctor loves us all, on this, his favourite planet.

Mawdryn Undead was my touchstone, for years. From grade school until college. Whenever we had a timed test, I knew I would finish first but not be allowed to leave. I carried my Target novelisation with me everywhere. It has indentations on the back where I must have written on it, needing it to be close enough to touch, for strength. I have read it and read it and read it, so many times, and when I read it again last night, after many years, I could hear the actors' voices in my head. I'm amazed it's not falling apart. These days I have the old style Seal of Rassilon tattooed upon my ankle, and I draw my strength from the knowledge that the Doctor is always with me. But before my tat, it was always, and will always be, *Mawdryn Undead*.

Terminus

Terminus by **Andy X Cable**, 44, Liverpool, UK

When mum died I felt much the same as I did when I first saw *Terminus* starring the youthful performer Peter Davison. It had been a busy few weeks for the Doctor having been bothered by lots of people he'd already been bothered by in the past including the Brigadier who was now very, very old and knew how many beans made five (it's five, I counted).

The evil snake The Mara had come back and tried to get lots of people to look into a blue crystal just like the third Doctor, played by the panel show host and singer Jon Pertwee, had tried to do many years previously. I don't know if this means the third Doctor is really the Mara or that the Mara was really the third Doctor but I do know they both liked blue crystals, but not as much as the massive spider queen. She loved crystals a lot and shouted about it all the time in a voice that sounded like a sharp-flavoured jelly being grated on a grater made of really sharp metal (steel?).

Tegan had also come back to menace the Doctor in *The Arks of Infinity* and she'd changed out of her air hostess outfit (presumably because she'd been sacked for never having gone to work) and they all went to Gallifrey where the sixth Doctor (possibly the Mara in disguise again but hard to tell because it's all so confusing) killed the fifth Doctor twice and then it turned out he wasn't dead at all.

Then in *Terminus* no old monsters came back to haunt the Doctor at all. But people say the whole season had returning monsters. Well I can't and mustn't allow this to continue because the Black Guardian doesn't count. He's just an old man (or woman? Not sure) on a screen shouting at Turlough for being stupid. I remember at the time they said that Ice Warriors would be in it and Ice Warriors is a stupid name for a monster because really they're Martians. Nobody called the Daleks the Static

Terrors did they? It's a really, really stupid name for them. I think if people called them Martians then the Ice Warriors wouldn't be so cross all the time. Also they're not even made of ice, they're made of green scaly stuff (skin?) and hiss a lot. They should be the Green Hissers or the Wheezing Lizards if they're going to be recognised by everyone they attack. But on the Moon there's no ice in the base and they're still Ice Warriors. There's no ice in the story at all, not even some snow - it's all foam or something that comes out of balloons if they pop which is why on my eighth birthday I had a nervous breakdown and mum had to take me to hospital because a balloon popped and I threw myself through the patio door glass out of terror and cut my arm, leg and eye and cost dad a lot of money which is probably why he left us.

But *Terminus* had something very special to me. Nyssa was in it and Nyssa was a really good friend to the Doctor and she was really pretty and nice and kind. Nyssa isn't real, she was played by an actress called Sarah Sutton and Sarah Sutton had a twin sister who also appeared in *The Black Orchids* playing Nyssa's twin. I bet you didn't know that! Sarah Sutton didn't know that either when I met her at a convention once but I'm not allowed to go near her anymore thanks to the stupid police.

Nyssa was born on Traken and her dad was the Master who disguised himself as Tremas for her whole life so he could keep his pet Melkur thing in the garden. I haven't watched *The Keepers of Traken* in a long time so I can't be sure but I'm pretty sure that's what he was doing even though I'm not completely sure but I'm sure that David Howe or Stephen James Walker would be able to tell you for sure. They know everything about **Doctor Who**.

In this story Nyssa doesn't wear many clothes towards the end which is very brave of her as it must've been really, really cold on that space station or whatever it was. Even with all that really hot radiation in there. She stays behind to help the people with blankets on their heads get better because they've got 'flu or something. I had a cold once and it was horrible. I was sniffing for days and sometimes when I sneezed stuff went everywhere and one time I put my hand up to stop it and it all hit my hand and gave me sort of webbed fingers like a Kaled mutant (a Kaled is what sits inside a Dalek. It's like a Dalek but spelt differently). I played with it for a while by putting my hand under a pile of receipts and clawing at the counter in the shop until stupid Karen told me not to and then screamed and told me to wash my hand because it was disgusting. It wasn't meant to be disgusting, it was meant to be scary and/or mysterious. She's dead too now.

So Nyssa was going to make some medicine to make them all better and didn't want to go back to the TARDIS with the Doctor, Tegan or Turlough not even for some clothes or her toothbrush or anything. If I was leaving home and my planet didn't even exist anymore, I'd at least take a change of shirt or something so I didn't smell. But Nyssa was happy to stay behind in just her underwear.

I liked Nyssa in her underwear. It was the first time I had a strange thought.

Sailing Ships and Strong Women

Enlightenment by **Vivienne Dunstan**, 40, Dundee, Scotland / First story: **The Ribos Operation**

Much of early 1980s **Doctor Who** was a blur for me years later. But I remembered *Enlightenment* as a highly imaginative story, with powerful images of old style sailing ships racing through space. I also remembered the Eternals, entities outside normal space and time, more powerful than the Doctor. Even on a recent watch of much classic **Doctor Who** it was clearly one of the stronger concept stories. It is similar in this respect to *The Pirate Planet*, where whole planets were gobbled up, but is, if anything, more mind expanding the more you think about it. And how much I liked it is a measure of its strengths: I'm usually not so keen on more space-set and sci-fi stories. However what struck me most recently were gender aspects. These should have impressed me as a young girl watching in 1983, but they passed me by. Only as an adult could I appreciate them properly.

This was the first story in televised **Doctor Who** written by a woman, Barbara Clegg. Given how imaginative it was it is a shame no more of her stories were broadcast. She would be followed by Jane Baker and Rona Munro in the 1980s, and Helen Raynor in the new series. There would be no more female screenwriters, at least until now as I write. It would be simplistic to search too hard for aspects of her gender in the writing. However I do find some aspects of the characterisation interesting.

Particularly striking is Captain Wrack. It was not unknown in classic **Doctor Who** to have strong female guest characters, indeed there were quite a number in Peter Davison's run of stories. However Wrack was a particularly strong example, a standout among the Eternal captains, easily the most powerful, and easily the most interesting to watch. Admittedly she relied on the Black

Guardian for some of her powers, and she was ultimately defeated by the Doctor. But this does not diminish her as a fascinating character on screen, and a strong female in a story so male dominated.

Also interesting is the depiction of companion Tegan. In some ways she plays a more passive role, and is being wooed actively by the Eternal Marriner. But she resists his advances, and asserts her authority, before helping the Doctor to figure out what the crystal is for.

As a story of its time *Enlightenment* was highly unusual in terms of its imagery and ideas. But it was also important, and certainly made an impact on me as an adult viewer, for gender reasons, both on screen and also behind the scenes. Now if only I'd noticed and been inspired by that as a ten-year-old…

Turn Right
The King's Demons by **Jonathan Potter**, 42, Headley,
UK / First story: **The Sea Devils** Omnibus

The King's Demons; an insignificant two-parter, industrial action, Warhead should have been the explosive climax to Season 20, a bit of Ainley tomfoolery, blah, blah, blah. You know the drill. I can't really tell you much about *The King's Demons*; I haven't seen it in over twenty years. But I can tell you what happened after the credits to Part Two. A trailer. A trailer for an event. A feast of clips from the series heralded **Doctor Who**, A Celebration: 20 Years of a Time Lord. A two day jamboree, to be held over the Easter Bank Holiday Weekend at Longleat. I was twelve and you should believe the hype, it really was the best time ever to be a fan.

    We made a few mistakes. Like everyone else we didn't realise how many were going to make the trip on Easter Monday and we hadn't bought our tickets in advance. The queue was immense but the Doctor saved the day. The fifth Doctor to be precise. Peter Davison made an appearance to placate the ever increasing queue which parted like the Red Sea. Everyone wanted a piece of Davison and my mother took advantage of the excitement and discretely slipped into a gaping hole in the middle of the queue. We made it in but there was undoubtedly someone who didn't because we cheated. Sorry about that.

    I wish I could tell you all about the Cinema Tent and the panels but I can't because it was sheer bedlam and we didn't get anywhere near them. We just queued to look at the set and costume displays and caught the end of a Peter Howell talk in the Radiophonic Workshop Tent. The one thing that really fascinated me was the DWAS stall in the Merchandise Tent. I had enough money to buy one publication (when I wanted to walk away with a bagful of **TARDIS** fanzines). The one that caught my eye was the **DWAS Yearbook 1982**. A man who I now know to be Ian

McLachlan tried to persuade me to take the latest **TARDIS** (I think it was cheaper and he felt sorry for me) but I wasn't for turning.

I read it all the way home to Port Talbot in South Wales and was riveted. This was a whole sub-culture I had discovered and it was fascinating. All these different people who seemed to know each other, writing great reviews and talking about Letraset, local groups and Douglas Camfield. I loved the convention reviews and stared in awe at artwork by someone called 'Drog.' I joined the Society and it felt like I knew David Howe, Dominic May and David Saunders through the various departmental columns published in **Celestial Toyroom**. I wanted to be a part of it but I was only twelve and Port Talbot seemed a million miles away from such glamour. Maybe if I knew a fellow fan at school things might have been different but I didn't.

So I kept my distance. I was fascinated by fandom but never joined in. I'd love a Time Beetle to see what would have happened if I'd made the effort, to see the sort of person I'd have grown into. Would my circumstances be massively different? Probably not. Instead of chewing the fat with J. Jeremy Bentham at The Fitzroy Tavern with Ian Levine hanging on my every word I'd have ended up sneering at losers with carrier bags asking inane questions to convention guests. That's because all **Doctor Who** fans are autistic, even the ones who think they're not. Here's an actual quote from a fan on an internet forum: 'I'm an introvert who dislikes social situations, mainly because I don't like large groups of people. That's just my preference, and it has no relation to autistic tendencies.' Of course, the fact that I'm sitting here, writing this article makes me autistic as well and the only reason I know this (and our friend on the forum doesn't) is because one of my children is profoundly autistic and I've learnt a hell of a lot about it since 2001. My Time Beetle trip would show me in 2001 ridden with guilt for every sneering and sarcastic comment made about socially inept

'Ming Mongs' (as one überfan so charmingly once described them).

I started socialising with **Doctor Who** fans around seven years ago. Last year I attended my first proper weekend convention and loved it. I had a nice conversation with a young man about Dalek livery in the 1970s. I didn't laugh at him and I didn't mock him. I would have in 1987 and not realised the irony of *me* explaining to *him* why the Daleks in *Death to the Daleks* aren't gun metal grey.

So even without the benefit of a Time Beetle I'm pretty certain that fate dealt its hand kindly. And now this book allows me to send a message to all those fans whose entrepreneurial efforts inspired me in my general outlook on life. Jeremy Bentham, Gary Russell, Richard Marson, Andrew Pixley, David Howe, Stephen James Walker, Justin Richards, Peter Anghelides, Anthony Brown, Gary Leigh, Kevin Jon Davies, Richard Bignell, Colin Brockhurst, Julian Knott, Rob Hammond and Matt West; fans who got up off their arses and did wonderful things that mean a great deal to me. I salute you.

Anyway, *The King's Demons* and a message to those of you who mock Ainley's accent and make-up as Sir Gilles and say how obvious the 'disguise' was, it wasn't. There was a collective gasp in the Potter household as our hero's sworn enemy was revealed.

'You escaped from Xeraphas?'

'Oh my dear Doctor, you have been naive!' Cue credits.

An Immortality Tale
The Five Doctors by **Barnaby Eaton Jones**, 39, Gloucestershire / Earliest memory: Being told to watch *Logopolis* because my Dad said it was going to be 'special'

When *The Five Doctors* aired on television, I recorded it on a Betamax tape and I was really (and very selfishly) annoyed that **Children In Need** kept flashing a pledge banner across the bottom of the screen, telling those of us who weren't die-hard fans how much the charity total had gone up in the last half an hour and how to donate more. It took me out of the show and back to reality. But, that's not the story I want to tell...

I did donate to **Children In Need** in the future by doing my own charity event when I was at school, by the way; such was my guilt at the rage directed towards that scrolling banner. But, that's not the story I want to tell either...

In fact, I've donated to *loads* of charities since then. I'm really rather generous. But, I digress...

I mean, I'm always the first one to pledge a fiver when a friend does the 'Race For Life.' It often nearly bankrupts me every year.

Anyway...

I just want you to know that I'm not a bad human being for hating the fact that **Children In Need** interrupted the 20th anniversary story.

So, um, where was I? Yes, *The Five Doctors*. That's right.

My story is about *The Five Doctors* being the perfect satisfying end for the urge I had to write comedy about my first love; the good Doctor and his adventures in time and space (and the quarries of Middle England).

For those fans who attended any conventions in the UK between 2003 and 2006, I was pretty much omnipresent with my little touring theatre company, doing original comedy stuff based on the show (sketches, full-length and one-act plays, etc). Then, we were invited to the USA in 2007 to perform at the Holy Grail of conventions – 'Gallifrey' – as their big Saturday night entertainment. This it was decided should be our final show, a full-length play in two acts, and I needed to write something celebratory and instantly accessible, very much like *The Five Doctors* is and was.

So, I just re-wrote it.

Myself and Ron Brunwin (my co-writer, who has the sort of name you can only say in full and in an American accent) drafted an outline called *The 2 x 5 Doctors*. This morphed, thankfully, into the simpler title of *The Ten Doctors* (and, thankfully, avoided the title *Red, White & Who*). The first half consisted of David Tennant's tenth Doctor taking the fifth Doctor's role and all his previous incarnations being snatched up by that pesky Black Triangle of Borusa's. The second half consisted of them all trying to get to the Dark Tower, in the Erogenous Zone (you can see the level of wit we were aiming for). It was written to run in two 45-minute Acts, with an interval. We rehearsed it diligently, we recorded video footage to insert and interact with, and we were sure that our timings were spot-on but we didn't have time for a final run-through in America at the venue. On the night we performed, the first half alone ran for the 2 x 45 minutes that the entire play was supposed to be. But, people stayed. They continued to laugh at the jokes. We sighed with relief.

For me personally, it was special because I was riffing on my very favourite episode of the show. I know that 'anniversary' stories are a poisoned chalice, as they are built up to be more than they can be ('A man is a sum of his memories, a Time Lord even more so'). But, I loved *The Five Doctors* when it was shown and I still love it now. It's perfect even though it isn't. Each Doctor gets their moment, the villain is suitably evil, there are companions aplenty, and the script is overflowing with references, wit, and quotable lines, whilst the inclusion of never-before-seen *Shada* footage, representing Tom Baker's fourth Doctor, felt exactly right. He wasn't there to overshadow but he was there to be seen (unlike in the publicity shots for the show, where he'd been taken over by the Nestene Consciousness). The last-minute script by Terrance Dicks, when Robert Holmes pulled out of his commitment to writing it, is a master class of structure and economy. I'm a big fan of Uncle Terrance and his writing style; especially his novelisations of **Doctor Who** stories. The main job of a writer is to entertain. If you're not entertaining, then you can't make people think or showcase your opinions or keep people interested or ... well, you get the idea. Nowhere is this more evident than in *The Five Doctors*. It entertains in spades. In fact, it exists to merely entertain. So, to try and ape that in a comedic homage for stage was of paramount importance. We needed to keep the audience entertained. My previous co-writer on a couple of the first **Doctor Who** shows we did thought that comedy wasn't working if you weren't offending someone. His were the lines that usually got trimmed in the final edit or, if they didn't, they were the ones that caused several people in the audience to laugh very loudly but had the majority muttering and shifting uncomfortably in their seats. He never understood that fans were attending conventions to have fun. They don't mind a gentle ribbing of their show in parody form but they don't like a Bill Hicks-style vitriolic rant on something as forgettable as the scenery wobbling.

    The second half of *The Ten Doctors* was interrupted by a fire alarm towards the end of the play, when everyone was gathered to solve the riddle of the Dark Tower. Nobody moved. We carried on. It took the disembodied voice of convention organiser Shaun Lyon (via a microphone) to inform everyone that it wasn't part of the play, it was real, and the hundreds of seated audience members should become unseated at pace and vacate the room.

    When we returned to finish the play half an hour later, it felt like we'd run a marathon. Possibly for charity. Definitely for **Children In Need**. I think the audience who survived the entire running time also felt like this. We'd done it. It was *The Five Doctors* doubled and it was a huge celebration of the show, my love for the story, and the four-year journey we'd all travelled to perform our affectionate homages to the greatest show in the galaxy. Two writers became Terrance Dicks for a night (the Ron and I), nine actors played sixty iconic characters (Dave, Kim, Gaz, Lizi, Ian, Kathryn, Francis, Bob and myself) and one person had produced, directed and controlled it all with the wisdom of Rassilon himself (thanks, Kim!).

Oh yes, and Colin Baker had a specially-written cameo as Commander Maxil, which the audience greeted as if it was the height of Beatlemania and John, Paul, George and Ringo had just stepped out of the TARDIS. He elegantly chewed the scenery and effortlessly stole the show.

It wasn't until I was on my way home, and the only one awake on the flight from Los Angeles to London, that - like President Borusa in *The Five Doctors* - I realised I had unknowingly craved immortality by trying my hardest to get somewhere in the world of **Doctor Who** (I knocked on the door of BBC Books and Big Finish) to have my name live on in years to come via my favourite show. But, I had come to the realisation that I was always happiest, like the Doctor himself, away from big professional organisations and just doing things that made me happy and that made others happy. To lose is to win and he who wins shall lose. Fortunately, there wasn't a portly Jimmy Edwards, with a Disco Ball placed underneath his chin, hovering over me as I realised this. If there had have been, I would have also realised that sleeping pills really don't mix with red wine.

I wanted to wake my wife up, sleeping peacefully next to me, and say I'd figured it out. I'd started writing comedy for the stage when I was a teenager. My first play was about five Doctors, oddly, and was seen by about sixty people. Here was I, having written a play about five Doctors again that was seen by six hundred people, desperately wanting her to ask me a question like: 'So, you deliberately decided to write a parody of *The Five Doctors* for the stage, with a rickety old theatre group, to entertain as many people as possible?' Then, I could reply, in my best Peter Davison voice…

'Why not? After all, that's how it all started.'

Cue 'Starfield' End Credits.

The Pictures Are Better...
Warriors of the Deep by **Alan P Jack**, 42, Dawlish, Devon, UK / First story: **City of Death**

A lot of people were looking forward to *Warriors of the Deep* prior to its transmission, and I was one of them. The first I had heard about it was in the **Radio Times** 20th Anniversary Special at the end of 1983, which outlined all the stories in Season 21. The return of the Silurians *and* the Sea Devils; what an amazing prospect. Being an eager thirteen-year-old and not having a hope of ever seeing the previous stories featuring either of these creatures, I was very excited.

Warriors of the Deep is a significant landmark in my Whovian journey for several reasons. It was the first story I followed and knew about before its transmission, for it was about that time I started getting **Doctor Who Monthly**. Those tantalising spoilers were amazing currency in the school yard.

In 1984, the video cassette recorder was an expensive luxury. They were in no way ubiquitous and we were in the majority by not having one. If I wanted to preserve a television programme, the only way I had of doing so was by recording the audio. This was a practice I had started in the summer of 1983 with the repeat of *The Visitation*.

By the time *Warriors of the Deep* was broadcast, I had perfected the recording process: the microphone the right distance away from the speaker, and the right levels on the television and the tape recorder to ensure that the recording was neither too quiet nor too loud. It was quite a laborious process but worth it in the end. I was so excited about seeing the Sea Devils and the Silurians for the first time. There would be a two-second clip of an old story that was shown within this other story and it would be a one-time event. The prospect of ever seeing a repeat of an old story was practically nil, and this is why it was so important to record the audio. Audio gives the listener a chance to relive the programme in a more manageable form. You can be doing other things whilst listening such as tidying the house, driving in the car, or falling asleep at night (yes, something I've often done. I am so glad that I now have the whole of the classic series on audio on my computer so that I can dip into it and not have the worry of being woken up by the tape stopping. It is also good to know how long you have slept by how much you have missed).

Parts One, Two and Three, there were no problems. Part Four was a different story; it clashed with my guitar lesson. Why did John Nathan-Turner put the show on on week nights...? So many people stopped watching at the time. When you are thirteen and a **Doctor Who** fan who does not have a video recorder, is not likely to be getting one, and never even considered that you might end up with the story on video and DVD format, let alone be able to see the programme on YouTube or dailymotion, this was a life event. At least I had the audio evidence but this did not make up for the fact that I missed it at the time. I would not hazard to guess that I am not the only **Doctor Who** fan who has been emotionally scarred by having missed the show when they were young. I say emotionally scarred... It felt like it at the time. It was not until 1992 that I actually got to see Part Four in its entirety. I was not disappointed.

Nowadays, we have all forgotten how horrible it was to miss the show, I think. 1984 seems a universe away from today, when you need never miss an episode. Although being there at the time is the optimum option, there is no longer the overwhelming imperative that there once was. It was an event. Having one's tea and having to do one's homework before **Doctor Who** was a good means of social control, and was used by my parents to manage me a little. The threat of being banned from watching **Doctor Who** was the ultimate in deterrence against any thought of malfeasance. The children of today do not know they are born! It just does not seem fair... They all seem to have it on a plate... Oh dear, I am sounding like my parents... But this accessibility and flexibility with when and how you watch the show has meant that, horror of horrors, there have been times when I have forgotten that the show is on. When I forgot something that my mother had told me to remember she used to say, 'You wouldn't forget it if it was to do with **Doctor Who** now would you?' Well, sometimes I do. Being a fan has been so much a part of my life for the last thirty-odd years that my degree of fandom has changed. I am still the excited thirteen-year-old who has those tantalising little bits of knowledge prior to the viewing of an episode, but then there is an adult part of me which has to live in the real world.

I have a great affection for *Warriors of the Deep*, and overall I still like it – despite having seen in it some of the loopholes that time and the adult eye cannot hide. There is a propensity to analyse and analyse and reduce and reduce to the point where you criticise everything and have nothing left to enjoy. Yes, the Myrka was ... flawed, shall we say. I still do not think Preston needed to die. And I never even noticed that the Silurians had not tucked their vests in on the first viewing.

I just enjoyed it.

Stepping Inside the Television

The Awakening by **Matt Barber**, 35, Falmouth, UK
First story: **City of Death**

I grew up on the border between Hampshire and Wiltshire, an area I like to think of as '**Doctor Who** heaven.' *Pyramids of Mars*, *The Android Invasion*, *The Dæmons*, *The Hand of Fear* and others were filmed within an afternoon's trip of my childhood home. I was born slap-bang between the M4 and M3, the main search areas for the London-based location scouts, and this has undoubtedly changed the way I watch certain **Doctor Who** stories.

When I learnt to drive I visited as many local **Doctor Who** locations as I could. I now can't watch *The Dæmons* without recalling the excitement of finding the village of Aldbourne – and the even greater excitement of finding that the barrows were actually just up a track from the church. In fact, this nostalgic extra-textual dimension has made these stories some of my favourites, not because of what happens on screen, but because of the recollection of the first time I spread my wings.

The Awakening was filmed in Tarrant Monkton in Dorset. This was a more ambitious trip out for my friend and me requiring sandwiches and, I'd like to imagine, weak lemon squash. But visiting the location of *The Awakening* was different from the others. Before I went to Aldbourne or Stargroves, or East Hagbourne, I had already watched *The Dæmons* and *The Android Invasion* repeatedly on video and was too young to have seen any of these stories when they were originally transmitted. With *The Awakening* the reverse was true. I hadn't seen the video at the time, but I had strong recollections of watching the story in the early 1980s. In January 1984 I was six-and-a-half – an age I believe is the start of the ideal period for watching the series. I watched the story in that glorious state of half-believing it was real – a state that is impossible to return to as an adult. Back when I was six, I was completely absorbed by the strange imagery and completely terrified by the ghosts and the Malus. The plot went completely over my head – but even then I found myself recognising the sunny, pastoral appeal of the village; the Panglossian perfection of the church and the green. When I visited Tarrant Monkton, therefore, I wasn't stepping inside the television as with Aldbourne, I was stepping inside my mediated memory of childhood. This alters the way I watch the two episodes. When I watch these stories set in familiar locations, I believe in them absolutely; they are, to me, *real*.

The plot of *The Awakening* is perhaps excessively rich for only two episodes. A modern village is hosting a Civil War re-enactment, but an alien, the Malus, concealed behind a wall in the church is causing a pandemic of madness amongst the villagers, whilst simultaneously bleeding time zones together. The two-part story has a narrative that, given the short amount of screen-time feels curiously stretched; however despite this, the Doctor, Tegan and Turlough and the supporting cast seem to spend much of the story running, walking or riding horses up the same stretch of road. Ironically, this is one of the appeals for me: the road, the houses, the church and the surrounding landscape are all familiar, not just from visiting the village but from the familiar landscapes of my childhood. In many respects the chalk down-lands of the south of England where I grew up shapes 1970s and 1980s **Doctor Who** as much as the music of Dudley Simpson or the sound effects of the Radiophonic Workshop. And this works for me. I'd imagine that children living in or close to Cardiff may feel the same way in years to come – indeed it's tempting to see the rebooted series as Russell T Davies' attempt to relocate the narrative of **Doctor Who** in the urban, suburban and rural landscapes of his own childhood.

The whole idea of stories such as *The Dæmons*, *The Android Invasion* and *The Awakening* is that a sense of normality is breached by something abnormal, something *alien*. The methodology is to start by installing a feeling of cosy familiarity in the viewer: of pubs and locals; of trees and churches and thatched cottages. When the audience has been lulled into this false sense of domestic and pastoral security they are hit in the face with the devil, or androids, or ghosts. *The Awakening* has been accused of being derivative of *The Dæmons*: it's set in a village that has been cut off, it features the reanimation of a long-sleeping, mythological creature, and it ends with the destruction of the church. I believe that at worst the story is a thinly veiled homage to the 1970s story, but at best it is simply drawing on the same rich vein of narrative material – of the tensions between the present and the past, of collective madness, of the clash between the preternatural and the scientific. These are all, at their core, **Quatermass**, but with the extra layer of pleasing eccentricity and playfulness that comes with **Doctor Who**. These types of stories, so popular when they were transmitted, seem now to be an acquired taste. In the present time of science-fetishism, of new Atheism and Brian Cox and Stephen Hawking, the inspired blending of fantasy and magic with science is often regarded as a step too far.

For me these stories go beyond plot or narrative. The feelings they summon span my life from childhood to adulthood. They tap into something far deeper and far more personal. For me, stories like *The Awakening* beat with the pulse of my own, fondly remembered, past.

'The TARDIS has been destroyed!'

Frontios by **Ian McArdell**, 38, Merstham, Surrey, UK
First story: **The Leisure Hive**

During the late Tom Baker era I became a regular viewer of **Doctor Who**; with two older brothers it had always been on in the house. Like most boys of my age, I enjoyed the programme and acted it out in the playground with friends.

As the show's 20th anniversary approached, something changed. I moved from viewer to fan, beginning to actively look forward to **Doctor Who** in all its forms. I attribute this change in my level of engagement to a range of things including repeats and Target books, but one thing I recall with absolute clarity; my first sight of the **Radio Times** 20th Anniversary Special.

I spied it on the local newsagent's shelf but only flicked through it, as I did not have the £1.50 cover price, high currency to a nine-year-old in 1983. Returning home, I was lucky enough to be treated to the cash by my visiting Nanna and haired back up there to bag my copy.

Cover to cover I devoured it, every photo and every line. The magazine was stuffed full of past Doctors, monsters and even a poster, but as well as chronicling every adventure, there was a brief section which trailed the show's upcoming 21st year and the incoming sixth Doctor Colin Baker. While I was not too sure about the looks of him and frustrated that he shared the surname of a former Doctor, it was the tease for *Frontios* that caught my eye: 'The third story, *Frontios*, concerns a group of survivors of a destroyed Earth, far in the future, establishing a colony on the planet Frontios. They will find that an external force is wreaking havoc with their settlement. The Doctor will also find that a Gallifreyan's TARDIS is not always his castle.'

Of course, it was the nebulous final line which led to months of head-spinning speculation, from November until the following January. What could it mean? Was the TARDIS to be invaded by Cybermen again? My friend Adam and I were certain there must still be one wandering the corridors after the events of *Earthshock*! Would it be damaged or crash dramatically? Of course, the tabloid press were no help as, spurred on by the show's Hawaiian shirt-wearing master of spin, they gleefully printed rumours that the time machine was to be axed from the show.

As well as excitement in the run up to the programme's return in January, there was heartbreak too. The move to a Thursday and Friday evening slot meant a clash with Cub Scouts and thus I was condemned to learn about the first and third episodes of a tale second hand, either from an inattentive family member or in the playground the following day.

Soon *Frontios* rolled around and it did not disappoint. A crashed colony ship and doomed humanity struggling to survive in the far-flung future. Of course, that troubling sentence came to pass too, with the ship seemingly destroyed at the end of the first episode. Not that I saw it of course, merely heard of it at school and waited tensely to see if it was really true.

It *was* destroyed, the Doctor seemed utterly convinced of it. Before I knew it, lunacy seemed to take hold and nothing was off limits. The TARDIS hat stand was brandished about weapon-like and the Doctor was improvising heart defibrillation with a large battery full of green gloopy acid. People were sucked bodily into the hungry earth and Turlough was having some sort of panic attack, turning a sickly colour and dribbling about Tractators.

Another thing that grabbed me was the notion that the Doctor had gone further forward in time than he ought to. As well as apparently destroying the TARDIS, which is a great conceit, writer Christopher H. Bidmead plants the thought that there are limits on what the Doctor can do and this fascinated me; that there might be rules on time travel and a point in the future where the all-seeing Time Lord's knowledge runs out. An upper time limit if you will. It is something that is not often touched on, as these days we hear romantically that he has access to, 'all of time and space, everything that ever happened or ever will.' In addition, there is the notion that there are occasions in the universe he really ought not to be, perhaps the genesis of Russell T Davies' fixed points in time.

There is still more to *Frontios* though, with its sober view of humanity struggling in a desperate, low-tech future. With the rule of law failing, we see the beginning of mob mentality. Their transport gone, the TARDIS crew find themselves becoming involved in the affairs of the colonists; Turlough begins to figure things out with Norna and the Doctor gravitates towards the heart of the mystery. Meanwhile Plantagenet seems quite keen on Tegan's company; perhaps it is the leather skirt as it surely can't be her personality! Turlough enjoys some much needed character development also, with his race memory scenes, brought on by the sight of the monster, being terribly effective. Not only that, but it serves as proper confirmation once again that he is indeed alien and something more than just an oddly knowledgeable schoolboy.

Of course, these days I can also see the crippling limitations of the Tractator costumes and the reuse of the **Blakes 7** Federation Trooper helmets, with Peter Gilmore's performance as Chief Orderly Brazen clearly pitched at scenery chewing level. What I revel in now are the ideas at play, with the colony attacked from both above and below and, of course, that tremendous line from the Part One cliffhanger, uttered with such conviction: 'The TARDIS has been destroyed!'

Confessions of a Plagiarist!

Resurrection of the Daleks by **Guy Lambert**, 38, London, UK / First story: **Logopolis**

I committed a crime during *Resurrection of the Daleks*. There, I've said it, and in print, so now it's public. The crime was plagiarism, and it was on a massive scale! So after nearly thirty years, I feel it's finally time to admit all in an open letter to the man I wronged:

>Dear Mr Eric Saward,
>
>I very much enjoyed your **Doctor Who** serial *Resurrection of the Daleks* back in 1984. I didn't quite understand the 'Movellan War' references, who Davros was, or what a Dalek was (I'd only seen one briefly in *The Five Doctors*) but I really enjoyed it. So much so that it inspired me to write. So much so that it inspired me to steal.
>
>After the final episode had transmitted, I ran behind the sofa! Not to hide from the Daleks, but to write my first ever **Doctor Who** story. But it wasn't really mine, it was yours. I'm sorry to say that I copied your story and almost word-for-word.
>
>I spent about an hour writing it on lined-paper with a ball-point pen. It just came gushing out. I changed a few things, like giving the Doctor a new companion (I thought that would be original and ground-breaking) and I think there was a lot more running up-and-down corridors. And probably more Daleks. And probably appalling dialogue. But essentially it was your story, retold, with a few less scenes, and a lot more things blowing up for no reason.
>
>My script editor was the one to spot it. He read the entire document (some 4 x A4 pages) and exposed the lie. We chatted about it over a cup of tea in the lounge while mum made the dinner.

Oh yes, I should explain: my script editor was my dad, and I was nine. Does that make it okay?

All the best,

Guy Lambert.

I wonder what Eric would think if he saw that? I hope he'd be amused, and very happy. You see, **Doctor Who** was a huge inspiration for me. Peter Davison my hero, and I loved the monsters, the imagination, and I loved the stories. Moreover it was during *Resurrection of the Daleks* that I first remember discovering that I didn't just love watching stories, I also loved telling them too.

Not only was my dad on hand to give praise, and point out the plagiarism, but during our *Resurrection of the Daleks* chat he was the first person to ever reveal a vital story-telling concept. 'All stories,' dad pointed out, 'have a beginning, a middle, and an end.' That changed everything. From then on I thought seriously about writing, all thanks to the inspiring tales of **Doctor Who**.

So hot on the heels of my copied-and-pasted epic, I sent the **Doctor Who** office my proposal for *The Four Doctors*. Oh yes: Jon, Tom, Peter and Colin would all team up for this epic story about a monster that had lost four eggs and needed them found. Basically it was like The Key to Time ... but with eggs ... and about ten minutes long! I was so convinced that it would be produced that I wrote to Colin Baker asking if he would be willing to appear in it. I'm pretty sure he said, 'Yes.' (So technically I could dig out the story, write it up for Big Finish, and force him to star in it!)

I also wrote four, proper TV scripts for a story entitled *Attack from the Sea*. Andrew Cartmel was extremely encouraging to new writers, and although I'm sure he never had time to read a word of my scripts his office gave the impression that he was interested. To a young boy desperate to break into TV, that was incredibly motivating.

In the early 1990s, I wrote for my local **Doctor Who** club's fanzine, **The Who St Kids Magazine**. At the time **DWM** was publishing short, original fiction, and we decided to do the same. Oddly enough one of the first stories I wrote was a kind-of sequel to *Resurrection of the Daleks*. This involved the seventh Doctor returning to visit Tegan to apologise for involving her in his violent world. They were watching news reports of wars playing on a TV in a shop window at the time: to me, that was deep and meaningful stuff!

Since then I have written a vast number of scripts for television, most of which you wouldn't have heard of, and produced a lot too. Nowadays I read lengthy books discussing the 'three act structure' and the nuances of dialogue. But ultimately it still all comes down to that simple lesson learnt during *Resurrection of the Daleks*: beginning-middle-end.

So what of the *Resurrection of the Daleks* itself? I adored it. I loved the action, the fast pace, the true sense of danger. I loved the thrilling image of the High Council being attacked by the Doctor's clone! That was a whole adventure in itself, and one my mind happily created. In many ways, it was almost my generation's Time War - what a story that would be!

Plus there was the history of the show, all presented in flashbacks of every Doctor and companion (well, nearly every; poor Leela). As a child I suddenly became aware of this show's mammoth past: how could I see all this stuff? Where was it? Like a mini history lesson of worlds and people that had many stories of their own to tell.

Most of all I loved it because it was amazing television. This story inspired me, encouraged me, and helped make me the writer I am today.

So how to end this brief look back at *Resurrection of the Daleks*? Well, let's go back to the beginning and my letter to Eric Saward. How about this for an ending:

P.S. Thanks for the inspiration, Eric.

The Beginning Came On a Beach in Lanzarote
Planet of Fire by **Abby Peck**, 38, New York, USA
First story: **Planet of Fire**

Parts of this essay have appeared before in two **Doctor Who** fanzines. But it's my story and it's why I chose *Planet of Fire* as my entry.

To make a long and tragic story short: I was thirteen, out of sorts, bad home life, acting out in ways that thirteen-year-olds shouldn't. One night, after a particularly disgustingly debauched and drunken evening in a downtown apartment with some random older guys, I snuck into my dark and angry house at 2am and decided, in typical thirteen-year-old dramatic fashion, to end it all. I hated my life and I hated myself. But first, I thought, I'll just see if anything good is on TV.

I turned it on only to see the most bizarre show flickering across the screen – and just like that, my life changed. I watched, confused, as the action in front of me played out in something called *Planet of Fire*. Who the hell were these people? Why was everyone running around, freaking out about some weird triangle? Why was this guy called 'the Doctor?' He didn't seem to be doing anything particularly medical. People kept going in and out of a disappearing and reappearing blue box and being completely dramatic on a beach. This kind of stuff didn't happen on **The Cosby Show** or even the über-adult and super-boring **LA Law**. At the end of the show I went upstairs to bed, baffled, my mind swirling – but any thoughts of killing myself had quietly slipped away.

And just like that – things started to change. My illicit nights out with people twice my age began to dwindle, my self-harming behaviour, which had reached a crisis point, lessened, and even my failing grades started to slowly right themselves. I didn't want to go out and lose myself in doing the wrong thing and acting out; that wasn't what the Doctor would do. Stealing and getting wasted seemed to take a backseat to wondering about what was going to happen this week on **Doctor Who**. There was no internet, so there were no forums, no people squawking about 'spoilers' on Twitter. I didn't want to tell anyone that I was watching, because I had a reputation to uphold of 'tough, cool girl,' and I was so afraid that people would make fun of me. I was alone, but that was okay. My imagination, which seemed to have dried up when I started drinking the vodka from my parents' liquor cabinet to numb everything around me, ran full force and I spent hours thinking about the characters I had grown to love and find comfort in. In short – I learned to be a kid again. Life at home was still a constant nightmare and I seemed to always be one phone call away from being sent to juvenile hall or a psych ward, but my existence had meaning now. Maybe it was the escape factor – wasn't the Doctor himself running away from an unsatisfactory life on Gallifrey? I think it was that plus the undeniable fact that the Doctor was a father figure, teacher and best friend all rolled up into one.

And even Peri, poor Peri in her skimpy outfits and stuck being everyone's sexual harassment plaything – I admired her sassy 'tude, her spunk, her desire to run away and have some adventure. Things obviously weren't going so well (say what you will, but that dream she has where she's crying out to Howard indicates some Funny Stuff was happening at the Browns' house) and she needed to escape. I identified with her and even got my hair cut in a cute little Peri bob (dyed purple) because at last, here was someone I could look to and admire who wasn't a) all cheerleader fake like or b) scary far too old for me punk.

So *Planet of Fire*, known for bikinis and the Master and Turlough's Speedos, became for me the touchstone of my decades-long love affair with **Doctor Who**. It may not be the best episode – it ain't no *Genesis of the Daleks* – but it certainly isn't something as mind numbingly soul crushing as *Galaxy 4*. It's a nice little story. It's got some heart. It was the beginning of me.

The End Is The Beginning

The Caves Of Androzani by **Simon Thorpe**, 32, Ipswich
First story: **The Caves Of Androzani**

This is a story that should need no introduction to anyone even vaguely interested in **Doctor Who**; Peter Davison's swansong, deservedly winner of **Doctor Who Magazine**'s Mighty 200 poll and, quite simply, the greatest story in the programme's illustrious history. It's also the very first story I ever saw, on a grainy pirate video in the summer of 1990. And it gave me high expectations for the series that it's never quite managed to live up to since.

It wasn't my first introduction to the world of **Doctor Who**, however. As a child, I'd always been a prolific reader, helped by the fact that the local library was on my road. Two years earlier, I'd read a book called **Cry Vampire!** which won't mean much to many of you, but when I say it was written by a man called Terrance Dicks, you'll see where this is headed. For a seven-year-old, that's quite a memorable name, so when I saw another book by him a couple of days later, I quickly grabbed it. Over the next few weeks I read and re-read all of his **Baker Street Irregulars** series, but they didn't have anything else and I moved on to another author.

It wasn't until the following summer that I found, hidden at the back of the bottom shelf, a book that would influence the next 25-plus years; **Doctor Who and the Loch Ness Monster**. I had no idea who this Doctor Who person was, I just remembered the author's name and wanted to read about the monster. But that was it, a love affair was born. I read the book that afternoon and it was obvious that there had to be more of them. The following day brought another trip to the library. Nothing in the 'd' section, but there were several by another author, Malcolm Hulke. **The Sea Devils** and **The Dinosaur Invasion** looked the most interesting and they were dispatched just as quickly, as was the rest of the library's small stock. That would probably have been it, if one of the assistants hadn't been helpful and suggested I might like to order some in from elsewhere. Before long the staff were buried under a mountain of Target novelisations as I exhausted the rest of the county's stock (I should probably thank the staff of Stowmarket library at this point. I must have been a pain in the proverbial, but their patience was unending).

Skipping forward another year and **Doctor Who** was still purely a literary world. I'd missed out on the 'classic' run, mainly because I didn't even realise it existed. I was aware of the concept of regeneration, although it meant little to me. The Doctor was the Doctor as far as I was concerned, it didn't matter what he looked like. As long as he had the TARDIS ready to whisk his companions away for another exciting adventure, I was happy. That all changed one fateful afternoon. My mother was catching up on some paperwork at her school, so I was sitting in the staffroom, discovering Peladon. My reading was interrupted by the headmaster who, seeing what I was reading, offered to let me watch one of the **Doctor Who** videos in the school's library. **Doctor Who** was on video?! Soon after he was back with the video and a bag of sweets. He put the video in the machine and left me to it.

The starscape exploded into life and I was transfixed. The sweets were soon forgotten and I was completely engrossed in the story. As the Doctor and Peri were prepared for execution, I almost fell off the old leather sofa. I knew the Doctor would survive, he could just regenerate, but surely he couldn't let his companion die? As the credits rolled, I was left completely dumbstruck, how could they survive this? The remaining episodes flew by and I loved every second. The schemes of Morgus, the insanity of Sharaz Jek, the army and the gunrunners, android duplicates, murder, intrigue, revenge; the Doctor caught in the middle of it all, trying to stay alive, the Magma Beast... No, I haven't lost the plot, I did just say the Magma Beast. Because that's why I love this story so much. Robert Holmes' script is brilliant, the castare all on top form and they're superbly directed by Graeme Harper, but nothing can make the Magma Beast look good. It's a typical BBC monster, a man in a cheap rubber suit with a roar that wouldn't frighten an easily startled deer. Even as a nine-year-old, that wasn't going to frighten me. Strangely, though, at an age where I was starting to laugh at cheap effects, I was able to forgive this slip-up. Probably because everything else was so good; I'm not sure I'd have been as forgiving if I'd been sitting in front of *Timelash*. *The Caves of Androzani* is probably the closest the programme has ever come to perfection, but it has that fatal flaw that makes it even more lovable.

The Caves of Androzani will always hold a special place in my heart. It's the story that made me a fan; the one I can always go back to, no matter how many times I've seen it. It's the perfect summation of why Davison is my Doctor: the fallibility, the determination to do the right thing, trying desperately to save his friend no matter what the cost to himself. Most of all, it's the reason I will keep watching, no matter what. There have been times when I've thought about giving up on the new series, especially during the nauseating pre-regeneration sequence in *The End Of Time*. I'm glad I've kept going though, because there have been many more highs; for every *Fear Her* there's been an *Empty Child* or *Blink*. But nothing has yet matched the brilliance of *The Caves of Androzani*. One day something will and I want to be there when it happens. That's what keeps me coming back for more. I don't know what will happen then, but I can't wait to find out...

The Sixth Doctor Who

The sixth Doctor Who was born in a turbulent fashion, and this seems to have set the precedent for his incarnation – both on-screen and off.

Eschewing the normal pattern for new-born Doctor Whos, then-producer John Nathan-Turner decided to introduce Colin Baker's incarnation one story before the end of Season 21, rather than in the opening story of the following run. But Baker's debut was a troubled creation, in terms of both the writing and of the production (it being the custom at the time for the money to run out before the shooting schedule did), and so it was that the sixth Doctor Who's tenure was established as being a noisy and unstable one. Sometimes, these initial impressions can be hard to shake off.

With a production team at odds with one another and never fully behind his interpretation of the role, Colin Baker was destined never to be given a fair run at the part; being the 'face' of the show meant he was the most obvious target for blame and replacement when things went wrong. And things went so very badly wrong.

But the mid-1980s were also an exciting time in terms of the series' presentation, and whether the changes that came were initiated successfully or not, there was at least a sense that the programme was attempting to adapt to the times. Back on Saturday nights, trying out a new 45-minute format, and ultimately incorporating the entire 23rd series into one 14-week story, the **Doctor Who** of the period was among the least typical and most outrageous the show had ever presented. Teatime terror for tots was a thing of the past, with the programme moving into new territory and attempting to reinvent itself as a hard-bitten, hard sci-fi series for (young) adults.

This was also the first time an entire Doctor Who's term had been broadcast into a world that could comfortably no longer need to experience it 'as-live.' The prevalence of domestic video recorders now meant that the series was no longer challenging its competition simply to be seen, but instead that there was room for both in the audience's viewing schedules. Unfortunately, this too was to have a lasting effect on the show's fortunes...

In spite of a changing world and a changing formula, there is still much that can be drawn from the sixth Doctor Who and his stories. An ultimately well-liked actor and companion combination, the return of any number of popular and crowd-pleasing foes, and about as much food for fan debate as has been provided by any other period in the series' existence.

It was the best of times for being the worst of times, perhaps. And for that at least we should celebrate it.

The Guy Who Likes The Twin Dilemma

The Twin Dilemma by **Andrew Philips**, 38,Reading, UK
First story: **Terminus**

Dear JNT,

I'm sure you've noticed with dismay, as I have, the way that **Doctor Who** fandom has repaid all the hard work and effort that you and your team put into Colin Baker's debut story. Poll after poll is conducted, and in every single one of them it comes stone cold last. It's the butt of a thousand jokes, and the topic of a thousand vitriol-fuelled threads on all those Internet forums. As the producer of that story, I can only imagine how disheartening you must find such a reaction, which is why I feel compelled to write to you about it. You see, I find it dispiriting too. Because I'm The Guy Who Likes *The Twin Dilemma*.

Perhaps it helped that I didn't grow up in the 1970s, for which so many fans have nostalgic affection. My eight-year-old self only discovered the show in 1983, so *The Five Doctors* was the only memory I had of previous Doctor Whos. Having a new Doctor all my own was exciting, especially as he was such a contrast to Peter Davison, and right from the moment he brightened up **Blue Peter**, I cherished every moment that Doctor Number Six appeared on screen.

As for the story, I never thought it was significantly better or worse than most of the others I'd seen. I remember thinking it was very 'indoors', which is hardly surprising coming after the three location-heavy stories which ended Peter's run. But that's no bad thing – I'm not a particularly outdoorsy person myself. And looking back at it from 2013, it probably does have a TARDIS scene or six too many, but let's face it, that coat looks far better in the studio than it does in the street –

you only have to watch *Attack Of The Cybermen* to realise that.

And whilst we're talking about the coat, I have to confess ... I love it. Unreservedly. I want one. **Doctor Who** should be the brightest, loudest, alienest, eye-catching-est show on the box, and even at the height of the 1980s' most ridiculous fashion excesses, the sixth Doctor's coat ensured the programme was exactly that. You've told us you now think the coat was something of a mistake. I disagree. The mistake was how your writers and designers treated it. Instead of running it down, they should have used it to draw the villain's eye away from the companion sabotaging their evil master plan in the background. Instead of making the sets brighter, they should have drabbed them down to make it stand out *even more*. Don't you think it looks best against the plain white TARDIS set?

The Twin Dilemma should be praised for giving **Doctor Who** so much potential to do something different – not an easy feat for a show that's over two decades old. The sixth Doctor had a personality that matched his outfit – loud and confrontational. This script, more than any other he received in **Doctor Who**, enabled Colin to display his considerable range of acting skills. His violent moments of insanity contrast with his touching performance when Azmael passes away, not to mention the traditional Doctorish scenes of working out Mestor's plan in the egg-chamber, and his playfully rude departure scene at the end. And all of it peppered with difficult dialogue, which Colin delivers perfectly, every time.

So fandom is wrong. This isn't the all-time worst **Doctor Who** story. It's quotable, it's striking, it's got some fantastic model work and set design, it's well-acted (well, by the adults at least), and it's epic in scope, taking in three planets and a spaceship. It's all too easy to pick on the eponymous twins and the strangling scene (actually completely justified in the script), but these are mere moments. *The Twin Dilemma* is, in fact, great, and is a very, very easy story to stick up for in an argument...

...which is where I come in. Because I'm The Guy Who Likes *The Twin Dilemma*. With capitals, because it's like a title or an accolade. And in that role, I've had to defend *The Twin Dilemma* very many times. I once wrote in some obscure fan publication or other of how my post-millennial fandom all takes place online, separately to Real Life™. When you meet other fans in person, it's easy to make an impression, but on an internet forum with tens of thousands of other faceless dafties to interact with all at once? It's much harder to stand out there, no matter what colour coat you're wearing. But *The Twin Dilemma* has given me an instant identity. I've unwittingly become its champion. It's not that it's one of my All Time Top Five or anything (Hell, it's not even one of my All Time Top Five Colins), but for reasons which I still genuinely cannot fathom, it's a controversial one to like, and it's given me the best online signature in fandom. Whatever I've posted about **Doctor Who** on the internet, however outrageous, it's always followed by that quick disclaimer '...but then again, I'm the guy who likes *The Twin Dilemma*, so what do I know?' Whatever I've said, that signature proclaims loud and clear that it's only an opinion, and it's the opinion of someone who knows what it's like to be in a minority.

And fandom became that little bit more fun as a result. I've lost count of the number of times someone has started a thread on *The Twin Dilemma*, only to be warned, 'Don't let Wilf hear you say that!' Or even, on one occasion, 'Don't let Wilf hear you say that, or he'll be along in a minute to give you fifty reasons why it's the best story ever, with footnotes and everything.' I duly obliged. I actually had to leave nine reasons out to keep to the number.

And then there was the time **Doctor Who Magazine** ran their Mighty 200 poll, after the broadcast of the 200th **Doctor Who** story. No prizes for guessing what came in last place. I had to write in – I did it as a limerick to make sure it made the letters page the following month. They credited me as Andrew Philips, but then gave a short reply using my online nickname, with no explanation. That must surely have confused a lot of readers, but I figure they did it because they knew that a good percentage of them would go, 'Oh, it's all right, it's only him again,' when they saw it.

So I want to thank you, JNT, from the very bottom of my heart, for making *The Twin Dilemma* exactly the way you did. Not only did you give me four more wonderful episodes to enjoy, but more than that, you gave me an identity, a reputation and a catchphrase, for which I will always be grateful.

And even if I'm the only one who doesn't think of *The Twin Dilemma* as the worst ever **Doctor Who** story, it's still **Doctor Who**, which means it's still a damn sight better than 90% of the rest of television.

Gastropodically yours,

Andrew Philips (who is also called Wilf).

No Need For Cryon...
Attack of the Cybermen by **John Scott**, 39, Whitley Bay
First story: **Pyramids of Mars** (It gave me nightmares)

Like many fans of a certain age, my relationship with the good Doctor has gone through a series of peaks and troughs. Whilst I'd always enjoyed the show, it wasn't until **The Five Faces of Doctor Who** repeat series that my fan-gene was fully activated. Suddenly I was leading (or was that dictating?) playground re-enactments of episodes inspired by the repeat run. One week I'd be the Doctor to my mate Bazz's Chesterton; the next he'd be Jamie to my Troughton. I can't remember what we did once we hit the third Doctor's stories – I'm guessing that Bazz didn't much fancy dragging up as Jo Grant – but the bug had well and truly taken hold. From that point on I was no longer just a slightly over-enthusiastic viewer, I was a *fan*. That Christmas I received the World anthology of stories from previous **Doctor Who** annuals, its cover festooned with images of the first four Doctors in full colour and one sepia-tinged painting of Tristan Farnon. My parents might just as well have given me crack cocaine. There was no going back.

Three years on, unsurprisingly, I mourned the demise of the fifth Doctor. He'd had a good send-off – though I'd enjoyed *Resurrection of the Daleks* much more than the slightly dull *The Caves of Androzani* – and his time had come. Whereas back in 1982, Davison's ubiquity at the BBC meant that it felt like an old friend was taking over the role, Colin Baker was little more than the bloke who'd appeared wearing a jacket fashioned from deckchair material at his press-call and whose face beamed out somewhat smugly from the latter pages of the **Radio Times** 20th Anniversary Special. Never a one to embrace change, my dear, I waited with some anxiety for his first story.

And then, disaster. The fates conspired to keep me away from the television throughout all but the last ten minutes of *The Twin Dilemma*. A birthday party here, a trip to the dentist there and it was almost all over. Even the Betamax video recorder seemed to join in the conspiracy against me as it took one of its regular vacations to the repair shop to have its recording heads replaced. So when Colin Baker announced at the end of Part Four that he was the Doctor whether we liked it or not, I could do little more than shrug and rue the run of bad luck that had seen me cruelly deprived of his debut tale. Of course, in hindsight, I couldn't have had better luck. I was spared the horrors of Jaconda, the sixth Doctor's murderous instability and the woeful weactions of Womulus and Wemus. For this viewer, the sixth Doctor's era would begin with *Attack of the Cybermen*.

And it couldn't have been any better.

Attack of the Cybermen had it all: a new Doctor, the Cybermen, the return of Lytton, one of the most memorable scores of the 1980s, ice-tombs, Telos, death, destruction, explosions and blood. It even had the actors behind Davros and the Tetley Tea Men unmasked and sharing scenes together. For many a latter-day critic, hidebound by received wisdom, this cornucopia of continuity and carnage is a serious misstep, the beginning of the end, a story that, along with the rest of Season 22, gave Grade the green light to axe the show. For this twelve-year-old boy, it was perfection. Grade was wrong.

I can think of few moments from the series that have stayed with me for as long or as vividly as some of those from *Attack of the Cybermen*. Bates and Stratton roaming the wastes of Telos, harvesting dead Cybermen to affect their disguise; the blackened Cyberman patrolling the sewers of London; the horror – the real, visceral horror – of Lytton's conversion and the Doctor's genuine remorse at his lack of judgment. Even the much derided Cryons, a race who look like they've stumbled through a time-eddy from the Hartnell era, have a strange, ethereal nobility to them and are impossible to forget.

As for the new lead, he was just great. I've yet to take to a Doctor as quickly. Maybe it was the teenage rebellion about to kick in, but I loved this acerbic, arrogant, self-righteous smart-arse of a Doctor. Looking back at it now, I can see why: he was the twelve-year-old me in a harlequin-suit; to this day, I can't walk past an organ or keyboard without playing a burst of Bach's *Toccata and Fugue in D Minor* in his honour. The fact that he also had the most attractive companion I'd ever seen in Nicola Bryant undoubtedly helped; they may have bickered all the time, but so what? Have you met many twelve-year-olds recently? When they're not talking in text-speak, bickering is their second language. Anyway, it wasn't the bickering I was looking at; even Julie from **Fame** hadn't had this effect on me.

The following years would see the deepest trough in my relationship with **Doctor Who**. A combination of hormones and a hiatus would drain my enthusiasm as I discovered other, more anarchic ways to soothe my teenage angst. I didn't go off it for long, but I missed more episodes between 1986 and 1988 than at any other time in my life. Even when I returned to the fold, I wrote off much of the show's latter years as a mistake. Received wisdom got hold of me around the neck and strangled me. It wasn't until *Attack of the Cybermen* came out on DVD a few years ago that I really *got* it again. Watching it with my eight-year-old son, I was transported back to those heady days of 1985 as one of the show's new generation of fans lapped up the adventure with as much enthusiasm as I had more than quarter of a century before.

Forget received wisdom. Watch without prejudice. It's still a peak.

A Tail of Two Doctors
Vengeance on Varos by **Nabil Shaban**, London, UK
First story: **The Daleks**

I was ten years old in 1963 when I first saw **Doctor Who**. It was the second episode of *The Daleks*. I had missed *An Unearthly Child* and the first episode of the Dalek story, because the children in my family group (I was an inmate in a special boarding school for disabled children) were banned from watching the much-heralded new science fiction show. You can imagine I was well pissed off with not being allowed to watch it, especially as my friends from the other family groups were gloating about how brilliant and scary it was. However, by chance, me and my best pal, Stephen Hawkings (no, not the world famous physicist) were invited one Saturday afternoon to have tea with our local G.P. and his family. It turned out that his son had become a **Doctor Who** fan, and insisted on watching episode two, while we were there. The doctor apologised at how rude it was to be watching TV with guests present, but I assured him we didn't mind, secretly overjoyed that I, at last, was going to view this notorious programme. My pal Stephen nearly wrecked this illicit opportunity; he was about to say, 'We are not allowed to watch **Doctor Who**,' but I stopped him in time. Imagine how thrilled I was to see the Daleks for the first time, and hear their chilling electronic voices shriek, 'Exterminate!' I was instantly hooked and *nothing* was going to stop me from watching the following week's episode and all subsequent adventures of the intrepid space and time explorer in his funny police-box. The following week when the woman in charge of my family group said we couldn't watch **Doctor Who**, I warned her that I would tell the local G.P. that it was unfair that his son, who was the same age as us, could watch this programme, when we couldn't. I reminded her that it would make the institution look bad in the eyes of the town. The Children's Home was very proud of its compassionate reputation, and so she quickly gave in to my demands, and I became a **Doctor Who** addict for the next 12 years, finally giving up on the show when I became a university student at the age of 25.

However, it was always a fantasy of mine to, one day, be involved in **Doctor Who**, either as a writer or as an actor. During the 1970s, I attempted to write scripts and outlines, but I lacked the courage to send them to the BBC. Then when Roger Delgado, who played the first Master, died, I did have the temerity to write with the suggestion that since the Master was a Time Lord and therefore capable of regeneration, the series could still retain the character with a different actor in the role, and I would make a perfect replacement. I was still a student at the time, and had only acted as an amateur, and being disabled as well, I never had a hope the Beeb would take my letter seriously. Of course, they didn't. My next attempt to inveigle my way into **Doctor Who** was in 1981, when the BBC announced they were looking for someone to replace Tom Baker as the new Doctor. I wrote to Jon Nathan-Turner, and informed him (tongue firmly in cheek) that I would make the perfect Doctor Who. He wrote back saying the part was now cast, but he would keep me on file should something come up. Little did I imagine that 'something' would come my way three years later, when I was offered the part of the deliciously evil Sil.

Funny enough, JNT had no recollection of me writing to him earlier, and the idea of casting me as Sil belonged entirely to Ron Jones. Actually, it was Martin Jarvis and his wife who thought of me, after remembering me from an Arena TV documentary about my disabled theatre company Graeae, they had seen in 1981. Ron auditioned me, and when I finished reading for the part, said, 'I'll put my cards on the table. I want you for the part. Are you interested? I promise we won't cover your face with an ugly monster mask. You will be a real character.' I mischievously replied, 'Oh, you think my face is ugly enough without a mask?' This made him laugh. Then, he said, 'You will have to work on the Sil laugh, though.' I agreed, 'I know it was crap. Don't worry, when we next meet, it will be just right.' I knew the laugh of Sil was key to his character and crucial to his notoriety. I was determined to make Sil so scary that all the children would be back hiding behind the sofas, just like I was when I was a kid. I felt **Doctor Who** had gone soft on terrifying the little brats, probably because of the unhealthy influence of such nannies as Mary Whitehouse.

The factors which helped me create Sil, were devising a laugh which was both reptilian and slug-like, and Gollum in Tolkien's **The Hobbit** and **Lord of the Rings**. This was, of course, before Andy Serkis' portrayal in Peter Jackson's movies. I always wanted to play Gollum, so I decided I would recreate elements of how I imagined him in my evocation of Sil.

My first day of rehearsal for *Vengeance on Varos* seemed to be blessed by an encounter with Patrick Troughton in the lift at the BBC rehearsal rooms. I was too shy to tell him this was my first day on **Doctor Who**, but I felt sure his close proximity to me was a good omen. At the end of the read-through with the entire cast, Forbes Collins who play the Chief came up to me, and whispered, 'You can't fool me. You've learnt all your lines.' I didn't try to deny it. 'Well, when I'm against all you heavy-weights, who are so much more experienced in telly acting,' I replied, 'I have to make sure I'm several steps ahead of the game.' Forbes nodded, and then as we parted company, he turned and said, 'Great nasty little laugh you invented. It'll make you the star of the show. You scene-stealer, you.'

Lip-Gloss and Leather
The Mark of the Rani by **Jennie Stayner**, 34, London
First story: One of Sylvester McCoy's!

I don't remember the first time I saw **Doctor Who**, where I was or who I was with, I just have a vague memory of thinking Ace was really cool. I was brought up in a matriarchy, my mother and grandmother raised me from the age of six to the age of eleven when my mum remarried. My formative understanding of womanhood was therefore predicated on a very 1980s view of manhood - a woman needs a man like a fish needs a bicycle. It's me that builds the flat packs in our house. It is perhaps for this reason that I love the Rani. I mean that, I love her. Whisper it - I think she's better than the Doctor, well the sixth Doctor anyway. Yes, she may enjoy using the human race for experiments and her idea of giving someone wood is turning them into a tree, but she does it with style. She's no-one's assistant.

I hadn't given much thought to **Doctor Who** in the intervening years but had an open mind when my then-boyfriend (now husband) wanted me to watch some of his DVDs with him. I had heard the general criticism of the weakness of the female characters but I wanted to see for myself and, as I say, Ace had been pretty awesome to the 9nine-year-old me. I was hooked; the character of the Doctor has to be one of the most brilliantly conceived in television history. How can you not fall in love with the adventure? You can go anywhere in time and space with him. If he turned up I would have travelled with him in a heartbeat. Yes, there are some dodgy moments but they are of their time. Whilst Benny Hill was chasing women in their underwear around a park, the Doctor's companions were the least of feminism's worries.

Besides, there have always been assistants that have challenged the received wisdom that **Doctor Who** is sexist. The first Doctor has the beautiful and composed Barbara who provides a great counterbalance to the screaming Susan. Doctor number two has the genius alien Zoe. Even the third Doctor has Liz Shaw, scientist with UNIT and not always required to just make the sandwiches. And of course the wonderful Sarah Jane Smith, not so much assistant as institution with her own spin offs. Then we get to the fourth Doctor and the lovely Leela. Difficult to argue with the feminists there, except her aggression and violence are something of a foil to the tiny clothing. And then there's Romana, the Doctor's equal. We can ignore the whinging of Tegan and skip to Nyssa, the fifth Doctor's alien child prodigy. Then we reach the sixth Doctor and the less said about Peri and Mel the better. Onwards to number seven and the aforementioned Ace, Nitro anyone? The eighth Doctor has a doctor of his own in Grace and then we get into the world of Rose Tyler, Martha Jones, Donna Noble and Amy Pond. And who can forget River Song? The strong female characters are there if you look but all are the assistant to the Doctor. They faithfully follow him when he tells them to run, gaze in awe when he's said something clever and fall in love with him again and again.

This brings me back to the Rani. The Rani needs no-one. She travels in her art deco wardrobe TARDIS accompanied only by T. rex embryos and a shed load of self-tan. Exiled by the Time Lords for the murder of a cat by her genetically engineered mice, the Rani does everything the Master does but in heels, leather trousers, and shoulder pads. A pure academic, her motivation is intellectual rather than petty power struggles. Even the smug, know-it-all sixth Doctor is most interested in being viewed as a VIP by George Stephenson. The Rani on the other hand, like all good *femmes fatale*, quietly leaves her male subjects sleepless, violent and marked with a giant red hickey.

I love the Rani because she is an intellectual who takes the time to be tanned and glossy. She doesn't suffer fools, is uncompromising and has the best wardrobe of any of the characters in this story. Her serious scientific attitude is coupled with high glamour, a fabulous combination. Even the dust in the capsules she uses to knock Peri out so she and the Master can escape glitters. Poor Peri, blundering about the countryside in her dodgy dress and pink shoes, always on the brink of tears.

For me, the Rani, aside from Romana, is the character you can use to counter the sexism in **Doctor Who** argument most effectively, should you need to. It's true that there is a fair amount of 'something for the Dads' throughout the show's long history, not least in the guise of Peri and her pink bikini. But there are examples of female power that make the dodgy bits less important and the Rani is one of those.

You could argue that **Doctor Who** is just a kids' show so why does it matter? But we all know that's not true, not least because there is no such thing as *just* a kids' show, but mainly because this show is special. For so many people it is a clear part of their earliest memories and influences. I remember desperately wanting to be like Ace when I was little; she had exciting adventures, blew things up and came from close to where my Mum worked. Revisiting the show as an adult though, the others took their places in my feminist heart; Sarah-Jane, Romana, Nyssa and of course Ace are examples of women with intelligence, ingenuity and sensitivity. They are role models for the girls watching and exemplars of womanhood for the boys. If I'm honest though, the Rani is the most fun and fabulous of the strong female characters on offer. The companions are just too decent. Give me a mad scientist in lip-gloss and leather any day.

The Generation Game
The Two Doctors by **Suky Khakh**, 42, Willenhall UK
First story: **The Leisure Hive**

I was fourteen years old; two months shy of my fifteenth birthday. Saturday evenings I'd watch the wrestling on **The World Of Sport**, before switching over to BBC1 to watch **Grandstand** for the final football scores, so I could check my Dad's football coupon (I'd always watched the results on the Beeb as they were faster getting them on to the screen).

'Did we win?', 'No Dad' (30 years later and I'm doing the same with my lad – i.e. not winning – but it's the lottery this time).

And then it was the main event of the evening. I'd been enjoying the series so far. Loved all the fan references in *Attack of the Cybermen*, Sil's machinations in *Vengeance On Varos* and the one-upmanship between the three Time Lords in *The Mark Of The Rani*. Years later my opinion has sort of changed on all three stories.

I was most excited about the return of Patrick Troughton and Fraser Hines. But two weeks into the return of the Sontarans, catastrophe struck. The news broke that **Doctor Who** had been cancelled.

I couldn't believe it. I asked my Dad if he'd heard anything.

'No, I don't know anything.'

As this was midweek and I was still at school during the day, I decided to go to the library later and see if there was anything in the papers there.

Bilston Library – my second home from the ages of five to eleven before we moved house. It's an old stately building of modest size that had been converted to a Library and Art Gallery downstairs and an Exhibition of Bilston's history upstairs. It had ample-sized gardens where we would climb over the railings and play football using our jumpers as goalposts, before we got chased off every evening by The Caretaker or when Dad would come and fetch us after being told by Mom that the food was getting cold (it was nearly nine o'clock and we had been out since six after all the kids' shows had finished – can't do that these days!)

After we had moved house to about a mile away I would still go to the library to borrow the latest **Doctor Who** books. I'd check on the Microfiche machine for the latest releases. When I knew a title would be coming out I'd reserve a copy. This way I was up to date on most of the W.H. Allen hardbacks. The Target paperbacks with their glued-on plastic protection would come much later. Occasionally these books would be put on sale.

'Dad, can I have 10p to buy a book?' 'Here you go – don't be late getting back!' 'No Dad.'

The library had a reference room where old men or the unemployed would sit reading the day's papers – it was a way for most of them to read all the paper's without having to pay for them. You could sense the librarians would hope that some of them would get jobs and move on instead of skulking in a corner ogling the latest Page 3 girl or surreptitiously filling out the easy crossword in **The Mirror**.

I started walking to the library – it was going to take a while as I had decided to return some books and also renew **Doctor Who: A Celebration**, a book that my Dad couldn't have afforded to buy me, but I knew if I kept borrowing it from the library it would be the same as having my own copy. I had that book for nearly a year before one of the librarians cottoned on and took it off me – I've always wondered what happened to it. It had all my handwritten notes in the back few pages! (I'm looking at that book now and I've discovered that it's got the same handwritten notes in my own copy.)

When I got there I renewed 'my' book and then went into the Reference Room to find the papers. The news had hit during the day so the only newspaper that had anything on it was our local evening paper – the **Express and Star**. If memory serves me correctly it was just a couple of inches of news on the front page - nothing much but it did put me in a bit of a flap.

Walking home carrying my books I met my Dad who offered to pay for the bus to get home. We jumped on, and we were nearly home when he said, 'I have to get off here.' 'But our stop is the next one.' 'I know but I only put in enough for you to go to that stop but I'll get off here and have a smoke while I'm walking home.' 'No leave it Dad, the driver won't say nothing. Trust me.'

A few seconds later the driver called my Dad from his seat and asked him to either pay the extra fare or get off. Dad got off - he hadn't got the money. I waited for him at the next bus stop. His face was fuming. I tried to laugh it off but he was having none of it. We walked the rest of the way home in silence.

The following day I went back to the library and there were front page headlines on all the major papers and I sat there reading all the details. Statements from BBC sources had said that it had definitely been cancelled. I think I went to that library every day for the next few weeks just to see if there was any more news. There was no internet in those days - every bit of news came from the television, the papers or **DWM** (if you could find a copy - the library wouldn't stock that periodical, no matter how many times I asked them). During those days of sitting waiting for somebody to finish their crosswords I managed to gather more bits of news - it had not been cancelled; the money allocated for **Doctor Who** was being used to pay for the purchase of **Dallas**; there would be an 'awesome' charity record called *Doctor In Distress*.

If it wasn't for that library I wouldn't have known any of that (some of which I wish I hadn't have known - 'Doctor In Distress, Let's all answer his SOS!')

Bilston Library, Art Gallery and Exhibition is still open thirty years later but with reduced hours and the threat of closure from the council. Without local libraries like this most of the unemployed would have nowhere to sleep during the day and I would have had to travel to Wolverhampton for all my information. Wolverhampton!

Thanks for all those happy memories of playing footy in your gardens, borrowing the latest **Doctor Who** books and just helping me through a dark period of my life.

Me Dad died two months after the news of **Doctor Who**'s hiatus broke. Love you Dad.

Timelash Waits For This Man

Timelash by **Anthony Williams**, 25, Atlanta, Georgia, USA (formerly London) / First story: **The Time Warrior**

I am a member of the oddest generation of **Doctor Who** fans. That strange group that grew up and became fans when no new **Doctor Who** was being produced (with the exception of the TV movie in 1996! Oh what a glorious ninety minutes that was – but that's someone else's article!). My father got me into the show at the age of four or five, in 1992. For the next thirteen years, there would be no new **Doctor Who** on air. Dad only really liked the first four Doctors, and he bought me stories featuring those Doctors on VHS for most of my birthdays and Christmases.

But, of course, I wanted more than that. We got satellite TV at the beginning of 1995, and I quickly discovered the joys of the Sunday morning omnibus on UK Gold. This was something I looked forward to through the entire week, and I would eagerly check UK Gold's teletext to see what was coming up. It was really through this that I developed a love for all of **Doctor Who**, regardless of era.

Let's fast-forward a little, before this turns into a dull history of my viewing of all of **Doctor Who**. Soon, November 1996 came round. By this time, I had heard about *Timelash*, but not being on the internet at the age of eight, I had little idea of this story's poor reputation. I saw on teletext that it featured Paul Darrow, the actor who had played my favourite character in **Blakes 7** (a programme I had also discovered through UK Gold), and at this point, I just couldn't get more excited about this story!

So, Sunday 10th November, 1996 came around. A week before my ninth birthday. *Timelash* was due to air. But I couldn't watch it live, as my parents wanted to watch the Remembrance Sunday services. Not a problem, thought I! I will tape it, and watch it later! I carefully set up the VHS recorder, and set the timer. Being only eight years old, I had decided that the best thing would be to have the BBC1 footage of the service showing via the Sky box, then I could switch it over for **Doctor Who** and turn to BBC1.

Sadly, my plans didn't quite work out. I forgot to turn the channel over, and subsequently missed all but the last ten minutes of *Timelash*. I was *devastated*! I had been looking forward to this for absolutely weeks. I knew it would eventually come back around, but it would surely be another two or three years, right?

Wrong. It wasn't meant to be at that stage. A year later, I got really into **Star Trek**. My **Doctor Who** videos all went into storage, and I just didn't care about the show for three years. What a fool I was! *Timelash* came and went twice on UK Gold, and I missed it. I was too busy obsessing over Captain Janeway's next encounter with the Borg, and how she would handle it, to care about *Timelash*.

The new millennium came in, and in the summer of 2000, my parents were sorting out the cellar. My VHS tapes came out of storage, and my father encouraged me to watch them again. I put *The Claws of Axos* into the VHS player, and absolutely loved it. I gave up collecting **Star Trek** on VHS (how fickle I was!), and got back into **Doctor Who** in a big way. I bought **Doctor Who Magazine** for the first time, started getting some of the eighth Doctor novels, and I had memories of this story called *Timelash* – my holy grail of **Doctor Who**.

There were other stories I hadn't seen, but that near miss with *Timelash* gave it a near-legendary status in my mind. I started looking at the UK Gold schedules to see when it would be on. I watched through some of those other stories that I hadn't seen before. But *Timelash* was never far from my thoughts.

Finally, the day came. UK Gold had moved from Sunday morning omnibuses to being on both days of the weekend. Saturday 8th December 2001. I was now fourteen years old. Older, more mature. I had just dipped into online fandom, with the BBC message boards. People were saying bad things about *Timelash* online, but I didn't care. I had to see this story that I had missed so unfortunately five years previously.

Eventually, the day came around. I watched with excitement. I watched through the terrible acting, the terrible costumes, sets that looked like they might fall over if you blew on them too hard. And, of course, Paul Darrow's excessively camp acting. But I just didn't care about any of that. I loved this story for all that it was.

Yes, it's terrible. Yes, it's camp. Yes, it's kitsch. Yes, they could have got actors who could act. Yes, they could have made Herbert less annoying. Yes, they could have asked Darrow to tone it down a little. But I had finally seen it. And regardless of its flaws, it didn't disappoint me. I suspect that its status to me as 'the one that got away', combined with everyone online being mean about it, meant that I had this strange juxtaposition in my head of it likely to be terrible, but that I was still looking forward to it.

And you know what? It worked. *Timelash* is still a story that I love, even in my mid-twenties, when I can look at it with a critical eye. It still has that magic to me, it still has that status of the story that I foolishly waited five years to watch, because of my idiotic flirtations with **Star Trek**. I dread to think what my wife (yes, she's a fan) will think of it when I expose her to it...

You Only Die Twice
Revelation of the Daleks by **John Davies**, 40, Manchester, UK / First story: **The Android Invasion**

'I know, I'll take you to...'

As the recent horse meat scandal focused our minds on what we were actually eating, it was only natural for my **Doctor Who**-head to drift back to 1985 and the show's Davros-infused take on **Soylent Green**. However, it didn't stay focussed on the 'meat' of a story in which Ruby from *Upstairs Downstairs* pines over Richard Bucket and Mr Balowski plays pop songs to jolly up the atmosphere for long. This story's theme was, and is, death (well, it was written by Eric Saward), and in 1985 death was very much on my mind. But not *physical* death – and, at the age of thirteen, not John Donne's Elizabethan take on death, either.

They say you only die once. The truth is ... you only die twice.

A man is the sum of his memories... So very true, Doctor. Our memories make us, and one of the most painful is that moment, or quick succession of moments, in which the secure bubble you have lived in since birth is prodded for the nth time and bursts ... leading to the death of certainty, and the death of childhood. My certainty, at least in a **Doctor Who** sense, and my childhood – yes, also in a **Doctor Who** sense – met their maker in 1985.

While every childhood is unique, each generation will share certain memory-traits. Together with the base line that sees us all put teeth under our pillow, and all believers in Christmas go to sleep on the 24th of December wondering, 'What will that jolly man who made us cry in a toy store two weeks ago leave under the tree?', to most people of my generation the telephone number 01 811 8055 will have been as familiar as their own home number. In addition to that the post code W12 8QT was probably the first one they truly memorised. To this kid, though, there was also a televisual certainty and a special first line of an address. **Doctor Who** had always been there on television from the day I was born, and always would be – *it had to be* – and there was also *that* address: 111 Central Promenade.

'I know, I'll take you to...'
Prod...

As the sixth Doctor dangled from cables at the end of Part One of *The Two Doctors*, Sue Lawley calmly, and professionally, took my Linus Blanket away from me and announced **Doctor Who** was cancelled.

Prod...

And then, in October 1985, the doors closed on...

111 Central Promenade...

'I know, I'll take you to....'

Blackpool.

Prod...

Famously the last word in the Doctor's 'destination chat' with Peri in *Revelation of the Daleks* ('Blackpool!') was cut due to the Lawley-announced hiatus. The planned rematch between the Doctor and the Celestial Toymaker would have to go (or, rather, *go into* abeyance until novelised and transformed into audio by Big Finish). However, my parents would often take me to Blackpool as a child – to Ron and Barbara's B&B (I know – Ian and Barbara's would have been amazing, but hey ho). It was a delight every time. Aside from the majesty of the tower, the dazzling magic of the lights, the lure of the sea air, the thrill of the Pleasure Beach and that strange, baffling assurance that even on a bright, sun-drenched day, one shortcut down a back street would find you in a howling wind tunnel, there was something else ... something that allowed a young John Davies, sporting a bowl haircut and a hand-knitted jumper, to make his fictional television certainty a physical, tactile reality. On the street opposite the Central Pier I became a companion of the Doctor. On that corner, with his faces smiling down at me from a painted mural, I entered the TARDIS.

I am, of course, referring to the **Doctor Who** Exhibition that ran in Blackpool from 1974 to 1985.

Every year we went to Blackpool, I went there. Quite often, every day. After the first time, where my parents would walk around with me, though, they would see me in and then wait in the café; they had to endure endless cups of what my mum referred to as 'Cyber-pee' as they waited.

I can still retrace the steps leading down into the exhibition, the theme tune in my ears, K9 at the bottom of those stairs. I can still recall turning left, strolling down a short corridor looking at walled exhibits of props, scripts and record covers and then. - *oh! and then!* - I can still remember - as though it was *now* - the right turn that took me into the TARDIS console room. I didn't notice, or care, that the console prop was fan-made (heck, I didn't even know the term back then), nor did I mind that the entire room wasn't totally encased in white roundelled walls. There were **Doctor Who** monsters in there! I could press buttons and make them move! I could see Cybermen! *Real* Cybermen. The Malus, the Mandrells. I could hear Peter Davison say, 'Well, did you enjoy the exhibition Hmm? Well come again soon!' on a loop... I could live in a **Doctor Who** world while I was there, and no-one would judge me.

While the vast number of displays, live shows and exhibitions seen since the show's 2005 reboot might make the huge nostalgia I hold for that exhibition incomprehensible to recent generations, this was, to this Northern lad in the early 1980s, a unique place; almost a Mecca (no, not a Bingo Hall). It was a place where I could buy **Doctor Who** *things* - inside the TARDIS!

I would save my pocket money for weeks to go in there and buy postcards you couldn't get anywhere else. I can still remember one particular day (it must have been in 1983 for reasons that will be clear to fans), when I walked to the shop counter, my pennies in hand. There were two guys there already, American I think, looking at the Aladdin's cave on sale. As I stared at the Patrick

Troughton postcard I was going to buy the taller of the two guys pointed at a box on the wall. 'I'll have two of those to start with!' The box was the original VHS release of *Revenge of the Cybermen*. Alas, I didn't have Vogan gold dust on me so couldn't afford it myself. However, even though I felt a tad poor that day, looking back I think I was the richer. I believe I actually valued that postcard of Patrick more than they did those videos. Not only did they comment disparagingly on the cover ('Wrong logo, wrong Cyberman!'), I expect they'll be onto Blu-ray by now, the VHS forgotten (or eBayed). My postcard, however, is still Exhibition fresh - the only wear on it the age of my memories of *that* day, *that* place and *that* magical exhibition.

On the day we left Blackpool in 1985, the B&B owner, Ron, stopped me on the way out of his digs. There had been a poster for the exhibition on the wall the whole week I had been there.

'You've been looking at that all week,' he said. 'Do you want it?'

Giddy John bounced and said, 'Yes please!'

Ron, the man who had drawn smiley faces on my hard-boiled eggs for years, grinned, taking it down. 'The place closes this year, you might as well.'

Prod...

As I took the rolled up paper, the final *prod* burst my bubble and my childhood fell away, the smiley egg faces turning upside down in their cups.

The TV show was gone (but now just for eighteen months - *result!* - however the *certainty* of 'always there' was now irreversibly gone) ... and now the exhibition was gone (a *real* forever, it seemed).

In that exchange I also ceased being a child. I became ... the geek I am to this day (although some would say that this still involves being a child). As I clutched that poster I vowed, no matter what, to keep **Doctor Who** alive. It would always survive! It would survive through *me*!

And I've just realised something. The sixth Doctor *did* take Peri to Blackpool. No, not in *The Nightmare Fair*, but rather, in a trip to *that* place, *that exhibition*. And with Tegan! Forget fan-made – that's fan-fiction!

Pivots and Police Boxes
The Trial of a Time Lord by **Jez Strickley**, 37, Sistiana, Italy / First story: **City of Death**

1986 marked a change in the fortunes of **Doctor Who**. The period of hiatus stemming back to the early weeks of 1985 meant that, for the first time in more than twenty years, the BBC's New Year schedules were bereft of the Doctor's weekly adventures in time and space. Instead, myself and countless other fans were kept waiting until the final days of summer for the much anticipated return of Colin Baker's flamboyant sixth Doctor.

When the series finally returned towards the end of September 1986, Season 23 and its single, epic offering, *The Trial of a Time Lord*, proved to be nothing less than pivotal for the future of the programme. Relatively low viewing figures and a less-than-supportive BBC management saw the end of Colin Baker's all too brief tenure; whilst discontent behind the scenes culminated in the resignation of long-time script editor Eric Saward.

Yet as these broad brushstrokes reworked the canvas of the series, my perspective as a young and impressionable fan gradually shifted too, as the treacherous sands of late childhood drew me ever closer to the questioning cynicism of the teenager.

But all that was yet to come. For me, not yet ten years old when the hiatus struck, the protracted wait for new adventures felt like a lifetime. Indeed, as 1986 came into view, Season 22's unashamed monster mash had already become the stuff of distant memory. To keep myself in the loop, I wrote to **Doctor Who Magazine** asking to know something of what lay in store in the coming season. The then editor, Sheila Cranna, promptly replied to tell me that the production was still underway, and that the working title for the first four episodes was the intriguing *The Mysterious Planet*.

With my curiosity slaked just a little, I guess it wasn't until the slow August days of my school summer holiday that Season 23 really began to take shape before me. Finally, after eighteen months of waiting there would be that familiar explosion of sound and starscape as the title credits rolled once more. I couldn't wait.

I don't remember what I was thinking when I finally sat down on that Saturday teatime to watch my favourite programme. But I do clearly recall being very perplexed upon first hearing Dominic Glynn's haunting interpretation of Ron Grainer's iconic score. As the weeks passed, the new version of the theme music, with its almost mournful quality, began to become the norm, very much as Saturday teatimes once again played host to a twenty-five minute helping of original science fiction.

As the season unfolded its mighty tale, I was drawn into its strange mix of past, present and future, in amongst which I was devastated when the wonderful Peri was apparently murdered by the slippery Mentors of Thoros Beta, and the energetic Mel joined the Doctor amidst a space-bound whodunit. It was the latter outing which saw this adventure take a dramatic turn for me, as the highly-charged cliffhanger to Part Nine presaged Part Ten's even more frightening ending with the unveiling of the Vervoid-infected human, Ruth Baxter. When the subsequent week's instalment finally arrived, I took shelter by way of my newly-diagnosed myopia! More precisely, by discarding my new prescription spectacles and moving to the back of my parents' living room, the now blurred television screen allowed the reappearance of Doland's tragic assistant to be that bit more bearable. This sense of genuine trepidation – a real behind-the-sofa moment – was the last I was to experience as a young fan. Later seasons came and went with far less effect, as adolescence drew nearer and I simply wasn't as affected by what I was watching. Whether this change was due to the cynical attitude I alluded to earlier, or something else, it revealed the signal importance of this story's place in my life as a fan.

And it didn't end there. Pip and Jane Baker's lively murder mystery with liberal doses of alien horror led into two of the most gripping episodes I had ever seen. In fact, not since the final moments of *Logopolis* had I been so totally mesmerised, as I was by the twists and turns of Parts Thirteen and Fourteen of *The Trial of a Time Lord*. The incredible revelation of the Valyard's identity, the baffling duel in the Matrix culminating in one of the best cliffhangers in the series' original run, and the superb unmasking of Mr Popplewick to reveal the malign features of the Doctor's court antagonist; each set off a veritable maelstrom of thoughts and ideas in my mind. It was utterly compelling.

As the final episode's end credits rolled on a dark Saturday teatime in early December, I was convinced that the sixth Doctor would be back the following year to do battle with yet another collection of nasties. After all, in the wake of such a fantastic finish surely things could only get better?

Coincidentally, the next Saturday was my birthday and my parents' present to me consisted of a pair of walkie-talkies. That evening, with my mother in one room and myself in another, I used my new means of communication to regale her with the long and complicated tale to which I had been avidly attending over the previous fourteen weeks. That evening was one of childhood innocence, as I lost myself – and my poor mother! – in the somewhat labyrinthine machinations of the Valeyard, the true identity of a mysterious Earth-like planet named Ravalox, the devious dealings of Sil and Kiv, and a space liner replete with foul play and an all-new monster threat.

Things were never quite the same after that. The naïveté of childhood waned and I saw later seasons with a somewhat jaded eye. As time wore on I began to realise that the Doctor's lengthy trial had become a sort of pivot for me, as thereafter my more innocent perspective on the Time Lord and his TARDIS gave way to the unrelenting scrutiny of the teenager.

And yet that innocence is still somehow preserved, if you will, in those fourteen episodes, which remind me of a different, much younger me, who still hid behind sofas and dreamt of travelling with the Doctor in his mystifying police box.

Carry On Up the Totem
The Mysterious Planet by **Tony Jordan**, 53, London, UK
First story: **An Unearthly Child**

'It was the best of times, it was the worst of times, it was the age of wisdom, it was the age of foolishness, it was the epoch of belief, it was the epoch of incredulity, it was the season of Light, it was the season of Darkness, it was the spring of hope, it was the winter of despair, we had everything before us, we had nothing before us, we were all going direct to Heaven, we were all going direct the other way.'

In many ways, the opening paragraph of Charles Dickens' **A Tale of Two Cities** perfectly reflects what it was like to be a **Doctor Who** fan, and indeed organised fandom itself, in the mid-1980s. A triumphant 20th anniversary year, and an ever growing global fan base had, in less than two years, become a show in crisis with a fragmented following. It's long been my view that this situation was deliberately created by Jonathan Powell and Michael Grade following their senior appointments within the BBC. Their misjudgement at the response to the 'cancellation' of a show they disliked in early 1985, its subsequent re-instatement but in a much reduced and diminished manner, and the slow lingering demise that finally concluded on December 6th 1989 reflects badly on both men to this day.

But facts are facts, and the planned Season 23 was on ice. The proposed stories had sounded half decent, including the return of the Celestial Toymaker, the Ice Warriors and Sil, and the Autons. However at some stage, bearing in mind the cynical reduction from thirteen 45-minute episodes to fourteen 25-minute ones, a decision was made to scrap all existing plans.

Producer John Nathan-Turner has, for decades now, been a controversial figure – often derided for his lack of drama knowledge, and regularly criticised by those to whom he gave employment; in particular then-script editor, Eric Saward, who has on several occasions stuck the knife in.

There is, perhaps therefore, a supreme irony to the fact that it was Saward who suggested the idea of having the Doctor 'on trial' for the whole of the revised Season 23, in an unsubtle narrative parody of what was actually happening at Television Centre. JNT (in my opinion) foolhardily took this proposal on board, and we were left with *The Trial of a Time Lord*.

Paralleling the crisis within the show, fandom had descended into chaos. Schisms had developed during the 'cancellation crisis', following on from which the **Doctor Who** Appreciation Society (DWAS), the officially recognised fan club, found itself thousands of pounds due in the red. DWAS took drastic action to increase income and reduce costs, the single biggest project being its annual Panopticon convention. By the end of 1985, this had been scheduled for the weekend of September the 6th and 7th 1986, taking place at Imperial College, London. The event itself was a great success, and ensured the future of the Society. However fate decreed that the opening day of the event would also be the day of the first episode of **Doctor Who** in eighteen months. Part One of *The Mysterious Planet* would be broadcast on the giant screen in the Great Hall to an expectant, and packed, audience of over six hundred people...

Legendary writer Bob Holmes had been tasked with writing the first four episodes. He was a master of the great double act, from Jago and Litefoot to Stotz and Krelper, and many more besides. For this new story Holmes came up with what, sadly, proved to be his final pair, Glitz and Dibber. They were undoubtedly one of the highlights - unfortunately counterbalanced by the miscasting of Joan Sims as Warrior Queen Katryca. Now, Joan was an actress I loved but her drinking problems seemed palpably clear on screen.

But let's return to Imperial College. It's 5.45pm, the atmosphere in the Great Hall is euphoric, and not just because **Roland Rat The Series** has finished. This is followed by a trailer for the new autumn season on Children's BBC, culminating with **Dungeons and Dragons**. A brief countdown leads into the eruption of party poppers. Unfortunately it's a case of premature epoppulation, as the continuity announcer delights in telling us about the new series of **Telly Addicts**, which will follow in 25 minutes.

But, at long last, Dominic Glynn's new take on the famous theme plays as the credits roll, leading into *that* remarkable space station sequence filmed using a top of the range motion-controlled camera. Blimey, this is brilliant...

Unfortunately what we get for the remaining 24 minutes, and indeed subsequent three episodes, fails to live up to that opening scene. It's almost as if all the eggs had been placed in one small basket. I remember having a terrible feeling that Part One had actually been boring in places. And that was a problem for the whole Trial idea. The narrative could never flow well enough for long enough, before being broken up (*Mindwarp* perhaps being the sole exception). That night, September 6th 1986, Charles Dickens' words were going around in my brain – well at least until the alcohol kicked in.

Ultimately the high hopes that greeted *The Mysterious Planet* were, in reality, a false dawn. Within three months Colin Baker, a fine actor whose reputation as the Doctor has rightly been re-evaluated over the years, would be removed and nothing would be able to stop the BBC's slow but measured and inexorable destruction of one of its greatest ever assets.

Mindwarp: Minus Five Weeks

Mindwarp by **Matt Goddard**, 32, London, UK
First story: **The Ultimate Foe**

'An interior. A dark corridor of chiselled cave walls. Disorientated Thoros Alphan slaves waltz. Their ponchos bounce off each other and the stone. The caves are in panic, an alarm echoes continuously... But behind the rock, steady hands undertake an operation that will change the universe...'

It's the kind of thing I find myself craving for in a lot of science fiction tales now. Okay, not the ponchos – but the momentum, the threat, the hard science-fiction: all the things that can change the universe. I've loved all these facets in **Doctor Who** during its run, but not in *Mindwarp*. Not first time around... Because I missed it. In fact, I missed it by precisely five weeks.

I suspect that my first **Doctor Who** memory is also one of Michael Grade's favourites and Mary Whitehouse's least. The sixth Doctor drowning in quicksand. Or to be more accurate, quickgravel. Speckled, salt and pepper quickgravel. With hands. *The Ultimate Foe* scared the hell out of me so much that I didn't watch another episode until *Remembrance of the Daleks* two years later. By then the Daleks were far more approachable than those homicidal 'Carrie' hands. Also, my pre-ten nightmares had found reliable new reserves in **Bergerac** Easter specials. I wouldn't realise what I'd missed for seven years.

'In the flurry of whirling confusion, three figures desperately hurtle through the rock caves. They're not waltzing, they're single-mindedly racing for the laboratory, desperately hoping they're not too late...'

It wasn't too late to catch-up. The luxury of that *Trial of a Time Lord* VHS box set in 1993, with its primary coloured classic logo and its small blue 30th Anniversary banner... I think I stared at that logo more than anything else that year. That tin, first Doctor image on the base of course, is still my premium TARDIS reproduction with its wonderful Alister Pearson interior artwork hidden inside, just slightly torn. It was on 27th December 1993 that I carefully removed the black cassette and realised what I'd missed. Well, I say realised... In fact, my recent teen self just hadn't got a clue.

'A multi-coloured figure, his patchwork and cat broach discernable in the strobe, is caught in the confusion. Separated from his companions, he shakes his head, frantically searching for the right path...'

While I enjoyed the season, any analysis of *Mindwarp* left me shaking my head. While that's hardly a surprise, its multiple ambiguities were intriguing. *Mindwarp*, the standard schlock brain swap; *Mindwarp*, the confused protagonist playing a triple-bluffing game; *Mindwarp*, shoddy evidence; *Mindwarp*, Peri falling for Ycranos!

All those different possibilities and the name of the serial didn't even appear once.

'The desperate jester runs through the caves, as beside him a rectangle of white light dissolves with a slight rasping sound. The light resolves as a blue box. A blue police box. The figure stops in his tracks, as if caught in headlights.'

Like car headlights, very, very slow car headlights, *Mindwarp* was to catch up on me. I began to appreciate its storytelling in the great **Doctor Who** tradition. While parodying the series' controversial predicament – a sequel to *Vengeance on Varos*, yes! – the Trial season also managed to reinterpret revered prime slices of Baker (Tom). *The Mysterious Planet* presented *The Face of Evil* technology worship, while those **Ten Little Indians** – or *The Robots of Death* – would reappear in floral form. The serial would end in Dickensian melodrama, but in the middle, this little oddity added something more than just faux-*The Brain of Morbius*.

Even now, I'm astounded how much is packed into what the Valeyard calls the Doctor's 'next frightening adventure.'

Mainly, there was horror: **Frankenstein** body shock, lycanthropic mutations and lagoon monsters all in one place. There was civilisation meddling and the return of possibly the last great classic **Doctor Who** villain Sil (cue Nabil Shaban's laugh...). Then there was that rare companion death, possibly – forever etched into my mind alongside the Bowie lyrics, 'squawking like a pink monkey bird.'

'Fixed in a trance, the colourful character begins walking backwards in a perfect arc, straight into the open doors of the newly materialised blue box. The doors close, the box fades away.'

Time ultimately showed Trial to give the Time Lords a proper sign-off. I was always a fan of Robert Holmes' post-*The Deadly Assassin* Time Lords. To me they were so much more than a **Gormenghast**-lite bureaucratic satire. I was fascinated by the entropy of a civilisation rendered Time's Vampires. By Trial, the High Council were unseen, only noticed by a trail of interference, corruption and murder. Maybe.

'The foraging party have more success, breaking through the corridors to their goal, only to pause. They are trapped in time a time bubble until everything is in place.'

It's a savage end for what might be the funniest script in the **Doctor Who** canon. The casting is immaculate, from Patrick Ryecart and his tea to Brian Blessed and his 'scum.' They make me laugh every time.

Yes, five weeks later I would see the Valeyard *bamfing* his way through dunes, and that frock coat clashing with the speckled sand pebbles, almost ten years to the week since the fourth Doctor first entered the Matrix. That my first **Doctor Who** memory is the *death* of the Doctor is my personal mindwarp, but to think I missed the real one by five weeks... If you see me in the street, perhaps waltzing around, whatever you do don't mention it.

It would be like adding salt to a Mentor.

'Out in a space and time of blurring star fields, Time Lord engineers complete their magic. A pillar of light snares a blue box. At last, the eight episodes old Trial of a Time Lord can actually begin.'

Co-Incidences (Parts 9 - 12)

Terror Of The Vervoids by **Graeme Ferris**, 32, Edinburgh, UK / First story: **The Awakening**

Co-incidences? To be honest, I've never really believed in them. Chance maybe... But a full blown co-incidence?! As the Doctor says to Donna Noble... 'Sometimes I think there's way too much coincidence around you, Donna.' However, that changed; no blonde girl said two words in my ear; it involved my mother and a Christmas Tree... [*Cue Theme Music*]

What the hell was that though?! That though, was my first instinct, aged thirteen, when I put on videotape three of my *Trial of a Time Lord* (TARDIS-tin) box set, a set my dad bought me for Christmas. Who'd have thought it tonight? I'm still a bit baffled... Here I am, helping my mum put the last of her dishes away and having the usual random kind of conversation with her – nostalgia, putting the world to rights, latest family politics – when the conversation ends up tumbling onto the time I had chickenpox, aged six. It hit me bad apparently. I'd had it for weeks; was even delirious at one point... Except that's not how I remember it! I thought I'd laid on that sofa a week...

I hadn't been 'delirious'... Mel screaming in the Hydroponics Centre? The Doctor and Mel finding a half-turned Vervoid (that vein throbbed!) and the Black Hole of Tartarus! Three amazing cliffhangers and okay, it's four episodes, but I'll get to Genocide later! I blame my Dad... He liked watching it. After **Grandstand**. No, Dad! I'll never understand how to kick a rugby ball, but yes, thanks to him, my favourite stories are *Pyramids Of Mars* and *The Robots Of Death* and I thought for a long time that Tom Baker was a movie-Doctor like Peter Cushing... (Edit together *Terror of the Vervoids*, show it to your six-year-old child and he may end up writing about it 28 years later!) Sir George Hutchison being 'eaten' by the Malus, *Attack of the Cybermen* guest starring Thomas the Tank Engine (thanks to my mum taping over it for my brother), these are the only four episodes of **Doctor Who** that were as I remembered...

So why had I gone for videotape three? That would have made *such* an *amazing* close-up 'on-face' cliffhanger! (Black Hole of Tartarus!) I do remember following the Trial season... Or as much as a six-year-old could. Parts One to Four had seemed quite dull, Parts Five to Eight made no sense, although seemed *very* pink and had that cool slug thing in it. Oh and Peri died! But then came *Terror of the Vervoids*... Co-incidence began, little did I know!

'And there you have it!' No, I'm not about to spend the next page defending Melanie Bush. Yes, she was introduced in this story and from what I've seen, heard and read that was enough to put the heebie-jeebies up most fans – to be honest, she's not even that bad in this one! She's eager for an adventure, getting herself into trouble, screaming and asking questions... She's the archetypal companion! This was the first story that scared me...

What was in the Hydroponics Centre? The Doctor could sense it; 'A great evil...' And then that first cliffhanger! 'Poor Edwardes' being electrocuted, Mel screaming (as she should!) and then something shooting out of one of the pods. What the hell was it?! That second cliffhanger! The Doctor and Mel break into the guarded Isolation Room. There they find some hybrid – half human, half Vervoid. That huge vein-thing throbbing on the side of its head and then the third cliffhanger – Oh no! Bruchner is piloting the ship into the Black Hole of Tartarus. Videotape three showed me every moment as I'd remembered! And yes, the Vervoids themselves! I will not hear anything bad about them; Steven Moffat listen up! Okay, they do look a bit rude but for a six-year-old they were absolutely terrifying. Being six years old, I knew of, and as a thirteen year old had read *The Day of the Triffids*.

That terrified me too! Weeping Angels weep... Vervoids could kill; a poisonous thorn injected out of their clasped hand... Genius! And they could puff poisonous smoke out of their mouths. The build-up to seeing them ... only occasional glimpses ... seen behind a grill, an oily leaf left behind, empty pods from which they have emerged.

Co-incidences though? Flash forward to the future.... And no, it's not Genocide yet! I hadn't forgotten. Are you keeping up? It's Parts Nine to Twelve and a BBC recap may be needed before each sentence now! This excursion is only going twenty years into my future... I'll explain all this to my mate. 'This is a brill story to watch! Ignore X, Y and Z... Hopefully, one day they'll edit out those trial scenes... Yeah she's the Oxo woman...' . I've skipped straight to disc three of a DVD box set... One that my Dad's given to me for my 28th birthday... That same series my Dad introduced me to when I was a four-year-old (*The Awakening*)... Mum and camomile lotion (it was pretty serious; I was delirious – that rhymes!) on its original showing... thirteen years old and skipping straight to videotape three in my TARDIS *Trial Of A Time Lord* set. (Colin Baker was on the bottom!) But yet... *Terror Of The Vervoids*... Who cares?! That's what I know it as! The BBC have put a sticker on the front of the third DVD calling it that! And yeah, despite the very man who got me into **Doctor Who** in the first place buying this said box set for my 28th birthday (it was delayed by a month; Mum's estranged from him; separate reasons...) twenty-something years later, here I am helping her with the Christmas Tree, talking about baubles, chicken-pox and Vervoids. She's now watched it again since.

Actually... if a blonde girl came up to me and said two words – Terror, Vervoids – I'd know to point her in the direction of my Mum; she'd be the one who knew how to explain co-incidences (and definitions) to a six-year-old...

The Last Movement
The Ultimate Foe by **Will Ingram**, 34, Hampshire, UK
First story: **Logopolis**

1986 wasn't a good year to be a **Doctor Who** fan. You'd had to wait an entire year-and-a-half for the new series, and when it arrived it was barely half the length it was supposed to be, and what's more the original stories had been discarded in favour of one epic (don't get me started) storyline where the Doctor was effectively on trial for his re-commission.

Fortunately in 1986 I wasn't a fan. I'd never even heard of the word 'hiatus', let alone used it. I was just an eight-year-old, into stickers and climbing trees, and therefore was far better qualified to actually enjoy what was being shown on Saturday on BBC1. Yes including **Roland Rat: the Series**.

Strangely enough, I have only very patchy memories of the opening eight episodes of Trial when they went out; I'd barely even noticed Peri being killed off. Perhaps there was an exciting import on what we simply used to call the other side, and I'd missed a few episodes along the way. Maybe our family had simply had a busy social calendar that autumn? It wasn't until Season 25 that **Doctor Who** had taken such an important place in my life that to watch it became the law, an immovable object that needed to be planned around.

Then, the *Terror of the Vervoids* episodes made me sit up and take notice. I had no prejudices about Bonnie Langford, other than perhaps the vaguest of assumed second-hand sneers. *Terror of the Vervoids* had it in spades, whatever it was. A classic whodunit plot, interesting characters, decent acting, nifty design and pacy direction. Not to mention two of the best cliffhangers of the sixth Doctor's whole run, not including the end of Part Twelve itself. At last the Valeyard ups the stakes to threaten the Doctor's very existence, arguably several episodes late.

So, the Vulvoids dispensed with, we have the finale. The bit where everything would tie up neatly into a satisfying conclusion and point the way forward. Or at least should have done. As every fan knows, fate intervened and robbed us of Robert Holmes before those pesky ends could be properly tied up. The Eric Saward / JNT partnership imploded, and the drafted ending went up in a puff of legal smoke, emitted in the wake of the swiftly departing script editor. The Bakers were swiftly recruited to create a conclusion from scratch in two weeks, using only chicken wire and a thesaurus. It was a right mess.

No of course it wasn't. Of course 'the fans' would decree that it was bound to be awful, and that Bob Holmes' Part Fourteen would have been far superior. Are these the same fans who largely dismiss his Parts One to Four as a tedious runaround? The eight-year-old version of me loved Part Thirteen too. 'The Master is involved? Wow! The Valeyard is the Doctor? Whoa! The Doctor's chasing the Valeyard into a virtual universe? Fantastic!'

I was several years too young to have seen *The Deadly Assassin*, so the Matrix was a new concept. Clearly *anything* could happen, as made shockingly clear by those arms thrusting out of the water barrel. Following the lovely scene with the two Popplewicks, the Doctor is pulled down into the shingle by more grasping hands and both times it's the anonymity which sells the horror. Years later, when I saw George Romero's **Day of the Dead**, the opening dream sequence brought this scene to mind in a second. And the echoes continue, the voice-over of the Valeyard recalling those of Goth in the earlier story.

The madness continues into Part Fourteen. What's not to like? Yes the Bakers' script is quirky, but it's also remarkably entertaining, chock-full of colourful dialogue and literary references. The fact that it's hard to place some of them (for this patchily educated wretch at least) is neither here nor there.

One of the highlights is the reveal of the fake courtroom, which in production terms is perhaps sold a little short by the limitations of the SFX. However, dramatically it's a masterstroke, at least to the eight-year-old of 1986. Even now after many years and repeated viewing it still works exactly as it should and no amount of over-egging the pudding by Bonnie and the Bakers can spoil it.

Alas, the Doctor's cunning plan is thwarted by his new chum, and they move to confront the Valeyard via the most convincing example in the series' history of removing a rubber mask (though it's mostly up against masks of Roger Delgado that are themselves only marginally more believable than Michael Myers' impression of Bill Shatner). Still, he does have time for a quick Dr Evil moment after revealing his rather unimaginative plan.

Meanwhile Gallifrey is turning to shit (apparently) and the Master is twirling his moustache at the court room as he prepares to take over. But of course it doesn't quite go to plan, either for him or the Valeyard. They both get a sonic something up the bracket and the Time Lords duck and cover. The Inquisitor takes charge, as the Doctor bids farewell, assured that Peri is not dead after all. Don't have nightmares, kids.

However, it's no damp squib final episode, just a conventional one. It might not be a great Part Fourteen, but it makes a pretty decent Part Two. I never knew anything back then about the troubles behind the scenes, I could only take it all on face value. With these final two episodes, **Doctor Who** had never been bolder, madder or more colourful, and I loved it. As Sid Sutton's credit sequence faded for the last time ever, it'd been a damn entertaining ride. And isn't that all that matters?

The Seventh Doctor Who

If the **Doctor Who** of the 1980s had hitherto been moving further and further away from its successes in the salad days of the 1970s, then the arrival of the seventh and final incarnation of the original run heralded instead a brave new period of reinvention and reengagement with the series' core concepts.

Gone were the adult styling and backwards-looking continuities that had dogged the tenancy of the seventh Doctor Who's predecessor, in place of which an emphasis on originality and a more cartoon-like approach were the order of the day. This new Doctor Who was as likely to find himself in the kind of metaphorical landscape that his black-and-white forerunners had occasioned to visit as he was the gritty action-adventure backdrop of his immediate precursor. The series seemed to be finally coming of age, by embracing its heritage as a children's show that the whole family might enjoy.

But that's where the problem lay. In this new era of time-lapsed viewing, and positioned against one of the behemoths of modern television, the **Doctor Who** of the late 1980s was destined not to swim but to sink, official viewing figures falling to among the lowest the programme had ever recorded. Which is not to say that people weren't watching the programme any more, they simply weren't watching it as it was broadcast. It wasn't as if people didn't care either, for although the seventh Doctor Who and his signature companion Ace might have divided reactions among fans who had been more used to the show growing up with them, these characters are now among the most fondly-remembered of the series' last decade.

All this was taking place simultaneous with a new competitor for the contemporary **Doctor Who** follower's affections; the home video release. By the late 1980s, BBC Video were slowly finding their feet in the domestic sell-through market, with the popular third and fourth incarnations of the character gradually finding regular representation in the homes of fans, a situation that had (Target book adaptations aside) never occurred before. Suddenly the current Doctor Who wasn't the only Doctor Who to which enthusiasts had access, and in this brave new world of viewing-to-demand, it was inevitable that comparisons would be made and contrasts drawn.

By the time the 1990s arrived and the series departed the broadcast wavelengths ('**Doctor Who** will return in a new series next year,' was the usual end-of-season sign-off, or words to that effect; but this time, there *were* no words to that effect), it was the seventh Doctor Who and his imaginative but evocative progress that became the template from which a new kind of **Doctor Who** would spring ... but that's a story for another book.

Time and Time and the Rani

Time and the Rani by **Andrew Blair**, 27, Edinburgh, UK
First story: **Pyramids of Mars**

March 2008: I see the VHS of *Time and the Rani* in the British Heart Foundation charity shop on Bell Street in St Andrews. Because the cover – which I seem to remember liking – is pink, I buy it for my friend Ali, who likes pink. Not wanting her to get the wrong idea about this gift, I explain that she is the only person I know with a VCR in her flat. She remains somewhat bemused by this chain of events.

September 1987: I am almost two years old. I have probably never heard of **Doctor Who.** *Time and the Rani* is broadcast and I remain completely unaware. In all likelihood I am sitting on a brown carpet in a bungalow in Fortrose trying to cram multicoloured shapes into the back of Thomas the Tank Engine. That sounds like the sort of thing I would have done.

April 2008: I am in House 36 in Albany Park Students' accommodation in St Andrews, one of a series of small semi-detached pebble-dashed greynesses. The North Sea loiters outside. Dog walkers are trying to remain upright in the constant bluster, and Americans are wearing shorts for no readily discernible reason. The BBC ident and jingle austerely hover on screen, then a CG TARDIS is tumultuously buffeted around by rainbows fired from Kate O'Mara's massive weapon. The girl is left, for it is the man she wants. A giant bat staggers into view and turns over Sylvester McCoy, whose features blur and morph into those of Sylvester McCoy.

'It's not always this camp,' I say.

Twenty-five minutes later I am finding it increasingly hard to defend this statement.

December 2012: Ali and I are sitting in our flat. We are about to watch the DVD of *Time and the Rani*.

'Do you remember when I bought you the video of this?' I ask.

'Yeah,' Ali says, 'You texted to tell me and I thought you meant it for someone else.'

April 2008: 'Why do the aliens run like that?' Ali asked me, probably.

'It seemed like a good idea at the time?'

'Why did that alien decide to pick up Mel and carry her off?'

'It seemed like a good idea at the time?'

'Why are we watching this?'

'...'

December 2012: We watch *Time and the Rani* again and are amazed to discover that **Doctor Who** beat **The Thick of It** to 'Quiet Bat People' by twenty-five years. We speculate as to exactly what sort of relationship do Urak and the Rani have. We ask ourselves 'Why does *everyone* trip up on that step?' and 'How do the Lakertyans know how to spell 'Einstein' upon hearing the word for the first time?'

The problem with *Time and the Rani,* I conclude, is that it does not maintain its effervescent insanity beyond the first episode. Episode Four has its own charming disregard for sense, which leads me to think that *Time and the Rani* might well be a brilliant 45-minute romp of the ilk that the show now pulls off effortlessly. It's got the Doctor being weird and Matt Smithy! It's got a giant talking brain! Einstein and the Doctor arguing! Lots of running! Giant bats! Elvis references and a big meteor made of rubbish science! 'Imagine!' I say to Ali.

She nods and continues playing Tetris.

But come on, imagine *Time and the Rani* with *time* on its side. For all its impressive deployment of nascent CGI, it needs a tone meeting and someone to say 'No' when the idea of using tinsel to decorate a tunnel is mooted.

And the guy who plays Brendan in **Hollyoaks** as the Rani's henchman.

September 1987: A two-year-old boy in Fortrose is unaware of **Doctor Who.** He is preoccupied with the removal of plastic colourful shapes from a plastic replica of Thomas the Tank Engine, and trying to eat chocolate mousse from a carton without the aid of cutlery. He fails to notice an old bearded man at the window, holding a brightly coloured plastic box.

'Hey,' the man shouts, 'Don't ask how I got here – but it was *brilliant* – just remember this cover...'

The boy stares at the man in the window, and the glaring pink object he is brandishing...

'Remember it,' the man shouts. 'It'll be surprisingly helpful.'

The boy ignores this and squeezes chocolate mousse over his face, then giggles for a bit and throws a plastic yellow star across the floor.

'Oh,' says the man. 'So that's where that photo came from.'

He leaves the toddler gleefully spreading mousse across his face. Soon he will be found in this state by his mother and photographed for posterity.

December 2012: 'Do you think,' I say hesitantly, 'That watching *Time and the Rani* made any difference to us getting together?'

'No,' Ali replies.

'Oh.'

'I mean, I quite like *Time and the Rani*, because it's very silly. But "proper" **Doctor Who** fans don't like it, do they? You don't *like* it.'

A pause.

She's right. I don't like it.

'Although,' she adds, 'I suppose it prepared me for the fact that **Doctor Who** fans take everything way too seriously.'

I have issues with these statements. I don't dislike *Time and the Rani* because it is silly. It's because it's not silly *enough*. If it managed to remain about as sensible as a Cornish piece of hate weeping shards of Monday up a chimney throughout its four episodes, then I think it'd win people's hearts through sheer perseverance.

And furthermore, **Doctor Who** fans don't take everything way too seriously.

Just **Doctor Who**.

July 1995: *Time and the Rani* is released on VHS. My brother buys it and I buy *The Mark of the Rani*. While neither are our favourite episodes, we certainly don't hate them.

I prefer the cover of *Time and the Rani* though. To this day I have no idea why.

Paradise Regained
Paradise Towers by **Beth Ward**, 28, Bristol, UK

I have a friend. He's a good friend; we've known each other for a few years now. Our friendship is almost entirely predicated on a mutual love for **Doctor Who** and sustained by endless disagreements on the subject. Our formative experiences of the programme are very different. He grew up in the 1970s, discovered **Doctor Who as** a boy and watched serials unfold week on week with his peers. He still not so secretly thinks of Jon Pertwee as his dad and speaks mournfully of the injustice of missing an episode of *Terror of the Zygons* when forced to attend some family function or other. I, on the other hand, came to the series on Sky television in the mid-1990s, during school holidays and sometimes in term time, swaddled in a blanket with a hot, lemony drink. As a result of this my Doctor seemed to change his face week on week, and to make a critical distinction between any of these new idols was inconceivable. I was ten years old for every incarnation, and I loved them all (I don't remember seeing much of the sixth Doctor at the time).

My friend claims to have stopped watching when Tom Baker left, a declaration he'll make at any and every opportunity. Apparently he was too old and Peter Davison was too camp, but he admits to appreciating Tegan's charms. He has little to say on the subject of Colin Baker, and the purest vitriol is reserved for the seventh Doctor, utterly unfairly in my eyes and he proudly admits to never having watched an episode script edited by Andrew Cartmel. At least he did. My friend also insists that as a true fan there is no **Doctor Who** he truly hates. He has a tendency to contradict himself. I accept it as part of his charm.

I have a great affection for *Paradise Towers* and have never understood why it's so looked down upon, but that's an argument for another book. Having said that I'd struggle to attach great sentimentality or significant personal epiphanies to it, nothing so much as a superficial but heart-warming coming of age story. If asked to name a serial that punctuated a definitive point in my life, or resonated with some fundamental belief I held this would not be it. But that's my life; and this story isn't really about me, it's about my friend.

I'll confess to testing Sylvester McCoy's proverbial waters somewhat cautiously, supervising my friend's first viewing with *The Curse of Fenric*. I'd already gifted him a copy of *Paradise Towers* by this point and was determined to see him sit through it no matter how he fared with the Season 26 story. To his great surprise *The Curse of Fenric* saw him rapt. I probably said something smug about never having doubted that it would. There was praise for performances and production, and deep contrition for years of being a self-described 'Sylvester denier.' The preparatory screening was an unqualified success.

A few weeks later when I arrived at his house to find *Paradise Towers* still sealed I was insistent. This was met with a surprising level of resistance considering how well *The Curse of Fenric* had been received, but after some initial grumbling, a grunt of displeasure and a few derisive snorts the shrink-wrap came off. Soon that most beautiful of utterances rang out across the room, those innocuous words that tell you something special is about to happen, the calm and reassuring tone that incongruously engenders skin tingling excitement, 'To select audio navigation press enter now.'

For obvious reasons I navigated past the main menu screen as quickly as my chubby little sausage fingers would allow. Having checked that we were both sitting comfortably we began.

After the first episode my friend turned to me, paused for breath, cocked his head to one side, said nothing, turned back to the screen, back to me... Once I was confident that he wasn't having a stroke I asked him what he thought so far. He asked me why he'd been told that Richard Briers overacted in this serial, as he thought the portrayal of a bureaucratic megalomaniac was wholly appropriate. The mood was good, we forged ahead.

His enthusiasm was such that we didn't stop to dissect Part Two, we went straight for the third episode, with another, brief objection during the opening credits as to why the Chief Caretaker was criticised so widely for what was clearly such a subtle and nuanced performance. I nodded in agreement, but moved the bottle of rum out of his reach.

For the better part of two hours we sat at right angles to one another, him transfixed by the screen, and me watching his reactions as closely as I could without being hit in the face when he flailed with delight. Very occasionally he would turn to me, point at the television and declare a some bit of business or line of dialogue particularly noteworthy, but there was no time to talk about why, as to do so would risk missing some other spasm-inducing set piece.

Halfway through the final episode he looked at me, stony faced and asked if 'this' was what the fuss was about regarding Briers' performance.

I may be misremembering for the sake of my own anecdote, but believe I saw some tears during Pex's memorial. I'm fairly certain there were tears. I'm sure there were tears. Without a shadow of a doubt, there were definitely tears.

When it was over I asked my friend, the man who so loathed the seventh Doctor for a quarter of a century, what he thought.

'That was top!'

Here's To The Future
Delta and the Bannermen by **Christopher Bryant**, 36, Woking, UK / First story: **Full Circle**

In 1987, I used to make up **Doctor Who** stories all the time. I was eleven years old and full of creativity which had yet to be harnessed or shaped – or stifled – in any way. So I poured it all into an unending stream of **Doctor Who** stories.

Some of these stories were acted out with my two best friends, Fred and Richard. I'd started playing **Doctor Who** in the playground way back at primary school; I recall using a bike shed as a spaceship as my friend Wayne (playing Tegan) was sucked out of the airlock. But in 1987, these stories usually began in the TARDIS (a bin on a desk played the console) which would land somewhere and we'd all go out to investigate. After some exploring, the Doctor would vanish as I went and hid behind a curtain, so that I could switch roles and re-emerge as the story's villain. I'd declaim something like, 'Nya-ha-har! I am Scaroth!' and we'd all sing the theme tune because it was the cliffhanger. Then I'd sit down to explain to Fred and Richard exactly who the Jagaroth or the Ogrons or the Monoids were.

Some of these stories were created using my **Star Wars** figures. I had a lot of these, but it was rare indeed that they were called upon to re-enact anything from **Star Wars**. Instead, the seventh Doctor (played by Luke Skywalker: Jedi Knight) and Ace (Princess Leia: Hoth Outfit) would arrive in the TARDIS (old bubble bath bottle) and battle against the Master (Imperial Commander), a Cyberman (Death Star Droid), an Ice Warrior (Greedo) or whoever else I felt one of my toys looked a little bit like. In four-episode epics.

Some of these stories were created in very primitive comic strips, many of which would be sequels to a novelisation I'd read recently (I definitely created a Peladon sequel before Gary Russell). On one occasion, I recall creating a version of **The Twelve Tasks of Asterix** but with the Doctor instead of Asterix. It wasn't very good.

Some of these stories were created in essay form, as I would twist whatever task I was given to fit my own agenda. An essay on Lady Macbeth's 'Things without all remedy should be without regard' became a re-telling of the Doctor's two-strands dilemma in *Genesis of the Daleks*. 'The day I'll never forget,' became the story of how the Doctor met his old enemies in mixed-up form: so, a half-Dalek/half-Cyberman, for example. He saw each new threat off by shooting it, then left in the TARDIS. I even remember writing a bastardised version of *The Robots of Death* without robots: instead, it was Kerril who killed everyone with a weird mouth-zapping-thing.

Over the course of my life – hell, over the course of 1987 alone – I must have created more **Doctor Who** stories than the BBC have in fifty years. But do you know what? At no point have I ever – *ever* – created anything even remotely like *Delta and the Bannermen*.

How on earth did Malcolm Kohll come up with this? How did he even conceptualise it, let alone think that it would be perfect for **Doctor Who**? 'A refugee, the last of her race, flees from a genocidal warlord and hitches a lift on a space bus full of tourists which pitches up in a 1950s Welsh Butlins with a beekeeper, two FBI agents and a motorcycle-riding rock'n'roll singer.' It's impossible to imagine in any season other than the twenty-fourth, the least-loved season of them all.

Perhaps the key, though, is to consider that this idea, this script, this mayhem was commissioned and approved by incoming script editor Andrew Cartmel. He obviously thought this was exactly the sort of thing he was after. It does, if you squint, have its roots in **Doctor Who**'s tradition: the Bannermen marching around the Welsh countryside is no stranger than Zygons in Scotland or Dæmons in Aldbourne. The eccentricity of some of the supporting characters can be found in *The Talons of Weng-Chiang* or *The Three Doctors*. But it moves beyond those roots to create something unlike anything we've ever seen before. No wonder people hated it.

Once you consider the surprising idea that *Delta and the Bannermen* represents the script editor's idea of what **Doctor Who** should be like in 1987, then Season 24 starts to make sense. *Paradise Towers* and *Dragonfire* hark back to the Hinchcliffe era in their basic set-up, but are realised through the Cartmel prism. The results are unsatisfying, predictably so. All three stories are compromised by their creators' attempts to fit into more than one box at once. *Delta and the Bannermen* succeeds on its own terms – not on ours.

I think it's probably a good thing that the show didn't continue in this style. I shudder to imagine a world where every story from 1988 and 1989 mimicked this escapade. But Cartmel did continue to preside over new forms of **Doctor Who**: there's nothing else in the canon quite like *Ghost Light* or *The Happiness Patrol* either. With *Survival*, he effectively produced a pilot for the Russell T Davies era (not to mention *Delta and the Bannermen* foreshadowing the entire series upping sticks and moving to Wales in the 21st century).

We always say that one of **Doctor Who**'s best qualities is that it can go anywhere and do anything. Thank goodness for visionaries like Cartmel and Kohll, who allow it to do just that. Without them, the series would be as repetitive and uninspired as my own creative efforts back in 1987; as uniform and unimpressive as Gavrok's faceless army. The **Doctor Who** universe needs mavericks like the Doctor, like Goronwy and like *Delta and the Bannermen*.

Don't Get Your Delicates in a Twist

Dragonfire by **Scott Burditt**, 37, Cheshire, UK
First story: **Earthshock**

'Leave the girl, it's the man I want.'

I love *Dragonfire*. It's my favourite story. It's full of classic moments, witty one-liners, and tight inspiring direction and comes straight off the back of the equally amazing *Delta and the Bannermen*. Oh, who am I kidding? To be honest, I'm sulking. I wanted to write about *Time and the Rani* but it was already taken. 'Leave the girl, it's the man I want.' It would have been nice to have used that line as my opening gambit. I'm going to use it anyway.

Dragonfire eh? If you feel like moaning about new **Doctor Who**, find a time traveller and go back in time and watch all of **Doctor Who** in 1987 (or watch a DVD if you find that easier) and you'll soon change your mind.

Dragonfire won't be paid much attention by many because Season 24's offerings sit right at the bottom of the huge pile of stories you could spend your valuable spare time watching for a very good reason. I count myself as one of the lucky ones who didn't share the awful experience of *Dragonfire* with a friend or family. I was safe from the flushed cheeks and the awful sinking feeling that the BBC no longer cared if you travelled with **Doctor Who** or not. To this day I'm still sulking that the BBC didn't produce another series of **The Tripods** instead of **Doctor Who** to finish off the story properly. At the time it felt epic. The music alone gave me goose bumps. Oh well. After the shockingly awful *Delta and the Bannermen*, my **Doctor Who** viewing went deep underground. Every week until its demise in 1989, I would watch the series in my bedroom on a black and white television. We weren't a rich family and we only had one VHS tape each at my house (with our names on) and it was already full. So I watched *Dragonfire* on a very old monochrome 12-inch screen which I had been given to play games on my Commodore 64. I would plug in my bright orange sponge-covered headphones and eat chocolate biscuits, drinking milk without interruption.

What is now considered a worthy and prominent series, **Doctor Who** was a very different beast in 1987, but luckily this pantomime version ended after one season. *Dragonfire* was a turning point in quality, not that I noticed at the time. For me, Ace saved the series. A sulky, teenage, explosive-loving arty type with her comedy 'youf' speak. Wicked!

From what I remember of it first time around, *Dragonfire* was a story full of lies. There was no recognisable Dragon, no fire and no treasure, just inept physical comedy. Mel provides the biggest shock when she suddenly proves an interesting companion by running off with loveable rogue Glitz right at the end! Oh, how I'd love to have seen how that one would have played out.

Having viewed *Dragonfire* properly on shiny DVD for the first time in years, the last time was from a colour VHS in the mid-1990s, I can honestly say that the very literal cliffhanger at the close of Part One is not the much derided piece of crap I once thought it was. For me, it's an absolute joy. Why anyone (including the director) now seems to think it's a problem is totally beyond me. That lovely sinking-feeling music that's played over it never fails to have me in stitches when I see it.

If you look carefully at the end of Part One, the gantry below the Doctor as he hangs from the end of his brolly is clearly visible in the final shot, and the drop isn't actually that far. If you take away the Doctor's height plus the brolly, it is approximately just the height of the Doctor to the next level. It's not, as some fans would have you believe, magically added in Part Two. What's more surprising is the Doctor briefly touching Glitz's crotch as a thank you for rescuing him.

Kane is a great villain in this story. It's a nice twist, to have what is effectively a male version of the Snow Queen. The satin white Nazi-esque clothing he wears along with the white make-up is effective and I would love to have that in my wardrobe.

I'm still confused why the woman from the café and especially her daughter, were so prominent in this story as they add nothing, apart from getting Ace the sack and wasting a bit of time in Part Three.

The return of Glitz (unfortunately without Dibber) is very welcome. You begin to wonder if he could have been replaced with Rodney from **Only Fools and Horses**. There is also an actor in the background of the café that at the time I thought looked like Prince Andrew. From this point onwards for no reason whatsoever Ace refers to the Doctor, annoyingly, as Professor, presumably just to wind him up. After Mel and Ace are told they can't come along by Glitz because it's too dangerous for girls, Ace calls him a 'male chauvinist bilge-bag.' Bilge-bag, to this day, is a term I've never heard anyone say. I really like the bit where the Doctor is leaving this scene though. He sees what looks like a cuddly baby Tetrap and goes to tickle it and it surprises him by growling. Made me laugh then, still makes me laugh now.

I think if the Dragon had been generally more impressive, it would have been more memorable. The VHS cover would lead you to believe it was amazingly powerful. For me, I still think this story played better as I remember it, in black and white. I'll leave the last words to Ace then.

'This is naff. This is mega-naff.'

Remembrance
Remembrance of the Daleks by **Nicholas Blake**, 29, Nottingham UK

'Leave your daydreaming outside the classroom,' the teacher said, dragging me back to reality. 'There's plenty of time for that at break.'

Was he talking about me? I wasn't a daydreamer. I was a goody two-shoes who paid attention during lessons. But yeah, at this point I was a tad distracted. I was counting down the days until I would finally get hold of something. It seems a bit silly now. But it wasn't to me. I was so excited about it.

It was a video box set. Or a 'Superb Limited Edition Souvenir Tin', according to the advert Dad found in the newspaper. I remember it vividly, mostly because I cut it out and stuck it to my wall with my other clippings about the 30th anniversary in 1993.

The box set was simply called: 'The Daleks'. And if there was one thing I loved, it was Daleks. I loved them *so* much.

I loved the yellow ones which could turn themselves invisible in *Planet of the Daleks*, one of the stories repeated the previous year. I adored the metallic black ones eerily gliding through *Genesis of the Daleks* (also repeated). But I especially loved the white and gold ones in *Revelation of the Daleks*. They got me so excited I kept rewinding the video I'd taped the episodes onto and making everybody in my family see the strangely-coloured Dalek. When the black Daleks also turned up at the end and they all had a scrap, I was thrilled.

I had to have that box set. There was nothing I'd ever wanted more in my nine years of life. The only trouble was, it cost £29.99.

Now, £29.99 was a lot of money in 1993. And when you're nine, it's a fortune, especially when you only get £1 a week pocket money which you usually squander on sweets.

Well, I reasoned, I just wouldn't buy any more sweets. A quick calculation soon revealed that it would take thirty weeks to raise enough money to buy it. Which was, to be honest, far, far too long. I went to my parents with my conundrum. Where does money come from and how can I get hold of it to buy this armour-plated Dalek extravaganza?

The answer turned out to be 'jobs'. Each weekday I would do four helpful things around the house, for five pence each. That made twenty pence a day, a whole extra pound a week. Add on a tenner I'd been given for my birthday, and we'd cut the waiting time down to ten weeks. Easy.

So I spent my free time after school vacuuming, stacking and unstacking the dishwasher, dusting, polishing, and laying the kitchen table. When Mr Jones from next door gave me a pound for helping collect apples for him from our tree, Mum pleaded with me not to waste it on my video fund. 'Buy some sweets or something,' she said. But I wasn't going to waste that money on delicious ephemeral treats! That pound represented a whole week's work! Even when we went on holiday to Spain I still begged to be given jobs to do to earn my box set money. I had to carry on or I wouldn't get my daydreaming fix.

The daydreaming continued. Also, I drew Daleks. Lots of Daleks. At school during wet breaks I would draw even more, larger and larger, dinner ladies leaning over my shoulder to say things like, 'Someone's a **Doctor Who** fan!' Large A3 effigies I'd created appeared on my bedroom walls: black and white Daleks, in battle as I slept. 'Why are they shooting each other?' my Dad asked when he saw it. He didn't understand that Daleks were so evil they even hated their own race just because they were different colours.

I wondered if there would be any white Daleks in the video box set. That's what I really wanted. I wanted white Daleks versus black Daleks. Oh, and Davros. Also I wanted the real Doctor, not any of the other actors pretending to be the Doctor. The true Doctor had a panama hat and question mark brolly. Would he be in it? I studied the newspaper advert every day, wondering if I'd suddenly see something that would reveal what the videos were about. But beyond saying it contained *The Chase* and *Remembrance of the Daleks* (two stories I'd never heard of), there were no other clues.

Sure, there were low points. During my darkest moments I would even doubt if the box set had anything to do with Daleks whatsoever. I mean, sure, it said 'The Daleks' on the advert, and there were things which looked like Daleks in the image, but maybe 'Daleks' means something else to grown-ups. Something not to do with **Doctor Who** at all. The advert didn't mention **Doctor Who**; the videos could contain anything. Only time would tell.

But at school I continued daydreaming, visions of white Daleks and black Daleks zapping each other in laser battles, explosions filling my head as I would swing around and around a pole in the corner of the playground. There were plenty more long days to crawl by before I could go to WH Smiths with my thirty shiny pound coins and collect my prize. But would it all be worth it? Would it satisfy my intense childhood longing?

Twenty years later, my Dalek box set is battered, crumpled and rusting. One of the cardboard slipcases is missing. Both videos are replaced by DVD versions. Yet I'll never throw it out. I dreamt of that box set for months, and it didn't disappoint. *Remembrance of the Daleks* is still my favourite **Doctor Who** story.

Time did tell. It always does.

Happiness is a Man Called Kandy

The Happiness Patrol by **Lewis Christian,** 19, Lancashire, UK / First story: **Rise of the Cybermen**

'If you want to view paradise, simply look around and view it.'

What do you get if you cross **Doctor Who** with Willy Wonka, Margaret Thatcher, and Bertie Bassett?

I adore this story, possibly more than any other in **Doctor Who**'s history. The only way to improve it, in my opinion, would be to add Whizzkid from *The Greatest Show in the Galaxy*. Everything about *The Happiness Patrol* is just brilliant. The story comes at a turning point in the Sylvester McCoy era – Season 25 sees the show change from camp to creepy, from daft to dangerous. This season, and this story especially, is the half-way point, successfully incorporating ingredients of the whimsical with side-servings of darkness.

These days, I've seen the McCoy era undergo a lot of re-evaluation within fandom and it warms my heart to see this because it's truly a magnificent period of the show. Creepy clowns, killer Kandy robots, Merlin mysteries, Cheetah people, explosive companions, Iceworlds, haunted houses, mythical Gods, camp Time Lords, deadly cleaners, ancient evils and, best of all, a world where it's illegal to be miserable. How can you not at least love the creativity and originality of this inventive era? It baffles me, it really does.

Maybe it has something to do with my age and my experience with Seasons 24 to 26. I was born in 1993, the year of the pickles and gherkins in a time jar (or something), and I therefore missed being able to see any of classic **Doctor Who** as it originally aired. I have therefore had to visit the past through books, forums and DVDs... I never got to see the classic series run 'decline in quality,' I never got to witness the backlash against McCoy, I never got to see the show 'become too violent,' etc. Instead, what I have been able to see is ... **Doctor Who**. The McCoy era, for me, is *just another era* of the show. And I'm happy to say it's my favourite era. I only wish it wasn't so short (but that's a discussion for another time, as I would've preferred the show to continue in the style of Seasons 24 and 25, rather than the new darker direction which crept in when Season 26 came along).

Whatever you think of the McCoy era, you really cannot deny the fact it was a breath of fresh air. It still had continuity from the past (hello Brigadier, hello Rani, hello 'President Elect of the High Council of Time Lords, keeper of the legacy of Rassilon, defender of the laws of time') but it was bold enough to head in a new direction. And, sure, it maybe delved a little too far into the mythical and the fantastical, but at least it was daring to venture into new ground. It appears that JNT allowed the writers more freedom in the McCoy era and this did the show a lot of good. *The Happiness Patrol* and *The Greatest Show in the Galaxy* embody this – I mean, can you imagine the JNT of Seasons 19 and 20 allowing episodes like this to be written and produced?

McCoy's era was fantastic. Utterly bloody fantastic. And so now I've discussed the McCoy era quite generally, let's focus in on *The Happiness Patrol*.

It's full of ideas. It's fun, and it's creepy. It dares to tackle Thatcher's government. It has a manipulative and mysterious seventh Doctor, midway between his goofy Season 24 persona and his meddling Season 26 character. It's Ace's first trip to an alien world (not counting Iceworld) and she's given a lot to do. There are Oompa-Loompa Pipe People living in the sewers below the ground. There's *that* sniper scene. But, best of all, there's a giant evil Bertie Bassett robot in a multi-coloured Wonka-esque Kandy Kitchen, complete with deadly sweets and sinister fairground music!

The Kandyman himself is great – a perfect **Doctor Who** baddie. Many fans ridicule him but, again, I'm baffled as to why. Steven Moffat regularly aims to make the mundane quite scary – the darkness (Vashta Nerada), the monster under the bed (see: *The Girl in the Fireplace*), stone statues which come to life ... in a similar vein, Graeme Curry does the same thing about twenty years earlier. He takes kids' candy and turns it into poison. He takes the sweet shop owner and turns him sour. It's a genius concept, and the realisation is brilliantly effective. He may not be taken entirely seriously in-story (to stop him, simply spill some lemonade at his feet) but the mesmerising swirly eyes and childlike voice combine to make the most chilling and creepiest **Doctor Who** robot ever. It's just a crying shame he didn't get more screen time. He's the perfect monster to pit against the seventh Doctor. And, while I know for a fact it'll never happen, as many fans petition for the return of the Meddling Monk and the Zygons, I'll always be wishing for another delicious adventure with a rebuilt Kandyman.

I'll always champion Sylvester McCoy's seventh Doctor. I'll always defend Season 24. I'll always love Season 25. And, most of all, I'll always adore *The Happiness Patrol*. There's no other story quite like it, and there probably never will be again.

What's that? Is that the sound of empires topping? No, it's the sound of fandom crying out in horror. Oh, happy days.

Special Edition
Silver Nemesis by **Stephen Candy**, 35, Haywards Heath, UK / First Story: **Logopolis**

Enjoying a show like **Doctor Who** as a child and then growing up into a dedicated adult fan is an exciting journey of discovery, full of little steps and realisations. When *Silver Nemesis* was broadcast in 1988 as **Doctor Who**'s 25th anniversary story, I was eleven years old. I had enjoyed the show for all my childhood and had already begun reading some of the 'behind the scenes' books (although, despite a collection of early **Weekly** issues I was not – yet – a regular reader of **Doctor Who Magazine**). The Cybermen had established themselves as my favourite monsters through repeated viewings of *The Five Doctors*, hired from our local 'Mr Video' rental store, so seeing them return in *Silver Nemesis* was a real treat. Sadly I did not make a home video recording of the story and this gave rise a few years later to that fan rite-of-passage of borrowing episodes from fellow fans on tape. A friend had the whole McCoy series and I was glad to re-visit those I had not recorded myself.

Growing up can also mean growing more critical and it was not until I was a regular reader of **DWM** in the early 1990s that I realised that the story had not been universally well-received! The concepts of 'plot-holes' and 'nit-picking' – embraced and even enjoyed by adult fans – are mainly lost on more innocent childhood viewers, making my first encounters with them something of an awakening, and it happened that it was criticism of this particular story that was my first encounter with them.

More important than that, though, was the sense of anticipation and urgency that came with the news that *Silver Nemesis* was to have a 'Special Edition' release on video, with not only extra scenes re-edited into the episodes but also a behind the scenes documentary. In this modern time of **Doctor Who Confidential**, websites, and the ability to Google any aspect of production even before a story has aired, we perhaps forget how rare the chance to see 'Making of...' programmes once was. Although I had *The Curse of Fenric* Special Edition, it had already been released when I found out about it and so I didn't experience that keen feeling as the release date approached. Knowing something special is on its way and that you *must* have it as soon as it comes out is a feeling that, I think, enthusiastic fans not just of **Doctor Who** but of any interest, share.

Finding ten pounds and ninety-nine pence for the upcoming release – or for any video release – was a big deal for me. (To give a sense of proportion, my weekly pocket money at the time was one pound.) To enable us to expand our video collection, my brother, Paul, and I combined our earning powers via the 'Who Box' – a red plastic dodecahedral money box that had come free when saving tokens from a popular breakfast cereal. Into this box we put our pocket money each week, as well as any extra amounts earned for helping around the house and, once there was enough in there for whatever we were saving towards, we could go to WH Smiths and buy it!

As it turned out, the bulk of the money for *Silver Nemesis* came from Paul and so the video was notionally his. (These things are important to keep track of, as any sibling will tell you.) As the big brother, though, the videos all lived on shelves in my bedroom. Later, as adults, the matter of who owned a VHS tape turned out to be something of a non-issue, since today you cannot *give* the things away!

At the time, though, getting our hands on the tape was a cause for celebration and excitement. The mythos around the concept of a Special Edition, containing something new and previously unavailable, was novel and exciting. Even though we were too young to watch it, the hype around the **Aliens** Special Edition VHS was around the same time and, to me, the *Silver Nemesis* release was even more exciting! (To this day I have watched those Sylvester McCoy episodes many more times than the Sigourney Weaver film.)

We dedicated fans appear to love a standardised appearance to things – so much so that the modern DVD releases have reversible covers to enable uniformity for those of us who collect the whole range and wish to avoid inconsistencies in the layouts. Even the VHS range had a fairly standard appearance, but *Silver Nemesis* eschewed this with a special bright green and silver foil version of the normal design. This added to the feel that it was indeed something special. By this time Banks and Skilleter's amazing **Cybermen** book had had a great impact too, so the combination of a Cyber-story *and* behind the scenes interviews was an extra treat.

Watching the story was no disappointment and having the additional scenes included in the episodes was good. I was disappointed that they were reduced to mere 'deleted scene' status on the eventual DVD release. Hopefully the **Doctor Who** Restoration Team, creators of the DVD range, will see their way to producing a feature-length version in the style of the versions they made of *Battlefield* and *The Curse of Fenric*. After years of watching the cut material as part of the episodes, I really miss it now that it is not there.

Perhaps it is a cliché, and yes, it wasn't in the broadcast version, but the journey of discovery is reversed and my childhood is rekindled whenever I hear the Cyberleader say, 'So, Doctor, a new appearance, otherwise our anticipation of your presence has proved entirely accurate.' Time, I hope, for one more Special Edition.

Always the Greatest Show
The Greatest Show in the Galaxy by **Jon Arnold**, 38, Newport, UK / First story: **City of Death**

By the late 1980s the future didn't look much like **Doctor Who** any more. Hollywood had shown us the wide open vistas of time and space. The future looked like **Star Wars**, **Blade Runner** and **Aliens**; even on the small screen it looked like **Buck Rogers** and **Battlestar Galactica**. **Doctor Who** might have had storytelling and imagination on its side but that hardly mattered in the onslaught of the best special effects money could buy. At times it seemed as if the show lacked the verve and direction to survive, thrashing about in its own past for answers while trying to ape the shiny bleakness and expensive dilapidation of the big screen. Trying to copy Hollywood on a shoestring budget was a zero sum game – all too often, **Doctor Who** looked cheap and tacky. Combined with that audience-killing 18-month break and scheduling which looked like the BBC trying to dig the show's grave, it meant that just us geeks were maintaining a lonely vigil. And our love was a weapon in the hands of the harder schoolyard kids, stigmatising us as sad. It was tough to stay true when the object of your affection was in one hell of a state and I got little but grief for it. Even worse I was at the dangerous age where the distractions of teenage years can take you away from the obsessions of youth, football, books and girls providing a slew of other distractions. For a while I abandoned the show. After the logo faded at the end of *Dragonfire* I quietly stopped buying **DWM** and the Target books, opened the curtains and let some light in.

I should've noticed during Season 24 that the times were a-changin'. Sure there was a grinding of gears between the way things had been and the way they were going to be, but the show had a twinkle back in its eye. But self-absorbed teenagers lack perspective and just pick up perceived flaws – Langford, cheapness and guest turns from the uncool likes of Ken Dodd. What was this, light entertainment or the show I'd grown up with?*

Then, in October 1988 the Doctor swaggered back onto my screen. It took precisely 25 minutes to reclaim my heart, conjuring with the Doctor's past to create something new and thrilling. A cliffhanging Dalek-eye view of an about-to-be-exterminated Doctor? Sold. I'm back next week. I adored the opening story, then the skewed strangeness of Terra Alpha. Strange was back in for the Doctor, if he still wasn't cool with others then it was okay. Sure the silver anniversary story fell a little flat with Queen impersonators, comedy Americans and unintentionally hilarious neo-Nazi skinheads diluting the potentially explosive cocktail of Cybermen, living statues**, magic and jazz.

I honestly wasn't expecting much from the last story. I knew little about it, even though I'd begun picking up **DWM** again the day after my re-conversion. What I got was the story that reaffirmed my faith in **Doctor Who** and cemented it seemingly permanently. The story that told me that show I'd always loved was still the same show and that really, those flaws that had annoyed me last year were actually a sign it was getting some mojo back.

Those flaws were still there, the odd duff performance, a strange choice of first cliffhanger and budgetary limitations occasionally showing through the ingenious means used to overcome them. But as with *The Happiness Patrol* imagination was there, and the ability to tell gloriously unhinged stories that didn't depend on violence, cynicism or the show's past. Above a host of fine performances, there were TP McKenna's perfectly pitched bore Captain Cook and Ian Reddington's Chief Clown, Reddington bringing out the sinister undertone inherent in a profession which hides behind make-up and masks and insists you have a good time – their good time. And for a fifteen-year-old there were clear allusions to the TV production process behind it all. Like Holmes and Hinchcliffe the intelligent early teenager was being targeted again; however this didn't riff off old Hammer films but was clever and entertaining on its own terms. This was the **Doctor Who** that sustained my faith, even when it was battered by the cynicism of **DWB** and rec.arts.drwho. I'd grown up with the show through the 1980s and finally I had the **Doctor Who** I'd always hoped and wished for, my classic era to match the Lambert, Lloyd, Letts and Hinchcliffe. And this was an era that carried on into the New Adventures, the default setting of **Doctor Who** for ten years until the TV Movie and BBC Books wrenched it into another shape.

Fast forward to Christmas 2012 – my son has generously offered to share all my **Doctor Who** DVDs, this year including *The Greatest Show in the Galaxy*. And, at the first opportunity (after *The Snowmen*) he insisted on watching it before he went to bed as he wanted to see it so much. The seventh Doctor and Ace had become his favourite TARDIS crew. He loved it, sitting rapt all the way through even as the clever metaphor that beguiled me as a teen flew over his five-year-old head. He simply watched and adored. *Blink*, *The Caves of Androzani* and *The Talons of Weng-Chiang* are all justifiably revered and fly high in fan polls, but at moments like this ranking stories in a 'my favourite's better than yours' way loses any meaning; what really matters is the memories and the joy that the right story at the right time can provide.

* It's actually both, of course, the understanding of which was part of the genius of Russell T Davies' approach to the show.
** Any then Paisley based writers taking note?

'I Just Do The Best I Can'
Battlefield by **Andrew Foxley**, 30, Liverpool, UK
First story: **The Mind Robber**

When you grow up reading about **Doctor Who**, in magazines, books or on the internet, you soon come across what is often referred to as the 'received wisdom' of fandom. That certain stories are classics, and others ... aren't. It was very much in evidence when I discovered the show in the early 1990s, when **Doctor Who Magazine** appeared to be akin to a holy text when it came to determining the relative success or failure of a particular aspect of the show. It was understandable - whilst we could read about old episodes, you'd be reliant on BBC Video's schedules or the brave new world of satellite television to be in with a chance of seeing many of them. Today, 'received wisdom' is arguably less relevant than ever, as more and more fans have access to virtually every episode in some form or another, and have numerous outlets (most notably the internet) where they can make their feelings known. No more do they have to rely on someone else's viewpoint, when they can, relatively easily, make up their own mind and have their voice heard.

Many people's view of the show is influenced by who 'their' Doctor was, growing up. I had the rather unusual experience of being introduced to the show more or less by watching one story per Doctor in sequence, thanks to BBC Two's 1992/93 repeat season, and so I like to think I'm more even-handed than most in considering the merits of different eras. After a good run of stories, which included *The Dæmons, Genesis of the Daleks* and *The Caves of Androzani*, the season eventually reached the McCoy era with *Battlefield*.

At this point, I knew *nothing* about the McCoy era, so sat down with no particular expectations as to what I was going to see... and loved it. If I'd come to it primed by 'fan wisdom,' I'd probably have picked holes in various aspects of the production. It's easy to do. Looking back from a more mature, perhaps cynical perspective, there are numerous problems with it. The editing and script could do with a bit of tidying up in places, one or two of the performances are perhaps a little too broad to be wholly effective, and Keff McCulloch's music hasn't aged well.

But none of that mattered the first time around. Because I found a great deal to like about *Battlefield*, and even as I've grown older, more cynical or even discerning in my tastes, I've never shaken that off on repeat viewings. It has an admirable scale of ambition, for one thing. Armies of knights battling UNIT troops, and each other. A mystical spaceship at the bottom of a lake. A powerful sorceress and her pet demon (the Destroyer being one of the best-realised **Doctor Who** monsters of its time), poised to destroy the world. And a role for the Doctor that makes perfect sense – he's Merlin. Of *course* he is. An enigmatic mentor figure, of uncertain origins and with many guises, whose numerous adventures have passed down into legend. Given Andrew Cartmel and Ben Aaronovitch's desire to restore a little of the mystery and magic they felt had been lost in the Doctor's character over the previous quarter century or so, the prospect that he might just be one of the most famous mythical figures of all time is an intriguing one, though it's appropriate that much of this is ultimately left ambiguous.

It has a terrific cast, too. Jean Marsh is compelling as Morgaine, whether being the menacing villain of the piece, or the more ambiguous character seen in her final confrontation with the Doctor – a lovely, quiet scene where she realises that she will never see Arthur again, and all the chaos and bloodshed has been for nothing. Angela Bruce and Marcus Gilbert are terrific fun as Bambera and Ancelyn, whose clash of personalities provides the comic relief. And then there's Nicholas Courtney, looking so much older but feeling like he's never been away as Brigadier Lethbridge-Stewart, in a rare example of an old character being revived in the show's later years that felt entirely fitting and appropriate.

The Brig gets some of his best material here, particularly his noble attempt at self-sacrifice to save the Earth. He was seldom served this well even in his heyday, fighting alongside the third Doctor.

So many of my favourite **Doctor Who** stories are triumphs of chutzpah over time and budget. Much of Season Seventeen looks like it was made on a shoestring, especially *Nightmare of Eden* – but it also happens to be insanely ambitious in many ways. *Invasion of the Dinosaurs* was woefully incapable of portraying a London beset by terrifying prehistoric monsters, though in other respects it's a fascinating and imaginative tale. *Battlefield* isn't the strongest of productions, but if you're able to come to it with a forgiving attitude, there is plenty to appreciate. **Doctor Who** has lasted for fifty years because generations of viewers have looked beyond the limitations of its production and been captivated by its ingenuity.

In that sense, *Battlefield* exemplifies the spirit of **Doctor Who**, and what I love about it – imaginative storylines, sometimes putting their own spin on familiar ideas and themes, brought to the screen by a production team who must know, deep down, that they lack the time and resources to make everything turn out exactly as it should. But they do it anyway, and aim to do the best they can. They did this in 1963, creating neolithic landscapes and distant alien planets in the confines of a BBC studio in London, and now a new generation are doing much the same thing today in Cardiff. Isn't that brilliant?

The Day Light Dawned
Ghost Light by **John Davies**, 40, Manchester, UK
First story: **The Android Invasion**

'We all have a Universe of our own terrors to face...'

Yes, Doctor, we do ... and in 1989 being a seventeen-year-old **Doctor Who** fan was one of them. The show simply wasn't cool anymore. The glow from the 1960s and 1970s had faded to such an extent that even the fans were tearing it to pieces – and not just between themselves. The fall-out was painfully public – and even televised. To the outside world **Doctor Who** fans were simply compounding the view that the show was tired, daft and well past its sell-by date. But not this fan. I was still its champion – even if that was to the amusement of most of my friends.

However, I wasn't wearing rose-tinted glasses. I knew from both memory and BBC video releases that recent years had been lacking some of the substance of the 'halcyon days' but I never admitted to that publically. I couldn't. I had my fan card and loyalty to uphold – especially after the recent hiatus. I had to be **Who** and proud. It was, after all, still **Doctor Who** and, as a result of that, good by definition. Happily, the late 1980s were making this 'lacking' easier not to admit to as the stories were emphatically re-affirming my never-ever-really-in-doubt love for and belief in the show. In 1989, the year *Ghost Light* aired, I was thrilled by the upswing in quality seen in the programme from the moment a scene in *Remembrance of the Daleks* Part One made this teenage fan-boy's neck hair tingle. That epoch-changing moment when a Dalek first glided up a staircase was fresh in my mind and the sheer verve and enthusiasm seen on-screen was a bold series-rejuvenation that flowed through the rest of Season 25 and on into *Battlefield*.

So, although I knew the show was still great I still had to live with the sneers, the jibes and the incredulity that I liked it so much. It wasn't easy to avoid this attitude and comments either. I was well known as a committed fan and when kids see an Achilles' heel they will try to kick it until the ankle breaks. Every day following a new episode I would hear the far from subtle 'whispers' behind me.

'Well, that was crap again, wasn't it?'; 'It's not as good as it used to be!'; 'I don't like the current Doctor!'; 'Bertie Bassett?!'; '**Doctor Who**? Doctor Why more like!'; 'What does John see in this?'

But I carried on liking and carried on defensively facing the whispers, the terrors, 'On my own terms.'

And then came *Ghost Light*.

My seventeen-year-old thoughts are recorded in the diary I kept at that time. After a lengthy transcript of the narrative, scribbled under October 4th 1989, I conclude, 'Now, I love tales of haunted houses. I also love the Victorian era – how can it fail? So far, it hasn't. Twenty-five minutes of class! Unadulterated brilliance! Wonderful stuff!'

Despite my rather subdued appreciation of the story so far (yes, I am being sarcastic), on the morning of October 5th 1989 I walked to school expecting business as usual. With my mind a whirl of haunting music, tantalising questions, the Doctor's cruel manipulation of Ace and the overwhelming atmosphere of what I watched the night before I sat down for Registration counting down to the inevitable.

It didn't happen.

Instead, a friend called Peter walked over to me and said, 'I watched **Doctor Who** last night. Best episode I've seen in ages. Really creepy.'

Incredulous, I asked, 'You mean that?'

'Yeah,' Peter said, 'Really good. Well ... until those stupid monsters popped up wobbling about. They were crap.'

I still remember the glow and the laugh I stifled at that moment. In the words of Stan Marsh I learned something that day. Sometimes you need those terrors in your life. You can become too blinkered by your commitment to any life hobby. You can become too immersed, too keen to show the rest of your world why they should love what you do. That will never happen. You have to accept that your passion is your passion and not force it on others. You can be so busy defending something that you can deny, overlook, over-apologise and over-compensate for any failings that are genuinely there. In so doing you can actually miss the impact a really good moment can have on an outside observer. Daleks floating? Fantastic for a fan but, considering that the 'Daleks can't climb stairs!' gag is still being paraded in 2012, especially after the RTD-era presented sweeping armies of air-borne Daleks, it meant far less to the public. Peter, however, will probably still remember a 'really creepy episode' of **Doctor Who** he once watched as a teenager. He won't remember the title. He won't remember the plot. He won't remember that it happened on 4th October 1988 and he certainly will not know that that story has the dubious honour of being the last in-house story to be made in the show's original run. Why should he? He will, however, remember the moment and that is probably just as important as knowing that Daleks can fly.

I also learned that in life praise and compliments will often be delivered via the back-handed method. This has put me in good stead in many situations, especially on-line.

And I have *Ghost Light* to thank for that.

Touched By the Curse
The Curse of Fenric by **Mikael Barnard**, 28, Leighton Buzzard, UK / First story: unknown (I was so young, I have no idea which was my first!)

The most difficult part of this essay was choosing to write about this story over all others. I whittled my list of candidates down to eight titles and five of those were from Patrick Troughton's last season. Every story in that season is immensely precious to me for a whole host of reasons, so why did I cast them, *Death to the Daleks* and *The Myth Makers* aside and choose to write about a story made two whole decades after that wondrous season of 1969?

My response to the question, 'Which story has had the most enduring impact on me?' is intimately linked with the stories that meant most to me as a child. A key reason I continue to adore **Doctor Who** is that it is perhaps the *only* constant in my life that has always, without exception, given me nothing but total happiness, even in the darkest of times, and provided a concrete, visceral link to a period when I felt totally safe, happy and contented. Since I have never felt quite like that since the age of six, that basically gives me *The Ark in Space, Death to the Daleks, Terror of the Zygons, The Curse of Fenric* and most of Patrick Troughton's last season as the stories that are the most dear to me. That is also why I will never throw away my VHS copies of those stories.

The Curse of Fenric was the first story I recorded from the original transmission. It pains me now as a multimedia archivist to recall throwing that tape away many years ago. It snapped in the machine and I had no idea then that it could even be repaired, let alone how. *The Curse of Fenric* is also one of the few stories from the classic series that I have memories of watching during its first transmission, particularly the end of episode three: 'We play the contest again, Time Lord.'

I wanted to try and be clever here and write an erudite, witty, analytical and academic study the way that

Tat Wood does in the **About Time** series of books, or the equally wonderful Philip Sandifer does on his blog 'TARDIS Eruditorum: A Psychochronography in Blue,' but even if I were up to the task, what more could I say? Yes, *The Curse of Fenric* is an excellent story filled with metaphor, imagery, psychology and all the other things that make **Doctor Who** infinitely more interesting than so many other television programmes, but these things operated on a purely subconscious level to me when I was a child (which is probably why I find certain stories far more scary as an adult than I ever did all those years ago!). However, even as a child those subconscious elements still mattered; I was just less aware of them, and this story provides one of those most tremendous fusions of sound, vision, writing and acting talent that I have ever seen. Dinsdale Landen is worth the proverbial ticket price alone.

Ultimately though, the deciding factor for *The Curse of Fenric* was, not so much that it means more to me than other stories (*Death to the Daleks* stands out above it for reasons that are far too abstract and incoherent to put into words) but that it has continued to exert a strange physical presence in my life at various stages. In 2003, during the first year of my undergraduate degree in *Music and Film, Radio and Television Studies*, I was required to produce three short adverts such as might be transmitted on radio. The DVD of *The Curse of Fenric* had just come out so I chose that as my product. At about the same time I acquired the CD of the soundtrack and for a long time the first few bars of the *Commander Millington* cue was the message alert tone on my mobile phone. Then on 27th June 2008 I had the unexpected, wonderful pleasure of meeting Mark Ayres, the composer of said soundtrack, at a symposium held to celebrate the life and works of Daphne Oram. He was kind enough to sign my programme, shake my hand and spare me some time for a chat. And did I stand there and think, 'I'm talking to the genius who composed the score for *Ghost*

Light?' Of course not; wonderful though his other **Doctor Who** scores are, it was *The Curse of Fenric* all the way!

Then, later in 2008, a friend and I visited all the locations in Kent used in the story (except Crowborough which I have yet to visit and will sadly only be able to photograph from afar.)

In May 2012 I embarked upon a massive location photographing trip, covering locations in Wiltshire, Dorset and Gloucestershire. Sixteen hours driving in two days! One of the places I visited was Lulworth Cove and it was another of those locations I just danced around in pure ecstasy with a massive, stupid grin on my face.

But *The Curse of Fenric* doesn't just continue to affect me every few months or so, it affects me on a weekly basis. As those of you who read my essay in the first volume of this book will know I work for an organisation called The Projected Picture Trust, an independent museum currently based within the grounds of Bletchley Park. A major project I have undertaken as archivist for this organisation is a major re-cataloguing programme which involves some pretty menial data generation and filing tasks. I therefore make no apologies for taking the occasional DVD with me to have on in the background. There is nothing quite like watching *The Curse of Fenric* within the grounds of the park itself, and as I walk the corridors of the place where all those incredible, intelligent, amazing heroes once walked, the ghost of Dr Alan Dinsdale Judson-Turing never seems all that far away.

Cheetah Your Fate
Survival by **Charles Daniels**, 35, Oxford, UK (born in Sacramento, Cal.) / First story: **Spearhead from Space**

One of my earliest memories is of my uncle Tony showing off this elaborate home taping kit he'd assembled some years before. Tony was always obsessed with gadgets and kits and the newest, greatest, most bleeding edge things you could get your hands on. He showed me an incredibly ropey looking, black and white recording of *Spearhead from Space* Episode 1, and gave me a very enthusiastic potted history of **Doctor Who**. He had enjoyed it greatly when he lived in England and was now sharing it with me in Northern California. It probably would have remained the crazy little tape my uncle once showed me, if it wasn't for KVIE, Channel 6, which began showing Jon Pertwee some short time later. My life in Northern California was not a terribly happy one. My father had completely disappeared when I was three years old, my mother was losing a battle with alcohol and drugs, and for the most part I was left being raised and looked after by some Irish uncles, whom for some reason my mother's sisters had been importing with regularity.

I felt overwhelmed by just about everything in my life, except for my brief escapes every Saturday night from 10pm onward, when I would watch omnibus cuts of **Doctor Who**.

It took a long time to dawn on me quite why it was such an escape, but once the penny dropped it was intensely potent. This weird show - which seemed beamed in from a totally different world, far removed from inner-city California - featured British people solving problems not with guns, or drugs, or crime, but by being terribly clever. I was at that weird age when you start noticing deeper patterns of cause and effect, but are still wonderfully naïve and believe that anything can happen. Week after week, this Doctor guy solved problems *just by being terribly clever*. And once this realisation struck me, I decided that it seemed a much better avenue than any other I saw going.

However, it wasn't easy to find the entrance or the start to that avenue. Take my school for instance, an underfunded nightmare where armed police stalked the corridors and guarded the entrance. In fact a few years after I left, my high school was shut down when an audit revealed only 25% of the students were functionally literate. While I was there I spent a lot of time in the library by myself. I felt there had to be something I could learn or understand which would get me away from this cycle of my life.

One respite I did have was being invited along to visit my uncle Tony's mother, who lived in Coventry. The first time this happened they had just started to air *The Trial of a Time Lord*, so I was able to catch *The Mysterious Planet* on first broadcast. I was aware then that the attitude in the house was, 'Well, this is a bit of a dumb show. But if you like it... Well, you're very young and we'll humour you.'

The *second* time I had the opportunity to visit Coventry, was when they were showing *Survival*.

I was insanely excited and my two slightly older cousins, Sean and Kevin, offered to sit down and watch it with me. Part One went fine ... until the Cheetah People showed up. After that, the floodgates opened. I was bullied and taken the piss out of so endlessly, that I skipped Part Two.

I was still reeling from their bullying a week after that, but decided I absolutely had to watch Part Three. And really my overwhelming memory of that was them screaming insults at how bad the show was, until they got bored and let me watch the last four or so minutes in peace.

In a way, it's a miserable memory to have of the end of the classic era, but it really drove home the difference between British and American attitudes at the time. Back in California, 98% of everyone had never even *heard of* **Doctor Who**. And the 2% that had heard of it, *loved it.*

I don't remember any Who Hate at all in America in the 1980s and 1990s. I remember Jon Pertwee and Peter Davison commenting on how much friendlier and more open American fans were, and explaining the criticism they constantly got from fans in the UK.

For me **Doctor Who** and my Uncle Tony, were what led me to pursue an intense interest in British culture; or my fractured understanding of it. I fell into the common trap of the anglophiles - trying to reverse engineer all of British culture using what scraps you can find; a twenty-year old comedy series, a novel by Arthur Conan Doyle, and a Cadbury Flake. To most anglophiles British people are either John Cleese or Sid Vicious; or perhaps the Queen. I wanted to understand what Britishness was, but my starting points were essentially **Monty Python** and Tom Baker, so of course my views on the subject were distorted. I was passionate, but it was hopeless. Looking at where my life was, the idea that I would one day live in the United Kingdom seemed a fantasy to me. It was as likely as a mountain climber coming over the crest of some impossibly misty peak and discovering a lost world of dinosaurs. So while I was fascinated with British culture, it always had the sheen of the unobtainable; which, come to think of it, is exactly the sort of thing which just makes something seem sexier.

I kept looking at where I was, and where I wanted to be, and did a slow grind of trying to inch toward my goal. To my amazement, I did end up in living in the UK and even settling down and becoming 'a proper adult.'

Perhaps even scarier than the idea of becoming a cheetah person, I became a father.

I started thinking about names. My partner Claire was very firm with me that she wanted to decide the name if it was a boy, but demanded that I come up with a good girl's name before she shared her idea. So I danced around different ones in my head and toyed with the notion of picking a name from **Doctor Who**. Claire doesn't know anything at all about **Doctor Who**, so I could have suggested 'Tegan Nyssa Daniels' if I wanted, and she wouldn't bat an eyelid. But one name kept coming back to me again and again.

'I know exactly what I want to call him, if he's a boy,' she said to me. 'Have you decided a girl's name, yet?'

'Well...' I hesitated. I couldn't really do this could I? Name my child after someone from **Doctor Who**? Isn't that what horrible, tacky parents do? Name their kids after pop stars, and actors, and places where they've had sex? No. The whole idea was very silly and stupid, and I was going to have to bite the bullet and just tell Claire I didn't have any ideas.

'Do you mind if I suggest a boy's name first?', she asked.

'No, go right ahead!' I replied, as I figured it would buy me a few seconds.

'Right. If it's a boy, I'd really like to call him Sylvester.'

I couldn't help but emit an unexpected laugh. She glared at me harshly.

'What's wrong with Sylvester?! I've always loved that name! I'm very serious about it. I really want the name Sylvester.'

'Oh! Sorry if that seemed weird. I was just surprised. Yes! Sylvester! Great!'

She smiled. 'So, what's your idea for a girl's name?' she asked.

I grinned, realising that my original idea was now absolutely perfect.

A few months later, I found himself holding my child, a little girl named Sophie. I did think it was terribly amusing all those months knowing that my child would either be Sophie or Sylvester. It might have been odd to name a child after an actor on a British telefantasy show, but in some way it would have felt even more unusual not to acknowledge something which I think has shaped and pointed along the direction of my entire life.

Survival has always stuck with me. Not just because I saw it on first broadcast. Or felt the brunt of my cousins' barbs. But because it ends with the promise that no matter what you achieve, there's always more to do. New things to see and experience. New worlds to conquer. There's magic, majesty, and mystery out there in the universe; and there's also time for a nice warming cup of tea – if you can get there before it goes cold.

The Diary of a Doctor Who Fan (age 7/8)
The Cancellation of Doctor Who by **Grant Bull**, 30, Isle of Wight / First story: **Remembrance of the Daleks**

5th – 26th October 1988
Keith at school is talking about **Doctor Who** non-stop! Apparently it's back on TV and on Wednesdays now. He said I should watch it so we can talk about it on Thursday at school – I wasn't sure but I gave it a go and it was sooo cool! The Doctor has a spaceship called the Tardis – I'm not sure what this means but Keith says it stands for something. Anyway it's a blue police box but when you go inside its massive, really massive. He has a friend called Ace. The story was split into parts over weeks and each one ends with the Doctor or Ace in trouble or something like that, so you have to watch next week to see what happens. This one was called *Remembrance of the Daleks* and Dad said he remembered the Daleks from when he was little, he said he used to hide behind the sofa from them... ha ha ha! It was wicked though, the Daleks were brilliant. My best bit was when Ace hit one with her baseball bat! The Doctor won in the end and beat them and their leader Davros. Me and Keith keep saying, 'Unlimited Rice Pudding,' the whole time, I nearly said it when our teacher took the register the other day! I can't wait for the next **Doctor Who**...

2nd – 16th November 1988
Doctor Who was only three weeks long this time but it was great. The monster was made of sweets and called the Kandyman. When we went shopping I got Mum to get me some liquorice allsorts, when we got home I tried to make a Kandyman with them but just got in a mess, so ate them! We played **Doctor Who** in school but no one wanted to be Ace, so I did, she might be a girl but she is a cool one, I'm

thinking of asking for a jacket like hers for Christmas – it's wicked!

23rd November – 7th December 1988
The Cybermen are my new favourite **Doctor Who** monster ... ever! They are like robots and are all shiny and evil. Dad said he had seen them before just like the Daleks. He said when he saw them they came out of the sewers from manhole covers. This scared me a bit; I haven't been jumping on manhole covers since ... just in case. I got in trouble for using all the tin foil trying to dress as a Cyberman.

14th December – 8th January 1989
The Greatest Show in the Galaxy – I am starting to think **Doctor Who** is just that. Each episode brings new wonders and adventures. The Doctor is so clever and a bit mad. It turns out this Doctor isn't the first one either. There was a book sale at school and we got to the look at the books during the day. There was this big **Doctor Who** book, full of writing and photos and there was loads I don't know about – other stories, other monsters, others who travelled in the Tardis and other Doctors. I really wanted the book, really badly, it was amazing. When Mum came at the end of the day we went to the book fair but I wasn't allowed the book, I got really upset – Keith got it. This time **Doctor Who** was about a circus, it was good but now it isn't on for a while. Mum and Dad said it will be back soon, I am going to look for it in the **Radio Times** each week, until it is back.

6th – 27th September 1989
Doctor Who is back! It was sooo good, it was medieval and cool. There were these army people in it call UNIT, imagine what it would be like to be one of them, helping the Doctor. I liked this story, it reminded me of my **Ladybird Myths and Legends** book. I've decided to start hassling my Nan to make me a jumper just like the

Doctor's, with question marks and everything – Keith will be so jealous!

4th – 18th October 1989
Ghost Light was really confusing, I didn't understand it at all but I didn't admit that in school. It was spooky in that old house and the characters were weird. Keith reckons he knows a house near us that has a Dalek in the garden; he won't tell me where it is though. I have been looking everywhere we go and can't find it – I want a Dalek in our garden. I think I am becoming obsessed with **Doctor Who** – it's all I think about, all I play and all I talk about. I am driving Mum and Dad mad with it, but its sooo cool!

25th October – 19th November 1989
Still no sign of the Dalek in the garden, I think Keith is winding me up. *The Curse of Fenric* was scary. It had zombies in it and they came from the sea. The monsters looked great. It is one of my favourites so far. Mum said she recognised the Vicar from somewhere and talked for ages trying to figure out who he was. I had to move right up to the TV to hear ... my ears are still ringing a little but I didn't want to miss a word the Doctor was saying.

22nd November – 6th December 1989
I've been practising rolling my letter 'r' like the Doctor does, its going pretty well but Mum has been wondering why my mirror is covered in spit! **Doctor Who** was fantastic; it had a baddie in it called the Master. He is like the Doctor's arch-enemy I think. People got turned into cats and there was another world with cat people on it. The ending was a bit different this time and I found out why...

    Mum and Dad sat me down on the sofa and said they had something to tell me – I knew this wasn't going to be good news. They said **Doctor Who** had finished. This wasn't a break either; this was the end, for good. I didn't know what to say. I thought maybe they had it wrong, there had been a mistake; there hadn't though. I went to my room and lay on the bed. I stared at the ceiling and started to cry ... and cry. I'd fallen in love with this programme, its world had become mine and now it was gone forever. I thought it would go on and on like it had before. It had been going since the 1960s and now it had to end when I started to enjoy it. The Doctor wasn't coming back, Ace wasn't coming back and nor was the TARDIS, which I know now stands for Time And Relative Dimension In Space. I can't believe it and don't want to but I have to. I wanted to wear one of those black armbands but Mum said that was going too far - I didn't feel like that to me though. I had lost something very special.

I'm giving up on this diary; it doesn't feel worth writing now I don't have **Doctor Who** to write about. I'm going to miss you Doctor, so much ... goodbye.

27th May 1996
The Doctor is coming back...

Afterword by Tom MacRae

I was only ever scared once watching **Doctor Who**.

As a child, **Doctor Who** didn't frighten me. This wasn't because I was particularly brave, or TV savvy, or had in any way lost the ability to suspend my disbelief – it was simply that I knew The Doctor would always save me. End of story. Cue credits. Woo-ooo-ooooh. And so there was never any need to be genuinely, literally, go-and-have-nightmares-Tom scared by any of it.

Except, that is, for this one time.

I loved **Doctor Who** with a passion (I still do, but it's different when you're a kid and you believe it could all be – might all be – should all be actually real) but to me it was thrilling, more than scary. God knows what I'd have made of it now, with cutting edge CGI and Murray's Miraculous Music to send me spiralling into a panic, but as a boy I was able to take it on the chin, and I never hid behind the sofa. Did anyone ever actually hide behind the sofa? Do they still? If it is actually true, I'm going to invent a sofa monster in a future story just to properly fry their brains forever. Ha!

Anyway. I was telling you about what scared me. And what scared me...was hands.

The Trial Of A Time Lord was one of my earliest memories of **Doctor Who**. I was just getting my head around what the show was and who The Doctor was and I loved the idea of the trial and the court and the Matrix and the silly hats. Because that meant they were important you see. Because of the silly hats. If you don't believe me, check out an Archbishop.

I thought the Master being inside the Matrix was brilliant. It made no sense, but Anthony Ainley maybe needed some spending money for beard wax so someone nicely crow-barred him into a story he didn't belong in. An appearance of Sil was always a joy, and he ate really really big bogies, which of course was the best thing ever. Fantastic. And then the Vervoids came along...

It's that one shot of the thorn in the palm of the human who has foolishly tried to shake hands with them (what an idiot, that's like asking a Dalek to unblock your sink) that chilled me and scared me and gave me nightmares. Something about the intimacy of it being in your hand - in the palm of your hand - that just freaked me out. The first and only time it ever happened. Cybermen - cool! Kandyman - brilliant! Davros - good to see you! But a thorn in the palm of your hand that killed you ... now we're talking Therapy Time.

Which is why I decided that hands were scary, creepy, odd things with wriggly fingers that you shouldn't look at too closely. And so, to complete the circle, when I was trying to come up with some cool, memorable monsters for *The Girl Who Waited*, my memory flashed back to the Vervoids and that hand. That simple human hand. And ... well you see where I'm going with this.

Thank you **Doctor Who** for an amazing fifty years. This is a kindness!

Tom MacRae
London
January 2013

Acknowledgements

Warmest, most heartfelt thanks to the following people:

Gary Russell, **Richard Kirby**, **Andrew Philips**, **Michael Russell** and **Tony Green** for providing the inspiration behind these books

Robert Hammond (particularly for the wonderfully silly and outrageous cover art), **Phil Ware** and especially **Matthew West** (literally a human teddy bear) – also known as **The Miwk Men**; not many people have the ability to perform genuine magic, but in allowing me to put this book together, these three men granted at least one of my wishes

Mike Royce for encouragement and lots of other things

Tim Hirst, for believing in something, even if he wasn't quite able to see it achieved

Christopher Bryant, my second incarnation, for stepping in and taking over – and also **John Davies**, my subsequent third incarnation

and **Mother** and **Omes**, my life and my motivation, but not on account of their patience, of which there is none.

But of course, the biggest and warmest thanks go to the people who wrote this book.

You folk are legends, each and every one of you.

You Have Been Reading...

7   Introduction by J.R. Southall

The First Doctor Who

13   An Unearthly Child by Si Hunt
17   The Daleks by Wayne W. Whited
20   The Edge of Destruction by Anthony Zehetner
23   Marco Polo by Steve Herbert
26   The Keys of Marinus by Grant Foxon
28   The Aztecs by Paul Stuart Hayes
31   The Sensorites by Anthony Townsend
35   The Reign of Terror by Kate Du-Rose

38   Planet of Giants by Jo West
39   The Dalek Invasion of Earth by Tom Henry
42   The Rescue by Antony Wainer
45   The Romans by James Gent
48   The Web Planet by David O'Brien
51   The Crusade by Andrew Orton
57   The Space Museum by Andrew Hickey
60   The Chase by Michael Seely
63   The Time Meddler by Sam Hemming

65   Galaxy 4 by Kevin Jon Davies
68   Mission to the Unknown by Christian Tarpey
71   The Myth Makers by Andrew T. Smith
75   The Daleks' Master Plan by Jim Sangster
78   The Massacre by Donald Tosh
80   The Ark by John Rivers
83   The Celestial Toymaker by John S. Hall
86   The Gunfighters by Michael S. Collins
89   The Savages by Alun Harris
92   The War Machines by Allen Dace

94   The Smugglers by Tim Hirst
100   The Tenth Planet by Greg Bakun

The Second Doctor Who   103

- 105 Power of the Daleks by Paul Butler
- 109 The Highlanders by Nick 'Diskgrinder' Livingstone
- 112 The Underwater Menace by Ash Stewart
- 115 The Moonbase by Nick Mellish
- 119 The Macra Terror by Matthew Fitch
- 122 The Faceless Ones by Gareth Kavanagh
- 125 The Evil of the Daleks by Tony Jordan

- 128 The Tomb of the Cybermen by Cliff Chapman
- 131 The Abominable Snowmen by Peter Nolan
- 134 The Ice Warriors by Shauno Eels
- 140 The Enemy of the World by David O'Brien
- 143 The Web of Fear by Peter Crocker
- 147 Fury From the Deep by Peter Webber
- 150 The Wheel in Space by Mike Morgan

- 153 The Dominators by John Davies
- 156 The Mind Robber by David Agnew and Robin Bland
- 161 The Invasion by Sebastian Wilcox
- 164 The Krotons by Christopher Bryant
- 169 The Seeds of Death by John Dorney
- 172 The Space Pirates by Mikael Barnard
- 175 The War Games by Alys Hayes

The Third Doctor Who   178

- 180 Spearhead from Space by Tony Green
- 183 Doctor Who and the Silurians by Gary Russell
- 186 The Ambassadors of Death by Jef Hughes
- 189 Inferno by Bill Albert

- 192 Terror of the Autons by Simon Brett
- 195 The Mind of Evil by Matthew West
- 198 The Claws of Axos by Benjamin Adams
- 201 Colony in Space by Steve Roberts
- 203 The Dæmons by Tony Jones

206   Day of the Daleks by Richard Dinnick
210   The Curse of Peladon by Amanda Evans
214   The Sea Devils by Christopher Luxford
216   The Mutants by Philip Newman
220   The Time Monster by Blayne T. Jensen

222   The Three Doctors by David Guest
225   Carnival of Monsters by Tom Jordan
228   Frontier in Space by Jon Cooper
231   Planet of the Daleks by Jack Dexter
234   The Green Death by Brad Jones

237   The Time Warrior by Tony Kenealy
240   Invasion of the Dinosaurs by Ion Williams
243   Death to the Daleks by Andy Davidson
246   The Monster of Peladon by Steven Dieter
248   Planet of the Spiders by Colleen Hawkins

The Fourth Doctor Who   251

253   Robot by Bob Furnell
256   The Ark in Space by Stuart Douglas
258   The Sontaran Experiment by Alister Davison
261   Genesis of the Daleks by Daniel J McLaughlin
265   Revenge of the Cybermen by Tony Green

268   Terror of the Zygons by Al No
271   Planet of Evil by Christine Grit
274   Pyramids of Mars by Robert Morrison
277   The Android Invasion by Richard McGinlay
280   The Brain of Morbius by Paul Driscoll
285   The Seeds of Doom by Al No

288   The Masque of Mandragora by Mietek Padowicz
291   The Hand of Fear by Anthony S. Burdge
294   The Deadly Assassin by David Busch
298   The Face of Evil by Andrew Stark
301   The Robots of Death by Paul Mount
305   The Talons of Weng-Chiang by Rob Irwin

- 308 Horror of Fang Rock by Jenny Shirt
- 311 The Invisible Enemy by Alan Hayes
- 314 Image of the Fendahl by Tony Eccles
- 317 The Sun Makers by Matt Hills
- 320 Underworld by Felix Dembinski
- 322 The Invasion of Time by Nicholas Hollands

- 325 The Key to Time by Naomi Padowicz
- 328 The Ribos Operation by Mark Trevor Owen
- 331 The Pirate Planet by Peter Nolan
- 334 The Stones of Blood by Michael Russell
- 337 The Androids of Tara by May Norwood
- 339 The Power of Kroll by Gareth Kavanagh
- 342 The Armageddon Factor by Dean Hempstead

- 345 Destiny of the Daleks by Nicholas Hollands
- 348 City of Death by Mark Cockram
- 351 The Creature From the Pit by Hugh Haggerty
- 354 Nightmare of Eden by Terry Cooper
- 357 The Horns of Nimon by Tony Cross
- 360 Shada by Isobel Tolley

- 363 The Leisure Hive by Simon Hart
- 366 Meglos by Alun Harris
- 369 Full Circle by Tony Green
- 372 State of Decay by Andrew Clancy
- 375 Warriors' Gate by Matt Hills
- 378 The Keeper of Traken by Robert Day-Webb
- 382 Logopolis by Chris Orton

The Fifth Doctor Who 387

- 389 Castrovalva by Neil Thomas
- 391 Four to Doomsday by Kevin Stayner
- 394 Kinda by Simon Fernandes
- 398 The Visitation by Richie J Haworth
- 401 Black Orchid by Robert Hammond
- 405 Earthshock by Stuart Flanagan
- 408 Time-Flight by Ian Wheeler

411 Arc of Infinity by Giles Milner
414 Snakedance by Colleen Hawkins
419 Mawdryn Undead by Susan L Coleman
421 Terminus by Andy X Cable
424 Enlightenment by Vivienne Dunstan
426 The King's Demons by Jonathan Potter
429 The Five Doctors by Barnaby Eaton Jones

434 Warriors of the Deep by Alan P Jack
437 The Awakening by Matt Barber
440 Frontios by Ian McArdell
443 Resurrection of the Daleks by Guy Lambert
446 Planet of Fire by Abby Peck
448 The Caves Of Androzani by Simon Thorpe

The Sixth Doctor Who   451

453 The Twin Dilemma by Andrew Philips

457 Attack of the Cybermen by John Scott
460 Vengeance on Varos by Nabil Shaban
463 The Mark of the Rani by Jennie Stayner
466 The Two Doctors by Suky Khakh
470 Timelash by Anthony Williams
473 Revelation of the Daleks by John Davies

478 The Trial of a Time Lord by Jez Strickley
482 The Mysterious Planet by Tony Jordan
485 Mindwarp by Matt Goddard
489 Terror Of The Vervoids by Graeme Ferris
492 The Ultimate Foe by Will Ingram

The Seventh Doctor Who   495

497 Time and the Rani by Andrew Blair
501 Paradise Towers by Beth Ward
504 Delta and the Bannermen by Christopher Bryant
507 Dragonfire by Scott Burditt

510   Remembrance of the Daleks by Nicholas Blake
513   The Happiness Patrol by Lewis Christian
516   Silver Nemesis by Stephen Candy
519   The Greatest Show in the Galaxy by Jon Arnold

522   Battlefield by Andrew Foxley
525   Ghost Light by John Davies
528   The Curse of Fenric by Mikael Barnard
531   Survival by Charles Daniels
536   The Cancellation of Doctor Who by Grant Bull

Afterword by Tom MacRae   540

Made in the USA
Lexington, KY
19 March 2015